ALSO BY MILES J. UNGER

Magnifico: The Brilliant Life and Violent Times of Lorenzo de' Medici

The Watercolors of Winslow Homer

MACHIAVELLI

A Biography

———

Miles J. Unger

SIMON & SCHUSTER

NEW YORK   LONDON   TORONTO   SYDNEY

Simon & Schuster
1230 Avenue of the Americas
New York, NY 10020

First Simon & Schuster hardcover edition June 2011

SIMON & SCHUSTER and colophon are registered trademarks of Simon & Schuster, Inc.

For information about special discounts for bulk purchases, please contact Simon & Schuster Special Sales at 1-866-506-1949 or business@simonandschuster.com.

The Simon & Schuster Speakers Bureau can bring authors to your live event. For more information or to book an event contact the Simon & Schuster Speakers Bureau at 1-866-248-3049 or visit our website at www.simonspeakers.com.

Designed by Joy O'Meara

Manufactured in the United States of America

10   9   8   7   6   5   4   3   2   1

Library of Congress Cataloging-in-Publication Data
Unger, Miles.
Machiavelli : a biography / Miles J. Unger.—1st Simon & Schuster hardcover ed.
p. cm.
Includes bibliographical references and index.
1. Machiavelli, Niccolò, 1469–1527.   2. Statesmen—Italy—Biography.   3. Intellectuals—Italy—Biography.   4. Political scientists—Italy—Biography.   5. Authors, Italian—Biography.   6. Italy—History—1492–1559—Biography.   7. Florence (Italy)—History—1421–1737—Biography.   I. Title.
DG738.14.M2U54 2011
320.1092—dc22
[B]
2010054130

ISBN 978-1-4165-5628-2
ISBN 978-1-4391-9389-1 (ebook)

To Dad and Debi, with love and admiration

To Dad and Debi, with love and admiration

CONTENTS

SELECT CAST OF CHARACTERS

Cesare Borgia, Duke Valentino (c. 1475–1507)

Rodrigo Borgia, Pope Alexander VI (b. 1431, Pope 1492–1503)

Biagio Buonaccorsi, friend and correspondent of Machiavelli

Charles V, Hapsburg Holy Roman Emperor (1500–58)

Charles VIII, King of France (1470–98)

Francesco Guicciardini, Machiavelli's friend and correspondent, historian, governor of the Romagna (1483–1540)

Louis XII, King of France (1462–1515)

Bernardo Machiavelli, father of Niccolò (c. 1425–1500)

Niccolò di Bernardo Machiavelli, Second Chancellor of Florence, political theorist, playwright (1469–1527)

> Marietta Corsini, wife of Niccolò Machiavelli
>
> Children: Primavera, Bernardo, Lodovico, Guido, Bartolomea, Piero

Maximillian I, Hapsburg Holy Roman Emperor (1459–1519)

Giulio de' Medici, Pope Clement VII (b. 1478, Pope 1523–34)

Lorenzo de' Medici, *Il Magnifico* ("The Magnificent") (1449–92)

Sons of Lorenzo the Magnificent:

Piero de' Medici ("The Unfortunate") (1472–1503)

ℙ ⌐ Giovanni de' Medici, Pope Leo X (b. 1475, Pope 1513–21)

Giuliano de' Medici, Duke of Nemours (1479–1516)

Lorenzo de' Medici, Duke of Urbino (1492–1519)

ℙ ⌐ Giuliano della Rovere, Pope Julius II (b. 1443, Pope 1503–13)

Girolamo Savonarola, Prior of San Marco, prophet (1452–98)

Ludovico Sforza, *Il Moro* ("The Moor"), Duke of Milan (1452–1508)

Piero Soderini, Gonfaloniere of Florence (1450–1522, Gonfaloniere 1502–12)

Giovanni Vernacci, nephew of Niccolò Machiavelli

Francesco Vettori, Machiavelli's correspondent, Florentine ambassador to Pope Leo X (1474–1539)

Italy in the Late 15th Century

Florence
Milan
Naples
Papal Territory
Venice

FRANCE

DUCHY OF SAVOY

Milan

Venice

OTTOMAN
EMPIRE

Genoa
Sarzana

Bologna

DUCHY OF
FERRARA

Imola

ROMAGNA

Lucca

Pisa

Florence

Urbino

THE
PAPAL
STATES

Siena

Ligurian Sea

Corsica
(Genoa)

Tiber R.

ITALY

Adriatic Sea

Rome

Naples

Sardinia
(Spain)

Tyrrhenian
Sea

Mediterranean Sea

Palermo

Sicily

AFRICA

N
W   E
S

0   100 miles
0   100 kilometers

Quarters and Gonfaloni of Florence

I
S. M. Novella
Viper
Unicorn
Red Lion
White Lion

Porta al Prato

Por Faen

Leon Bianco
(White lion)

S. Mari Novella

I

Unicorno
(Unicorn)

Leon Ross
(Red lion)

Drago
(Dragon)

III
S. Spirito
Ladder
Shell
Whip
Dragon

O L T R A

Nicchi
(Shell)

P. P

III

Ferza
(Whip)

Porta Romana

| 0 | 200 | 400 meters |
| 0 | 200 | 400 yards |

N
W E
S

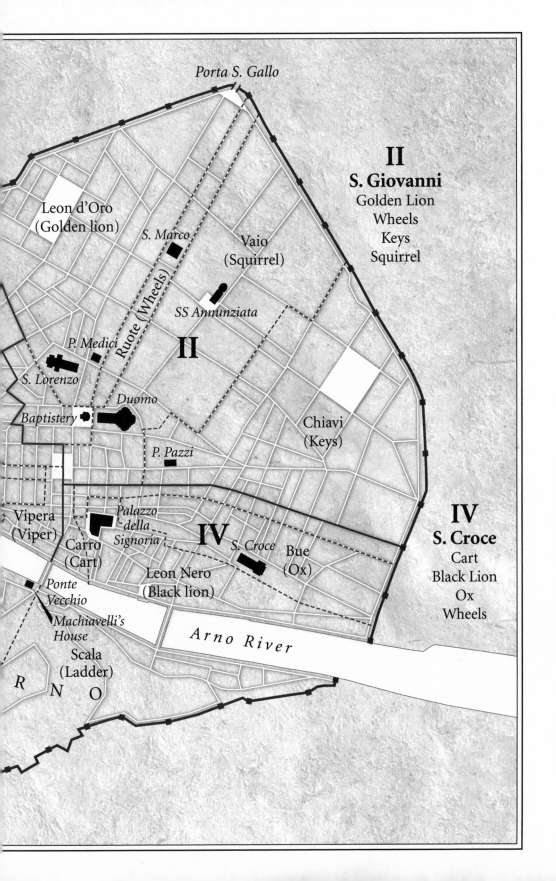

Machiavelli

THE MALICE OF FATE

"I have written down what I have learned from these conversations and composed a little pamphlet, De principatibus, in which I delve as deeply as I can into the subject, asking: What is a principality? How many kinds are there? How may they be maintained and why are they lost?"

—NICCOLÒ MACHIAVELLI,
LETTER TO FRANCESCO VETTORI, DECEMBER 10, 1513

IT HAD BEEN A BAD YEAR FOR NICCOLÒ MACHIA-velli. Not only had he lost his job—"dismissed, deprived and totally removed," read the decree that singled out the Second Chancellor of Florence with vindictive thoroughness—but the republic he had served faithfully for the past fourteen years had fallen beneath the tyrant's boot. His friends fled as foreign armies descended upon the city, replaced by people with little reason to wish him well. To those who had followed Machiavelli's career and recalled his abrasive manner, his current isolation came as no surprise. Often during the years he had served in government he had spoken a little too bluntly or pushed his agenda with more enthusiasm than tact, and now that he was in need of allies in high places they proved to be in short supply.

These repeated blows were all the more painful since it was hard to deny the fact—and, were he inclined to forget it, his many detractors were only too happy to remind him—that Machiavelli's policies were largely responsible for the disaster. The citizen militia that had been his proudest creation had disgracefully turned tail at the first contact with the enemy, abandoning the neighboring city of Prato to sack and pillage and doom the independent Florentine Republic.

Worse was to come. With his friends disgraced and his enemies triumphant, Machiavelli's name appeared on a list compiled by a man captured while plotting to overthrow the new regime. On February 18, 1513, Machiavelli was arrested and thrown into prison. Dragged periodically from his dank, vermin-infested cell in Le Stinche, only a few short blocks from his old office, he was tortured with repeated drops of "the rope" in an attempt to extract a confession of guilt. It was an ordeal that might have broken a less resourceful man, but Machiavelli, making the best of a grim situation, chose to regard it as something of a character-building exercise. Only a few weeks later, still recuperating from his injuries, he wrote to his friend Francesco Vettori: "And as for turning my face toward fortune, you should take at least this pleasure from these troubles of mine, that I bore them with such stoicism that I am proud and esteem myself more highly than before."

His dignity, in fact, was about all he had salvaged from the disaster of the past months. Machiavelli's state of mind can be gauged by a sonnet he composed during his prison stay. The honesty and grim humor are typical, as is his capacity to laugh at himself:

> *I have, Giuliano,* on my legs a set of fetters,*
> *with six pulls of the cord on my shoulders;† my other miseries*
> *I do not intend to recount to you, since so the poets are treated!*
> *These broken walls generate lice so swollen that they look like*
> *flies; never was there such a stench. . . .*
> *As in my so dainty hospice.*

Rather than wallowing in self-pity, Machiavelli was inclined to meet his reversal with a wisecrack and a shrug. The image of his "dainty hospice"

---

* The sonnet was addressed to Giuliano de' Medici, one of the leaders of the newly restored Medici dynasty. It is doubtful whether the sonnet was ever sent to its intended recipient and, if so, what Machiavelli hoped to gain.

† One of the most common forms of torture, called the strappado, was to bind a prisoner by the arms and drop him from some high place, often dislocating the shoulders and causing various other painful injuries. As Machiavelli indicates, he had undergone this excruciating ordeal six times.

crawling with lice who fatten themselves on the wasting flesh of prisoners is half farce, half tragedy—a play of light and shadow that runs through both his political and literary works. "So the poets treated are treated!" he snorts, making light of his predicament and, with more than a hint of self-mockery, placing himself among the long line of artists who have suffered for their craft. One of the clearest signs that his spirit remained strong was that he found the time to take a swipe at one of his favorite targets, the pious fools whose answer to life's every problem was prayer:

> *What gave me most torment was that, sleeping near dawn, I*
> *Heard them chanting the words: "We are praying for you."*
> *Now let them go away, I beg, if only your pity may turn itself*
> *Toward me, good father, and loosen these cruel bonds.*

Who but Machiavelli would insist that having to listen to prayers all night was more painful than a session with the state torturer? He would have been mortified if in a moment of weakness he suddenly embraced religious beliefs he had scoffed at most of his adult life. He was not one of those fair-weather skeptics who deny God in the good times only to rediscover Him in their hour of need. He refused to accept the easy comfort of religious pabulum, preferring to take his chances with fickle *Fortuna* rather than place an existential bet with the priests he regarded as little more than charlatans and swindlers.

In any case, it was not the power of prayer that freed him after a three-week sojourn in his "dainty hospice," or even the charm of his jocular little poem, but his captors' grudging admission that they lacked any real evidence he was involved in the plot.* But his release was not the end of his difficulties. Even after he was freed Machiavelli remained under a cloud of suspicion. He was barred from government service, the only career he had ever known and the only one in which he could employ his distinctive talents. Short of losing his life—something that seemed more than likely

---

* Giuliano himself admitted that, outside of the two ringleaders, "the others who were accused and imprisoned have been set at liberty as innocent men" (Villari, *The Life and Times of Niccolò Machiavelli*, II, 34). The immediate occasion of his release was as part of a general amnesty following the election of Giovanni de' Medici as Pope Leo X in 1513. The Medici would never have spared him had they really believed him to be a threat. All the available evidence suggests that while Machiavelli's name appeared on the list of potential sympathizers, he was never actually contacted by the plotters.

at one point—it his hard to see how the past twelve months could have brought more disappointment and sorrow.

These days he rarely made the journey to Florence, a few hours' ride by mule or on foot along the winding road that led through the olive groves and vineyards of the Tuscan countryside. The handful of friends who had remained loyal to him during his recent troubles could now find him living in obscurity at his farm in the village of Sant' Andrea in Percussina, trying, without much success and even less enthusiasm, to eke out a meager living from his modest patrimony. From his fields he could see the red-tiled rooftops of his beloved Florence, crowned by the soaring arc of Brunelleschi's dome and the angular tower of the Palazzo della Signoria, the government building that had been his place of work in recent years.* But far from providing solace, the view was a constant reminder of a life in shambles. The depth of his anguish can be felt in a note he scribbled in the margins of a document he was working on: "*post res perditas*," it read, "after everything was lost."

One consolation was that without a real job he had plenty of time on his hands to philosophize, to put his troubles behind him, and to try to draw larger lessons from his own experience. As he wandered beneath the bright Tuscan sky and gazed at the city shimmering in the distance, he gained new perspective on the human condition. On occasion he gave vent to his bitterness, but even when his mood darkened he tried to see the bigger picture. In a poem titled "On Ingratitude or Envy" he contemplated the dismal fate of those who served their country well, only to find themselves repaid with slander:

> *Hence often you labor in serving and then for your good service*
> *receive in return a wretched life and a violent death.*
> *So then, Ingratitude not being dead, let everyone flee from courts*
> *and governments, for there is no road that takes a man faster to*
> *weeping over what he longed for, when once he has gained it.*

---

* The Palazzo della Signoria (also called the Palace of the Priors or the Palazzo Vecchio, the Old Palace) was the capital of the Florentine Republic. The Signoria (Lordship) was the chief executive, consisting of eight Priors and the Gonfaloniere di Giustizia (the Standard-Bearer of Justice or titular head of state). The Signoria served for only two months at a time. Frequent elections and rapid rotation through office made the government weak and easy prey for ambitious families like the Medici, who manipulated the system for their own advantage.

However sound this last piece of advice, Machiavelli himself was incapable of adopting it. Like someone who keeps returning to an abusive relationship, he would no doubt have leapt at a chance to exchange his current indolence for the government halls from which he had been banished.

To his friend Francesco Vettori, who was complaining about the minor inconveniences of life in Rome, where he was serving as Florentine ambassador to the Holy See, Machiavelli replied with a touch of sarcasm: "I can tell you nothing else in this letter except what my life is like, and if you believe it is worth the exchange, I would be happy to swap it for yours."

Few people were as ill suited to the quiet life of the countryside as Machiavelli. He was a man of the city who thrived on sociability and the stimulation that came from lively conversation. A keen observer and unsparing chronicler of the *human* animal, here among the beasts of the field he found little to excite his imagination. He did what he could to maintain his mental agility, but the company he now kept was a far cry from the cardinals and dukes with whom he was used to spending his time. "I wander over to the road by the inn," he reported, "and chat with the passersby, asking them news of their countries and various other things, all the while noting the varied tastes and fancies of men." In other words he trained on the local rustics those same sharp eyes that were once so quick to size up the ambition of a king or discover the inscrutable designs hidden in a bland ambassadorial dispatch. There is the same insatiable curiosity, the same need to examine the smallest incident or quirk of character for insights that might hint at universal laws. But there was no denying that his singular talents were wasted as he puttered about his small property, tending to the petty chores that seemed to puzzle him more than the intricacies of an international treaty.

Perhaps out of frustration, or merely to relieve the boredom of his existence in Sant' Andrea, he engaged in petty quarrels with his neighbors and then described them in letters to friends. They would have gotten the joke immediately. A few months ago he was dining with kings; now he was reduced to butting heads with peasants. "Having eaten," he wrote to Vettori,

I return to the inn where I usually find the innkeeper, a butcher, a miller, and a couple of kiln workers. With them I waste the rest of

the day playing cricca *[cards] and backgammon, games that spark a thousand squabbles and angry words, and though for the most part we are arguing over only a penny or two, you can hear us yelling all the way to San Casciano. Thus, cooped up among these lice, I get the mold out of my brain and lash out at the malice of my fate, content to be trampled upon in this manner, if only to see whether fortune is ashamed to treat me so.*

But even as he slummed with the locals he began to plot a return to public life. While fate (*Fortuna*, as he often calls her) had treated him shabbily, Machiavelli had not given up hope of returning to active duty. He would wrestle this capricious goddess to the ground and wring what he could from her, "for," as he was soon to write with more pugnaciousness than gallantry, "fortune is a woman and in order to be mastered she must be jogged and beaten."

And so in the winter of 1513 he conceived a plan to ingratiate himself with those who now called the shots in Florence—the Medici and their henchmen, whose return to the city had marked the beginning of all his troubles. To some of his former colleagues, his eagerness to beg a job from the same people who had toppled the democratically elected government was inexcusable, and Machiavelli's apparent about-face has continued to earn him the scorn of generations of critics. At best it seems like rank hypocrisy, at worst the sign of a man willing to betray every principle to further his career. But neither charge is fair. It is true that Machiavelli had been an ardent supporter of Florentine democracy. He had toiled on behalf of its elected government for fourteen years, at great cost to both his health and his pocketbook. He had stood by his feckless and ungrateful colleagues when less conscientious men had shirked their duty or profited at the public's expense, and instead of enriching himself with bribes that fell so easily into the pockets of those who worked in government service, he left office no better off than he had entered it. As he himself noted, "my loyalty and honesty are proven by my poverty."

The truth was that no matter how much he favored Florence's republican institutions, his patriotism was something far more visceral. His love of country was an intense and irrational passion. This was a rare

weakness in a man who famously spurned conventi
celled at exposing human foibles. Few were more a
religious believer in the tangle of his own contrad
delight in ridiculing the amorous gymnastics of an old
ing over a young beauty. Friends forgave the barbs launched by
they dubbed *Il Machia* (the spot or the stain) not only because he usually
delivered them with disarming humor, but also because he was happy
to offer up his own delinquencies to the ridicule of others. But when it
came to the fierce loyalty he felt toward his native land, he would neither
examine nor question it. "I love my city more than my own soul," he once
confessed (a statement that perhaps says as much about his disregard for
his immortal soul as it does about his patriotism) and it is this nationalist
fervor that is the guiding passion of his life, the one fixed point toward
which all his thought and action pointed.* It explains all the apparent
inconsistencies in his politics and absolves him of the charges of hypocrisy that have dogged him for almost five hundred years. Now that the
country he loved was the property of the restored Medici dynasty, he was
determined to swallow his pride, if not his principles, and make his peace
with those who ruled the state.

This would be no easy task. True, all charges against him had been
dropped, but the authorities, slightly paranoid like all new regimes of
questionable legitimacy, continued to snoop around, looking for any piece
of incriminating evidence that might put the troublesome former Second
Chancellor away for good. Machiavelli's rehabilitation would have been
a simpler task had either his pedigree or his bank account been more
impressive, but lacking the means to bribe his way back into the good
graces of the current rulers, he would have to fall back on his native ability, offering his potential masters the only gift he had: the insights he had
acquired in a decade and a half of loyal service to the state. As he sat down
to compose his masterpiece, the brief work that would ensure his place in
history, he had rather limited goals in mind. Indeed, had he been a better
businessman it is unlikely he would ever have turned to writing and his
name would have been quickly forgotten, a fact he himself seemed to rec-

---

* Though Machiavelli's patriotism never wavered, his definition of country evolved over time. For
the most part, he gave his loyalty to his native Florence, but in his famous epilogue to *The Prince* he
expanded his horizons to encompass all of Italy.

gnize: "fortune has arranged it that because I can speak neither of the silk trade nor the manufacture of woolen cloth, nor of profits or loss, I must speak of matters of state."

It in no way diminishes Machiavelli's achievement to point out that his greatest work was written with prosaic goals in mind; often it is the specter of the wolf at the door that stimulates an artist's best work. Without his civil service salary Machiavelli had difficulty providing for his family, a needy brood that now included a wife and five young children. "I am wasting away," he complained, "and cannot go on like this much longer without becoming so reduced by poverty. And as always, I desire that these Medici princes would put me to work, even if that means beginning by rolling a stone."

So it was that he set about distilling all he had learned in a single slender volume—"this little whimsy of mine," he called it dismissively—which he intended to dedicate to Giuliano de' Medici, brother of the current Pope and a man whose friendship he had to cultivate were he to have any hope of prospering in Medicean Florence.* Machiavelli himself sketched the scene as he sat down to write his most famous work. The charming picture he conjures of the scholar at his desk, putting aside his worries to commune with the ancients, is curiously at odds with the sinister reputation of the book and of the man who wrote it:

> *Come evening, I return to my house and enter my study; on the threshold I take off my ordinary clothes, covered with mud and dirt, and wrap myself in robes meant for a court or palace. Dressed appropriately, I enter the ancient courts filled with ancient men where, affectionately received, I nourish myself on that food that alone is mine and for which I was born; where I am unashamed to converse and ask them to explain their actions, and where they, kindly, answer me. And for four hours at a time I feel no boredom, I forget all my troubles, I have no fear of poverty, or even of death. I enter their lives completely. . . . I have written down what I have learned from these conversations and composed a little pamphlet,* De principatibus, *in*

---

* By the time Machiavelli completed the work, Giuliano de' Medici was dead. As it has come down to us, *The Prince* is dedicated to Giuliano's nephew Lorenzo, son of Giuliano's older brother Piero.

which I delve as deeply as I can into the subject, asking: What is a principality? How many kinds are there? How may they be maintained and why are they lost?

Thus was born *The Prince*, the most notorious and influential political tract ever written.* It is difficult to imagine a quieter entry onto the stage of history for Machiavelli's infamous title character. Indeed, they are something of an odd couple—the bloodthirsty tyrant, pitiless in the pursuit of power, devious, ruthless, and cruel, and the mild-mannered scholar in his threadbare robes and slippers—and it is safe to say that the contrast has done nothing to help Machiavelli's reputation. He has been caricatured as a real-life Dr. Frankenstein, one of those intellectuals who pursues their version of the truth regardless of the consequences, blithely setting loose upon the world a monster they can't or won't control. People might have been more willing to forgive Machiavelli had he himself been a man of action. Instead, he comes across as one of those armchair dispensers of mayhem, the first in a long line of faceless bureaucrats who, from the safety of their studies, justify every cruelty with that all-purpose excuse—*raison d'état* (reason of state).

It is a picture of the man so ingrained in the popular imagination that his name has been turned into an adjective to describe any cynical act or the pursuit of power without conscience. The image is not a new one. He was barely in his grave when one prominent churchman described him as "an enemy of the human race," and it took only a few years more for the Pope—in a move that the anticlerical Machiavelli might have taken as a backhanded compliment—to consign the entire body of his writings to the Index of Prohibited Books. In fact one can attribute much of his posthumous fame to the quality and virulence of his opponents, who turned

---

* Competitors for this dubious distinction might include Karl Marx and Friedrich Engels's *The Communist Manifesto* and Adolf Hitler's *Mein Kampf*. In both cases, however, one might argue that the ill repute into which they have fallen resulted more from the abuses of the political systems they spawned than the works themselves. *The Prince*, by contrast, remains notorious despite the fact that it is difficult to attribute the crimes of any one regime to its influence. This is not from lack of trying; in the sixteenth century, Cardinal Reginald Pole made the case that the court of Henry VIII used Machiavelli's book to inspire its "criminal" break from the Church of Rome. Arguing almost the opposite case was Innocent Gentillet, a French Protestant, who argued in his *Contre-Machiavel* ("Against Machiavelli") that his writings inspired the St. Bartholomew's Day massacre of the Huguenots by the Catholic regime.

the obscure civil servant into the Devil incarnate,* father of a philosophy stripped of ethics, conjurer of a world in which human society, bereft of religion and lacking the sanction of a benevolent God, is reduced to a war of all against all and dedicated to the blind pursuit of power.

Machiavelli owes his sinister reputation above all to this one slender volume, written as a job application for the Medici lords of Florence. It is ironic that while *The Prince* failed in its immediate objective to restore him to the good graces of the lords of the city, it has secured him a permanent place in the history of ideas. It might have amused Machiavelli—as it almost certainly would not have amused his would-be patrons—to witness the curious reversal of Fortune that made this minor functionary far more famous than the lords from whose table he hoped to take a few small crumbs.†

When he sat down to write *The Prince*, his desk piled high with books of ancient history he treasured and his head filled with the lessons he had learned from years of practical experience as a diplomat, Machiavelli was forty-four years old, just on the far side of middle age for a man of the early sixteenth century.‡ He thought of himself as a failure, and few of his friends would have disagreed. Despite a respectable record in the upper ranks of the state bureaucracy, he had done little to distinguish himself from his anonymous colleagues toiling at their ledgers in the Palazzo della Signoria. To those who recalled him at all, it was primarily as the author of Florence's worst military fiasco in recent memory.

But, as he liked to observe when chronicling the lives of the great leaders of the past, there is nothing like a bit of adversity to test the mettle of

---

* In his 1827 work on Machiavelli, Lord Macaulay wrote: "Out of his surname they have coined an epithet for a knave, and out of his Christian name a synonym for the Devil." The English pseudonym for the Devil, Old Nick, derives from Machiavelli's first name.

† Lorenzo and Giuliano de' Medici, the two men to whom Machiavelli dedicated *The Prince*, were singularly fortunate that their own mediocrity was redeemed by the talented servants who surrounded them. Giuliano was the youngest son of the famous Lorenzo the Magnificent; the Lorenzo to whom *The Prince* was dedicated was his grandson. Not only did Machiavelli dedicate his most famous work to them, but Michelangelo's Medici tombs in San Lorenzo were built to house the remains of these two obscure members of the famous family. Michelangelo seemed to recognize this when he responded to criticism that the portraits looked nothing like their subjects, claiming "that a thousand years hence no one would be able to know that they were otherwise."

‡ Machiavelli's older contemporary, the statesman Lorenzo de' Medici, died at forty-three; Michelangelo, six years his junior, lived to be eighty-eight, a remarkable age for the time. A man of Machiavelli's age might, on average, have anticipated a decade or more of productive life ahead of him.

a man—and Machiavelli had more than his share of this particular commodity.* Facing financial ruin and with the prospect of a dull, unproductive retirement stretching out before him until such time as decrepitude
and finally death overtook him, Machiavelli chose to resist the dismal
grave fate seemed to have prepared for him. He had been tested but not
broken, and the ordeal seemed to have renewed his faith that he had
something original to offer the world. From the solitude of his hilltop farm
the vast panorama of history spread out before him. Deprived of the lively
give-and-take he loved so much, the voices of the dead haunted his mind,
whispering those universal truths that until recently had been drowned
out by the frenetic pace of his daily existence. In their company he seemed
to pry out the secrets of the human heart, mining past and present to discover the laws that govern the fate of nations.

---

* For instance, Machiavelli asserts that the more difficult it is to seize power, the more secure that
power is once achieved: "Those who become princes by virtue of their abilities . . . acquire dominion
with difficulty but maintain it with ease" (*The Prince*, VI, 26).

I

BORN IN POVERTY

"I was born poor and learned early on to deny myself rather than to enjoy."

—NICCOLÒ MACHIAVELLI TO FRANCESCO VETTORI,
MARCH 18, 1513

AS HE CONTEMPLATED THE WRECKAGE OF HIS ONCE promising career, Machiavelli consoled himself with the thought that he was, after all, no worse off than he had been when he had come into this world. Only his dreams of something better had been shattered. "I was born poor and learned early on to deny myself rather than to enjoy," he recalled, finding comfort in the thought that he had nothing left to lose.

At first glance Machiavelli's characterization of his circumstances seems willfully misleading. The Machiavelli were an old and respected family and by most measures the particular branch into which Niccolò was born in the spring of 1469 was solidly middle-class.* Niccolò's father, Bernardo, was a man of property. He owned a house near the Ponte Vecchio, one of a cluster of buildings occupied by various cousins, grouped about a small courtyard with a loggia known as the *chorte di Machiavelli.* This alone was enough to lift the family above the great majority of the urban poor, who owned little more than the ragged clothes on their back.

---

* It is difficult to classify Florentine families like the Machiavelli using familiar terms, either those that come out of the traditional divisions of feudalism or those that come out of modern sociology. They had ties to the feudal aristocracy, but were deemed *popolani,* i.e., men of the people, or members of the prosperous merchant class. They were aristocrats in the sense that they belonged to the governing class, but they were distinguished from "magnates," who were barred from holding office. The Florentine ruling class combined elements of bourgeois merchant values and aristocratic privilege.

Nor was this Bernardo's only piece of real estate. Furnishing the city house with wine, oil, eggs, meat, and fresh vegetables was his farm in Sant' Andrea in Percussina, situated some ten miles south of Florence along the road to Rome. Even in lean times the family could fall back on its own resources to feed and clothe itself.

The status of the Machiavelli in Florence was measured by more than material possessions. Bernardo could claim descent from the minor nobility (through the Castellani family), a connection that, while it brought little in the way of tangible profit, conveyed real benefits in the form of prestige. In the countryside Bernardo's superiority to his neighbors was marked by quaint ceremonial gestures that carried a distant echo of once vital feudal obligations: every Saint Peter's Day, a member of the parish of San Piero a Nebbiavole offered in tribute a half pound of candle wax, and when the priest of the local church of San Michele a Mogliano died, Bernardo, in recognition of his role as fatherly protector of the community, was among those consulted in naming his successor.

In the city the family was equally well established. For centuries the Machiavelli had belonged to Florence's ruling elite. Niccolò's ancestors had been prosperous bankers and merchants, dealing mostly in the lucrative wool and silk industries. Bernardo himself, though he never held elective office, was a friend of some of the most powerful and prominent men in the city. One of them, the Chancellor of Florence, Bartolomeo Scala (an intimate of Lorenzo de' Medici himself), called Bernardo his "friend and familiar" and estemed his erudition so highly that he made him a principal character in his *De Legibus*, a philosophical dialogue on the origins of the law. Nothing indicates his high standing in the community as surely as this: Bernardo Machiavelli was someone in whose mouth Scala could place learned paraphrases of Plato and Cicero without fear that contemporaries would find the image ludicrous.

In other words Bernardo Machiavelli was an intellectual. He had earned a reputation as an amateur scholar and expert on legal matters, something confirmed by the honorific *messer* used by his peers when greeting him on the Ponte Vecchio or Piazza della Signoria. He was the prototypical scholarly dilettante. Years after his death, when it was brought to Niccolò's attention that strangers had been mistakenly buried alongside his father in the Machiavelli family crypt in Santa Croce, he quipped: "Well, let them be, for my father was a great lover of conversation, and

the more there are to keep him company, the better pleased he will be." Bernardo had both the inclination and the leisure to cultivate his mind, secure in the knowledge that his various properties would provide sufficient income to support his family.

But despite this solidly bourgeois standing, Niccolò was not mistaken in characterizing his origins as less than promising. True, he never suffered the dire want of many of his neighbors for whom even a slight economic downturn meant hunger; nor did he ever have to endure the humiliation of begging charity from his richer relatives. But in the world of late-fifteenth-century Florence, both Bernardo and his son Niccolò lived uneasily on the margins of respectability. In fact the earliest surviving documents in Niccolò's hand—two letters from 1497 written when he was twenty-eight years old—reflect a painful recognition of social insecurity. They involve a property dispute between his family and the powerful Pazzi clan. Hoping to counter the uneven odds, Niccolò put his case before the influential Cardinal Giovanni Lopez. In the first letter Machiavelli refers to his own kin as "pygmies . . . attacking giants." In a follow-up letter to this same cardinal, he seems anxious to remind his correspondent that, despite appearances, the Machiavelli are at least as respectable as their more powerful rivals: "And whoever would wish justly to weigh the merits of our house against that of the Pazzi, all other things being equal, would declare ours the greater in liberality and manliness of spirit." Of course, as Niccolò knew, the scales were never fairly weighted, and any contest between unequal combatants would favor the strong over the weak. As he remarks bitterly in his play La Mandragola, "a man who doesn't have pull with the government of this city . . . can't find a dog to bark at him, and we're good for nothing but to go to funerals and to meetings about some marriage, or to sit all day dawdling on the Proconsul's bench." Surprisingly, at least for those who regard him as the preeminent exponent of ruthless power politics, Machiavelli's natural point of view was that of the vulnerable. This marginality, the sense that he was on the outside looking in, was vital to Niccolò's self-conception. This self-conception in turn was vital to the formation of his thought.

Niccolò Machiavelli was born on May 3, 1469, in the family house just south of the Ponte Vecchio. The modest residence stood on the Via Romana, which led from the city's oldest and busiest bridge to the southern gates. From his bedroom window young Niccolò could watch not only the steady stream of farmers on their way to market, but also more exotic figures who were a reminder of the vast international reach of Florentine commerce: walking shoulder to shoulder with the humble peasants were long-distance merchants with their mules piled high with goods from Turkey, Arabia, and far-off India, as well as tourists—including numerous dukes, duchesses, cardinals, and even an occasional emperor or king— who had come to worship at the city's many sacred shrines and delight in Florence's unparalleled works of art and architecture.

The house in the heart of the Oltrarno—the section of Florence on the south bank of the Arno River that is still among the most charming in the city—no longer stands, but the surrounding urban fabric is largely intact. The neighborhood in which the young Machiavelli grew up, identified by the ancient heraldic symbol of the shell (*Nicchio*),* is one of narrow streets and tiny, shaded squares, of small shops and unpretentious eateries. On summer days when the Arno became sluggish, a foul stench rose from the mud along the riverbank, a miasma made even worse by the dyers and tanners who used the waters to scrub away noxious liquids. It was then that plague-carrying rats multiplied, bringing contagion that ravaged the neighborhoods of rich and poor alike. Then, as now, it was not the most fashionable address in the city, but a few imposing palaces tucked in among more modest apartments were a reminder that powerful families lived among them. A few minutes' walk from the main civic and religious centers, the Oltrarno was close enough to participate fully in the hustle and bustle of the thriving metropolis.

Within this busy urban neighborhood there was little to distinguish the Machiavelli home from dozens of others in the vicinity. By the late fifteenth century the most powerful families of Florence—like the Medici, whose palace on the widest street of the city, the Via Larga, set the stan-

---

* In the fifteenth century the city was divided into four main quarters: San Giovanni, Santa Croce, Santa Maria Novella, and, across the river, Santo Spirito. These quarters were each further subdivided into four *gonfaloni*, forming the sixteen traditional districts of the city. The *gonfaloni*, or banners, were the heraldic devices under which medieval Florentines marched into battle. Though by the time of Machiavelli's birth the militia was a thing of the past, these ancient divisions still had political significance. The Sixteen *gonfalonieri*, or bannermen, were among the leading officials of the city. Florentines might also refer to their neighborhood by the name of the local church.

dard for those that followed—advertised their wealth and status by constructing splendid homes that dwarfed their neighbors,' but the Machiavelli residence would not have made much of an impression on the passersby. No architect had imposed his newfangled ideas of classical order on the rather haphazard collection of medieval buildings; the conglomeration was decidedly unostentatious, suggesting shabby respectability rather than vaunting ambition.

Like most Florentine families, the Machiavelli were unable to trace their origins back more than a couple of centuries, though, unlike some more pretentious or deluded lineages, they felt no need to invent fictitious pedigrees out of dragon slayers or Trojan heroes. In the centuries before Niccolò's birth they had prospered as the city prospered, making a solid if not spectacular contribution to a metropolis that was becoming a center of trade, manufacturing, and finance.

The location of the city house, as well as the various properties scattered about the countryside in the hills just south of the city, indicates that the Machiavelli originated in the Val di Pesa, in the wine-making region of Chianti. As the population of Florence swelled in the twelfth, thirteenth, and fourteenth centuries, largely through immigration from the *contado*, the rural area just outside the city limits, families tended to settle in districts closest to the gates through which they had first entered. The less densely populated Oltrarno was a popular destination for new immigrants, particularly those from the region south of the city. It is almost certain, then, though there are no documents prior to the thirteenth century to prove this, that Niccolò's distant ancestors were among those nameless tillers of the soil who, since before the days of the Roman Empire, cultivated grape and olive on the sloping, rocky hillsides that lie between Florence and Siena.

The insecure respectability that marked Niccolò's life and that fueled much of his creative fire was the result of fortunate decisions made by long-dead ancestors and unwise choices made more recently. If Niccolò burned with ambition, it was due at least in part to the gap he perceived between the prestige of the Machiavelli name and the precariousness of current circumstances. In his dedication to *The Prince* he refers to himself as "a man of low and poor station," a perspective that encouraged him to break with convention and propose startlingly new solutions to old problems. Had he been richer or more careful of his dignity, it is unlikely he would have made his career in the civil service, a form of employment too close to real work to be suitable for a gentleman and one that provided vital insight into the cruel economy of power. Equally important, the nagging sense that his family was in decline left him with a fierce ambition to make his mark.

The Machiavelli first enter history during the thirteenth century as adherents of the Guelph party, the group allied with the papacy in their often bitter quarrel with the Ghibellines, followers of the Holy Roman Emperor. Though these factions, which existed in most of the cities of northern and central Italy, ostensibly owed their allegiance to one or the other of the great universal lords of Europe, abstract geopolitical considerations often were less significant than the fact that party solidarity provided an opportunity to settle purely local scores. In the streets of Florence, as in Milan, Pistoia, and Siena, Guelphs and Ghibellines organized themselves into armed factions and slew each other with abandon as first one and then the other gained momentary advantage, burning down the houses of their enemies and driving the survivors through the city gates. Time and again the same bloody drama played itself out. While the victors celebrated, the exiles made their way to the nearest friendly city, where they plotted revenge on their insufferable compatriots. The most famous iteration of this familiar story involves the great Florentine Ghibelline Farinata degli Uberti who, after the triumph of the Guelphs in 1250, headed to Siena, where the Emperor's men still clung to power. Demonstrating that loyalty to party and family meant more than loyalty to country, Farinata led the armies of Siena against his hometown, defeating them at the battle of Montaperti and briefly reasserting Ghibelline ascendance in Florence.[*]

One of the earliest mentions of the Machiavelli family comes in the context of this Ghibelline triumph, when a contemporary chronicler listed them among the prominent Guelphs whose houses were plundered by

---

[*] Farinata degli Uberti is one of the most memorable characters in Dante's *Inferno*, where the poet places him among the heretics. When Dante, a prominent Guelph, describes his family, Uberti replies: "They were fierce enemies to me and to my forebears and to my party, so that twice over I scattered them" (*Inferno*, X). Apparently hatred between Guelph and Ghibelline was intense enough to be continued in the afterlife.

their enemies. Fortunately for the Machiavelli and their allies, the quarrelsome and faction-ridden Ghibellines failed to consolidate their victory and by 1267 the Guelphs, the Machiavelli among them, had regained control. But the Guelphs proved equally belligerent, repeating the worst excesses of their ousted foes. This particular round of destruction was not entirely unproductive since the torching of the houses of the Ghibelline Uberti clan created much needed open space in the crowded heart of the city. The smoldering ruins of the Uberti towers were paved over and transformed into Florence's main civic square, the Piazza della Signoria—a peculiar but effective bit of urban renewal.

The triumph of the Guelphs brought no peace to the city. The crumbs of the victory feast had barely been cleared when they themselves split into rival factions—the Blacks and the Whites—who now went about slaughtering each other with equal gusto.* The Machiavelli, once again fortunate in their loyalties, joined the victorious Blacks, the faction that, under the lead of the Donati family, banished Florence's most famous citizen, the poet Dante Alighieri, who had the bad luck to belong to the Whites. As a bitter, rootless exile, Dante took his revenge on the city that had betrayed him by providing eyewitness testimony that "through Hell [Florence's] name is spread abroad!"

Niccolò's ancestors joined in the street battles that were a feature of daily life in medieval Florence, ransacking the houses of their neighbors when they were on top and suffering the same fate themselves when Fortune reversed herself. If Niccolò would one day become the world's most famous cynic, given his own family history and that of his native city, it is a view he came by honestly. While the Machiavelli were not among the leaders of the victorious Black Guelphs, by the mid-fourteenth century they were named as one of the "notable" citizen families of the Oltrarno neighborhood. Equally significant, contemporary accounts list the Machiavelli as *popolani*—that is among those prosperous merchants who were slowly pushing aside the old feudal aristocracy as the ruling class of the city.

The annals of medieval Florence chronicle a tragic cycle of murder and arson that was one generation's legacy to the next, but viewed from a

---

* True to form, the Blacks also split into rival factions once they had driven their rivals from the city. The civil war led by the Cerchi and Donati families chronicled by Dino Compagni in the early fourteenth century was between two factions of the Black Guelphs.

distance a more constructive picture emerges. In his *Florentine Histories*, Machiavelli admits that "if in any other republic there were ever notable divisions, those of Florence are most notable. . . . From such divisions came as many dead, as many exiles, and as many families destroyed as ever occurred in any city in memory." But he perceived that her greatest fault revealed her greatest virtue, for "in my judgment no other instance appears to me to show so well the power of our city as the one derived from these divisions, which would have had the force to annihilate any great and very powerful city. Nevertheless ours, it appeared, became ever greater from them." However violently and spasmodically, Florence was wrenching itself free from ancient feudal bonds and asserting its autonomy in defiance of both Pope *and* Emperor. By the end of the thirteenth century, despite periodic orgies of bloodletting, Florence had transformed itself into a vital and independent state, dominated by merchants and bankers grown prosperous on the revived trade between East and West that was an unintended by-product of the Crusades.

In the Ordinances of Justice of 1293, Florence established a government that reflected the new order; the right to vote and to hold office would no longer be the privilege of the landed aristocracy but would be based on membership in one of the city's merchant or professional guilds.* Flexing their newfound muscle, these merchants now sought to rein in the lawless magnates whose arrogance and violence had for so long disturbed the peace. Merchants and shopkeepers formed themselves into a citizen militia powerful enough to challenge the armored knights who were the source of the feudal aristocracy's military power. First they tore down the towers in the city from which the great lords had waged war on each other, and then marched out into the countryside, smashing their castles and forcing them to swear allegiance to the commune. "[H]aving eliminated their nobility," Machiavelli wrote in his *Florentine Histories*, "the republic was left in the hands of men nurtured in trade."

The Machiavelli were among the families benefiting from the government established by the Ordinances of Justice, and from the end of the thirteenth century their name crops up regularly among the Three Ma-

---

* The original Ordinances included seven recognized major and nine minor guilds. The major guilds were comprised of mostly large-scale merchants and capitalists, while the nine minor guilds were mostly comprised by artisans, small tradesmen, and shopkeepers.

jors, the chief elected offices of the land.* The social transformation that brought families like the Machiavelli, the Medici, and the Pitti to the fore while marginalizing such feudal "magnates" as the Tornaquinci and the Pazzi, did not constitute a full-scale revolution in which one class seized power from another, but rather an evolution within a population in which such distinctions were already thoroughly confused. This confusion can be seen in microcosm among Niccolò's own ancestors. In 1393, two Machiavelli brothers, Buoninsegna and Lorenzo di Filippo (Buoninsegna was Niccolò's great-great-grandfather) inherited the run-down castle of Montespertoli in the Val di Pesa, formerly the possession of the noble Castellani. Thus, while their descendants continued to earn a living in the city as merchants, bankers, and lawyers, their titles and property in the countryside provided both income and social standing.

By the mid-fourteenth century the Machiavelli were firmly ensconced in the Oltrarno. The property on the Via Romana was purchased by the family from the powerful Pitti clan in the late 1300s. By that time, they were also in possession of various properties in the Val di Pesa south of Florence, including Sant' Andrea in Percussina, where Niccolò would retire to write *The Prince*. But while the Machiavelli prospered along with the commune, they did not stand out from dozens of their colleagues. In the tax rolls of 1427, for instance, no Machiavelli is listed among the top bracket of households assessed at more than 10,000 florins.† Nor did they stand out in the political arena. The great struggle for supremacy between the Albizzi faction and the rising Medici clan that dominated the early decades of the fifteenth century saw the Machiavelli discreetly on the sidelines, poised to retain their modest standing whichever side ultimately prevailed. When, in 1434, Cosimo de' Medici, following a year of exile, drove his opponents from the city and established himself and his allies

---

* Between 1280 and 1530, the Machiavelli name turns up 130 times among the Three Majors. Compared to the record of powerful clans like the Medici, whose members served 196 times over the same period, this was a more than respectable showing (see *Online Catasto of 1427*).

† The tax roll (*Catasto*) of 1427 is one of the best-studied documents of Renaissance Florence. Of the 9,780 households listed, including eleven bearing the Machiavelli name, only 137 (approximately one in 70) had an assessed worth exceeding 10,000 florins. Niccolò di Buoninsegna Machiavelli, Niccolò's grandfather, had a declared net worth of 1,086 florins, all of it in the form of real estate. This placed him in the upper third in terms of total wealth, but far behind such plutocrats as Palla Strozzi (162,906) or Giovanni di Bicci de' Medici (91,089), grandfather of Lorenzo the Magnificent (see *Online Catasto of 1427*).

as the dominant power in the land, none of the Machiavelli suffered in the wholesale changing of the guard.

Like most Florentine families, the Machiavelli identified closely with their own neighborhood, investing not only their financial but their spiritual capital in the local community. Opposite the Machiavelli compound was the parish church of Santa Felicità, where the family claimed patronage rights over the small chapel of San Gregorio. Here young Niccolò spent many a Sunday morning gazing up at Domenico Ghirlandaio's fresco of Christ's deposition from the cross, commissioned by his cousin Alessandro, an experience that seems to have done little to instill in him either piety or an aesthetic sense.

If the overall picture of the Machiavelli as the fifteenth century unfolded was one of comfortable prosperity, in the decades before Niccolò's birth there were signs of future difficulty. The source of these troubles was largely Bernardo himself. Though Niccolò never seems to have reproached his father, for whom he showed a deep affection, it is clear that Bernardo had none of the characteristic Florentine aptitude for business. One can comb through his diary, which he kept for thirteen years of his adult life, and still have no idea what Bernardo did to earn a living. The pages are filled with various mundane transactions—the sale of wool or firewood from the farm at Sant' Andrea in Percussina, a dispute with a butcher over payment for a delivery of spring lambs for Easter, endless haggling over the dowry for his daughter's wedding—but he never seems to have contemplated the possibility of adding to his modest patrimony through investment or hard work. The frugality of the family budget is suggested by numerous transactions recorded with one Matteo, a dealer in secondhand clothes, justifying Niccolò's claim that growing up he "learned to deny myself rather than to enjoy." The impression left by Bernardo's diary was that he was singularly lacking in ambition, particularly when compared with his compatriots, who were known throughout Italy as shrewd businessmen, greedy for gain, and ambitious as the devil.

Bernardo had been trained in the law, but there is little indication that he ever earned money by pursuing this potentially lucrative career. On his tax return of 1480, he wrote: "*messer* Bernardo . . . practices no gainful employment"—a statement that seems as much a boast as a plea for understanding. Whatever his financial circumstances, he was too much a gentleman to consider bolstering the family fortune through work. His circumstances and attitude are remarkably similar to that of Michelangelo's father, a member of the minor nobility, who proudly told the ruler of the city: "I have never practiced any profession; but I have always up to now lived on my slender income, attending to those few possessions left to me by my forebears, seeking not only to maintain them but to increase them as much as possible by my diligence."

The most tangible result of Bernardo's education seems to have been the acquisition of debt he had difficulty repaying and that served as a handy excuse whenever he fell behind on his taxes. Like his son, he was both garrulous and gregarious and preferred to spend his time discussing the news of the day rather than earning a florin. He was a man in no particular hurry, content to rely on an inheritance sufficient to allow him the leisure in which to pursue his intellectual interests.

This fecklessness determined the trajectory of Niccolò's life. The fact that Bernardo was in arrears with his taxes meant that he was officially listed as *a specchio* (literally on the board), that is, barred from holding office. This was both a political and a social impediment since election to political office was the medium through which Renaissance Florentines measured their status.* Even during the height of the Medici regime, when real power was concentrated in a few hands, politics still played a central role in the Florentine citizen's life. The traditional legislative bodies continued to meet and debate in the Palazzo della Signoria and, to a large extent, social standing was determined—and useful connections made—by success in elections that were hotly contested even when the offices to which they led had been reduced to futility.

Thus Bernardo fell short on the most significant measure of a Florentine citizen's social standing. His friendship with Chancellor Bartolomeo Scala reveals that the debt preventing him from holding elective office did not exclude him from polite society, but it did mean that he was always a marginal, even eccentric figure. This was the way Bernardo preferred things. His daily itinerary shows him puttering about his estates, tending in desultory fashion to the meager economy of his household, reading

---

* Bernardo's tax problems may also have been the source of a curious incident in Niccolò's career when his enemies tried to claim he was ineligible for government service (*see chapter 8*). Ironically, his debt may also have interfered with his ability to make a living since those declared *a specchio* were also barred from practicing as notaries, a profession for which his legal training qualified him (see Atkinson, *Debts, Dowries, Donkeys*, 43).

his books in quiet and generally enjoying his life as a cultured gentleman of modest means. This impression is only reinforced by the most ambitious undertaking recorded in the pages of his diary: the compilation of an index for a new edition of Livy's monumental history of Rome.* The project, which required him to provide a list of "all the cities and mountains and rivers that are mentioned" in the text, involved a good deal of scholarly detective work, a task in which he was aided by the loan of a rare volume of Ptolemy's world atlas. This was his true calling: to sift through ancient books in search of obscure facts—a pedant's dream of paradise. It speaks to Bernardo's priorities that the only payment he received for all his hard work was a copy of the precious volumes for his own library, a transaction that suggests the Florentine's love of classical learning but an atypical disdain for hard cash.

While Bernardo's diaries provide only the most grudging glimpses into his life, Niccolò's own writing may shed some additional light. Niccolò's satirical play *Clizia* includes a description of an elderly Florentine gentleman, one Nicomaco, who sounds a lot like his own father, a modest man of affairs and an amateur scholar: "He spent his time as a good man should," recalls his wife, Sofronia.

> *He got up early in the morning, heard mass, bought the provisions for the day. Then, if he had business in the public square, in the market, with the magistrates, he attended to it; if he didn't, he either joined with some citizen in serious conversation, or he went into his office at home, where he wrote up his ledger and straightened out his accounts. Then he dined pleasantly with his family, and after he had dined, he talked with his son, advised him, taught him to understand men, and by means of various examples, ancient and modern, showed him how to live. Then he went out. He spent the whole day either in business or in dignified and honorable pastimes. When it was evening, the* Ave Maria *always found him at home; he sat a little while with us by the fire, if it was winter, then went into his office to go over his affairs. At nine o'clock he had a cheerful supper. This ordering of his life was an*

---

* This project of Bernardo's was particularly significant for Niccolò, since his most sustained work of political writing is his commentary on this work of ancient history, his *Discourses on the First Ten Books of Titus Livius.*

*example to all the others in the house, and everybody was ashamed
not to imitate him.*

The pleasant domesticity Sofronia describes offers a window onto the
household in which young Niccolò grew to manhood. Particularly revealing is the passage in which Nicomaco guides his son's moral development,
drawing lessons from both ancient and modern examples just as Bernardo
must often have done with young Niccolò.

Niccolò often complained about his own poverty, but he never blamed
his father. In fact, father and son were cut from the same cloth. His admission that he knew nothing of "either the silk or the wool trade, or profits or
losses," could as easily have come from Bernardo's mouth.

Father and son resembled each other in other ways, too. Both were
sensitive about the family honor, which they guarded as a precious commodity even as they allowed more tangible assets to slip through their
fingers. One incident stands out from the rather dry recitation of daily
transactions that forms the bulk of Bernardo's diary. It concerns the
pregnancy of the serving girl Lorenza, who had been seduced, perhaps
even raped, by one Niccolò d'Alessandro Machiavelli, a second cousin
and neighbor in the Oltrarno, while she was living under Bernardo's roof.
Throughout the investigation of the incident and the bitter recriminations
that followed, Bernardo seems motivated primarily by a desire to uphold
his reputation. Typically for a man of his class, he is less concerned for the
unfortunate girl than for his good name, which had been besmirched by
the recklessness of a young relative.

The importance of the incident to Bernardo is reflected in the number
of pages he devotes to it, but a more serious blow to the family's reputation is passed over in silence. This concerned another relative, also a
second cousin, by the name of Girolamo Machiavelli. Though a far more
distinguished citizen—he was a professor of law at the University of
Florence—Girolamo more seriously damaged the family name than the
lecherous Niccolò d'Alessandro. In the summer of 1458, during one of
the periodic struggles between the ruling clique and a faction seeking
more democratic representation, Girolamo spoke out forcefully against
the electoral controls imposed by Cosimo de' Medici and his henchmen.
This courageous act resulted in Girolamo's arrest and, when he persisted

in agitating against the regime, eventual imprisonment. This was a rare instance in the annals of the Machiavelli family when one of its members had stood apart from the anonymous crowd of respectable *popolani*, but the results of this bold act would not have encouraged his kinsmen to follow in his footsteps. Girolamo's rashness only served to reinforce Bernardo's aversion to politics.

A clue to Bernardo's attitude toward his wayward cousin comes in Bartolomeo Scala's *De Legibus*, where the author attributes to his friend the following bit of political wisdom, won presumably from hard personal experience: "For it often happens that men who are just and principled risk losing their good names and reputation because they are the innocent heirs or relatives of someone in disgrace." But if Bernardo had actually vented these bitter feelings to his friend, he seems not to have heeded his own advice. In 1458, the same year that Girolamo spoke out against the government, Bernardo, then a mature man of thirty-three,* compounded his kinsman's indiscretion by marrying Bartolomea, widow of the apothecary Niccolò Benizi. Other members of the Benizi family, though not Niccolò himself, had been implicated in Girolamo's machinations against the government and had been among those exiled for sedition. It is unlikely that Bernardo intended by his choice of bride to make a political statement but the questionable association certainly did nothing to deter him. If this speaks well of Bernardo's independence, it also confirms his impracticality.

Despite the association with a politically suspect family, Bernardo's marriage was conventional in other respects. The Benizi were neighbors of the Machiavelli in the parish of Santa Felicità, and the young widow must have seemed like an eminently suitable match for the scholarly bachelor. "Above all else stick together with your neighbors and kinsmen," wrote the Florentine patrician Gino Capponi, advice Bernardo apparently took to heart. In the fractious, violent world of Florence, such local alliances were often the best guarantee of family survival.

---

* This was not an unusual age for a Florentine male to be married. While girls tended to marry in their late teens, boys were allowed a period of irresponsibility before settling down to raise a family.

•   •   •

Niccolò was the third child of the union between Bernardo and Bartolomea. He had two older sisters: Primavera, born around 1465, and Mar-
gherita, born 1468. Niccolò, born the following year, was the oldest son,
and in this patriarchal society his arrival was a momentous occasion since
it all but guaranteed that the family name would endure and prosper.* The
birth of a son after two daughters was particularly welcome since the cash-
strapped Bernardo was already having difficulty salting away sufficient
funds to provide the older girls with adequate dowries. To young Niccolò
would fall the honor and the burden of carrying on the family name, a task
made increasingly difficult by Bernardo's carelessness.

As for Bartolomea, her individuality, like that of most of her sex in this
male-dominated society, has largely been lost to history. Niccolò himself
almost never mentioned his mother, and never provided any insight that
would have put flesh on the bare bones of her biography. Bernardo makes
frequent reference to "la mia donna" or "la Bartolomea" in his diary, but he
leaves no room for the expression of feeling in the dry recitation of facts
that make up his entries. What we can glean from these pages is that Bartolomea was a practical woman, a frugal housekeeper and helpmate to her
husband in managing their modest properties. Only in the scandal over
the pregnant serving girl does Bartolomea play a significant role; here,
where sexual mores were involved and discretion required, a woman's
delicacy was used to elicit the truth where a man's blunter approach might
have proved ineffective. When it came to confronting the offending party
and negotiating the financial settlement, however, Bernardo once again
took matters into his own hands.

The only glimmer we have that Bartolomea was anything more than
the typical middle-class housewife is the family tradition that when Niccolò was young she composed some religious verses for her son, a rare
achievement in a world where many girls, even from good families, were
barely literate. Employing her talents for pious ends reflects a conventional cast of mind, but the fact that she took the time and effort to write

---

* It would be another six years before another child lived beyond infancy, Niccolò's younger brother
Totto. There was also a stepsister, Lionarda, born in 1457, Bartolomea's only child with Niccolò Benizi.
She did not grow up in the Machiavelli household and little is known of her.

original poetry suggests a woman of more than ordinary ambition and ability.

It is difficult to determine Bartolomea's contribution to Niccolò's development. Like most Florentine mothers, she no doubt tended to his day-to-day needs while his father saw to his moral and intellectual development. Her apparent piety, in any case, made little impression on her son, whose career was marked by a disdain for priests and a contempt for religious hypocrisy. Niccolò may well have inherited from her his literary flair, but it is safe to assume that the conventional Bartolomea would have been horrified had she known the use to which he would put his talents.

It is easier to trace his father's influence—not only the shared love of books and of history, but also the impracticality when it came to money, intertwined traits that give to both father and son the air of absentminded scholars whose heads are too filled with grandiose schemes to pay attention to the mundane details of daily living. But in the most important decision of his life—to enter government service and dedicate his life to the state—Niccolò ran in the opposite direction. It is above all Niccolò's passion for public service that distinguishes him from his father. While Bernardo rarely set foot in the Palazzo della Signoria, center of Florence's political life, Niccolò never felt more at home than within its crowded chambers, bent over his desk, where he handled much of the government's correspondence. It is plausible to assume that his dedication to public service stemmed from a subconscious need to erase the political and financial failure of his father. Often the most patriotic men are those who feel politically and economically marginalized, who compensate for their social insecurity by more fiercely attaching themselves to the state that spurned them. Clearly, Niccolò set out upon a much different path than the one traversed by his father, but there is a strange sort of symmetry to their journeys. Niccolò's passionate attachment to politics suggests a deep psychological need, perhaps born out of a sense that his father was a somewhat pathetic figure in the eyes of his peers.

Given the copious documentation for his later life, much of it provided by Machiavelli himself, Niccolò's early years remain frustratingly obscure. It is as if he walks onto the stage of history fully formed at the age of twenty-eight. What we know of his life before his memorable debut consists of a few dry facts indifferently recorded in Bernardo's diary; one learns more from these pages about the two oxen he purchased to plow his fields than about his son. The copious correspondence, both personal and official, that opens an intimate window onto Machiavelli's life begins only when he enters the public sphere. This is a pity, since Niccolò's own voice—sardonic, insightful, and always fresh—would surely have vividly evoked the scenes of his childhood.

Even without the benefit of his unique perspective the view is fascinating enough. Machiavelli was a product of a remarkable city at the most remarkable period in its history. The small, independent Republic of Florence was something of an anachronism in an age of rising nation-states, a pygmy among giants, to paraphrase Machiavelli's memorable description of his own family. Florence itself numbered no more than about fifty thousand souls—less than half its peak population reached in the mid-fourteenth century before the coming of the Black Death—while her Tuscan empire included merely a handful of small cities and rustic hamlets. The form of government that had evolved during the Middle Ages was republican; frequent elections and multiple, overlapping jurisdictions made for a lively, if inefficient, political system. The franchise was restricted to wealthy merchants and more modest artisans, but while the urban masses were excluded from any role in political life, Florence remained perhaps the most democratic state in Europe. At least in theory. In fact, the institutional weakness of the government invited its own subversion. Throughout the years of Machiavelli's youth, real power was held by a single family—the fabulously rich Medici—and their cronies, a situation that elicited much grumbling and occasional violence from families who felt they had an equal claim to rule.

One way the Medici consoled their compatriots for the loss of any real say in their own government was by keeping the city prosperous and splendid. During his boyhood some of the greatest minds of the age were assembling in Lorenzo de' Medici's palace on the Via Larga, and many of history's greatest works of art were taking shape in the studios about town: Sandro Botticelli, favored by the Medici family, was conjuring a mood of pagan sensuality in his *Primavera* (1478) and *Birth of Venus* (1482); Andrea del Verrocchio, churning out masterpieces of painting and sculpture assembly-line style, had just taken into his busy studio a talented young apprentice, Leonardo da Vinci, who startled the city with precocious works that surpassed those of his master; while his chief competitor, the equally industrious Domenico Ghirlandaio and his students—among whom was the young Michelangelo—frescoed the walls of the city's churches with narratives in which holy miracles unfolded on the familiar streets of the city while its leading citizens looked on.

Nor was creativity confined to the artists' studios. Impeding traffic and filling the streets with dust and noise were the massive building projects that proclaimed the taste, wealth, and vanity of the richest citizens, including the imposing palaces of the Pitti family, a few blocks to the south of the Machiavelli compound, and of the Strozzi, just beginning to rise near the Old Market. But if the bankers and merchants of Florence had abandoned medieval prohibitions against extravagant display, they still felt sufficiently uneasy to expiate their sins by spending lavishly on the city's great ecclesiastical institutions. The interior of every sacred structure, from the Duomo to the local parish church, gleamed with gilded altarpieces and jewel-encrusted reliquaries paid for out of the profits of the city's thriving wool and silk trade; bankers and lawyers vied with each other in the generosity of their bequests to charitable institutions, while others served the public good by opening the world's first public libraries.

It was, in short, an exciting time to be alive. In many ways the city of Florence seemed to be the center of the universe, but there is little evidence that Machiavelli was deeply affected by the unparalleled visual culture of the city. Of greater interest to a young man whose gifts were literary and interests political were the remarkable poets and philosophers who congregated at the home of Florence's leading citizen, Lorenzo de' Medici. Not only was *Il Magnifico* a fine poet in his own right, but he attracted the greatest writers and thinkers of the day to the city, including the philosophers Marsilio Ficino and Pico della Mirandola, and the poet and scholar Angelo Poliziano. "This is an age of gold," wrote Ficino in an understandable burst of pride, a verdict that history has largely confirmed.

Machiavelli grew to maturity in one of the most peaceful interludes in the turbulent history of Florence. Through the tireless diplomacy of Lorenzo de' Medici the city became, in the words of Machiavelli's friend and contemporary, Francesco Guicciardini, "the fulcrum of Italy"—the keystone in an elaborate system of alliances that prevented the rival states of Italy from destroying each other and that kept greedy foreigners from swooping in to pick up the pieces. In his *History of Florence*, Guicciardini summed up the mood of the city during the last decade of Lorenzo's reign:

> *The city enjoyed perfect peace, the citizens were united and in harmony, and the government so powerful that no one dared oppose it. The people every day delighted in shows, revelries and other novelties; they were well fed, as the city was plentifully supplied with victuals, and all its activities flourished. Men of intellect and ability were contented, for all letters, all arts, all talents were welcomed and recognized. While the city within was universally enjoying the most perfect peace and quiet, without her glory and reputation were supreme because she had a government and a leader of the highest authority.*

Fourteen years older than his friend, Machiavelli recalls that time with equal fondness, declaring that until Lorenzo's death in 1492, "Florentines lived in very great prosperity. . . . For when the arms of Italy, which had been stayed by Lorenzo's sense and authority, had been put down, he turned his mind to making himself and his city great." Both men looked back on the years of their youth as an idyllic time that stood in stark contrast to the disorder that followed Lorenzo's death when, in Machiavelli's words, "discordant Italy opened into herself a passage for the Gauls and suffered barbarian peoples to trample her down." Machiavelli's pessimistic view of the human condition was forged when a peaceful childhood was violently shattered. The "ideal" ruler he conjures in *The Prince* is not made for times of peace but is a grim figure at home in troubled times.

It would be a mistake to exaggerate the peacefulness of Florence during Machiavelli's childhood. Even under Lorenzo de' Medici's firm guiding hand, there was plenty of political discord and even an occasional outburst of civic violence. It was only compared to the disastrous period that followed, that Lorenzo's reign appeared to embody political and social harmony. Crucial to the development of Machiavelli's political thought were the institutions that made Florence a laboratory of republican government and that fostered a vibrant, if often contentious, political climate. However firmly the Medici remained in control of the government, a daily round of commotions and recriminations formed the backdrop of daily life. Every citizen was a politician; debate did not end at the doors of the Palazzo della Signoria but spilled out onto the streets and piazzas, enlivening every conversation and coloring every relationship. Even during Lorenzo's reign there was sufficient turmoil to stimulate the imagination of the budding political scientist. In fact it is hard to imagine the systematic study of politics originating anywhere else but here in Florence, where the average citizen expected to share in his own government and young boys were schooled in Cicero, Aristotle, and Livy to prepare them for the debates they would later hold in the Palazzo della Signoria.

Niccolò was nine years old when the bloodiest upheaval of *Il Magnifico's* reign occurred—the Pazzi Conspiracy in which Lorenzo and his brother were set upon in the Cathedral of Florence. Lorenzo's brother, Giuliano, was killed in the attack, while he himself was wounded. The assassination set off weeks of reprisals more sanguinary than anything seen for centuries in the streets of Florence. The sight of bodies being torn apart by angry crowds, as well as the anxiety provoked by rumors of foreign armies approaching the city gate, must have left a mark on the psyche of the young man, reminding him of the savagery that lay just beneath the surface of even this most cultivated city. This spasm of violence, as well as the lively factional quarrels that were more typical of Florentine political life, provided Niccolò with a unique opportunity to study the passions that drove men to compete in the civic arena, the thirst for power and the love of liberty, the tug of ambition and the belief in community, whose opposing imperatives kept the city at a constant boil.

When it came to raising his children Bernardo shared the priorities of his compatriots. On May 6, 1476, Niccolò, who had just turned seven, began his formal education with "*Maestro* Matteo, master of grammar whose school is located at the foot of the Santa Trinità bridge, where he goes to learn to read his *Donatello.*"* In 1480, the eleven-year-old Niccolò switched from studying Latin to studying "abacus," that is, applied

---

* This refers not to the famous Florentine sculptor but to Donatus, author of a Latin grammar that dates back to ancient times and was used as the initial primer for students of the Renaissance.

mathematics, an important subject in a town built on banking and trade. Niccolò's education was typical of boys of his class, though it is clear that time spent delving into classical texts was more fruitful than time learning arithmetic. Like his father, Niccolò had no head for business, preferring to lose himself in a volume of poetry rather than pore through his own account books. Throughout his career and in his writings Machiavelli demonstrates a familiarity with the poetry, history, and philosophy of the ancient world, though there is little indication that, in addition to Latin, he mastered the newly fashionable but still esoteric Greek.*

For Florentine schoolboys of the Renaissance, being conversant with the major works of the classical past provided more than the basis of an elegant style or the dusty furnishings of the pedant's mind. Dropping the names of Roman generals or quoting obscure Greek philosophers was essential to success as a public speaker, and success as a public speaker was essential to getting ahead in Florentine politics. The young read Scripture to prepare their souls for the world to come, but read Cicero, Aristotle, and Plato to learn how to tackle the responsibilities of civic life. The fact that Machiavelli largely rejected traditional religious doctrine did not mean that he rejected any ethical framework. "For when a child of tender years begins to understand," he wrote in *The Discourses*, "it makes a great difference that he should hear some things spoken of with approval and some things with disapproval, since this must needs make an impression on him, by which later on his own conduct will be regulated in all the walks of life."

Educated Florentines like Machiavelli found their moral bearings not by emulating the lives of the saints but by studying the deeds and adopting the attitudes of the ancient Greeks and Romans. "We call these studies liberal," wrote the fifteenth-century pedagogue Pier Paolo Vergerio, "which are worthy of a free man: they are those through which virtue and wisdom are either practiced or sought, and by which the body or mind is disposed towards all the best things." These studies were also called *bonae*

---

* Machiavelli often quotes Plato and Aristotle and was clearly familiar with their work and with the history of ancient Greece, but he always seems to have relied on Latin translations of their most important writings. Fluency in Latin would have been a normal acquisition for someone of his time and education, while knowledge of Greek continued to be reserved for true scholars. (See Villari, *The Life and Times of Niccolò Machiavelli*, I, 239ff for a fuller discussion.)

litterae (good letters) or *litterae humaniores* (human letters) and the stories of great men and great achievements, as well as the salutary lessons to be learned from wicked men who received their comeuppance, provided a template against which to measure one's own behavior. The constant back and forth between ancient history and current events that forms the structure of *The Prince* and the *Discourses* is not unique to Machiavelli, but is the product of an educational system that encouraged students to interpret the present in light of patterns set down long ago. Whenever he was in danger of succumbing to despair, Niccolò found solace in the great literature of the past. "Leaving the woods, I go to a spring," he recalls in his famous letter to Francesco Vettori: "and then to one of the spots where I hang my bird nets. In my arm I carry a book: Dante, Petrarch, or one of those minor poets like Tibullus, Ovid. I read of their amorous passions and their loves and recall my own, and lose myself for a while in these happy thoughts."

Machiavelli reached maturity without having done anything to distinguish himself from his peers. Florentines had a term for such young men: they were called *giovani* (youths), men who were no longer children but had yet to take on the adult responsibilities of marriage and child-rearing. Given the fact that Florentine men typically married in their late twenties or early thirties, they represented a large and potentially explosive element in the social fabric. Much of the violence that had plagued the city in earlier centuries can be attributed to these lawless young men who roamed the streets in search of adventure. One Florentine patrician summed up the general attitude toward these good-for-nothings who did little but "threaten bar keepers, dismember [statues of] saints, and break pots and plates."

The young Niccolò Machiavelli was no worse, though not much better, than most of his peers. The best one can say is that while he can boast no record of achievement for these years, neither did he appear on the rolls of the *Otto* (the Eight), the police who patrolled the streets and attempted to curb the worst excesses of the *giovani*. Though he was certainly not living in monkish denial, much of his time was spent in study, either formally through the Studio, Florence's university, or by delving into the numerous learned volumes in his father's library.

In appearance the young Niccolò was unremarkable. He was of average

height and possessed a wiry frame that would serve him well on many a
harrowing voyage in service to his country and during his weeks of imprisonment, ordeals that would have overwhelmed a less robust constitution. His nose was aquiline, his lips thin, features that gave him a sharp
and somewhat birdlike aspect. But the impression of hardness was relieved
in conversation when his face lit up and his eyes sparkled with mirth.
Unfortunately, there are no contemporaneous portraits of him, but those
painted shortly after his death and based on the memories of people who
knew him well emphasize the sardonic smile and curious expression that
suggest both his keen intelligence and the impudent sense of humor that
won him as many enemies as friends. In the best of them, there is a hint
of kindness behind the wry smile, of sympathy as well as cynicism. Given
the absence of a likeness taken from life, one must content oneself with the
few descriptions available. The most precious comes from his wife, Marietta, who, upon the birth of their child, reported to her absent husband:
"For now the baby is well. He looks like you, white as snow, with his head
a velvety black. . . . Since he looks like you he seems beautiful to me"—a
clue, if only an oblique one, as to his true appearance.

For a bright young man from a family with little money and little influence, literary talent was one of the few means of gaining entrée into elite
circles. Early on, Machiavelli took the first tentative steps on the route to
success already traveled by the poets Luigi Pulci and Angelo Poliziano.
These talented but impecunious youths managed to parlay their gifts into
a coveted seat at Lorenzo de' Medici's table, and Machiavelli saw no reason
why he might not duplicate this feat of upward mobility. As part of this
effort he dedicated one of his earliest works, a carnival poem titled "Pas-
torale," to Giuliano de' Medici, youngest son of *Il Magnifico*. This minor
work offers a tantalizing clue that Machiavelli wished to join that glittering circle of poets and artists who congregated at the palace on the Via
Larga. The unoriginal verses, in which local shepherds mingle familiarly
with Apollo, Diana, and Jupiter, followed the erudite formula perfected by
Angelo Poliziano, Lorenzo's closest friend, and seem calculated to appeal
to the refined tastes of his teenage heir. Given his father's friendship with
Bartolomeo Scala, another Medici client, it is clear that the Machiavelli
were members, if only marginal ones, of the city's dominant faction. Thus,
despite later complications, Niccolò's connection to the Medici began

early. When in 1513 Machiavelli wrote to Giuliano de' Medici from his prison cell, he was not an anonymous supplicant but an old acquaintance hoping to remind the young lord of happier times.

Perhaps Machiavelli's failure to secure a place for himself at the Medici court owed something to his prickly personality. Though he never lacked for friends, those close to him knew he could be his own worst enemy. A few years later, when he was just beginning his career in the civil service, his friend Biagio Buonaccorsi had to intervene to prevent him from alienating his colleagues. "Write to Niccolò Capponi," Buonaccorsi pleaded, "who grumbles and complains that you have never written him, and tell that asshole *Ser* Battaglione to ease up. . . . I spoke to Fantone about what I wrote you yesterday: he told me that four other lawsuits had been brought against you." Everyone seemed to recognize his intelligence, but throughout his life he was hampered by his inability to flatter his superiors—a defect exposed most glaringly when his gift of *The Prince* was spurned by those who preferred servility to brilliance.

Even as he made a halfhearted stab at launching a literary career, Niccolò indulged the many pleasures the city had to offer. He was a frequent visitor to both the brothels and the taverns that lined the streets near the markets and that catered both to dissatisfied husbands and young men who were expected to spend the years between boyhood and married life sowing their wild oats. Even as a married man with young children, Niccolò made no effort to hide his taste for whores and the raucous conviviality of the tavern, habits he picked up early on.

His taste for low pleasures, however, did not distract him from his true passion. When he wasn't at the whorehouse—or perhaps even when he was—his head was often buried in a book, most likely a volume of Greek or Roman history or one of the great triumvirate of modern Tuscans—Dante, Petrarch, and Boccaccio. Like Callimaco, the hero of his play *La Mandragola*, Machiavelli might have described spending his own youth "partly in studies, partly in amusement, partly in business." His writing, rich in learned allusion but also earthy and filled with the crude vernacular of his native city, demonstrates an education that took place both in the classroom and on the streets.

At the age of twenty-eight there was little to distinguish Niccolò from countless equally directionless young men. He seemed content to live off his modest properties and spend his free time—of which he had plenty—in conversation with friends, and his money—of which he had less—on whores and gambling. "Because life is short," he later wrote in the introduction to *Mandragola*,

> *and many are the pains*
> *that every man bears who lives and stints himself,*
> *let us go on spending and wasting the years as we will,*
> *for he who deprives himself of pleasure*
> *only to live with labor and toil*
> *does not understand the world's deceits.*

He had by this time a fair amount of experience in "spending and wasting." Half his life was over and he had little to show for it.

But despite the rather aimless course his life had taken so far, he burned with ambition. This, too, was encouraged by the get-ahead mentality of Florence. As one influential educational text claimed, men are motivated primarily "by eagerness for praise and inflamed by love of glory," words Machiavelli will paraphrase in *The Prince*. He wanted to make his mark, to achieve something that would cause his name to be remembered by future generations. Not particularly well connected or well heeled, he lacked only the opportunity to demonstrate the singular talents of an obscure young man of modest means.

I I

A SWORD UNSHEATHED

"O Italy! O Princes! O prelates of the Church! the wrath of God is upon ye, neither is there any hope for ye, unless ye be converted to the Lord. O Florence! O Italy! these adversities have befallen ye for your sins. Repent ye before the sword be unsheathed, while it be yet unstained with blood; otherwise neither wisdom, power, nor force will avail."

—GIROLAMO SAVONAROLA

ON THE MORNING OF MARCH 3, 1498, MACHIAVELLI left his home near the Ponte Vecchio and set out for the monastery of San Marco on the northern outskirts of town. Here, far from his accustomed haunts—and in a departure from his usual routine—he attended a sermon delivered by Girolamo Savonarola, the charismatic monk whose messianic visions had alternately inspired and convulsed the city for six tumultuous years.[*]

Savonarola was not a prophet of peace but a preacher of fire and brimstone, and his apocalyptic sermons unhinged a populace already agitated by years of war and civil unrest. So intemperate were his jeremiads that the Pope himself had issued a decree forbidding the friar to speak in public, a policy meant in part to silence denunciations launched against the Holy Father and the church he led. Throughout this Lenten season, and despite calls from cooler heads for the people of Florence to follow the example of

---

[*] According to his own account, Machiavelli attended Savonarola's sermons at San Marco on two consecutive days, March 2 and 3.

Jesus, the city was torn apart by factions whose approach to settling political disagreements was to hurl abuse at their opponents or even to resort
to the dagger and the club. Most numerous were the *piagnoni* (weepers
or snivelers), pious followers of Savonarola who dominated the councils
of government and policed the streets for signs of immorality. Arrayed
against them were a variety of parties, like the *arrabbiati* (angry ones), or
the aristocratic *compagnacci* (the rude companions), and the sinister *bigi*
(grays), a secret society plotting to restore the disgraced Medici to power.
The always bitter rivalries had recently turned even uglier, as angry words
gave way to acts of vandalism and intimidation. Now all eyes turned
toward the modest church where the friar was expected to issue his challenge to Pope Alexander VI, an act of defiance that could well plunge the
city into civil war.

On this late-winter morning the paths of two of the truly remarkable
figures of the Renaissance crossed, one ascending, the other headed even
more precipitously in the opposite direction. For the obscure young man,
an anonymous face in the crowd, it was a first tentative step on a rising
ladder, while for the famous preacher—who from his current perch atop
the pulpit stood a few steps closer to heaven—this was a final opportunity
to pull back before his plunge toward a fiery death. Years later Machiavelli
might well have had this moment in mind when he wrote of the "countless
men who, that they might fall to earth with a heavier crash, with this goddess [Fortune] have climbed to excessive heights."

There is no other place on earth where such an encounter could have
occurred. Not only are Savonarola and Machiavelli both monumental
figures in the history of Western thought, but one would be hard pressed
to find two men who embodied such divergent and mutually uncompre-
hending philosophies: one a religious extremist, spiritual father of fun-
damentalism, the other an ardent secularist who dared to contemplate a
world without God or morality. Nowhere but in this creative, contentious
city could two such remarkable, and remarkably different, men have been
thrown together by the hand of fate. It is not an exaggeration to say that on
this chilly morning at the beginning of March, in the modest church a few
blocks south of the Porta San Gallo, two worlds collided.

Unlike most of the crowd packed into San Marco that day, Machiavelli had not fallen under the spell of the charismatic Dominican friar.

As Savonarola thundered from the pulpit, those in the audience wept and sighed, shouted their agreement or turned inward, gnawed by some secret guilt exhumed by the speaker. "O Italy!" he cried. "O Princes! O prelates of the Church! the wrath of God is upon ye, neither is there any hope for ye, unless ye be converted to the Lord. O Florence! O Italy! these adversities have befallen ye for your sins. Repent ye before the sword be unsheathed, while it be yet unstained with blood; otherwise neither wisdom, power, nor force will avail." These were dark times, he proclaimed, but it was the deepest gloom that preceded the first faint glimmer of a new dawn. If only the citizens would turn away from sin they might step confidently into the light of a blessed day.

Machiavelli was unmoved. He passed a clinical eye over the scene of near hysteria, scoffing at the notion that the speaker was divinely inspired and instead dissecting the speech as if it were a performance in order to discover the tricks Savonarola deployed to keep his audience in thrall. "The people of Florence do not think that they are ignorant or rude," he wrote in *The Prince*, "yet Girolamo Savonarola convinced them he conversed with God. . . . [M]ultitudes believed him without ever having seen anything extraordinary to compel their believing it."

Though Machiavelli was outwardly conventional in his religious life, the kind of mysticism that was his stock in trade left him cold. In fact, while Machiavelli did not belong to any of the factions that were battling for control of the republic, his sympathies clearly lay with the preacher's opponents. He was an educated and sophisticated young man, steeped in the classical literature Savonarola deplored as a distraction from the Gospels and an avid consumer of those low pleasures for which Florence had once been famous. He had little use for the self-appointed guardians of public virtue who did their best to stamp out vice and corruption. From his point of view the friar and his "boys"—processions of youths dressed in white who patrolled the streets on the lookout for sins and sinners— were more than a minor nuisance since he was one of those whose morals were most in need of reform. Whenever one of these pious gangs came into view a cry went up, "Here come the boys of the friar!"—the signal for gamblers to pocket their dice, whores to scatter, and ladies of the better sort to hide their jewelry.

No doubt Machiavelli was one of the first to duck inside the nearest doorway. He had a certain grudging respect for the discipline and ardor of the friar's pious legions, but he objected to those grand spectacles of communal self-abnegation that were a feature of life in Savonarolan Florence. Chronically short of cash, he cringed at the sight of his wealthier compatriots casting their silks, jewels, and indecent *objets d'art* into the great "bonfires of the vanities" kindled in the Piazza della Signoria—extravagant gestures of repentance that only the rich could afford.

Machiavelli's skepticism toward charismatic religious figures like Savonarola is apparent in a letter he wrote some years later recounting the sudden success of another preacher, "a friar of Saint Francis who is half hermit and who, to gain more repute as a preacher, claims to be a prophet." Like his more famous predecessor, this cut-rate Jeremiah predicted that they would "suffer fire and sack," that "there would be a great dying and great famine." And just as they had a decade and a half earlier, Florentines flocked to hear this prophet of doom, demonstrating once again that nothing was more certain to fill the pews than forecasts of imminent apocalypse. While his friends shed tears of repentance and promised to mend their ways, Machiavelli saw no reason to change his habits. "I didn't actually hear the preacher," he admitted, "for I don't usually get involved in such matters." Still, he remarked sarcastically, the friar's gloomy prophesies did manage to demoralize him sufficiently that for one night at least he canceled a planned rendezvous with his favorite courtesan.

This morning, pressed by the crush of fervent disciples who credited Savonarola with the gift of prophecy—"I believe Christ speaks through my mouth," he proclaimed—Machiavelli listened with an attentive but skeptical ear. In fact it was his presumed immunity to the blandishments of the preacher that explained his presence in San Marco. He had gone at the request of Ricciardo Becchi, the Florentine ambassador to the Holy See, "to give you, as you wished," Machiavelli reminded him, "a full account of what is going on here regarding the friar." As far as we know it was his first political assignment, the moment when, after twenty-eight uneventful and unproductive years, Machiavelli walked onto the stage and took his place as an actor in the great political drama of the day. Admittedly, it is a small part—that of a witness standing in the wings and offering occasional asides while the star commands most of our attention. But it is a role that suited him well. Throughout his career as a diplomat, for which this assignment was something of an audition, Machiavelli proved himself a perceptive analyst of character. Attending this morning's sermon offered him an opportunity to exercise his critical faculties on the most compelling and controversial figure of the age.

The report Machiavelli sent to Ricciardo Becchi reveals both the strength and weakness of his methods. His indifference to spiritual matters certainly caused him to underestimate the appeal of Savonarola's message, but if he was blind to many of the friar's virtues—without which his hold on the people of Florence would be inexplicable—this handicap allowed him to see all more clearly the rhetorical devices the friar employed to win the impressionable to his cause. "[H]e began with great terrors, with explanations that to those not examining them too closely were quite effective," Machiavelli recorded. But while Machiavelli was inclined to view the great preacher as something of a fraud ("he follows the mood of the times and shades his lies to suit them," he declared), he appreciated the friar's courage in standing up to the most powerful lord of Europe: "[H]ad you heard with what audacity he began to preach," he told Becchi, "and how he proceeded, it would have stirred no small amount of admiration."

As always, Savonarola's exegesis of Scripture carried a pointed political message. Taking as his subject the book of Exodus, Savonarola told the story of God's chosen people persecuted by a cruel and corrupt potentate. "But the more they oppressed them, the more they multiplied and increased," he read, gesturing toward the crowd to make explicit the link between the ancient Hebrews and his own followers. In a characteristic act of hubris, he then proceeded to cast himself in the role of Moses leading them out of bondage. But if Savonarola was Moses, who was to play the vengeful Pharaoh bent on defying God's will? It was here that the Dominican preacher stepped onto dangerous ground, for he assigned the villain's role to Rodrigo Borgia, the corrupt and sensual man who now occupied the Throne of Saint Peter as Pope Alexander VI. "[H]e seeks to set all of [the people] at odds with the Supreme Pontiff," Machiavelli reported to Becchi, "and, turning toward him and his attacks, says of the pope what could be said of the wickedest person you might imagine."

As Becchi read Machiavelli's report he realized that Savonarola had no intention of backing down. The Florentine government was already in hot water with the Pontiff, and its continued inability or unwillingness to

rein in the disobedient friar had strained the relationship past the breaking point. The mere fact that Savonarola had delivered the sermon was a
brazen act of disobedience, since he was currently forbidden by the Pope
to speak in public.* "So," the Pope had recently grumbled to the Florentine
envoy, "you are allowing Friar Girolamo to preach again. I would never
have believed that you would treat me this way." Unless they dealt with the
rebellious monk, he told them, he would place the entire city under interdict. Such a ban would jeopardize not only the souls of Florentines but,
perhaps of more immediate concern, their worldly goods, since any merchant in a foreign land placed outside the protection of the Church risked
having his possessions confiscated. Torn between their loyalty to the Friar
and their own well-being, Florentines that morning vacillated between
hope and fear, resignation and anger.

Savonarola's address to the believers in San Marco was the climactic
moment in a bitter contest of wills between the Dominican monk and the
Pontiff. It also marked a critical juncture in the history of the republic after
four years of upheaval during which the entire peninsula of Italy—from
Naples in the south to Milan in the north, with Florence caught uncomfortably in between—descended into chaos. In 1504 Machiavelli wrote a
poem looking back on this gloomy period when the land lay "filled with
blood and dead men . . . when discordant Italy opened into herself a passage for the Gauls and suffered barbarian peoples to trample her down."
He treats the Dominican preacher with typical ambivalence:

> But that which to many was far more distressing and brought
> on disunion, was that sect under whose command your city lay.
> I speak of that great Savonarola who, inspired with heavenly vigor,
> kept you closely bound with his words.
> But many feared to see their country ruined, little by little,
> under his prophetic teaching.

That ambivalence was already present in his letter to Becchi of 1498,
written with the words of Savonarola still ringing in his ears. This was,

---

* The government's response to this demand was to prohibit Savonarola from speaking in the Cathedral, but they did not prevent him from delivering sermons at his own church of San Marco. This
doomed attempt at a compromise solution revealed deep divides within the ruling elite.

in effect, his first diplomatic dispatch, the first time he set pen to paper to offer his sober analysis of a highly fraught political situation. Future missions would take him to exotic courts and involve elaborate ceremony and official credentials, but few would rival the raw emotional intensity of this initial assignment. It would be another three months before Machiavelli took up his position in the government of Florence, but it was in San Marco, where he had gone as an emissary to an alien territory of the soul, that Machiavelli's remarkable career really began.

The age that made Savonarola's remarkable rise possible and precipitous fall inevitable, a chaotic time where frightened people turned to those who promised that present troubles were merely a prelude to certain redemption, had arrived four years earlier with the invasion of Italy by Charles VIII, Most Catholic King of France, at the helm of a massive army. The French invasion of Italy opened a psychic chasm, dividing time into a golden-hued "before" and an ash-gray "after." "With them," wrote Francesco Guicciardini of the marauding hordes, "a flame and a plague had entered Italy which not only overthrew states, but changed their forms of government and the methods of warfare.

"Before," he continued, providing a brief sketch of the world as he knew it in his youth, "Italy had been principally divided into five states: the Papacy, Naples, Venice, Milan and Florence, each seeking to preserve its own possessions, watchful lest any should usurp what belonged to another and grow so strong that the rest should fear him. . . . Now owing to this invasion of the French everything was turned upside down as if by a sudden storm; the unity of Italy was broken and shattered."* It was in this "broken and shattered" world that Machiavelli had his first professional success as a civil servant in the pay of the Florentine Republic and it was in contemplating the wreckage of his native land that his dismal view of the human condition was forged. It was a world of flame and ash, of chaos,

---

* For this period in history Guicciardini is a better guide than Machiavelli. Though at twenty-five Machiavelli was a grown man when Charles invaded while his friend Guicciardini was only eleven, Machiavelli's *Florentine Histories* ends with Lorenzo's death in 1492, while Guicciardini's *The History of Florence* and *The History of Italy* both cover the entire Savonarolan period. Machiavelli probably ended his *Florentine Histories* in 1492 so he would not have to deal with the unfortunate Piero in a book commissioned by his cousin, Cardinal Giulio de' Medici.

ruin, and disease.* It was a world that made possible not only the meteoric career of the Dominican preacher whose apocalyptic visions tapped into the troubled mood of the times, but also of the cruel tyrant Cesare Borgia, who dazzled all of Europe with his daring exploits before he too came to grief—a world presided over by capricious *Fortuna*, equally generous in her bestowal of sudden favor and sudden death. And it was a world that, ultimately, gave rise to Machiavelli's most imaginative creation, the ruthless antihero who strides across the pages of *The Prince*.

In *The Art of War*, Machiavelli provides a vivid description of Italy on the eve of the French invasion. Corrupt and complacent, greedy for profit and incapable of finding common ground for the common good, its leaders were singularly ill-prepared for what was to come:

> *Our Italian princes, before experiencing the shocks of foreign wars, were accustomed to believe that it was sufficient for a prince to be able to devise a sharp answer in his writing office, to pen a fine epistle, show wit and readiness in his words and sayings, be able to lay schemes, deck himself with gold and gems, sleep and eat with greater luxury than other men, surround himself with many sensual delights, rule his subjects with avarice and haughtiness, become rotten with sloth, confer military promotion as a favor . . . nor did the poor wretches foresee that they were thus preparing themselves to fall a prey to the first enemy that should assail them. Hence, in the year 1494, came terrible alarms, sudden flights, and miraculous defeats, and thus three of the most powerful States of Italy have been repeatedly pillaged and laid waste.*

It was late summer 1494 when Charles VIII, the twenty-eight-year-old king of France, crossed the Alps with an army of forty thousand well-trained and well-equipped men. This single impetuous and ill-conceived act put an end of the golden age of the Italian Renaissance, a time when the greatest artists, writers, and philosophers flourished under the indulgent regimes of the prosperous republics and minor principalities that

---

* This is literally true since the French army carried not only the usual arsenal of war but also the as yet unknown disease of syphilis, a contagion probably brought back from the New World by the Spanish ships of exploration.

divided the peninsula. These miniature polities, anachronistic survivors of the Middle Ages, were pathetically overmatched by the rising nation-states and their massive armies, as the King of France was in the process of demonstrating. Following the route of Hannibal's legions, Charles's battalions spilled row after row from the mountain passes and onto the fertile plains of Lombardy, heavy infantry—including the famed Swiss pike men, the most feared warriors of Europe—and armored cavalry carrying aloft banners bearing the fleur-de-lis of the royal house of France. Most terrifying of all were the bronze cannon hauled by teams of thickset horses, a gleaming array of firepower on a scale never before deployed on the battlefields of Italy.

One glimpse of this mighty host was sufficient to send shivers down the spines of the most battle-hardened *condottiere.** The ragtag bands of hired mercenaries with which the petty states of "discordant Italy" had for centuries been accustomed to wage war upon each other would scatter like dry leaves in the wind before the coming onslaught. That is if they could even be persuaded to act together, a doubtful proposition given the age-old enmities that existed between the myriad states of the peninsula and the selfishness with which each prince pursued his own private advantage. Italians of the Renaissance occasionally acknowledged a common kinship, particularly when threatened by "barbarian" forces, but if they were a family it was of the most dysfunctional sort in which fraternal rivalries were more potent than brotherly love.

It was one of their own, Ludovico Sforza, lord of Milan,† who had done the most to engineer the calamity. Known to history as *Il Moro* (the Moor) "because of his dark complexion and because of the reputation for cunning he had already begun to acquire"—it was rumored that he was in fact the bastard son of Duke Francesco Sforza and a slave girl—Ludovico had a streak of deviousness that in later centuries would undoubtedly have been

---

* These *condottieri*, literally "contractors," named for the *condotta*, or contract, they signed with the state that employed them, were mercenary captains employed by the various governments of Italy to fight their battles. Leading small bands of professional soldiers, these captains were specialists in avoiding bloody combat since death and destruction, at least for their own men, was bad for business. They had no compunction, however, in meting out the same to civilians who happened to get in their way.

† At the time, Ludovico was not officially the Duke of Milan, the title held by his young nephew for whom he was serving as regent. It was his desire to secure the title for himself that largely explains his machinations with the French.

described as Machiavellian. As it was, his contemporaries had no shortage of epithets to hurl at the man they blamed for their country's travails.

The disaster began with a dynastic quarrel between Ludovico and the King of Naples, one that Sforza thought might most elegantly be resolved by encouraging the French King to reassert his ancestral claim to the Neapolitan throne. It seemed at first glance a clever idea: have the French do the fighting while he, Ludovico, stood on the sidelines and enjoyed the spectacle of his rival's destruction. But the ruler of Milan, overly confident in his ability to control the forces he had unleashed, apparently lacked the imagination to picture the difficulties that would arise once the immediate objective was won. With a massive foreign army set loose upon Italian soil and with the other great monarchs of Europe itching to profit in some way, it was a strategy unlikely to accrue to the benefit of any Italian state.

For Florence, the arrival of the French army on Italian soil proved particularly challenging. At the time the republic was led by Piero de' Medici, the twenty-six-year-old son and heir of Lorenzo the Magnificent, a man who shared little with his illustrious father besides the family name. In his *Florentine Histories*, Machiavelli explains that the outcome might have been far different had Lorenzo, rather than his son, been at the helm: "for when Italy was left deprived of his advice, no mode was found for those who remained either to satisfy or to check the ambition of Ludovico Sforza. . . . Therefore, as soon as Lorenzo was dead, those bad seeds began to grow which, not long after, since the one who knew how to eliminate them was not alive, ruined and are still ruining Italy." For every virtue Lorenzo possessed, Piero seems to have substituted a corresponding vice. "He was a haughty and cruel man," wrote Guicciardini, "who preferred being feared rather than loved. Savage and bloodthirsty, he had on occasion attacked and wounded men by night and been present at the deaths of several. He lacked that gravity which was necessary to anyone in such a position, for amid these dangers to the city and to himself he was out every day in the streets publicly playing football."

Piero's first instinct was to resist the French invasion, but when it became clear that neither the other Italian states nor even his own people would follow him in such a rash undertaking, he beat a craven retreat. On the morning of October 26, 1494, with public opinion turning decisively against him, Piero, accompanied by a small retinue of loyal followers, secretly rode out of Florence and headed for Pisa, where Charles was en-camped with the bulk of his army. Hoping to be welcomed as a friend and ally, he was instead treated as a defeated enemy. Charles and his ministers were determined to extract the maximum penalty for his initial disloyalty, and Piero, desperate for some way out of the predicament he now found himself in, was more than willing to sell out his city to save his skin. In re-turn for handing over the Florentine fortresses of Sarzana and Pietrasanta to the French, without which the republic was left blind and defenseless on its northern border, Piero received a promise from Charles to support continued Medici rule in Florence. Even more disturbing to the citizens of Florence was the almost certain loss of Pisa, her ancient rival whom she had finally conquered in 1406. Behind the screen provided by the French army the Pisans were even now preparing to rise up against their over-lords and proclaim themselves once again an independent republic. While Charles made vague promises to restore the rebellious city after he had settled matters down south, it was clear to most Florentines that Piero's treachery had stripped them of their most prized possession. To add insult to these almost unbearable injuries, Charles also demanded that Florence contribute 200,000 florins to the cause of subduing Naples.

To Florentines the loss of Pisa was not only a military and economic issue: it was a symbol of their current impotence brought about by Piero's perfidy. Though no longer a vital international seaport—the silting up of the mouth of the Arno was slowly choking its once bustling harbor—its acquisition after centuries of bitter strife had elevated Florence in the minds of her citizens to the status of a great power. No sharper blow could be struck against her pride, and for much of Machiavelli's career the recon-quest of the wayward city was an undertaking—amounting almost to an obsession—that preoccupied the minds of those who toiled in the Palazzo della Signoria and upon which the majority of her blood and treasure was expended.

Piero returned to Florence on the afternoon of November 8 to face a population seething with anger. "[H]e threw out *confetti* [sweets], and gave a lot of wine to the people, to make himself popular," wrote one contem-porary, a desperate ploy that did little to instill confidence. When he and a few armed supporters tried to force their way into the government palace, those inside called out *"Popolo e liberta!"* (The People and Liberty), the ancient clarion call of revolution. The cry was quickly picked up by others gathered in the piazza, who drove Piero from the palace while the priors ordered the ringing of the great bell that from time immemorial had called the people of Florence to assemble in moments of greatest peril.

Soon the Medici and their partisans were being hounded from government buildings and accosted on the streets. When Cardinal Giovanni de' Medici, Piero's younger brother, tried to enter the square, he, too, was assaulted. Riding toward the family palace he called to his brother, "We're finished!" Later that day, the apothecary Luca Landucci caught a glimpse of the young cardinal through an open window of the family palace "kneeling with joined hands, praying Heaven to have mercy." By nightfall, both brothers, along with their closest allies, had fled the city, taking only as much of the fabled Medici treasure as they could shove into their saddlebags.

Thus ended, ignominiously, Medici rule in Florence, almost exactly sixty years since Cosimo, Piero's great-grandfather, had returned in triumph following his exile by the Albizzi family. It had been an almost bloodless revolution, carried out with a swiftness and ease that made those who led it ask themselves why they had not sooner thrown off a yoke that was so lightly fixed.

Eight days later Charles entered the city accompanied by seven thousand Swiss infantrymen. He rode in full armor, a baldaquin raised high above his head to signify his role as a conqueror. Met at the San Frediano gate by the Signoria in full ceremonial robes and escorted by a contingent of forty well-born youths, the King and his army paraded through the streets, passing within a block of Machiavelli's house. Machiavelli himself was undoubtedly among the citizens who lined the streets to watch as their city was occupied by foreigners. A few dutiful shouts of *"Viva Francia!"* could not disguise the general mood of despondency. The climactic moment came when the King dismounted between a double row of torches and ascended the steps to the Cathedral, though, "when he was seen on foot," wrote Landucci, "he seemed to the people somewhat less imposing, for he was in fact a very small man." As Guicciardini observed laconically, the ceremony was "a sight in itself very beautiful but scarcely appreciated, as all men were full of terror and alarm." The entrance of a foreign army was humiliating for a city that for centuries had jealously guarded its freedom, and though the citizens might console themselves with the thought that the occupation was accomplished without bloodshed or destruction of property, there was no getting around the fact that a once great power had been brought to its knees. Many of the top generals were housed in the palaces of the Florentine nobility that had been marked for the purpose beforehand by French officials, leading Machiavelli to observe sarcastically that "King Charles of France was allowed to conquer Italy with chalk."

If Florence had suffered a humiliating blow, the situation was not so bleak for the prior of San Marco, who had long foretold such trials and tribulation. Fra Girolamo Savonarola, a native of Ferrara, had come to Florence eight years earlier and had risen to fame by unleashing jeremiads against the corruption of his adopted city. His genuine concern for the plight of the wretched workers and his rage against those who exploited their labor won him a passionate following among the poor, but many wealthier citizens were also attracted to his message of salvation through mortification. His hair-raising sermons, often delivered before thousands packed into the Cathedral, had foretold the coming of another Cyrus to scourge Italy for her sins, and when Charles arrived at the head of a conquering army it took no great stretch of the imagination to convince the traumatized Florentines that his prophesies had been fulfilled. "[Y]our coming has lightened our hearts," Savonarola told the King after his arrival in the city, so "pass on securely and triumphantly, inasmuch as He sends you."

Passing on was something Charles was eager to do in any case since his real business was further south in Naples. Having secured his supply lines and replenished his bank account, Charles and his army left the city on November 28, heading for their confrontation with the overmatched armies of Alfonso, King of Naples.*

With the departure of Charles and his army, Florentines could set about the vital task of rebuilding their political institutions corroded by sixty years of domination by the Medici family. But as soon as they slammed the gates shut behind the departing Swiss pike men, the normal divisions that beset the ruling class of Florence began to reassert them-

---

* In return for Florentine promises of financial and logistical support, Charles agreed that as soon as he conquered Naples he would restore the fortresses of Sarzana and Pietrasanta, as well as the rebellious city of Pisa. Ultimately, he would deliver on none of his promises.

selves. As Machiavelli recalled: "After 1494 when those who had been princes in Florence were expelled from the city . . . there was no proper government, but rather a state in which anarchy and ambition were commingled and public business was going from bad to worse." It was a quarrelsomeness that, time and again in Florentine history, was resolved only by the strong hand of the tyrant. If that were to be avoided under present circumstances, the leading citizens must show a greater devotion to country and less devotion to personal interest than was usually the case.

The first months following the departure of the French were dominated by a struggle for power between the *ottimati* (optimates), who wished to retain the oligarchic nature of the Medici regime in which real power was shared only by a handful of rich and powerful families, and the *popolani* (populists), who believed that the only way to preserve their hard-won liberties was to enfranchise a wider and more representative cross-section of the citizenry. On December 14, under pressure from both sides to provide guidance, Savonarola made the fateful decision to jump, body and soul, into the political arena. "[T]he will of God is that the city of Florence be ruled by the people and not by tyrants," he proclaimed from the pulpit, throwing his immense prestige behind the popular party, which, with his backing, was able to drive their more conservative colleagues from the palace.

The most important feature of the new government was the Great Council, modeled loosely on that of their sister republic Venice, a representative body that would serve as a legislature and the pool from which the various executive officers were chosen. Unlike the Venetian model, however, in which membership was the privilege of a narrow aristocracy, the Florentine Great Council would be open to a wide spectrum of Florentine citizens, from wealthy bankers and merchants to small shopkeepers and artisans. In his "Treatise on the Constitution and Government of Florence," Savonarola set down his rationale for a more democratic system: "Now the Florentine people, having established a civil form of government long ago, has made such a habit of this form that, besides suiting the nature and requirements of the people better than any other, it has become habitual and fixed in their minds. It would be difficult, if not impossible to separate them from this form of government." This government was unrepresentative by modern standards, but it was a great advance over the tyrannies that dominated most of the Italian peninsula and over the

Medici oligarchy that preceded it. Though the urban proletariat—the unskilled labor that provided the muscle for the city's various industrial enterprises—was still excluded from representation, the council was perhaps the most democratic assembly in Europe.*

The establishment of the Great Council placed real power once again in the hands of an unwieldy body that not only spoke for but actually included a wide swath of the citizenry. As it was finally constituted it included 3,500 citizens, though only one third, serving a six-month term, were seated at any given time. Historians have calculated that, in a population of roughly 40,000 to 50,000, this council represented a little under half the male population over thirty, a remarkably expansive franchise for the day. Florence had reconstituted itself as a true republic, responsive to the will of the people to a degree remarkable in an age of deep social and economic inequality. It was this government, where in raucous sessions in the Hall of the Great Council butchers rubbed shoulders and matched wits with wealthy bankers in ermine-lined robes, that Niccolò Machiavelli would serve throughout his career as a civil servant.

There is no record of what Machiavelli was doing during these transformative days. In November 1494, when angry citizens drove the Medici from power, Machiavelli was already twenty-five years old, an age, even by cautious Florentine standards, when a young man might play a responsible role in the public arena. And yet there is no indication that he participated in any significant way in the great political upheaval. This might seem peculiar for someone who obviously thought deeply and felt passionately about politics. But a closer examination of his career reveals a certain passiveness, a tendency to stand on the sidelines and observe rather than thrust himself into the fray, particularly when the outcome was as uncertain as it was in the tumultuous days following the French invasion. In the service of his country Machiavelli was willing to risk life and limb, but when it came to determining what sort of government was best suited to

---

* To some extent the Great Council was not so much an innovation as a return to the pre-Medici forms when two large assemblies, the Popolo and the Commune, were said to embody the will of the people. But these two ancient councils had been marginalized by smaller and more tightly controlled steering committees.

make it prosper, that was a matter for intellectual inquiry rather than violent action.

This did not mean he was indifferent. A quarter century later Machiavelli analyzed the faults of the government he would soon be serving.* "After [the fall of the Medici], the city decided to resume the form of a republic," he wrote, "but did not apply herself to adopting it in a form that would be lasting, because the ordinances then made did not satisfy all the parties among the citizens." He believed that the government set up after the fall of Piero was deeply flawed, too weak to prevent the ruling class from splitting into rival factions, but he shared Savonarola's belief that any constitution that did not take into account the Florentine's natural love of liberty was doomed to failure. "Never will the generality of Florentine citizens be satisfied if the Hall [of the Great Council] is not reopened," he later explained to Giovanni de' Medici, emphasizing that a city accustomed to freedom would never embrace tyranny. As always with Machiavelli, the first consideration—to which all other things were subservient and, in fact, irrelevant—was: What works and what doesn't? The most elegant solutions on paper were worthless if they did not account for real human passions and failings, while the most morally repugnant systems should be considered if they improved the average man's lot in life. To this simple and irrefutable logic Machiavelli would cling all his days.

At the time, Machiavelli watched developments with keen interest, but he was not one of those hotheads who took to the streets agitating for radical change. This was simply not in keeping with his temperament. Wry bemusement was his normal response to those who fanatically pursued rigid ideologies. This detachment may be explained in part by his continued marginality: even with the change of government, his father's fecklessness guaranteed that his particular branch of the family was unlikely to reap any political reward, no matter how broad the franchise.

As Machiavelli continued along the meandering path first set out by his father, the city in which he lived and that was the sole object of his affec-

---

* Machiavelli's "A Discourse on Remodeling the Government of Florence" was written in 1520 at the request of Pope Leo X (Giovanni de' Medici). It is important to keep in mind the intended audience when analyzing Machiavelli's prescriptions. The main thrust of his argument is that Florence, as well as the Medici family, would be best served if the government were placed once more on sound republican foundations. Despite the need to tailor his arguments to suit his audience, there is no reason to doubt the sincerity of his conclusions, which correspond with those expressed elsewhere in his writings.

tion—the provider of intellectual stimulation and low pleasures—continued to bubble and seethe. Above all the continued defiance of Pisa rankled,
and the inability of the government to deal with it effectively undermined
its credibility. No Florentine could countenance the citizens of their former possession enjoying a liberty they themselves took for granted, and
while the new government strained every resource to reverse the humiliation—the Ten of War were soon renamed "the Ten Expenders"—Florentines found themselves impoverished by taxes that seemed to purchase
only defeat and incompetence. Despite the popular base of support, the
new government would be judged as the old had been, on whether it succeeded in preserving Florence's Tuscan empire. As Machiavelli put it in his
narrative poem, *The First Decennale*, addressing Florence herself:

> *So all Tuscany was in confusion; so you lost Pisa and those*
> *states the Medici family gave to the French.*
> *Thus you could not rejoice as you should have done at being*
> *taken from under the yoke that for sixty years had been crushing you,*
> *because you saw your state laid waste.*

Lacking the means to reconquer the city, the new government pinned
its hopes on Charles's promise to return Pisa. Florentines, as one might
imagine, followed the news of his progress to the south with more than
academic interest. At first all seemed to go well. So intimidating was the
French army that the southward journey was less a military campaign than
a triumphal progress. Pope Alexander VI, who had initially taken up the
Aragonese cause—the tilt of his policy confirmed when he married off
his second son, Juan, to Maria Enriquez, a cousin of King Ferdinand of
Aragon—reconsidered when Charles's vast army arrived on his doorstep.
Like Florence, Rome was forced to accept a French occupation, a humiliation the Pope would not soon forget or forgive. At the end of January 1495,
Charles finally set out to challenge the army of King Alfonso of Naples.
"So with his conquering army he moved upon the Kingdom like a falcon
that swoops or a bird of swifter flight," wrote Machiavelli, imparting epic
grandeur to what was in fact a rather pathetic affair. As expected, the Neapolitan forces were no match for the French. By February, King Alfonso
and his successor, his eldest son, Fernandino, had both abdicated in quick

succession, neither one able to muster more than token resistance, and on the 22nd of the month Charles entered the southern capital having barely struck a blow in anger.

But having labored so long for the prize, at the very moment he achieved his goal King Charles saw all his dreams turn to dust. Again turning to Machiavelli's evocative verse:

> *When the report of a victory so great and so easy came to the*
> *Ears of that first mover of Italy's distress [i.e., Ludovico Sforza],*
> *well he learned his folly clear, and afraid of falling into the*
> *trench that with so much sweat he had dug,*
> *and aware that his own might did not suffice, that Duke,*
> *striving to save the whole, along with the Pope, the Empire and*
> *Saint Mark [i.e., Venice], formed a huge army.*

As a more astute statesman might have foreseen, Charles's success had achieved what no amount of diplomacy could have—near unity among the quarrelsome states of Italy, who were now determined to drive the invader from their soil. It also should have come as no surprise that leading this effort was the treacherous Duke of Milan, who having invited in the French King had now decided that Charles had overstayed his welcome. Each man had used the other for short-term advantage, unable to grasp that their long-term interests made them natural rivals.

In March 1495, Pope Alexander, still smarting from his recent humiliation at the hands of Charles, called for the creation of a grand alliance to drive the French from Italy. The selfish motives of the signatories were glossed over by the Pontiff, who titled the new arrangement "The Holy League." Most worrisome for the French King, who knew he could sweep away any army the states of Italy could muster against him, was that his success had aroused the jealousy of the other great monarchs of Europe— King Ferdinand of Spain and Maximillian, Emperor of the Romans—who now saw an opportunity to join the game by casting themselves as the protectors of Italian liberty.*

---

* Emperor of the Romans was the title given to the man selected by the German Electors as Holy Roman Emperor but who had yet to receive his title from the Pope. This figure was the successor of Charlemagne, who was crowned Emperor by Pope Leo III on Christmas Day in the year 800, reestab-

The only major Italian power that refused to join this sacred cause was Florence, which, under the leadership of Savonarola, had its own ideas where righteousness lay. Guicciardini summed up his city's policy: "We were then pressed to join the league, whose princes hoped to unite Italy to discourage Charles from ever returning. This was rejected because they would not return Pisa to us, and if we did not have Pisa back, the unity of Italy was of no use to Florence. Disunity was more to our purpose." It was just this kind of selfish parochialism that had permitted the disastrous invasion in the first place, but Florentines—no different in this regard than the natives of Milan, Venice, Ferrara, Urbino, and countless other states— identified too strongly with their own locality to embrace the unity and common purpose that Machiavelli would urge so eloquently in *The Prince*.

With a hostile army now far in his rear, Charles was effectively trapped on the wrong side of the Alps. In the spring of 1495, he set out from Naples, reversing the triumphant march of the year before.* On July 6, the armies of Charles and the Holy League met at Fornovo, just south of the northern Italian city of Parma. It was one of the bloodiest battles ever fought on Italian soil—"a great slaughter" Guicciardini called it—but despite the effusion of blood neither the French nor the Italians could claim a decisive victory. Tactically the results were inconclusive, but strategically the French emerged the big losers. Charles had staved off utter destruction but his only option now was to retreat across the Alps and abandon the land that not many months before had seemed so ripe for the picking.

For Florence, and for Savonarola in particular, the result was disastrous. His decision to opt out of the Holy League placed him in a precarious situation. Not only had it enraged Pope Alexander, but the people of Florence were growing increasingly bitter as the promised benefits of the French alliance failed to materialize. "[Charles] ignored the treaty made with us in Florence and sworn so solemnly on the altar," Guicciardini complained. "[W]e kept faith with him so completely, giving him so much

---

lishing, at least in theory, the Western Roman Empire that had collapsed after the barbarian invasions. Throughout the Middle Ages the Emperor was a powerful secular lord who at times claimed absolute rule over the Germanic regions of central Europe as well as large portions of Italy. By the Renaissance, his power was often more symbolic than real, though in the person of Maximillian's successor, Charles V, the prestige of the title was combined with enormous political and military resources.

* He left a portion of his army behind to protect his conquest, but they ultimately proved insufficient to prevent the kingdom's recapture by Fernandino.

money and remaining his only allies in all Italy, and he perfidiously sold us and our possessions to our enemies."

But Savonarola had more important things on his mind, chief among them the renewal of the Holy Church through "scourgings and terrible tribulations." For the messianic friar, war and disease were to be welcomed rather than feared since the worse things got the sooner the day of rebirth would arrive. Likewise, the diplomatic isolation caused by his refusal to join the Holy League was to be embraced since it hastened the final reckoning with the institution he called a "false, proud whore."

Pope Alexander VI had so far been more than tolerant of the rebellious prior of San Marco. He looked on indulgently as Savonarola hurled abuse at him from the Cathedral of Florence, perhaps even acknowledging in private that much of what he said was true. As Guicciardini summed it up: "[Alexander] was not disturbed by those things which offended his honor as long as his profit and pleasure was not interfered with." It was only when Savonarola's spiritual crusade spilled over into foreign policy that Pope Alexander began to take notice. In November 1496, Alexander demanded that Savonarola place himself and his monastery under the supervision of the Lombard Congregation of the Dominican order, where he would be under more stringent supervision. When Savonarola refused, Alexander was forced to act. At first he tried to buy off the friar with the promise of a cardinal's hat, to which the Dominican monk replied with scorn: "It is not my habit to seek human glory. Away with that! . . . I want no hats, no miters large or small. I want nothing unless it be what you [my Lord] have given to your saints: death. A red hat of blood: this I desire."

Savonarola's confrontational attitude placed the government of Florence in an awkward position. No one had been more responsible for the successful transition from Medici to republican rule than he, and his followers the *frateschi* or *piagnoni* generally dominated in the Great Council he had done so much to establish. But while his popularity among the people remained undimmed—his sermons at San Marco and the Cathedral continued to draw thousands of tearful worshippers—his belligerent policies were threatening the profits of the international bankers and merchants who remained a powerful force in Florentine politics.

As the confrontation with the Holy Father shattered the consensus that prevailed in the early days of the renewed republic, the prior of San

Marco was unable or unwilling to address the growing divisions. Instead he focused on the spiritual rebirth of a city that had, in his estimation, long ago succumbed to luxury and vice. While their leaders quarreled in the Palazzo della Signoria, he organized young boys into religious confraternities and sent them marching about town to the sound of pipes and drums, carrying crucifixes and holy images and crying "Long live Christ and the Virgin, our queen." While some of their parents were moved to penitence, many others—like Machiavelli himself—maintained a resentful silence. The culmination of this program of spiritual reform came on February 27, 1496, when the followers of Savonarola erected a huge bonfire in the Piazza della Signoria into whose flames Florentines were expected to toss their vanities: mirrors, jewels, silks, revealing gowns and lascivious books, indecent paintings and unnecessary adornments—in short all those inessentials that distinguished Florentine life from that of a dreary provincial capital.

Savonarola, for all his personal virtue—his piety and incorruptibility—was a divisive figure. In curbing the worst excesses of life under the Medici, he also deprived the citizens of much that made life enjoyable. Savonarola himself, according to an early biographer, had found his true calling after a dream he had as a young man in which he was doused in icy water that "extinguished the carnal heat of desire, while its coldness froze in him every wordly appetite"—a remedy the preacher would no doubt have liked to apply to the Florentine population as a whole. As far as Savonarola was concerned, the greatest works of art and literature were little different from revealing gowns or ostentatious jewelry since both distracted impressionable minds from focusing on the important work of salvation. Some of his most violent opponents were young aristocrats who objected to his attempts to police their lifestyles, robbing them of the pleasures and privileges to which all wealthy young men feel entitled. Banding together under the title of the *compagnacci*, these well-born youths began a campaign of harassment and intimidation. Their boldest stroke came on May 3, 1497, when they sneaked into the Cathedral, dragging behind them the carcass of a dead donkey and smearing the pulpit with excrement just before Savonarola was set to deliver his sermon.

But if these delinquents hardly inspire our sympathy, they represented the class that had fostered the great artistic achievements that made Florence celebrated throughout the world. Their fathers and grandfathers had been the patrons of Donatello and Leonardo. Under Savonarola's more austere regime many men of genius fled or so transformed their art in response to the new mood as to become unrecognizable. The young Michelangelo was among those who hurriedly abandoned the city after the fall of the Medici, though this had as much to do with his close personal ties to the ruling family as to the uncongenial atmosphere created by Savonarola.* Among those who remained and fell under the spell of the charismatic preacher was Sandro Botticelli, but the works he painted in this period, filled with religious fervor and dark foreboding, are a far cry from the sensual and joyous works for which he is famous.[†] To Florentines like Machiavelli—worldly, sophisticated, addicted to carnal pleasures, and fond of open intellectual debate—the moral astringents prescribed by Savonarola and his followers were unwelcome medicine for dubious maladies. "Thus," wrote Francesco Guicciardini (whose own father was a supporter of Savonarola), "a great division and violent hatred had grown up in the hearts of the citizens, so that between brothers or between fathers and sons there was dissension over the question of the friar."

On June 18, Alexander's bull of excommunication against Savonarola was read in solemn tones in the churches of Florence; candles were snuffed out to symbolize the friar's exclusion from the community of Christian fellowship. Even devoted followers were shaken, torn between loyalty to their leader and their fear lest they, too, be cast out and denied the sacraments that were the only sure path to salvation. Luca Landucci, up until then a devoted follower, was disturbed when he witnessed the disobedient friar distributing the Eucharist: "[I]t seemed a mistake to me, although I had faith in him; but I never wished to endanger myself by going to hear him, since he was excommunicated."

The government was itself now almost evenly divided between the

---

* *Michelangelo had been discovered by Lorenzo de' Medici and for two years the first citizen of Florence had raised the young boy almost as a son in his palace on the Via Larga. Michelangelo's relations with Piero were more difficult, but after Piero's expulsion the artist feared he would be identified with the disgraced regime. The fact that he did not return to his native city for many years reflects in part the poor climate for art and artists there.

† It is hard to imagine that the artist who painted the terrifying *Saint Mary Magdalene at the Foot of the Cross*, with its backdrop showing a Florence aflame, is the same man who painted the pagan *Birth of Venus* some two decades earlier.

frateschi (followers of the friar), led by Francesco Valori, and an ever increasing number of citizens who were convinced that Savonarola's intransigence was leading them over a cliff. When Alexander tried to force their hand by demanding that they forbid Savonarola from preaching in public, ferocious arguments broke out in the Great Council. The case against Savonarola was perhaps most succinctly put by the merchant Giuliano Gondi, who advocated that the friar be locked away in San Marco:

> *This man preaches that the Pope is not the Pope, that we should have no belief in him, and other things of the sort that you would not even say to a cook. . . . Must we be against all Italy and the big powers of Italy and against the Supreme Pontiff as well? The Roman censures mean that we are in rebellion against the Holy Church, and many merchants have dispatched their goods to Naples and to other places so as not to be robbed or butchered.*

Among his fellow merchants, the core of the Florentine ruling class, these arguments struck home: while they might have been willing to gamble with their immortal souls, when it came to their worldly possessions they were less inclined to risk it all.

The atmosphere of crisis was heightened by the continued machinations of Piero de' Medici, who still deluded himself that the majority of Florentines would welcome his return. Backed by Venetian money and a papal blessing, he appeared on the morning of April 28 before the walls of Florence with about six hundred cavalry and four hundred on foot, expecting the grateful citizens to rise up against their oppressors, throw open the gates, and invite in their savior. When, after a few nerve-racking hours, the welcome failed to materialize, Piero turned tail and slunk away.

In the aftermath of the abortive attack it was discovered that Piero had been counting on more than spontaneous enthusiasm. An informant told the state police that a number of prominent Florentines had been in close contact with the city's former ruler and were plotting to seize the city gates and open them just as Piero's army arrived. Only a preemptive strike by the *frateschi*, who dispatched their own loyalists to man the walls, averted disaster. The conspirators included some of Florence's most distinguished citizens—men like Niccolò Ridolfi, Lorenzo Tornabuoni, and Bernardo del Nero. They were arrested, tried, and convicted of treason. Sentenced to death, they appealed the verdict to the Great Council on the basis of a law that Savonarola himself had advocated, but Francesco Valori and the other leading *frateschi* refused their petition, fearing that a prolonged trial would serve to rally the opposition. Ignoring the very law they had earlier promoted as a vital tool in the fight against despotism, they led the convicted men in chains to the Bargello where, in unseemly haste and in the dead of night, they had them beheaded. Even loyal followers of Savonarola were shaken by the brutal crackdown. The death of the young and handsome Lorenzo Tornabuoni in particular was mourned by all Florentines. "I could not refrain from weeping," wrote the Savonarola loyalist Luca Landucci, "when I saw that young Lorenzo carried past the Canto d' Tornaquinci on a bier, shortly before dawn."

In the short run at least, the pro-Savonarolan regime emerged from the incident intact, if not exactly covered in glory. But in elevating expedience above principle the government and its spiritual leader lost much of their moral authority. The incident is perhaps most intriguing for the light it sheds on Machiavelli's own attitudes. The self-serving reversal is exactly the kind of maneuver that he often recommends, and in other contexts one might well expect him to favor such a course. But in a discussion in *The Discourses*, Machiavelli takes a different position:

> *When [the accused] wished to appeal they were not allowed to do so, and the law was not observed. This did more to lessen the reputation of the Friar than anything else that befell him. For, if the right to appeal was worth having, he ought to have seen that it was observed. If it was not worth having, he should not have forced it through. The event attracted more notice in that this Friar in not one of the many sermons which he preached after the law had been broken, ever condemned the breach or offered any excuse. For, since it suited his purpose, to condemn it he was unwilling, and to excuse it he was unable. Since this made it plain to all that at heart he was ambitious and a party-man, it ruined his reputation and brought on him much reproach.*

This is from a chapter with the unwieldy title "It is a Bad Precedent to break a New Law, especially if the Legislator himself does it; and daily to inflict Fresh Injuries on a City is most Harmful to him that governs it"—a context that helps explain the unexpectedly principled stand Machiavelli takes. Rejecting the medieval scholastic tradition in which political theories were based on the notion that human institutions should conform to God's plan, Machiavelli was determined to test them in the harsh laboratory of experience. Savonarola's policy was flawed not because it is inherently evil to turn against a law when it no longer suits one's purpose, but because it undermined the source of his authority—his ability to persuade others of the righteousness of his cause. The man whom, in another context, he famously declared an "unarmed prophet," had forfeited through his moral cowardice the one real weapon he possessed.

In February 1498, Savonarola, defying the interdict placed on him by Pope Alexander, began to preach once again before expectant throngs in the Cathedral. "[T]his excommunication is a diabolical thing [and] was made by the devil in hell," he thundered from the pulpit. The Signoria, hoping to assuage the Pope's wrath while preserving its credibility among the still numerous *frateschi*, ordered him to retreat to the less public venue of San Marco. It is here that on March 2 and 3, Machiavelli attended two sermons, informing the Florentine ambassador to Rome that Savonarola was determined to force a confrontation. "[H]e seeks to turn all against the supreme pontiff and, using his own attacks against him, says of him as one would the wickedest person you could find"—a report that could hardly have encouraged Ricciardo Becchi, who, like the government he represented, was desperately trying to head off a violent clash.

As far as we know this is the only substantive contribution Machiavelli made to the dramatic events that led to the downfall of Savonarola. He did not play a prominent role in the opposition, but it is clear that he was sympathetic to their cause. Becchi, to start with, was an opponent of the *frateschi* whose appointment as Florentine ambassador to the Holy See was meant to demonstrate that the government had distanced itself from the rebellious friar. But despite their skeptical attitude toward Savonarola, neither Becchi nor Machiavelli belonged to the *arrabbiati* or the *bigi* whose hostility toward the popular party found expression in ever more brazen acts of defiance. Neither group would have appealed to Machiavelli since both were dedicated to reestablishing a more oligarchic form of government. Instead, Machiavelli should be counted among the growing number of citizens who cherished the popular democracy established after the expulsion of Piero de' Medici but who now saw that the greatest threat to its continued existence was the increasingly erratic and fanatical behavior of Savonarola himself.

On March 25, 1498, the struggle for the soul of Florence took an unexpected twist when a Franciscan brother, Francesco da Puglia, issued a challenge from the pulpit of Santa Croce to Savonarola: to walk with him through a gauntlet of fire to test the friar's claim that he was the appointed mouthpiece of God. For the past four years the Franciscans had watched helplessly as their rivals, the Dominicans, dominated the city's spiritual life and pocketed the lion's share of bequests from wealthy Florentines who believed that Savonarola and the order he led were in close communication with God. Once the bull of excommunication had been issued, and pronounced with ill-concealed joy in the Franciscan church of Santa Croce itself, those monks who had endured years of frustration and humiliation saw an opportunity to strike back.

This trial by fire—which quickly caught the imagination of the Florentine people, who were themselves perplexed as to how to judge Savonarola's claims—was a throwback to the more superstitious Middle Ages when supernatural intervention into the lives of the faithful was believed to be a normal occurrence. If God had recently cut back on such overt signs of his favor, the pious still believed in the possibility of miracles, and the climate of near religious hysteria fostered by Savonarola's sermons made the test proposed by Brother Francesco all the more plausible. The monastery of San Marco was itself the center of disquieting visitations. In the winter of 1495, one monk wrote, "diverse figures and monstrous animals would appear to disturb the sweetness of their prayers, and they often spoke ugly, dishonest, and filthy words to the friars, along with certain expressions exhorting them to seize the sensual pleasures of this life." This was to be expected in a city on its way to becoming a new Jerusalem as the demonic spirits, finding themselves under attack, made one final attempt to steal back the souls they had lost.

Given Savonarola's long-standing claim of prophetic powers, the challenge was difficult to dismiss. While Savonarola knew it was a cheap stunt meant to discredit him in the eyes of his followers, many of those closest to him enthusiastically embraced the opportunity to prove their faith. Among the most eager was his chief lieutenant, Fra Domenico da Pescia, who offered himself in place of his revered leader.

Now events proceeded with their own momentum. The trial had captured the public imagination not only, as some cynics claimed, because of excitement over what promised to be an entertaining spectacle, but because it was likely to relieve the almost unbearable tensions that had been building over the past months. For those Florentines, perhaps the majority, who were genuinely perplexed as to where righteousness lay, the trial offered a way to resolve their dilemma. Even the government, initially skeptical, ultimately agreed to give the test its sanction, setting up the pyre in the great square before the Palazzo della Signoria.

On April 7, 1498, the Saturday before Palm Sunday, the citizens of Florence flocked to the Piazza della Signoria to witness the great event. Snaking across the square was a large structure of pitch-soaked timber forming a tunnel more than seventy feet long. Once set ablaze, two men— Fra Domenico on behalf of Savonarola, and Fra Giuliano Rondinelli for the Franciscans (Brother Francesco having found a willing substitute)— would enter and proceed along the length of the two-foot-wide passage. Should Fra Domenico survive the ordeal unscathed it would be declared a miracle; Savonarola would be vindicated and the Pope, who had denied him the protection of the Church, would be exposed as an impostor and a fool.*

The Franciscans arrived first, two hundred of them gathering beneath the portico on the south side of the square. Then came the Dominicans, 250 monks from San Marco, trailed by Fra Domenico holding aloft a large crucifix. Finally came Savonarola himself, flanked by two monks who offered some protection from the restless mob that lined the street. With the arrival of the principals, all now seemed ready for the ordeal to begin. But as minutes lengthened to hours with no sign of action, the crowd grew increasingly hostile. A soaking spring rain did little to improve the collective mood. When, after hours of delay, heralds announced that the trial

---

* Fra Giuliano, having made no claim of divine protection, did not expect miraculous intervention on his behalf. It was, in effect, a suicide mission—which is perhaps why Fra Francesco had found an excuse to back out. (He claimed he would enter the fiery tunnel only if Savonarola himself agreed to go with him.)

had been called off, the citizens who had gathered hoping for a cathartic release turned ugly. They felt cheated and sought out someone to blame.

Though they focused their rage on Fra Domenico and Savonarola, the truth was that it had been the Franciscans rather than the friars of San Marco who were responsible for the fiasco. While the citizens of Florence waited in the rain, both Fra Francesco da Puglia and Giuliano Rondinelli were inside the palace quibbling over every detail—objecting, for instance, that the consecrated Host Fra Domenico intended to carry with him into the fiery tunnel might offer spurious protection—intending to drag negotiations out so long that the trial would have to be called off.

The Franciscans were certainly playing a cynical game, but who could blame the public for turning on Savonarola? It was he, after all, who had promised that the coming of the New Age would be marked by divine portents. For eight years he had preached his doctrine of trial and redemption to a people eager to accept his verdict that they were indeed God's new chosen people. If he could not even pull off the minor miracle planned this afternoon for their edification, what good was he? Even Luca Landucci, who was aware of the duplicitous role the Franciscans had played, was disillusioned: "[W]hen the dispute ended in the Franciscans leaving, the Dominicans soon followed them, causing great perturbance amongst the people, who almost lost faith in the prophet."

As Savonarola and the brethren of San Marco withdrew toward the monastery, they were forced to run a gauntlet not of fire, as had been intended, but of enraged humanity at least as dangerous to life and limb. Over the course of a single afternoon Florence had been transformed. Before the events of Saturday, Savonarola, for all the doubts that were beginning to bubble up, remained the most popular and influential man in Florence. Some in power had grown disillusioned with the Dominican friar but they were still afraid to move against him lest this provoke an uprising among his legions of devotees. Following the fiasco in the Piazza della Signoria he was almost universally reviled, and his opponents in the government were emboldened. In fact events had already raced past them. On Sunday morning, Savonarola's colleague Mariano Ughi, substituting for his master on the pulpit of the Cathedral, was pelted with stones and driven from the altar. Other known adherents of the monk were attacked in the streets, and soon the cry "To San Marco!" could be heard ringing across the city. By midday the monastery of San Marco was besieged by an angry crowd. Some had come spontaneously, responding to the sudden change in mood, but many belonged to organized squads of vigilantes organized by groups like the *compagnacci*, almost certainly with the connivance of the government itself. Shouting "Kill the traitor!" and "Dead or alive!" they began to launch stones at the buildings behind the monastery's high walls. The monks, not entirely unprepared, now rushed to gather arms—including battle axes, crossbows, and small artillery—that had been stockpiled in recent days.

Meanwhile, summary justice was being dispensed in the streets as the friar's most prominent supporters were set upon by angry mobs. Among those murdered was Francesco Valori, who had slipped out of the monastery through a secret tunnel only to have his skull split open by a man who struck him from behind. As for Savonarola himself, the moment he had heard the angry crowd assembling in the square below he retreated to the high altar of the church and prostrated himself in prayer. It was not physical cowardice that caused him to flee the battle, but mental anguish as he saw all that he had built over the years come tumbling down. The people he had hoped to lead into the Promised Land had turned against him; the New Jerusalem he hoped to found proved no more than a mirage.

His followers had demonstrated that they were prepared to fight to the death, but Savonarola knew the cause was lost. Wishing to avoid a bloodbath, he sent an emissary to the Signoria requesting a delegation tasked with negotiating his surrender. At 3 A.M., with the crowd having imparted a sense of urgency to the proceedings by setting fire to cloister doors, Savonarola, along with his trusted lieutenants, Fra Domenico and Fra Silvestro, was led from San Marco in irons. The man who only a few days earlier had been regarded as a prophet was now almost universally despised. He was kicked and spat upon as he stumbled along the streets leading from the monastery to the cell awaiting him in the tower of the Palazzo della Signoria; only the escort of heavily armed guards saved him from being torn apart by the enraged mob.

Over the course of the next month and a half Savonarola and his fellow prisoners were subjected to repeated rounds of torture meant to extract confessions that would justify retrospectively the harsh treatment they were receiving at the hands of the government. The procedure was complicated by interference from Pope Alexander, who claimed jurisdiction over members of the cloth and who hoped to have the miscreants shipped off to Rome, where he could render justice himself. But despite the tempting prospect of having the whole mess taken off their hands, the Signoria were reluctant to submit to a precedent that might in future lead to greater papal interference in their affairs. In the end, emissaries from the Pope— led by a Spanish expert in church law, Francisco Remolins—were allowed to conduct a separate interrogation where the unfortunate prisoners were once again subjected to the strappado in an attempt to add to the already voluminous confessions.

During these weeks of physical and emotional torment, Savonarola revealed something of his own conflicted soul. The official records of his confession were certainly manipulated to place him in the worst light, but they still manage to convey flashes of genuine human feeling. At first Savonarola told his interrogators exactly what they wished to hear: that he had been animated by a lust for worldly power and that his claims of prophecy had been a sham to persuade the gullible to follow him. "Regarding my own aim or ultimate purpose, I say, truly, that it lay in the glory of the world, in having credit and reputation; and to attain this end, I sought to keep myself in credit and good standing in the city of Florence, for the said city seemed to me a good instrument for increasing this glory, and also for giving me name and reputation abroad."

Read to the public in the Hall of the Great Council, this admission of worldly ambition, written in the friar's own hand, served its purpose, disillusioning those who still believed in Savonarola. "[H]e whom we had held to be a prophet," wrote Landucci mournfully,

> confessed that he was no prophet, and had not received from God the things which he preached; and he confessed many things which had occurred during the course of his preaching were contrary to what he had given us to understand. I was present when this protocol was read, and I marveled feeling utterly dumbfounded with surprise. My heart was grieved to see such an edifice fall to the ground on account of having been founded on a lie. Florence had been expecting a new Jerusalem, from which would issue just laws and splendor and an example of righteous life, and to see the renovation of the Church, the

*conversion of unbelievers, and the consolation of the righteous; and
I felt that everything was exactly contrary, and had to resign myself
with the thought.*

But in subsequent appointments with the torturer Savonarola regained
his true voice, recanting his previous confession: "Now listen to me. God,
you have caught me. I confess that I have denied God. I have told lies.
Florentine lords, be my witnesses. I have denied him from fear of torture.
If I have to suffer, I want to suffer for the truth. I did get from God what
I have said. God, you are giving me penance for having denied you from
fear of torture. I deserve it." Like Saint Peter before him, Savonarola now
embraced his punishment, not for the crimes cited by his tormentors but
for having, in a moment of weakness, denied his lord.

Now there was little to be gained by prolonging the agony. Both the
civil government and the Pope's ambassadors were determined to close out
this sorry chapter as quickly as possible. On May 22, Savonarola and his
two lieutenants were led to the scaffold erected in the Piazza della Signoria. First they were stripped of their sacred vestments (so they would not
go to their deaths still bearing the symbols of the Church) and their guilt
as heretics and schismatics proclaimed to the assembled crowd. Fra Silvestro was hanged first, followed by Fra Domenico. Savonarola came last, his
eyes downcast, murmuring a silent prayer. According to Landucci, who
witnessed the execution, a few of the remaining true believers lost their
faith then and there, since they had expected at this final moment some
sign from God that the dying men were blessed martyrs.

But even in death Savonarola had a subtle power over the minds of
men. To prevent his body from becoming the focus of a clandestine cult,
those who had hanged him now kindled a huge bonfire, turning the dan-
gling bodies into crumbling ash, which they then hauled away in carts and
dumped into the Arno.

As the crowd began to disperse, the citizens of Florence were gripped
by anxiety about the future. Some were relieved that the man who had
kept the city seething for years was now gone, anticipating, perhaps, a
return to the days of Lorenzo de' Medici when it seemed as if there was
more joy to be had, when full purses and peace abroad had made the city
sparkle and hum. Others mourned the dream that died along with the

three monks on the scaffold, of a world spiritually reborn with Florence as its capital. Whatever their political convictions, few Florentines took any pride in the grim spectacle they had just witnessed. It had been a dirty business and most were ready to forget and move on.

On Saturday, June 15, 1498, three weeks after Savonarola's death, Niccolò Machiavelli made his way to the Palazzo della Signoria, where he was nominated to serve as Second Chancellor of the Republic, an important post in the civil service of a government now seeking to regain its balance after the recent convulsions.

III

THE CIVIL SERVANT

"When you see a minister who thinks more about his own interests than about yours, who seeks his own advantage in everything he does, then you may be sure that such a man will never be a good minister, and you will never be able to trust him."

—MACHIAVELLI, *THE PRINCE*

JUNE 15, 1498, MARKS A TURNING POINT NOT ONLY IN Machiavelli's life but in the history of Western thought, for this was the beginning of his career as a civil servant and, as he made clear on more than one occasion, it was his years of service in the Florentine government that formed the basis of his political philosophy. "I have set down all that I know and have learnt," he wrote in the dedication to his *Discourses*, "from a long experience of, and from constantly reading about, political affairs." He opens the *Prince* in much the same way, pointing to "my knowledge of the actions of great men, learned by me from long experience in modern affairs and from continual study of the ancients." Citing his experience is not merely an attempt to establish his bona fides, though he was certainly conscious of the need to stress his professional credentials since he lacked the scholarly or aristocratic pedigree usually associated with intellectual ambition. Instead, he is offering a completely novel perspective: a view of human government seen from the trenches, by one who has been there and understands how things actually work. At another point he declares, "it seems best to me to go straight to the actual truth of things rather than to dwell in dreams." It is this approach that accounts for much of his originality, and also for much of the outrage his writings have provoked over the centuries, for in casting his unsentimental eye on "the actual truth of things," he discovers a world far different, and far more savage, than anything imagined by the philosophers who preceded him.

Given the undistinguished record he had compiled so far, his appointment to a responsible position in the bureaucracy comes as something of a surprise. At the age of twenty-nine, the minimum required for voting rights in the Great Council, this obscure young man with no experience, and from a family of little standing within the ruling elite, was about to be entrusted with one of the most important unelected offices in the Florentine government. There is nothing in his past to suggest such a career was in the offing. Like his father before him, he had spent his time cultivating his mind, familiarizing himself with the essentials of classical literature without which no Florentine could consider himself an educated man, but in no other way preparing himself for a serious career.

Instead, Niccolò seemed destined for the life of the country squire, managing the various Machiavelli properties in the city and the countryside, stretching their meager income to sustain a frugal lifestyle. Lately these responsibilities were consuming more of his time. As Bernardo grew more infirm, Niccolò took over more of the family business. His position as the effective head of the household was confirmed the year before when he was assigned the daunting task of writing to Cardinal Lopez when the family's privileges were being threatened by the covetous Pazzi family. But he remained to all intents and purposes a dilettante, a gentleman—though one of modest means—with plenty of time on his hands to prospect in the realm of ideas rather than profits.

One shouldn't overstate the honor Machiavelli was being accorded when he was nominated to head the Second Chancery. This was a bureaucratic office, one of the many paid positions offered by the government of Florence. But rather than signaling the dignity of the office, the salary— which started at 192 florins a year—was actually a mark of low status.* Florentines distinguished between offices deemed *onori* (honorable)—which included the top elected and appointed positions of the state where no

---

* This salary could provide a comfortable, if not luxurious, living. It was double what a skilled artisan would take home in a year. But given the expenses of the job—including travel on behalf of the government that was often not compensated—Machiavelli continued to struggle to make ends meet. Adriani, the Chancellor of Florence, was hired at a salary of 330 florins per year.

recompense was expected—and those deemed *utili* (useful or practical), positions of lesser importance that came with a salary. *Onori* were for gentlemen who could afford to work for free; *utili* were reserved for those who had to earn a living. No Medici, Pazzi, or Soderini would stoop to taking money for participating in government, but a Machiavelli couldn't afford to be so proud. At its highest levels Florence was ruled by amateurs, men who graciously volunteered to take time away from their normal pursuits to serve the greater good. This was the theory at least. In fact, by the fifteenth century those who circulated among the highest offices in the land were mostly practiced politicians who spent far more time running the state than they did managing their private affairs. For these influential men—amounting to a couple of hundred at most—political power was a prerequisite for economic success, since, as Lorenzo de' Medici once remarked, "it is ill living in Florence for the rich unless they rule the state." High political office, in addition to allowing the holder to tinker with the tax rolls in such a way as to reward friends and harass enemies, opened up the spigots of patronage. One of the main ways these gentlemen-politicians built up a power base was by providing *utili* to a long list of clients, who were then beholden to their patrons.

This was actually Machiavelli's second attempt to land a government job; at the beginning of the year he had unsuccessfully applied for the post of First Secretary to the Signoria. This came at a time when Savonarola's men were still in power, and Machiavelli's defeat offers one more clue that he was out of favor with the religious zealots.* But in the days following the arrest of Savonarola, Machiavelli's prospects began to look up as the government purged the *frateschi* from its midst. Among those who lost his job in the shake-up was Alessandro Braccesi, chief of the Second Chancery. Braccesi was closely associated with the disgraced preacher and his dismissal was part of a general purge of the friar's men. On June 15 the Eighty nominated Niccolò Machiavelli to serve out the remaining two years of Braccesi's term, beating out three other candidates. The appointment was ratified by a vote in the Great Council on June 19.

The hidden web of patronage that landed Machiavelli his job is dif-

---

* Diarist Marco Parenti declared that at this time Savonarola's "friends were approved [for election] and those suspect left outside" (Rubinstein, "The Beginnings of Machiavelli's Career in the Florentine Chancery," 80).

ficult to untangle, but it is clear he had friends and admirers among the moderates who now dominated the government. He almost certainly lobbied for the job since they were highly competitive and no one with the power to grant the favor was going to bestow it on someone who wasn't sufficiently grateful. It may have been Bernardo's friendship with the former Chancellor of Florence, Bartolomeo Scala, that first brought his son Niccolò to the attention of the new regime. Niccolò was also friendly with Alammano Salviati, Piero de' Medici's son-in-law, who was now a member in good standing of the ruling elite, and he was on cordial terms with the new Chancellor, Marcello Virgilio Adriani, a man who, like Scala and like all the chancellors before him, shared Machiavelli's taste for classical literature. Five years his junior, Machiavelli probably knew Adriani from his time spent rounding out his education at the Studio, Florence's university, while Adriani was a professor there.* Most significantly, perhaps, Ricciardo Becchi, the ambassador to the Holy See who had just employed him to snoop on the sermons of the friar, could have vouched for his anti-Savonarola views.

Machiavelli's politics made him acceptable and his connections brought him to the attention of the right people, but it was his literary skills that qualified him for the job. Unlike the First Chancellor's position, which was largely ceremonial and involved writing magisterial encomiums to the wisdom and greatness of the republic he served, the post of Second Chancellor was far less prestigious but equally important to the actual functioning of the government. The Second Chancery was tasked with handling the bulk of the state's correspondence. In theory, foreign affairs were under the jurisdiction of the First Chancery but, in typically Florentine fashion, the boundaries between the departments were porous, if not actually confused. Machiavelli did not limit himself to domestic matters but plunged almost immediately into diplomatic and foreign affairs. His role in the city's foreign service was made official in July when he was given the additional title of Secretary to the Ten of War and Peace, charged with handling the correspondence of this all-important body that oversaw the republic's military forces.

Machiavelli's role was not to set policy but to aid his superiors in

---

* Machiavelli's other sponsor was Antonio della Valle, Adriani's assistant in the First Chancery.

implementing it. His immediate subordinates at the Chancery included ten to fifteen notaries and secretaries, learned men of modest means who had the skill and command of both Latin and the vernacular to convert the often garbled instructions of their superiors into comprehensible documents drafted in a fine, legible hand. As worldly and well educated as those who ruled the state, they differed from their bosses to the extent that they needed to draw a steady income. Their office was located on the second floor of the Palazzo della Signoria, just off the Room of Lilies where their lordships dined in regal splendor beneath frescoes by Ghirlandaio.

Machiavelli was on friendly terms with many of these high dignitaries, but it was clear he was their employee, not their equal. Passing the highest office holders on his way to his office, he would bow before exchanging a few pleasantries. If he could not match them in terms of wealth or status, he was not far removed from their world. In fact he was in many ways a man of their class, equally well educated and with an old, distinguished family name. The distinctions were real but subtle, making Machiavelli's relations with his superiors complicated, ambiguous, and fraught with unarticulated tensions. When he came to write his great political and literary works, this marginality would offer a fresh perspective on age-old questions.

While in town Machiavelli would make the ten-minute walk daily from his house, across the Ponte Vecchio, to the palace where he would spend his days bent over at his desk piled high with the most important documents of the Florentine Republic. Working with him were his assistants Biagio Buonaccorsi and Agostino Vespucci, men who would become his friends and most reliable correspondents over the course of the next few years. Buonaccorsi was particularly close to his new boss. In one letter he describes how the two of them could be found on most days at adjacent desks, happily writing side by side as they shared the latest gossip and made snide comments about their colleagues. They had been friends before their appointment (on the same day) and it is largely thanks to their correspondence that we can paint a detailed portrait of Machiavelli's life in the first years of his career.

Though much of the work was routine, and always voluminous, Machiavelli clearly relished it. Plowing through the dispatches of various ambassadors, firing off letters of his own—sometimes encouraging but often, if he felt his correspondent had shirked his duty, acerbic—he was in his element. "If I have not written as often as I would have liked," Machiavelli wrote to one of his colleagues, "it is because I have been so busy"—a common complaint among those employed in the Second Chancery since the always parsimonious government tried to extract the maximum effort from its paid staff.

In part, his growing portfolio was a tribute to Machiavelli's native abilities, but it was also a product of the built-in inefficiencies of the government. Elected offices were usually of short duration—in the cases of the most important ones like the Priors and Gonfaloniere (Standard-Bearer of Justice), the titular head of state, as little as two months—which placed greater burdens on the permanent bureaucracy. While elected officers came and went, the salaried officials provided continuity and institutional memory.

This was all the more critical in this time of crisis. The wounds to the body politic in the wake of Savonarola's death were more than political and healing would require more than just a change in personnel. A few months earlier Florence was held spellbound by a leader who promised a wholesale reformation of the human spirit. During his first days in office, Machiavelli passed on his way to work a group of women who knelt in prayer on the spot where their leader had met his death, and they were not the only ones who found it difficult to turn their gaze from heavenly realms to gritty, earthbound realities. What could the current government of merchants and bankers offer to compete with Savonarola's metaphysics?

For the administration of which Machiavelli was now a part, the job was complicated by the fact that those who had brought about Savonarola's downfall did not necessarily share a common vision for the future. "[M]any," wrote Guicciardini, "believed that by overthrowing the friar the Great Council would be destroyed, and that was why they had worked so vigorously against him," but these reactionary elements were quickly disappointed "when they saw that many of their followers . . . and all the people wanted to keep the council." Chronic tensions between *ottimati*, who wished to preserve the dominant role of the traditional elite, and *popoleschi*, who continued to push for broader representation, made it difficult to implement consistent policies. The normal friction between the two groups threatened to erupt into chaos with each new fiscal challenge or military setback. In one heated debate over implementing a system of progressive taxation, a spokesman for the popular faction captured the resentments of his class. "[I]f [the *ottimati*] complain that this tax will impoverish them," sneered Luigi Scarlatti, "let them reduce their expenses; and if they can't keep their horses and servants, let them do as he does and walk to their country houses and serve themselves." The rich, for their part, suspected that legislation enacted by the popular faction was designed with the sole intent of ruining them. "What a disgusting thing it is," complained the wealthy and well-connected Guicciardini, "that among the city's leading citizens, who have the same interests and should have the same judgments about things, there is so little loyalty, so little unity, and so little courage in matters that one might say concern their very existence."

Machiavelli, less moralizing and more imaginative than his friend, drew different lessons from his city's fractiousness. Like James Madison, who structured the U.S. Constitution to resolve the conflicting needs of its citizens through a system of checks and balances, Machiavelli viewed such tensions as both inevitable and even creative. "[I]n every republic," he wrote in *The Discourses*, "there are two different dispositions, that of the populace and that of the upper class and . . . all legislation favorable to liberty is brought about by the clash between them." But while acknowledging the perennial conflict of interest among the haves and have-nots, and insisting that at least some level of conflict is a necessary precondition of liberty, he faulted his compatriots who shortsightedly pursued the interests of party, failing to recognize that their own rights would best be protected by acknowledging the legitimate aspirations of their neighbors. "The reason why all these governments [in Florence] have been defective," he explained, "is that the alterations in them have been made not for the fulfillment of the common good, but for the strengthening and security of the party." The problem was not with human nature, which he fully acknowledged was selfish and quarrelsome, but with those legislators who failed to put in place political structures that imposed equal obligations on all the citizens and, in return, offered a fair distribution of society's benefits.

Machiavelli's view of politics as an unceasing battle between competing groups and individuals came naturally to one intimately acquainted with Florentine politics. From the beginning of his tenure the government he served was divided both horizontally along class lines and vertically among multiple networks of patronage. Constantly bickering and with the blood of holy men on their hands, the current government lacked legitimacy in the eyes of many citizens. It was above all the haplessly conducted war to reconquer Pisa, whose only tangible result so far was to part Florentines from their hard-earned money, which served as the focus of popular discontent. The piling up of disaster upon disaster that had soured the people of Florence on Savonarola's leadership, would surely do the same for the current occupants of the Palazzo della Signoria unless they quickly did something to relieve the pressure.

A cornerstone of Machiavelli's philosophy is that success, particularly in the tricky realm of politics, depends on a willingness to adapt to circumstances. "[A] prince is successful," he writes, "when he fits his mode of proceeding to the times, and is unsuccessful when his mode of proceeding is no longer in tune with them." This commonsense observation, based on his own experience in the Chancery tailoring policies to the exigencies of the moment, is actually more radical than it seems since it leads ultimately to moral relativism. Unlike the philosophers who preceded him, Machiavelli does not seek to establish universal laws but only limited rules for individual cases. There can be no absolute notion of the Good when an approach that proves effective on one occasion leads to disaster on another.

This flexibility has outraged generations of critics who accuse Machiavelli of a deplorable moral slipperiness, but he would argue that sticking to principle when the facts have changed leads to human suffering. His was an elastic philosophy tailor-made for troubled times, hard won from years of toil on behalf of a weak and faction-ridden government.

Both Machiavelli's career and thought were shaped by war and by the unsettled condition of Italy following the French invasion four years before he took office. The reverberations from that cataclysmic event continued to rattle the fragile political structures that divided the peninsula, offering opportunities to a few adventurers but anxiety for the remainder who sought security in an age that seemed to offer little of that precious commodity. For the Republic of Florence, once again free to pursue its interests without distraction from messianic preachers, innumerable difficulties lay ahead. Fantasies of Kingdom Come had been jettisoned in favor of more obtainable objectives here on earth, but even with these more re-alistic and more limited goals in mind, those in government were forced to concede that the resources seemed inadequate to the task at hand. Floren-tines, who preferred to expend their coin rather than their blood but were inclined to be stingy with both, found the coffers almost bare as those they hired to do their fighting for them seemed more interested in prolonging the profitable enterprise than risking all in a decisive confrontation. As Luca Landucci observed, "The rule for our Italian soldiers seems to be this: 'You pillage there, and we will pillage here; there is no need for us to ap-proach too close to one another.'"

In retrospect it is clear that Machiavelli's service in the government of Florence at this particular moment in history provided the ideal education for the philosopher he was to become. It was a school of hard knocks that opened his eyes and toughened his spirit. It provided innumerable practi-cal lessons in practical politics, and he learned from both his occasional triumphs and his far more common setbacks.

Much of Machiavelli's writing, from *The Prince* to *The Art of War*, deals with military matters, since he concluded that it was pointless to discuss the proper form of government unless and until a state could adequately defend itself. "A prince must have no other objective, no other thought, nor take up any profession but that of war," he insisted. This bellicose attitude was a response to his frustration at Florentine fecklessness when it came to protecting itself from foreign aggressors. From the beginning of his ca-reer, Machiavelli found himself embroiled in endless quarrels between the cash-strapped government and the various generals in its employ. In March 1499, he was sent to the camp of one of the *condottieri* involved in the effort to reconquer Pisa, Jacopo, lord of Piombino, who was threatening to with-draw his services unless he received more money and more troops. Machi-avelli's mission was a success; he managed to persuade Jacopo to adhere to the terms already agreed to. More importantly, it was his first opportunity to witness the disastrous consequences of relying on soldiers for hire. As the war to conquer Pisa dragged on apparently without end and as Flor-ence sought protection against a host of foreign threats, relying on those who owed loyalty to no one but the highest bidder seemed to Machiavelli a dangerous and shortsighted policy unworthy of free men.

On a second junket, this time to Forli, a small state in the Romagna some fifty miles northeast of Florence, Machiavelli plunged more deeply into thickets of military strategy and diplomatic intrigue.* Setting out on horseback on the 12th of July, he arrived at the court of Caterina Sforza four days later. Here he plunged into negotiations with the Countess over renewing the contract with her son, Ottaviano Riario, as a *condottiere* in the service of the republic. On this, his first important diplomatic mission, he was brought face-to-face with one of the truly remarkable characters of the age. A woman of great courage and beauty (Biagio Buonaccorsi requested that his friend bring back a portrait for him to admire), Caterina was the illegitimate daughter of Galeazzo Maria Sforza, who had ruled Milan until his assassination in 1476. At the tender age of fourteen she had been married to Girolamo Riario, nephew of Pope Sixtus IV. It was Girolamo who, regarding Florence as the chief impediment to his ambition to carve out a state for himself in the Romagna, planned the murderous attack on Lorenzo and Giuliano de' Medici known as the Pazzi Conspiracy. A cruel and violent prince, he himself was assassinated by his long-suffering subjects in 1488. During the revolt, Caterina's young children were taken hostage; when the rebel leaders threatened to kill them unless she surrendered the fortress into which she had fled, she leapt onto the parapet, pulled up her skirts, and, pointing to her genitals, declared she was ready and able to make more.† When her second husband met the same fate as her first, she wreaked terrible vengeance on the people of Forli, executing forty suspected conspirators in the public square.

If her sex made her exceptional among the petty rulers of Italy, the frequency with which those close to her tended to meet violent deaths was only slightly above the norm. In the barely contained chaos of Italian politics, minor states were fought over by the larger ones like dogs snarling over a meat bone, and any petty potentate hoping to avoid being devoured needed to be both resourceful and quick on her feet. Caterina was both. She had survived this long through a certain ruthlessness and an aptitude for finding champions—neighbors, relatives, and husbands—who

---

* The Romagna was the province that bordered Tuscany to the east and north. Theoretically it was ruled by the Pope, but in reality it was divided among numerous, largely independent potentates. The tensions thus created were a source of endless headaches for the Florentine Republic.

† The children were spared.

would protect her from her covetous neighbors without demanding that she forfeit her independence. Her most recent marriage was to Giovanni de' Medici, son of Pierfrancesco,* and her court was, according to Machiavelli's report, "crowded with Florentines, who appear to manage all the concerns of the State."

With so many Florentines in positions of influence, Machiavelli hoped they would promote the republic's cause. But Caterina was a master at playing one power off against the other. Not only were Florentines here in force, but so were agents from the Duke of Milan, Caterina's uncle, who also hoped to retain Ottaviano Riario's services for his own impending battle with the French King. After days of haggling, Machiavelli thought he had struck a mutually beneficial arrangement, but the following morning he was called before the Countess and found her in close consultation with the Milanese ambassador. Now "having thought the matter over in the night," Machiavelli reported, "it seemed to her better not to fulfill the terms, unless the Florentines would pledge themselves to defend her state. That although she had sent him a message of a different nature the previous day, he ought not to be surprised at the change, since the more things are talked over, the better they are understood."

Machiavelli was mortified. He had already sent back optimistic dispatches to his bosses in the Signoria and now he would have to admit that he'd been misled. What was worse, he had been treated as a person of little consequence, an experience that would become all too familiar as he made the rounds of the courts of Europe. Caterina justified her change of heart on the grounds that Florentine words "had always satisfied her, whereas their deeds had always much displeased her." The undeniable truth was that Machiavelli's position was weak because his government was weak. Why should she place her faith in a state that had little by way of recent diplomatic or military triumphs to point to? In any case, she observed, the government of Florence was clearly not serious about forging a real alliance. Why else would they have sent to her court Machiavelli, a midlevel

---

* Pierfrancesco de' Medici belonged to the so-called younger branch of the Medici family descended from Lorenzo, brother of Cosimo—grandfather of Lorenzo the Magnificent and great-grandfather of Piero. Piero had exiled his cousins before his own expulsion brought them back to Florence. Giovanni de' Medici and Caterina Sforza gave birth in 1498 to another Giovanni, who grew into a famous mercenary general nicknamed Giovanni delle Bande Nere (Giovanni of the Black Band, the name for his renowned company). He, in turn, fathered Cosimo de' Medici, who became Grand Duke of Tuscany.

bureaucrat, rather than a full ambassador able to negotiate on his own behalf? Given such evidence of the Florentines' lukewarm feelings, Caterina
preferred to cut a deal with the ambassador from the powerful state of
Milan.

Machiavelli headed home frustrated that he'd achieved so little but wiser
in the ways of the world. He'd had his first taste of life as a roving representative of a second-rate power, and the experience was humbling. For a
patriot like Machiavelli, the derision with which Florence's ambassador was
greeted in foreign courts was unbearable. The reality of Florentine impotence, first encountered at the court of Countess Sforza but repeated many
times over the years, planted the seed out of which *The Prince* will grow.

On a personal level, Machiavelli's mission was more rewarding. He
was a naturally restless soul, never happier than when setting out on some
new adventure. His friend Agostino Vespucci once wrote of "that spirit
of yours, so eager for riding, wandering and roaming about," a wander-
lust that often irritated friends and family left to fend for themselves. His
bosses evidently took advantage of his taste for travel by sending him on
missions others would refuse. On this occasion, though in his own mind
he had accomplished little, they seemed well pleased by his efforts. Biagio
Buonaccorsi reported that his dispatches were "most highly praised" by
their superiors. One gets the distinct impression that the government
expected little from Machiavelli's efforts, and that is exactly what they got.

Buonaccorsi also kept him abreast of life back in the office, which, in his
absence, seems to have taken a turn for the worse. Antonio della Valle—one
of the men who had initially sponsored both Buonaccorsi and Machiavelli
for their current positions—was unhappy with the way the Chancery was
being run. A stickler for protocol, he complained of rowdy behavior and lax
attendance. "If you do as I advise," Buonaccorsi warned Machiavelli, "you
will bring back a lot of rose water to sweeten him [Antonio], since around
here you can't hear anyone else. He's already managed to get our Magnificent Lords to rake us over the coals. Let him shit blood in his asshole! Any-
way, that's how it is, though four rubs of the back have fixed everything. In
fact we all long for your return, your Biagio most of all, who speaks of you
every hour and to whom every hour feels like a year."

The warmth, coarseness, and high spirits of this letter are typical of
Machiavelli's circle of friends who shared a jaundiced but essentially tol-

erant view of the world. Life's earthy pleasures and low comedy were as worthy of their attention (and their wit) as weightier matters of war and peace. They had all suffered under Savonarola's puritanical reign and were inclined to let loose. Gone were the prepubescent spies and ubiquitous morals police who, if they did not manage to wipe out vice altogether, at least drove it underground. In a few short months Florence had reverted to the habits that earned it comparisons not to Jerusalem but to Sodom.

Machiavelli and his young friends took full advantage of the permissive climate, whoring, drinking, and gambling to their hearts' content. The year after his Forli junket, while Machiavelli was away at the court of the French King, his friend Andrea di Romolo described the pleasures he was missing back home, a "few little parties at Biagio's house" and other less innocent fare. "And just to prepare you: as soon as you arrive here she will be waiting for you with open figs. Biagio and I saw her a few evenings ago at her window like a falcon, you know who I mean . . . along the Arno by the bridge of Le Grazie."

This is the earliest reference to Machiavelli's well-known taste for whores. Throughout his life Machiavelli enjoyed the services of both common streetwalkers and high-class courtesans whose talents went beyond those normally practiced between the sheets. These cultivated and accomplished women could inspire in Machiavelli an adoration that was more than mere physical attraction. Neither marriage nor fatherhood dampened his appetite for illicit liaisons. Indeed he seemed to devote even greater energy to these escapades as he grew older, perhaps to compensate for disappointments in his professional life.

A few months after his return from Forli, Machiavelli was confronted with the first large-scale crisis of his tenure. It involved the captain-general of Florentine forces, Paolo Vitelli, who had been hired with great fanfare, and at great expense, just as Machiavelli was taking office. When Vitelli took the job in June 1498 he was greeted on the steps of the Palazzo della Signoria with an elegant Latin oration that compared him to the greatest generals of antiquity. But, as so often in the past, initial enthusiasm was a harbinger of later disappointment.

Vitelli began auspiciously enough, placing Florentine troops on a more aggressive posture and instilling in them much needed discipline. A year after accepting the baton he captured the strategic town of Cascina, and on August 7, 1499, word was received in Florence that their forces had broken through the Pisan defenses at Porta a Mare. They were now inside the walls of the city and its capture seemed imminent. So confident were Florentines that Pisa was about to surrender that, in a classic case of counting chickens before they're hatched, a lively debate began in the Signoria about how to punish the rebellious city. But the euphoria didn't last long. On August 29 the commissioners who had been overseeing the conduct of the war returned with the disturbing news that Florentine troops had retreated just as victory seemed within their grasp. With Pisan defenses shattered and nothing standing in the way of a breakthrough, Vitelli inexplicably ordered his troops to return to their camps. The Pisans repaired the breach and all the summer's gains were squandered. The commissioners hinted darkly that the cause of the reversal was treachery at the very highest levels. Machiavelli himself wrote in frustration: "We have granted the captain all that which he desired, yet we behold . . . all our trouble put to naught through his various shufflings and deceit."

The prospect that the war would now drag on indefinitely was particularly galling for the Second Chancellor, who had spent the previous months begging money from politicians already in hot water with the citizens who believed they were flushing their wealth down a bottomless hole. "[H]aving expended up to this date about 64,000 ducats* for this expedition," Machiavelli complained in early August, "everybody has been drained." Vitelli might have survived accusations of mere incompetence, but the bold predictions of success made only days earlier cast the failure in a sinister light. "We should have preferred defeat to inaction at so decisive a moment," Machiavelli despaired. "We neither know what to say, nor with what reasons to excuse ourselves before all these people, who will deem that we have fed them with lies, holding out to them day by day vain promises of certain victory." Suspicions of treachery were also fed by reports that Vitelli had recently been discovered in secret conversations with Piero and Giuliano de' Medici. To Florentines, the only explanation could be that he was plotting to bring their former rulers to power.

---

* The florin and ducat were roughly comparable. The florin was minted at Florence, the ducat at Venice. Both coinages were in use throughout Italy and Europe.

On August 28 the Florentine commissioners in camp invited Paolo Vitelli and his chief lieutenant, his brother Vitellozzo, to dine with them and discuss the future conduct of the war. When the Vitelli arrived the commissioners seized the *condottiere* and threw him in irons; Vitellozzo managed to escape by fleeing inside Pisan lines, which only served to confirm the suspicions of his former employers. Paolo was brought back to Florence, where he was first tortured and then put on trial for treason. Despite the fact that they were unable to extract a confession of guilt, on October 1 Vitelli was beheaded, his head mounted on a spear and shown to the people.*

Not everyone cheered the verdict and swift retribution. No firm evidence of Vitelli's guilt was ever offered, though secret deliberations of the Venetian government (unearthed only later) suggest that he had indeed come to some sort of treasonous arrangement with Piero de' Medici. Guicciardini, for one, believed that Vitelli was merely engaged in the typical practices of his kind, avoiding decisive confrontations in favor of tactical maneuvers that risked less and promised greater returns. Even Buonaccorsi suggested that an injustice had been done, remarking, "this was the end of Pagolo Vitegli, a very excellent man."

Machiavelli, however, refused to back down: Vitelli's treachery was obvious, he asserted, and the punishment just. Responding to his counterpart in the government of Lucca (a small Tuscan state, long a Florentine rival) who had condemned the execution, Machiavelli shot back: "[H]ad it not been for Vitelli's treachery, we would not be mourning our loss nor would you be rejoicing. . . . From his fault alone have arisen the countless ills that have befallen our campaign. . . . He deserves endless punishment." Not content with this analysis, Machiavelli concluded his letter with characteristic sarcasm: "And in brotherly love, I urge that in the future, should you want in your evil way to insult people without reason, you should do it in such a way that it makes you seem more prudent."

Both the content and tone of this letter are revealing. Given that even some in the Chancery doubted Vitelli's guilt, the hard line Machiavelli

---

* This practice happened surprisingly often in Renaissance Italy, perhaps one of the reasons *condottieri* felt little sense of obligation to their employers. The other famous case of a mercenary general beheaded by his employers was that of Carmagnola, a *condottiere* in the employ of Venice who was beheaded in 1432 after similar accusations of treachery. It is safe to say that relations between mercenary generals and the governments who hired them were marked by mutual suspicion.

took may strike the modern reader as excessively harsh. He remained unmoved by Vitelli's death, which had occurred only a few days earlier, defending his government's actions and verbally assaulting anyone who questioned the verdict. But Machiavelli was not being simply bloodthirsty. Given the enormity of the crime alleged, the punishment was fitting. Whether or not Vitelli was actually guilty of treason, Machiavelli had experienced firsthand the damage the *condottiere* had done to Machiavelli's beloved republic. Every day he had to listen to the abuse heaped on him and his colleagues by citizens who were fast losing faith in their government. For months he had worked to squeeze every additional florin out of citizens who could ill afford it, and to see his efforts undermined either through lack of zeal or out-and-out treachery was more than he could bear. For all his cynicism, Machiavelli's patriotism was real and deeply felt. His certainty that the country he loved had been poorly served by its top general forced him to conclude that Vitelli deserved his fate.

The letter's concluding jab offers perhaps the most telling insight into Machiavelli's personality. Never one to back down from a fight, at least if it was conducted with words instead of swords, he clearly enjoyed sparring with his Luccan counterpart, puncturing his rival's defenses with well-aimed barbs. For all the seriousness of the subject, Machiavelli's tone remains jocular as he wounds with scorn rather than with anger.

The Vitelli affair merely served to deepen Machiavelli's conviction that there was something profoundly amiss with Florence's military system. Only a year into the job, he was already contemplating a fundamental transformation of the way Florentines waged war. Mercenary armies, employed by all the major Italian states, were adequate as long as one's adversaries agreed to work within the same flawed system, but as soon as anyone found a more effective means of bringing armies into the field, the charm of such old-fashioned companies, with their aversion to shedding their own blood and preference for seasonal work, began to fade. Their limitations were amply demonstrated in 1494 when Charles's army—made up of French conscripts stiffened by the ferocious Swiss pike men—swept down the peninsula meeting little or no resistance. It is not that the mercenary armies employed by the Italian states fought poorly, rather, seeing what they were up against, they did not fight at all.

Analyzing failures of the recent past was sobering enough, but the prospect that the methods that had proved so ineffectual were about to be tested again was enough to frighten even the most optimistic statesman. Once more, the threat of a French invasion loomed over Italy. This time it was King Louis XII who would lead the invasion, having replaced his cousin Charles after his sudden death on April 7, 1498 (ironically the very same day of the aborted trial by fire that spelled the doom of his ardent supporter Girolamo Savonarola).

To all appearances the new King was more able and less impulsive than his predecessor. But while Louis was less prone to chase half-baked dreams of glory, he had no intention of abandoning what he believed were France's legitimate claims in Italy. His ambitions were, if anything, greater than those that had undone his predecessor. Not only did he covet the southern kingdom that had slipped through his cousin's grasp, but he hoped to pocket along the way the Duchy of Milan, to which he believed himself entitled through his grandmother, Valentina Visconti—a prize made all the sweeter by the fact that it would be won at the expense of the man most responsible for the disastrous conclusion of the last invasion, Ludovico Sforza.

Regarding this second anticipated conquest, his job was rendered considerably easier by Sforza himself, whose continued scheming had managed to alienate his former partners in the Holy League. "[J]udging the prudence and the intelligence of all the others to be far inferior to his own," Guicciardini wrote of Ludovico, "he expected always to be able to direct the affairs of Italy to suit himself and to circumvent everyone else by his cleverness." But rather than make his position more secure, the increasingly long list of broken promises produced an equally long list of enemies. When Pope Alexander, ever willing to adjust to the prevailing wind, reversed his previous antipathy toward the French, concluding he could more easily advance his family's fortunes by allying himself with that kingdom, Ludovico was effectively isolated.

This latest understanding between the Pope and the newly crowned King of France was perhaps the clearest indication that Louis was a far more canny statesman than his cousin. Charles's expedition had foundered when his initial success united his enemies, but even before he set foot on the peninsula, Louis had ensured that there would be no repetition of that fiasco. As soon as he ascended to the throne he dispatched ambassadors to

Rome with the outlines of a grand bargain that would more firmly tie the fortunes of the French crown to the house of Borgia. In exchange for an annulment of Louis's first marriage, which would pave the way for a more advantageous union with Charles's young widow, Anne, Pope Alexander's son, Cesare Borgia, would receive the minor French Duchy of Valence and a command in the French army that was poised to reenter Italy—a suitable launching pad for someone of his vaunting ambition.*

On July 29, 1498, Alexander issued a bull proclaiming Louis's first marriage invalid, clearing the way for his upcoming nuptials with Anne. The following month, the King of France, with Cesare Borgia by his side, recrossed the Alps and advanced toward Milan. The four years between the first and second French invasions had done nothing to erase the disparity between the mighty French army and the puny forces available to any of the Italian states. On September 2, facing the prospect of a siege and disillusioned with their lord, whose incessant scheming had brought them to this extremity, the people of Milan rose up against Ludovico and drove him from the city. Nine days later the French army entered Milan in triumph, having humbled one of the most powerful states in Italy merely by showing up.

For Florence, the return of the French should have come as welcome news. Ever since Piero de' Medici had thrown himself at Charles's feet, the republic had faithfully promoted the French cause, a commitment that had created no end of difficulties with her neighbors. But Florence had as yet little to show for its loyalty. The French government was generous in providing promises of help but stingy when it came to concrete action. Still, though they had been disappointed in the past, the government of Florence was ready to try again. On October 19 its ambassadors in Milan concluded a treaty with the French King that committed him to assist in the conquest of Pisa. In return, Florence promised to supply men and money to his upcoming Neapolitan campaign.

That expedition had to be postponed, however, when Ludovico Sforza, who had fled to Germany after the uprising, returned to Italy at the head of an army supplied, in part, by the German Emperor, who hoped thereby to thwart his rival's Italian ambitions. The fragility of Louis's Italian empire

---

* It is from this dukedom that Cesare took the title by which he is best known in Italy: Valentino.

was demonstrated by the ease with which the former Duke reclaimed his city. The people of Milan "who had opened the gates [wrote Machiavelli in *The Prince*], finding themselves deceived as to their opinions and their expectations, could not endure the burdens imposed by their new prince." Before Louis could set out for Naples he would have to deal with this threat in his rear. In April, the armies of France and Milan—each boasting contingents of the famed Swiss pike men—met on the plains of Lombardy. For years Ludovico had managed to evade the consequences of his actions, but now Fortune seemed to have finally abandoned the slippery Duke. Even before the battle was joined, a majority of his Swiss troops deserted his cause, citing wages owed and an unwillingness to shed the blood of their brethren across the field. With the battle lost before it began, Ludovico fled in disguise. He was quickly captured by the French and brought in chains to Lyons, where he was gawked at by the multitude. Ultimately confined to the Castle of Loches in Touraine, he would die, forgotten and unmourned, after ten miserable years in captivity.

Thus ended the remarkable career of the Moor, a man who imagined himself a paragon of cunning but whose short-term cleverness was accompanied by no real wisdom. "So his shrewdness was mocked," wrote Machiavelli with obvious satisfaction, a sentiment shared by a majority of his compatriots. It was due largely to his ambition that a great people now lay prostrate beneath the barbarian's boot, and it was only just that the author of this calamity should find himself caught in the web he had woven.

Among the first to congratulate the French King was the Florentine ambassador, Tommaso Soderini, who deemed the moment auspicious to remind him of recent commitments. Negotiations were conducted with Georges d'Amboise, Cardinal of Rouen,* a man whose business acumen and ability to drive a hard bargain were more typical of a merchant than a man of God. He finally agreed to lend the troops already promised—five hundred spearmen, four thousand Swiss pike men, and two thousand Gascons—but only at the exorbitant price of 24,000 ducats a month. Soderini acceded to the onerous terms reluctantly, hoping that a quick campaign would bring victory before bankruptcy.

---

* The elevation of d'Amboise, a favorite of the King, to the College of Cardinals was one of the conditions of the agreement between Louis and Pope Alexander. The red cardinal's hat was carried in the luggage of Cesare Borgia on his voyage to France.

But the expedition was doomed from the outset, largely because the two allies had divergent aims. For the French, Florence was of little use except as a bank from which to withdraw funds for the maintenance of their army on foreign soil; their strategy was to extract as much cash as they could up front, while providing as few troops as they could get away with. For Florence, the conquest of Naples was a matter of indifference unless Pisa was part of the campaign. The truth was that Florence needed France more than France needed the militarily insignificant republic. Soderini, like Machiavelli at Forli, was discovering the tribulations of representing a state regarded with contempt by its partners. The army was slow to set out, and once in motion moved with the leisurely pace, if not the tight discipline, of soldiers on parade. In fact the greed and unruliness of the French troops, who extorted money and provisions from every community they approached—friend and foe alike—undermined the cause of the city that employed them even before any blows were struck.

Hoping to bring order to a situation that was fast spinning out of control, the Florentine government dispatched to Cascina, ten miles to the east of Pisa where the army was now bivouacked, two commissioners, Luca degli Albizzi and Giovan Battista Ridolfi. Also included in the delegation was Machiavelli, who was to serve as secretary. Riding into camp, they found the troops close to mutiny. In the tradition of hired guns throughout the ages, the men complained of poor rations and salaries owed, turning their fury on their paymasters rather than on the enemy they were supposed to fight. Albizzi deemed the situation so dangerous that he told his colleagues, "He who is afraid may go back to Florence," an offer that Ridolfi immediately seized.

Despite friction between the Florentine representatives and the army, in late June eight thousand men advanced on Pisa, and on the 27th French artillery opened up on the walls of the city. But in a repetition of the Vitelli fiasco a year earlier, stalemate was plucked from the jaws of near certain victory, and this time the results were even more injurious to Florentine interests. On July 7, the Gascons deserted en masse, while the Swiss concluded that they risked fewer injuries if they stormed the headquarters of the Florentine commissioner rather than the Pisan fortifications. "It might . . . be well," Albizzi now wrote to the Signoria with calculated understatement, "whether it is desired that my life should be saved. . . . Let not your Excellencies think that cowardice moves me in this, since by no means would I flee from any peril, that should be deemed indispensable by my city." Machiavelli, who actually penned these letters dictated by his boss, was of the same mind, willing to do what he could but anxious not to lose his life in a doomed effort. The following day Albizzi was seized by the disgruntled troops, who threatened to kill him if he did not come up with the money they claimed they were owed; he was released only when he signed a guarantee that he would cover his government's obligations from his own bank account. But by this time it was too late to salvage the expedition. The army for which Florence had paid so dearly and from which so much had been expected no longer existed. It had dissolved before the walls of Pisa, taking with it much Florentine pride and treasure.

Machiavelli recalled this unfortunate episode in his *First Decennale*, which sets out in verse form the trials of serving a state that lacked the will and courage to defend itself:

> *But when they confronted the Pisans, the Gauls, full of confusion,*
> *struck by fear, did not show their forces at all prepared,*
> *but went away almost defeated and marked with severe disgrace;*
> *so the truth was known that the French can be conquered.*
> *And it was not an affair to pass over lightly, because if it made*
> *[Florence] groveling and servile, upon the French was the chief reproach;*
> *but you were not free from blame, although the Gaul*
> *tried to cover his shame with the failure of others;*
> *and your government too did not understand how to make decisions.*

Though he grants to the French "the chief reproach," he blames his native land almost equally. "Groveling and servile," Florence had allowed itself to become dependent on another nation, one, moreover, that proved itself inept as well as faithless. Failure to capture the puny city of Pisa revealed the weakness of both states. Under more settled conditions such a revelation might not have proved fatal, but with Italy fast becoming the proving ground for the armies of Europe, such an opening could not remain long without someone walking through it.

IV

SIR NIHIL

"The French are blinded by their own power, and only think those who are armed or ready to give money worthy of their esteem. They see that these two qualities are wanting in you, so they look upon you as Sir Nihil."

—MACHIAVELLI, DISPATCH TO THE TEN OF WAR

RODRIGO BORGIA, THE SPANISH-BORN POPE ALEXAN-der VI, was on intimate terms with most of the Deadly Sins. Greed, Wrath, Lust, Gluttony, and Pride: all these vices he possessed in more than full measure. It was as if he modeled himself on the Borgia family crest, whose heraldic device featured a black bull. Rather than conceal his failings, as his equally corrupt but more timid predecessors had, Rodrigo reveled in them, boasting of his sexual prowess and gargantuan appetites. In July 1501, Machiavelli received a report from Rome chronicling the misdeeds of the Pontiff. "Benefices are sold here like melons," Agostino Vespucci explained to his friend. "[E]very evening, from the Ave Maria to an hour after sunset, twenty-five or more women are brought into the palace . . . until the whole [Vatican] palace is turned into a brothel filled with every obscenity." In a break from the custom of the time, Rodrigo openly ac-knowledged his many children rather than passing them off as his nieces and nephews. He may have been no worse than some of the other recent occupants of the papal throne, but he embraced his sinful nature with un-usual gusto.

Machiavelli himself had a decidedly mixed opinion of this powerful figure "who, of all the pontiffs that have ever been, showed how much a pope—with both money and an army at his disposal—could accomplish." But, as Machiavelli also noted, his abilities were employed in pursuit of selfish ends, "to ensure the greatness not of the Church, but instead of the Duke [Cesare, his son]." In *The Prince*, Machiavelli treats him with grudging respect: "Alexander VI . . . never thought of anything but deception, and always found subjects on whom to practice this art. There never was a man who made promises more effectively, or affirmed an oath with as much solemnity, while observing them less. Nonetheless, his tricks always paid off, for he was well acquainted with this side of the world."

Alexander's oldest and most capable son, Cesare—known as Valentino—had followed his father into the Church. Elevated in 1493 to the College of Cardinals at the age of eighteen, he was insulated to some extent from the squabbles that set one minor state against the other. Of course the Renaissance Church was a highly political institution and, as his father's right-hand man, he was a force to be reckoned with in temporal as well as ecclesiastical matters, but since he was prohibited by the nature of his office from producing legitimate heirs and founding his own dynasty, he remained largely on the sidelines while others fought to rearrange the map of Italy to their liking. Within the Church his future was unlimited, and to one of a more placid temperament the prospect of ascending to the very pinnacle of power without risk to life and limb might have seemed an attractive alternative. But to Cesare, honors won by peaceful means seemed hardly worthy of a man.

Despite the fact that Cesare did not allow his office to interfere unduly with his lifestyle—even his generally tolerant colleagues in the Holy College complained that he preferred the doublet and hose of a courtier to the scarlet robes of a cardinal—he was restless and discontented. A handsome, athletic man, he was already exhibiting the telltale "flowers" of syphilis—the Gallic disease, it was often called by Italians, who believed it had arrived with Charles's invading army in 1494—proof that, like his father, he was not inclined to take his vow of celibacy literally. Another rule he apparently found onerous was the one prohibiting men of the cloth from engaging in acts of violence. When his sister Lucrezia was discovered in flagrante with a valet in her husband's employ, Cesare drew his sword and chased the man through the Vatican. The valet's life was initially spared when he threw himself at the feet of the Pope, but his body was later discovered floating facedown in the Tiber—the kind of unfortunate accident that seemed to befall those who got in the way of the Cardinal.

The one man whose mere existence stood between Cesare Borgia and his fondest ambitions was his brother, Juan, who received the title the Duke of Gandía after marrying a cousin of the Spanish King. Described by a contemporary as "a very mean young man, full of ideas of grandeur . . . haughty, cruel and unreasonable," Juan was nonetheless his father's favorite and, it seemed to Cesare, the undeserving recipient of all those titles that rightfully should have gone to him. In 1496 Juan was appointed by Alexander second-in-command of the papal armies, a post for which Cesare thought himself far better suited. Events seemed to confirm Cesare's judgment when Juan's incompetence led to the army's defeat at the hands of their own vassals, the insufferable Orsini counts, who were reluctant to submit to their papal overlord.

On the evening of June 14, 1497, the two brothers dined together at the home of their mother, the Pope's former mistress Donna Vannozza. Riding home that night the two parted company somewhere near the Piazza degli Ebrei, in Rome's Jewish quarter. When the Duke failed to return home, and when the following morning his bodyguard was found dead, his desperate father launched a massive search effort. After searchers spent a couple of days combing the slums and alleys of the Eternal City, a charcoal vendor came forward to report that on the night of the disappearance he had seen a body being tossed into the river near where the Duke had last been seen with his brother. (When asked why he had not told his story earlier, he explained that this was such a common occurrence he had not thought it worth reporting.) Dredging the Tiber, the Pope's men discovered the Duke's body, dressed in the clothes he had worn while dining with the Cardinal.

Suspicion immediately fell on Cesare, the man last seen in the Duke's company and the one who had most to gain by his departure from the scene.* This, at least, was the rumor whispered in the rooms of the Vatican, though only out of the Pope's hearing. Alexander was devastated by his favorite son's death, "shutting himself away in a room in grief and anguish

---

* Plausible candidates for the murder also include the various Orsini and their allies. It is unlikely the mystery will ever be resolved.

of heart, weeping most bitterly." When he finally emerged from his isolation he appeared to be a changed man. "Life has lost all interest for us," he
declared. "It must be that God punishes us for our sins, for the Duke has
done nothing to deserve so terrible a death."

But after a period of mourning, and a well-publicized campaign to
reform a Church that under his tenure had grown, if possible, even more
corrupt than before, Alexander reverted to his old ways, this time lavish-
ing on the likely murderer all the favors he had previously bestowed on his
victim. "Even more than by anger or by any other emotion," Guicciardini
declared, discovering in this simple formula the lodestar of all his policies,
"the Pope was motivated by his unbounded greed to exalt his children,
whom he loved passionately." Thrusting aside any suspicions he might
have harbored, Alexander was now determined to set Cesare on the path
to worldly triumph that had eluded his ill-fated brother.

The first step was for Cesare to exchange the robes of a prince of the
Church for the sword and armor of a secular lord. Fortunately, a likely
sponsor immediately stepped up in the person of King Louis of France,
whose ambitions in Italy could best be realized by forging an alliance with
the Pope. Soon Cesare was headed to France with the King's guarantee
of a dukedom in his pocket and, even more to his taste, the promise of a
prominent role in the army of invasion.

For the Republic of Florence the return of the ambitious Cesare Borgia
to Italian soil at the head of an army was about as welcome as the plague.
Papal relatives always proved troublesome since the territories in which
they could fulfill their ambitions abutted those of the Florentine empire
and often lay within what Florentines considered their sphere of influence.
During the reign of Sixtus IV, the Pope's desire to provide his nephew
Girolamo Riario with his own fiefdom embroiled Florence in a two-year
war that almost extinguished the independent republic. Geography alone
made the Pope and his spawn a threat to Florentine independence. To the
south lay the Papal States, the region near Rome that constituted the most
ancient possession of the Holy See; to the east and north the Romagna:
both regions owed theoretical allegiance to the heir of Saint Peter, however
much each vassal might act as if he commanded an independent state.
Should Alexander and Cesare succeed in forcing these unruly dependents
into submission, they would virtually encircle the republic. It is not sur-

prising, then, that in the Palazzo della Signoria news of Cesare's arrival in northern Italy was greeted with near panic.

Everything indicated that Cesare was unlikely to settle for less than his predecessors. As a newly minted lord with a high-sounding title but little real power, he now contemplated the patchwork of Italian states like a ravenous man surveying a mouthwatering buffet. The only decision was which delicacies he should pop into his mouth first.

Once Milan fell to the French—with Cesare, Duke Valentino, riding into the city triumphantly at the King's side—he was free to set off in pursuit of his own territorial ambitions. First to attract his covetous eye was Forli, the same small state Sixtus had bequeathed to his nephew and that was still in the hands of his widow, the formidable Caterina Sforza. The unhappy outcome of Machiavelli's earlier mission to Forli had resulted from Caterina's conviction that Milan, under her uncle Ludovico Sforza, was in a better position to rescue her from the clutches of the Borgia than the weak, vacillating Florentine Republic. With her uncle now driven from Milan by the French, it seemed she had placed her bet on the wrong horse. Nor was this her only misstep. "[I]t would have been safer for her," Machiavelli observed dryly, "had she not been hated by the people." Caterina had run out of champions. After a brief siege, Valentino's army stormed her last remaining citadel, captured the Countess, and threw her into prison.* Thus the son of Pope Alexander destroyed the last vestiges of the fiefdom his predecessor had hoped to establish for his nephew, Girolamo Riario, once again demonstrating how difficult it was to build a secular dynasty on a foundation of papal power.†

This sobering lesson was lost on Valentino, who was determined to grab as much as he could while his father still sat on the Throne of Saint Peter. After snapping up Forli, Valentino seized Pesaro and Rimini on the Adriatic coast. "This lord knows very well," Machiavelli wrote in a report to the Ten setting out the Duke's overall strategy, "that the Pope can die any day, and that he needs to think before his death of laying for himself some other foundation, if he intends to preserve the states he now has."

---

* Ever resourceful, it was said that the still attractive Countess captured the eye of Cesare and that the two became lovers.

† The first Medici Pope, Leo X, also tried to set up his relatives as feudal lords in the Romagna, with equally dismal results.

In the space of a few short months Cesare Borgia had shown himself to be a far more energetic and capable leader than his late brother, but far from satisfying him, each new success—enthusiastically recounted by Alexander, who sorely tried the patience of his visitors with tales of his son's exploits—merely whetted his appetite for tastier morsels.

Florence looked on with apprehension as the Duke picked off one small territory after another on the borders of Tuscany, but there was little it could do to slow his triumphant progress across central Italy. The one card Florence had to play was diplomatic. Both the Republic of Florence and Duke Valentino were clients of the same patron—the Most Christian King Louis of France. Though Louis had thus far turned an indulgent eye toward his new vassal—in fact most of Valentino's conquests were made with an army that included French troops—he also realized that his long-term success in Italy would be jeopardized if he lost the goodwill (and hard cash) of the Florentine Republic. To deal with this growing crisis, as well as the continuing stalemate before Pisa, the government of Florence appointed Francesco della Casa special envoy to the French King. Accompanying him on this critical diplomatic mission was the Second Secretary of the Chancery, Niccolò Machiavelli.[*]

Della Casa and Machiavelli set out for France on July 18, 1500, arriving on August 7 in Nevers, where the King's peripatetic court had temporarily alighted. With its throngs of ambassadors and clerics, lords and ladies—both great and small—ministers and secretaries, as well as countless hangers-on and supplicants attracted by the prospect of advancement or the hope of redress, the court of the Most Christian King was a far more splendid stage than any on which Machiavelli had previously performed. By comparison, Countess Sforza's castle in Forli had been little more than a rustic stronghold.

But if the stage was far grander, the part the two envoys from the Florentine Republic could expect to play was proportionally diminished. Their insignificance was made abundantly clear when della Casa and Machiavelli attempted to navigate the bureaucratic maze, competing for

---

[*] Francesco della Casa's superior rank was indicated by the larger stipend he was initially granted by the government. When it was clear that Machiavelli was doing most of the work, his friends and relatives succeeded in granting him parity (Machiavelli et al., *Machiavelli and His Friends,* letters 13 and 14). But even with this increase of salary, Machiavelli was required to spend more than he received.

attention with men who represented far greater powers and whose governments provided them with far more substantial resources. "The French are blinded by their own power, and only think those who are armed or ready to give money worthy of their esteem," Machiavelli reported to the Signoria. "They see that these two qualities are wanting in you, so they look upon you as Sir *Nihil* [Nothing]. . . . Our degree and quality, on an unwelcome errand, do not suffice to bring sinking things to the surface. . . . [The republic] should try to obtain by bribery some friends in France who would be stirred by more than natural affection, since that is what has to be done by all who have affairs at this Court. And he who refuses to do it is like one who would win a suit without feeing his attorney."

Though signed by both ambassadors, the dispatch—written in Machiavelli's own hand—reflects the pithy analysis of the junior partner. No one was quicker than the Second Chancellor to size up a situation and discover where real power lay. Whatever they were told by the Cardinal de Rouen or any of the King's other ministers, they would receive little satisfaction without something tangible to offer their hosts. As usual, however, the Signoria was trying to do diplomacy on the cheap, sending men of little standing who cut rather shabby figures at the glittering French court.

But in Machiavelli the Florentines always got better than they deserved. Despite complaining about the meager level of support, Machiavelli was zealous in carrying out his mission, promoting his government's policies and sending to Florence a series of dispatches filled with penetrating analyses. As if to compensate for their miserliness, his superiors at the Chancery were generous in their praise. "I don't want to forget to tell you," reported Biagio Buonaccorsi, "how much satisfaction your letters give everyone; and believe me, Niccolò, when I tell you, since you know that I have no talent for flattery, that when I found myself reading those earlier letters of yours to certain citizens, many of the highest rank, you were highly commended, and it pleased me greatly, and in a few words I artfully confirmed their verdict, showing how easily you did it."

Machiavelli's worth was proven even more emphatically when della Casa took ill, leaving his assistant to carry on without him. Most of his time at court, which by September had relocated to Melun, near Paris, was spent trying to patch up the quarrel that had arisen between the two states over the conduct of the war with Pisa. While Machiavelli suggested delicately that the disaster was attributable to the incompetence and treachery of the Swiss troops, the King pointed the finger at the Florentines, who failed to deliver the promised fee. Unless Louis were paid the 38,000 francs he claimed he was owed, Machiavelli reported, "he threatens to erect Pisa and the neighboring territory into an independent state."

The second matter Machiavelli raised with the King and his ministers was the increasingly threatening posture of Cesare Borgia. Sooner or later, he explained, Valentino's ambitions in Italy would clash with theirs. Sparring with the powerful minister of the King, Machiavelli more than held his own. "[W]hen the Cardinal of Rouen told me that the Italians knew nothing of war," Machiavelli recalled in *The Prince*, "I responded that the French knew nothing of statecraft, for if they had they would never have allowed the Church to grow so great."

Satisfying as it was to knock the arrogant French Cardinal down a peg or two, Machiavelli also advanced the republic's agenda by reminding Rouen of the dangers of unchecked papal power. Were Alexander and his son allowed to ride roughshod over the independent powers of Italy, how long would they tolerate Louis's ambitions on the peninsula? The uncomfortable fact, at least as far as the French were concerned, was that in striking a deal with the Pope they were emboldening a man who already had turned on them once before and whose interests were ultimately at odds with theirs. As Machiavelli wrote in October, "if the King had conceded everything for [Cesare's] expedition in Romagna, it was rather because he knew not how to withstand the unbridled desires of the Pope, than from any real desire for his success."

Machiavelli's strategy was to remind the French at every turn how dangerous Valentino was, a task made easier by the Duke's natural aggressiveness. While Machiavelli was pleading his case before the French court, Valentino was threatening to pounce on Bologna; he had even entered into negotiations with Pisa to have himself declared its Duke, demonstrating that his ambitions could no longer be contained within the borders of Romagna but extended to Tuscany as well. "The Pope," Machiavelli told his bosses, "tries by all means to compass the destruction of the King's friends, to wrest Italy from his hands with greater ease." Unfortunately, Machiavelli did not have the stage to himself. He had to wage a daily struggle with ambassadors from Pope Alexander who suggested that if only Piero de'

Medici were restored to Florence, the French would find the republic far easier to deal with. Machiavelli urged the Ten that the best way to counter this insidious campaign was to swallow their pride and pay the French the money they claimed was owed to them—a request his government quickly complied with. The arrival of Florentine ducats had an immediate impact; upon their receipt, the King conveyed a stern letter to Valentino ordering him to stop his meddling in Tuscany.

Machiavelli remained with the French court until late November, by which time the government had appointed Pier Francesco Losinghi to replace him. The five months he had been away from Florence had been difficult for Machiavelli. His penny-pinching bosses in the Signoria begrudged him every *soldo* so that he was forced to content himself with dingy, lice-infested lodgings and often showed up at court in robes worn at the cuff and too often mended. This was not only personally humiliating but also self-defeating since it was but one more indication in the eyes of his hosts that the state he represented was truly Sir *Nihil*.

The mission to France had come at a difficult moment in Machiavelli's life. His father Bernardo had died in May, which meant that just as Niccolò was setting out on this crucial assignment he was burdened with new responsibilities.* He was now officially the head of the Machiavelli household, with siblings and other relatives looking to him for advice as well as material support. During his months away in France his older sister, Primavera, died of fever and her thirteen-year-old son, Giovanni, seemed likely to follow her to the grave. Though, happily, the boy survived, this meant that Machiavelli's list of responsibilities was that much longer.† When his brother, Totto, begged the government to cover the additional expenses of Machiavelli's foreign posting, this was in part an acknowledgment that Niccolò's salary, even when combined with the rents derived from their properties, was still insufficient to meet the family's basic needs.‡

---

* His mother, always a shadowy figure in his life, seems to have died a few years earlier.

† Machiavelli took a lively interest in the welfare of his nephew, Giovanni Vernacci, and remained close. A number of letters survive between the two, attesting to their abiding affection. In one from 1515, Machiavelli declared, "I shall always regard you as my son" (Machiavelli et al., *Machiavelli and His Friends*, letter 248, p. 314).

‡ In fact while Totto managed to get the government to agree to an increased stipend, they apparently sent no additional money while Machiavelli was in France.

But in some ways it was an enormously exciting time for Machiavelli. After more than thirty directionless years, he had found his calling. This was the work he felt he was made for. Politics, which to the average Florentine citizen was a normal part of civic life, was his consuming passion, and nowhere was the game played more ferociously and for higher stakes than in the great courts of Europe. These were not places for the faint of heart or the easily deceived. Latin orations modeled on Cicero delivered by ambassadors dressed in cloth of gold and sparkling with pearls, the culture of flattery and obfuscation—Machiavelli saw through it all. Beneath the glittering surface something far more savage was taking place. Observing at close hand the palace intrigue and backstairs deal-making at the royal court, he discovered a window into the soul of men and a true picture of society built on unequal relationships. Here, brazen self-interest and naked aggression were ingeniously concealed, sweetened with lies and sauced with piety, until even the most unpalatable cruelties seemed refined enough for a king's table.

The mission to France was his first opportunity to view at close range the inner workings of one of the great power centers of Europe. The lessons he learned pleading before the King and his closest advisers were ones that would remain with him throughout his life and would shape his political philosophy. Perhaps the most important lesson was that, for all the high-sounding oratory, the only thing that mattered in those places where the fate of nations was decided was raw power. He who possessed it commanded the world, while he who lacked it could expect nothing but pity, a gift of the great to the less fortunate that was less than worthless. Machiavelli learned in France that he who could not bargain from a position of strength had better not bargain at all, for in any such exchange—as between a lion and a lamb—the stronger party was bound to devour the weaker. "There can be no proper relation between one who is armed and one who is not," he wrote in *The Prince*, "nor is it reasonable to expect that one who is armed will voluntarily obey one who is not." Any appeal to conscience or fairness was bound to fail when one party had his hands around the throat of another.

It was his profound understanding of this basic fact that transformed his difficult mission in France into a success. It was pointless, Machiavelli realized, to plead the justice of his case: he needed to demonstrate that the weak city-state of Florence and the powerful nation-state of France shared a common goal. To the skeptical Cardinal Rouen he pointed out that Florentines acted "not upon their good faith, but upon its being their interest to side with France," while, by the same measure, the Pope's ambitions for his son in Italy were incompatible with the extension of their power on the peninsula. In *The Prince* he elaborates on the arguments he used on the Cardinal to fashion one of his more memorable aphorisms: "[H]e who causes another to become powerful is himself ruined." In other words, by backing Cesare and Alexander in their campaign to dominate Italy, the French were sowing the seeds of their own destruction. By contrast, Florentine weakness actually made her a more valuable ally, for the mighty kingdom need not fear her as a rival for supremacy. In the end Machiavelli was able to persuade his own government to yield upon a matter of pride and remind the French of the value of continued Florentine goodwill. The arrangement ultimately hammered out was that the republic would continue to bankroll Louis's adventures in Italy in return for protection against her enemies, of whom the most dangerous continued to be Cesare Borgia and his indulgent father.

Burdened by the demands of his job and by continuing personal and financial worries, Machiavelli nonetheless kept up that good-natured and often ribald correspondence that no amount of anxiety could suppress.* Biagio Buonaccorsi, Agostino Vespucci, and his other friends continued to fill him in on the latest gossip. Office politics was often more compelling, and had more immediate impact on their day-to-day lives, than great affairs of state. In August, a colleague in the Chancery passed along an assessment of the grumpy Antonio della Valle in which he claimed to have discovered the source of their boss's perpetual nitpicking: "Every day *Ser* Antonio's stomach bothers him, but we're learning how to deal with it; I believe it's because he doesn't have his lady Agostanza here to warm him up and give him a workout on the seesaw."

If a discussion of *Madonna* Agostanza's bedroom habits was justified by the irritability it provoked in their boss, no excuses were needed to pass along an obscene anecdote or scurrilous rumor. Gambling, whoring, and

---

* Unfortunately, for this period we have many more personal letters written to Machiavelli than from him. Much of what we have from Machiavelli's own pen consists of official reports and analytical essays.

other unsavory escapades seem to have occupied a great deal of their free time, though often it is hard to tease out a thread of truth in the exaggerated yarns they spun. Machiavelli's own proclivities are hinted at by Andrea di Romolo, who tried to entice him back to the city with memories of one courtesan who lived near the Arno. More potentially damaging allusions are contained in a letter by Agostino Vespucci: "When in jest and to relax our minds we were speaking about you, how you so abounded in charm and drolleries, that we were so often forced to be delighted, to smile, even sometimes to laugh when you were present, Ripa added that there was no way you could stay in France without grave danger, since sodomites and homosexuals are stringently prosecuted there."

Though obviously offered tongue-in-cheek (Vespucci follows up his little joke with another more far-fetched tale involving sexual relations with a horse), the reference to sodomy—which in Florence was a crime punishable, in theory at least, by burning at the stake—can't be dismissed out of hand. The term, which encompassed not only sex between men but also "unnatural" sex with a woman, was one that attached itself from time to time to Machiavelli's name. His taste for whores, which he made no effort to conceal, and the various sexual affairs he conducted with more passion than discretion throughout his life, opened him up to slander by his political enemies who trafficked in sordid tales about his private life when they ran out of substantive arguments. Whatever the mechanics of Machiavelli's sexual performances, and whether or not, as has also been suggested, he occasionally engaged in such acts with boys, his behavior was unremarkable. Florence, both before and after Savonarola, was a city of sexual license where illegitimate children were commonplace, whores innumerable, and the lines between hetero- and homosexuality less precisely drawn than in our day.* As Machiavelli's own correspondence makes abundantly clear,

---

* In fact the morality of the age was less apt to make a distinction between the sex of the two partners involved than in the orifices employed. Anal sex with a woman was no less reprehensible than with another man. Thus accusations against Machiavelli that he engaged in sodomy do not tell us whether the crimes alleged were of a hetero- or homosexual nature. In fact Florentines did not recognize homosexuality as a fundamental aspect of human nature. Only sexual intercourse between married partners was approved. All other varieties, including prostitution and sex with teenage boys, was included in that wider category of illicit sexuality. In theory, sodomy was punishable by death, but the severest penalties were rarely enforced. The government cracked down from time to time on this "abominable" vice, but without much success (see Rocke, *Forbidden Friendships: Homosexuality and Male Culture in the Renaissance* for an illuminating discussion of the issue).

his own range of experience was no wider than that of his friends and colleagues. He was the first to admit he was no saint, but unlike some of his more pious compatriots, he at least had the honesty to admit his failings.

Upon his return from France in December 1500, Machiavelli found his desk piled high with urgent matters needing his attention. In the months he had been away his stock had risen, and with increased confidence in his abilities came increased demands on his time. In February 1501 he was sent to the Tuscan city of Pistoia to mediate between two rival factions, the Pantiachi and Cancellari, who, like the Guelphs and Ghibellines of medieval Florence (or like the Montagues and Capulets of *Romeo and Juliet*), seemed bent on painting the town red with each other's blood. Exposure to the hatred and violence of this provincial city—whose ferocity was disproportionate to the prize being contested—offered Machiavelli further evidence of the brutal nature of power politics. His attempts to broker a truce were ultimately futile. Here in one small city on the Arno was the world in microcosm, where hatred stoked over generations proved more compelling than reason, a bitter lesson that Machiavelli would remember when composing *The Prince*.

It was Valentino, however, testing the limits of his French confinement like a caged tiger, who continued to draw the attention of the Ten and the Signoria. If his master had shortened the leash a bit, forbidding him to gobble up Bologna and Florence, there was still other prey to stalk. Among the more tempting prizes was Piombino, a midsized city on the western coast of Tuscany. Valentino was not discouraged by the fact that to reach this seaport he would have to lead his army through Florentine territory. In fact, he seemed less interested in acquiring the city than in seeing how far he could go before his French overseers reined him in.

In early spring 1501, the lead divisions of Valentino's army began to stream through the Apennine passes and onto the Tuscan foothills, pillaging the towns of the Mugello foothills as they advanced. Thoroughly alarmed, the Florentine government sped a promised 38,000 francs to Louis along with a reminder of the commitments he'd already made to them. Fortunately, Florence was not solely dependent on French troops. While awaiting the French response the Florentines began to muster their own troops for the defense of the capital. Most of the organizational details fell to Machiavelli, Secretary to the Ten of War, who did not allow skepticism about the strategy his government was employing to interfere with his duties.

As always he worked zealously on behalf of the state, while using the daily frustrations of his office—the incessant quarrels with various captains over pay and dispositions—as grist for the analytical mill that was turning slowly in his head. He had received a traditional humanist education, built around the great classical authors and texts, so it was only natural for him to compare his own experience to the ancient models set forth in Livy, Plutarch, and Thucydides—almost always discovering that the present fell far short of the past. "I have heard," he wrote, "that history is the teacher of our actions, and especially of our rulers; the world has always been inhabited by men with the same passions as our own, and there have always been rulers and ruled, and good subjects and bad subjects, and those who rebel and are punished."

Comparing the professional soldiers of his own day with the citizen militias of the Roman Republic, Machiavelli extolled the virtues of the latter: "[A]s long as the Roman republic continued incorrupt," he would later write in *The Art of War,*

> *no citizen, however powerful, ever presumed to avail himself of that profession [of arms] in peacetime so as to trample upon the laws, to plunder the provinces, or to turn tyrant and enslave his country. . . . The commanders, on the contrary, contenting themselves with the honor of a triumph, returned with eagerness to their former manner of living, and the common soldiers laid down their arms with much more pleasure than they had taken them up. Each resumed the calling by which he had gotten his bread before, and none had any hopes of advancing himself by plunder and rapine.*

Compare this happy picture to the professional soldiers for hire Machiavelli was forced to deal with on a daily basis:

> *Mercenary captains are either skilled at arms, or they are not* [he wrote in *The Prince*]. *If they are, you cannot trust them, because*

they will always aspire to achieve greatness for themselves, either by suppressing you who are their master, or by suppressing others whom you wish to protect. If, instead, they are not courageous and skillful soldiers, they will ruin you just the same.

The habit of viewing current events through the prism of the classical past was not unique to Machiavelli, but few could speak with the authority of the Second Chancellor of Florence, who combined theoretical knowledge with a wealth of practical experience.

Even at this early stage Valentino had made a powerful impression on Machiavelli. His boldness stood in stark contrast to Florence's indecision. While Valentino led his own troops into battle, seizing the initiative through quick movements and judicious application of force, Florence depended on the favor of distant lords and mercenaries whose loyalty was to themselves rather than to their employers. The city's impotence was amply demonstrated in the spring of 1501 when Valentino was allowed to cross Florence's borders unchallenged.

Borgia's policy was to put as much pressure as he could on the republic without actually provoking a French backlash. In May, with his army on Florentine soil, he demanded they reward his insolence by offering him a *condotta* (contract) as a captain in their army. Reports of atrocities committed by his troops added to the urgency to strike a deal. "The whole morning," wrote Luca Landucci in his diary, "we heard nothing but the iniquities of Valentino's troops; among other things they sacked Carmigiano, and carried off all the girls they found there, who were gathered in a church from all the country round." Too weak to confront their tormentor on the field of battle, Florence was forced to buy him off by offering him a contract to supply three hundred men-at-arms in return for the exorbitant fee of 36,000 ducats.

This was less a traditional contract than a form of extortion, though in truth in the hiring of mercenary troops there was often little to distinguish the two. Valentino was proving that, in addition to his other talents, he was adept at running a Mafia-style protection racket. Fortunately the republic was saved from further bullying by Louis, who summoned his vassal to help with the reduction of the Kingdom of Naples, which, by the terms of the Treaty of Granada—signed secretly in November 1500—had been divided between France and Spain.* Valentino himself was ordered to capture the strategic city of Capua, which he treated with his characteristic brutality. "They killed without pity priests, monks and nuns, in churches and convents, and all the women they found: the young girls were seized and cruelly abused; the number of people killed amounted to around 6000." On August 19, the French army occupied Naples and, for a few weeks at least, Florence could relax while Valentino, with all the arrogance and cruelty of a conquering hero, enjoyed himself with a harem he created by seizing forty of the most beautiful women in the city.

At the same time Valentino was wading in gore and indulging in sensual excess in Naples, Machiavelli's life in Florence was taking a more domestic turn. Sometime in August 1501, Machiavelli—now thirty-two years old—married Marietta Corsini, a young woman from a distinguished family in the adjacent neighborhood in the Oltrarno, the *Gonfalone Ferza* (the Banner of the Whip). The Corsini, like the Machiavelli, were an old and respected Florentine family, well represented among the office holders who ran the city, though not among the great clans who dominated the halls of power. The union was professionally advantageous for Niccolò since Marietta's sister was married to Piero del Nero, a member of the Ten of War and thus, effectively, Machiavelli's boss. It was one more sign that Machiavelli was well regarded in the upper echelons of the government; in marrying Marietta Corsini, Niccolò was marrying up.

As head of the household Machiavelli conducted the negotiations for the marriage contract himself. Marietta remained in the background and had little say in the matter. Instead, Machiavelli haggled over the dowry over a period of months with Marietta's father, Luigi, and possibly her brother, Lanciolino. There is no question of a romantic motive.† Marriage in Renaissance Florence was largely an economic arrangement between two

---

* The terms of the treaty were left deliberately vague. Though the Aragonese dynasty in Naples was easily toppled, tensions over the division of spoils continued to simmer, shortly leading to all-out war between France and Spain.

† It is telling that the most famous romance in Florentine history—Dante's love for Beatrice Portinari—was an unconsummated passion between two people married to others. Love and marriage in Renaissance Florence belonged to separate realms. Lorenzo de' Medici famously gave a tournament for his lady love, Lucrezia Donati, even as he was engaged to Clarice Orsini.

families. At most, the groom would have examined his intended—either himself or through third parties—to determine whether she was physically suitable and of good character, while the prospective bride had little input, relying on the male members of her family to protect her interests.

We have no records of the various contracts or ceremonies involved, though we know enough about the process to paint a detailed, if somewhat generic, picture. After an initial marriage contract (*sponsalia*)—arrived at only after many offers and counteroffers—the bride would have been escorted to the house of her husband where the wedding feast was laid. Months or even years could pass between the initial *sponsalia* and the moment when the bride left her father's house to live under the roof of her husband. The wedding feast was the public face of a union that was as much civic as private, the moment when the community gave its blessing to the joining of two families. Given Machiavelli's modest means, this was unlikely to have been an elaborate affair, but it would have included not only members of both families, but also friends and neighbors who were politically and financially invested in the successful merging of two respected clans. Only after the plates were cleared and the guests had departed was a more intimate union forged as the couple retired to the bedroom to consummate marriage.

No doubt Niccolò and Marietta followed these time-honored customs, though neither the bride nor groom was an important enough personage to have the event recorded for posterity. Nor did Machiavelli himself feel compelled to memorialize the occasion. True, his marriage to Marietta Corsini marked a profound change in his life, the moment when he began to build his own household, looking forward to fatherhood and assuming the added burdens of supporting a family of his own. But it was also something prosaic, the next step in a logical progression from youth to maturity. It is telling that having taken this momentous step he saw no reason to alter his habits or his outlook on life. His passion continued to be his job; his time was taken up with work and with friends, who no doubt spent many a hilarious hour at the tavern making obscene jokes at the expense of their newly married friend. He found little time, and spared little thought, for the young bride who waited for him while he pursued his various pleasures.

Like Niccolò's mother, Bartolomea Nelli, Marietta remains a shadowy figure. But few Renaissance women—and almost all of these, like Caterina Sforza or Lucrezia Borgia, are members of ruling dynasties—are anything but two-dimensional. Custom relegated women to the domestic realm, to housekeeping and childrearing, and even in these limited roles they almost never received the credit they deserved. Writers on domestic issues tended to treat women with patronizing indulgence or, worse, with outright contempt. The Venetian aristocrat Francesco Barbaro in his influential essay "On Wifely Duties" speaks of the wife's "obedience [to her husband], which is her master and companion." In his *Books on the Family*, Leon Battista Alberti lists the characteristics of an ideal wife—"to wish to appear a woman of honor, to command the household and to make herself respected, to care for the welfare of the family and to preserve the things that are in the house." Even in this limited and distinctly female role, she can only hope to fulfill her potential by listening attentively to her husband, who should instruct her with the patience and forbearance one might use with a child.

A relationship in which the husband claimed absolute authority over his submissive wife was encouraged in Florence by the large age difference between the two. Marrying at thirty-two, Machiavelli fell within the normal range for men. Marietta's age at the time of her wedding is not known for certain, but she was almost certainly in her late teens. Though her family was at least as distinguished as her husband's, she was a young girl of far less education and worldly experience. For all his imagination when it came to matters of state, there is no indication that Machiavelli was more enlightened than his peers when it came to relations between the sexes. In fact one can glean from various remarks scattered throughout his writings that he possessed the usual prejudices of males of his class. "I hope I shall never be a husband if I can't get my wife to do what I want," remarks Callimaco, the hero of his play *La Mandragola*, an attitude of superiority reflected in somewhat softer terms by Callimaco's servant, who says, "with gentle words you can usually get a woman where you want her to go." There is no question of Machiavelli treating his wife, or any of the other women in his life, as an equal. Men who doted on their wives were considered fools and, in all likelihood, cuckolds who deserved what they got for having turned the natural order of their households upside down.

In his own writings Machiavelli enjoys skewering men who strayed from the "ideal" prescribed by moralists like Barbaro and Alberti. The

foolish husband whose wife runs rings around him is a stock comic character, and Machiavelli squeezes maximum laughs from such situations in
his two best-known plays, *Clizia* and *La Mandragola*. Here it is the men
who are weak, easily deceived, and done in by their own vices—lust in the
case of Nicomaco in *Clizia*, stupidity and greed in the case of Nicia in *La
Mandragola*—while their wives are both more virtuous and more capable.
In both cases Machiavelli gives the husband a name that is a variation of
his own, demonstrating a generous capacity to laugh at himself.

   This is not to say that these plays are necessarily an accurate depiction of his own marriage, but they do reflect a nuanced, if not entirely
unprejudiced, attitude toward the potential of both sexes. He certainly had
no trouble imagining strong, sensible women, women who, in the eyes
of the pompous Barbaro, would have been condemned for not knowing
their place. How much of Marietta is there in the character of Sofronia,
the long-suffering wife in *Clizia* who must hold the family together while
her husband recklessly pursues the object of his obsession? Perhaps a great
deal, but it is also true that comedy often depends on reversing the normal
order of things (which is why cross-dressing is such a staple of the genre).
Despite his sympathy for his female characters, Machiavelli was capable of
a misogyny distasteful to modern ears. Noting the vicissitudes of life, for
instance, Machiavelli wrote "fortune is a woman and in order to be mastered she must be jogged and beaten," words that elicit sympathy for the
flesh-and-blood woman forced to share a house, and a bed, with the writer.

   Marietta seems to have been devoted to Niccolò, but not so cowed by
the master of the house that she didn't feel free to lash out when she felt
she had been wronged. Her main complaint was that he was so often out
of town on business that she rarely got to see him. Only a year after their
wedding, while Machiavelli was away on government business, she was
berating him for abandoning her. "Lady Marietta," wrote Biagio Buonaccorsi—whose job, it seems, was to look after her while he was away—
"curses God, and says she has thrown away both her body and her goods."
Similar complaints are a regular feature of their correspondence, but a wife
whose main complaint is that her husband is never around is a wife not
entirely dissatisfied with her mate.

   The following year, 1503, Marietta wrote the one letter we have from
her hand. The short missive offers a precious glimpse into Machiavelli's
domestic world and is worth quoting in full:

My dearest Niccolò. You make fun of me, but without reason, for
I would thrive if you were with me. *You know how happy I am when*
you are not down there [in Rome]; and now more than ever since I
have been told how much disease is going around. How can I be con-
tent when I can rest neither day nor night. The happiness I find comes
from the baby.† So I beg you to send me letters a little more often
than you do, since I have only had three so far. Don't be surprised if
I have not written, because I have not been able to since until now I
have had a fever. I am not angry. For now the baby is well. He looks
like you, white as snow, with his head a velvety black, and he is hairy
like you. Since he looks like you he seems beautiful to me. And he's so
lively he acts as if he's been in the world for a year. As soon as he was
born he opened his eyes and filled the whole house with his cries. But
our daughter [Primavera] is not feeling well. Remember to come back
home. Nothing more. May God be with you and keep you safe.

I am sending you a doublet and two shirts and two kerchiefs and
a towel, which I have here for you.

Your Marietta in Florence

There's a tenderness to this simple note that belies the caricature of Machiavelli as a soulless hedonist, pursuing low pleasures while offering his
sardonic take on the world around him. In assessing Machiavelli the man,
one should recall these words along with seedier details revealed in his
letters and his plays. Though it could not have been easy putting up with
his infidelities and frequent neglect, there nonetheless seems to have been
genuine affection between husband and wife, a bond cemented over the
years by the shared love of their children.

Judged by the less sentimental measures favored by Renaissance Florentines, Machiavelli's marriage was an unqualified success. By March
1506, when it was the turn of Agostino Vespucci to assume the pleasant
chore of dropping in on Machiavelli's family and filling him in on their

---

* Marietta here uses the *voi* form of the word. This is more formal than the familiar *tu*, revealing, at least at this stage in their relationship, a certain stiffness.

† This is Bernardo, their oldest son. The daughter referred to later is Primarena, their oldest child, born in 1502.

progress, the household was already overrun by young children. "I'll go to your house before heading off to the chancellery, and before I finish I'll let you know what's happening with your little troop," Vespucci assured him. Later he reports: "I've just returned from your house, and took care of everything that you asked of me in your letter. All are well, excellent in fact, and Marietta was anxious for me to pass along her regards, as well as that of the children. As I said: all are well. Only Bernardo is a little bit fussy, but has no fever or other illness."

Machiavelli, in any case, had little time to bask in domestic bliss. By the autumn of 1501 Valentino was back in Tuscany and renewing his assault on Piombino, which quickly fell to his forces. New and alarming reports concerning Valentino's intentions landed on the Second Chancellor's desk almost daily, including one in December that the Pisans had reopened talks to have Borgia declared their Duke, a move that would put an end to Florentine hopes of regaining the wayward city. Borgia's promises to the French King precluded a direct assault on Florence but did not prevent him from toying with the republic like a cat with a wounded bird.

In June 1502, with Valentino making various provocative demonstrations in the vicinity, the citizens of Arezzo—a city some forty miles southeast of Florence that had been an important dependency since the fourteenth century—rebelled, offering to place themselves instead under the protection of one of Valentino's chief lieutenants. The man to whom they turned was Vitellozzo Vitelli, the brother of Paolo Vitelli, whose execution at the hands of Florence had transformed the surviving sibling into an implacable enemy. The dimensions of the threat were exposed when Vitellozzo was joined by Piero de' Medici, who hoped to use Arezzo as a launching pad for an attempt on Florence itself.*

Though Valentino disavowed his subordinate's action, he clearly enjoyed watching the squirming of a government he regarded as little more

---

* The one bright spot as far as Florence was concerned was the difficult relations between Piero de' Medici and the papal family. Piero was married to Alfonsina Orsini and had close ties to that baronial family. Despite the fact that Paolo Orsini served for the moment as a captain under Valentino, the Borgia detested that powerful family and were often in open conflict with them. Restoring Piero to rule in Florence would greatly increase Orsini influence in Italy, something the Borgia hoped to avoid.

than a collection of pusillanimous shopkeepers.* His poor estimate of the republic's fighting capacity was confirmed when a Florentine force detached from the Pisan campaign to rescue Arezzo turned back without striking a blow. All Florence could now do was go scurrying off once more to the King of France, whose friendship they had recently purchased at a high price.

Cesare Borgia clearly had the upper hand, but he still needed to tread carefully to avoid provoking Louis. It was a delicate three-way dance among partners who circled each other warily, daggers half drawn. Tensions only increased when Valentino added yet another state to his long list of conquests. His latest victim was the Duchy of Urbino, a mountain stronghold in the Marches about seventy miles east of Florence that he seized in a surprise attack on June 21.† It was from a position of strength, then, that Valentino now requested from the government of Florence a delegation to discuss a new arrangement, one that acknowledged his supremacy in the region. Appointed to head the mission was Francesco Soderini, Bishop of Volterra; in the now familiar supporting role was Niccolò Machiavelli.

Setting out on horseback, Bishop Soderini and Machiavelli arrived in Urbino on June 24, where they hurried to pay their respects to the new lord of the city. The palace to which the two Florentine envoys were now escorted remains one of the great monuments of the age. Begun some forty years earlier by Federico da Montefeltro, the successful *condottiere* and humanist patron, it projected an air of cultivation and refinement at odds with the violent profession of its master.‡ With its classically proportioned courtyard, fine library—one of the most extensive in Europe—and its famous study paneled in inlaid woods conjuring with startling verisi-

---

*   Machiavelli quoted the Duke as saying: "[I]t is true that Vitelozzo is my man, but I swear to you that I knew nothing of Arezzo" (*Legazioni, Commissarie, Scritti di Governo*, no. 103, p. 121).

†   The element of surprise was achieved in large part because the Duke, Guidobaldo da Montefeltro, had no reason to expect an attack. He was an ally of Pope Alexander and was often employed as a *condottiere* in the papal employ.

‡   Federico da Montefeltro was one of the great characters of the Renaissance. Learned patron of Giovanni Santi, a mediocre painter best known as the father of Raphael, and Piero della Francesca, he was also deeply involved in the Pazzi Conspiracy to murder Lorenzo and Giuliano de' Medici. Shortly after Machiavelli's visit, the castle was the site for those rarefied conversations between lords and ladies that made Baldassare Castiglione's *Courtier* the model of the refined gentleman for generations to come.

militude the trappings of a scholar's life, the palace was a monument to Renaissance ideals if not realities.

Only a few days earlier the palace had been home to Federico's cultivated but sickly son, Guidobaldo, and his accomplished wife, Elisabetta Gonzaga. The current occupant was a far more forceful figure, more along the lines of Montefeltro senior though without Federico's interest in books and other scholarly pursuits. What Valentino did possess, however, was a flair for theatrical display, at least when such display could be employed to intimidate his rivals. This aspect of Valentino's character was made immediately apparent to Soderini and Machiavelli, who were made to cool their heels in an antechamber, their anxiety and apprehension increasing with each passing minute while the new lord of the city spun his webs.

It was nearly midnight before the two envoys were admitted into the great man's presence. In a setting made portentous by the flickering torchlight, Machiavelli came face-to-face with the man who, more than any other, exerted a strange fascination on him and who—seen through the mists of intervening years, and then in idealized and exaggerated form— would serve as a model for the ruthless tyrant of *The Prince*.*

Unlike an earlier encounter with the equally charismatic Savonarola, this time Machiavelli did not prove immune to a great man's charms. The dispassionate distance he was able to maintain when harangued by the preacher dissolved before the victorious general surrounded by the spoils of victory. The impact of this initial meeting can be judged by the amount of space in Machiavelli's writings devoted to the career of Valentino, out of all proportion to his actual achievement. It is no exaggeration to say that Valentino was his muse, the mythical exemplar of the will to power that to Machiavelli was the engine driving all human history.

While the government Machiavelli served was weak, pointing this way or that as the wind shifted, or more often pointing no place in particular in the belief that it would thereby avoid offending anyone, Valentino was decisiveness itself. Machiavelli's admiration comes through in the dispatches he sent from Urbino. "This Lord is of such splendid and magnificent bear-

---

* As late as 1515, long after Valentino's destruction and after Machiavelli had written *The Prince*, the Duke continued to serve as a model. In a letter written to his friend Francesco Vettori, Machiavelli referred to "Duke Valentino, whose deeds I should imitate on all occasions were I a new prince" (Machiavelli et al., *Machiavelli and His Friends*, 313).

ing," he reported, "and in war so decisive that there is no thing so daunting that it does not seem to him a small matter; and for the sake of glory and in order to secure his state he never rests, nor does he know weariness or fear. He arrives at one place before one hears he has left the other; he treats his soldiers well; he has acquired the best men in Italy: all of which, in addition to his eternal good fortune, makes him formidable and victorious."

The admiration Machiavelli felt for Cesare Borgia was as much a product of emotion as reason. It resembles a schoolgirl crush, giddy and thoughtless. It was the adulation that literary types often feel for men of action. Though hardly uncritical of Valentino, particularly after his precipitous fall, Machiavelli was powerfully attracted to the Duke. Had Machiavelli ever summed up his feelings frankly, he might have declared: Here, finally, is a real man! Whatever his faults, Borgia made the most of his opportunities and through boldness and cunning put to shame a dozen states with more resources than he ever had at his command.

In the current circumstances, the awe with which the Second Chancellor regarded his host—an awe, incidentally, shared by the senior partner on the mission, Bishop Soderini—made him a less than ideal emissary. Valentino's response to their overtures was to step up his intimidation. "We heard," wrote Luca Landucci, "that Valentino had sent to say that he wished to make an alliance with us, or else he would come and attack us." Machiavelli's own report, though more nuanced, was essentially the same. "Well I know that your city is not well disposed towards me," he quoted the Duke, "and would abandon me like an assassin; they seek to get me in hot water with the Pope and the King of France." This scolding was followed by an explicit threat: "I have no love for this government, which I cannot trust; you must change it. . . . Know that if you refuse me as a friend, you will have me as an enemy."

Up to this point Borgia had played his cards shrewdly, but in raising once again the specter of Piero de' Medici's return he went a step too far. At this impertinence Soderini and Machiavelli bristled, declaring they were happy with the government as it was currently constituted and that, in any case, it was no one's business how they managed their own affairs. They also added that if he really wished to demonstrate his friendship the Duke would order his lieutenant to abandon Arezzo, something Borgia seemed unwilling to do.

The envoys were emboldened by the fact that for all his bluster, and despite the commanding military position he now occupied, Valentino was not free to act as he chose. Even as negotiations in Urbino dragged out inconclusively, another delegation was heading to the court of Louis to complain about the Duke's high-handed behavior. Valentino remained dependent on the King who had taken the Republic of Florence under his wing. Soderini and Machiavelli played for time, knowing that once Louis got wind of what Valentino was up to, he would put a stop to his vassal's bullying.

Machiavelli was unhappy at having to play this cowardly game, but before heading back to Florence he did manage a minor victory, extracting from Valentino a promise that he would do nothing until he had time to consult with his government. This was one of the few instances where the Florentine habit of avoiding hard decisions paid off. After a series of noncommittal responses to Valentino's demands, Florence learned in late July that Louis, alarmed by the situation in Arezzo, was sending six thousand cavalry (at a cost to the republic of 40,000 ducats) to restore order. They arrived in Tuscany in August, and on the 28th, with French soldiers on his doorstep, Vitelozzo agreed to return the rebellious city to Florentine control. With Vitelli's withdrawal the immediate crisis was over, though, as Landucci records in his diary, their French rescuers proved almost as destructive as their supposed enemies, looting the very people they were supposed to protect.

In September, Machiavelli was dispatched to the French camp before Arezzo as representative of the Ten of War. Busy as he was with details of provisioning and maintaining troops, his mind began to wander; he sought in the day-to-day frustrations of his job the outlines of a larger pattern. The fruit of this labor was his first concerted work of political philosophy. The brief essay, titled "On the Method of Dealing with the Rebellious Peoples of the Valdichiana," demonstrates in miniature many of the salient characteristics of his more substantial books.* One of the most

---

* The Valdichiana is the region south of Florence in which Arezzo is located. Scholars continue to debate when the essay was written and for what purpose. Originally it was thought to date from 1503, that is, almost contemporaneously with the events described, and that it was meant to be delivered as an official report in the Palazzo della Signoria. This, however, seems unlikely. Its style is aphoristic and literary, a far cry from the kind of report one might expect a secretary to deliver to his superiors. In it Machiavelli offers lessons to the government with an assurance inappropriate to one of his junior status. It is probable that it was meant to be incorporated into a larger work—perhaps his *Florentine Histories*—and the words placed in the mouth of a senior official.

striking features of this brief work is his tendency to interpret events he actually participated in through the lens of the past. The essay opens with a reference to a famous incident from Roman history: "Lucius Furius Camillus entered the Senate after having conquered the rebellious peoples of Latium, and said—'I have done all that war can do; now it is your turn . . . to assure your future safety as regards the rebels.'" From this historical parallel he swiftly extracts a universal lesson: "[T]he Romans knew that half measures were to be avoided, and that peoples must either be conquered by kindness or reduced to impotence." Just as the Romans eschewed the middle course, so should his own government adopt a policy and pursue it to its logical extreme:

> One can therefore approve your general course of conduct towards the inhabitants of the Val di Chiana; but not your particular conduct towards the Aretini, who have always been rebellious, and whom you have neither known how to win by kindness nor utterly subdue, after the manner of the Romans. In fact, you have not benefited the Aretini, but on the contrary have harassed them by summoning them to Florence, stripping them of honors, selling their possessions; neither are you in safety from them, for you have left their walls standing, and allowed five-sixths of the inhabitants to remain in the city, without sending others to keep them in subjection. And thus Arezzo will ever be ready to break into fresh rebellion, which is a thing of no slight importance, with Cesare Borgia at hand, seeking to form a strong state by getting Tuscany itself into his power. And the Borgia neither use half measures nor half way in their undertakings.

Thus Machiavelli subscribed to what one might call the "wasps' nest" theory of politics: if you must disturb the hive, make sure you eliminate the residents' capacity to do you harm. By harassing the rebellious Aretines with petty punishments that irritated them but didn't lessen their ability to retaliate, the Florentines were increasing the odds of getting stung.

This remains one of Machiavelli's favorite lessons. He returns to it time and again, most devastatingly in *The Prince:* "[M]en must either be coddled or destroyed, because while they avenge minor offenses they can do nothing against major ones. Thus if one must do harm to another, it must be such that it will not give rise to a vendetta." Those advocating mild measures, as he noted in the context of the bloody strife in Pistoia, often inflict the worst damage, since, like a surgeon too squeamish to amputate a gangrened limb, they allow a local infection to spread to vital organs. If there is one thing Machiavelli abhorred, it was the middle way—the route, unfortunately, most often taken by his own government.

V

EXIT THE DRAGON

"[We will be] devoured one by one by the dragon."

—GIANPAOLO BAGLIONI ON CESARE BORGIA

ON THE EVENING OF OCTOBER 9, 1502, BEHIND THE high stone walls of La Magione Castle overlooking Lake Trasimeno—where more than a millennium and a half earlier Hannibal annihilated the legions of Rome—many of the most powerful military leaders in Italy gathered in secret. Among them were Vitellozzo Vitelli, lord of Citta di Castello; Francesco Orsini, Duke of Gravina; Gianpaolo Baglioni, tyrant of Perugia. Most were captains serving Valentino and his father, Pope Alexander, but, significantly, Cesare Borgia himself was not included. In fact the guests went to great lengths to keep word of the meeting from reaching his ears, since on the agenda was a plan to raise the banner of rebellion against their Borgia overlord. Valentino's apparently insatiable appetite for new conquests—ominously demonstrated by his unprovoked attack against Duke Guidobaldo da Montefeltro in Urbino—had caused his chief lieutenants to fear for their own safety. As Gianpaolo Baglioni put it, they must rise up against Duke Valentino before they were all "devoured one by one by the dragon."

Up until then these generals had been happy to make war alongside Borgia, earning their pay as mercenaries and sharing in the plunder that followed his victories, but now they began to suspect that they had helped create a monster who would not stop until he had gobbled them all up. For the first time since Valentino had exchanged the life of a cardinal for that of a warrior, a coalition was forming powerful enough to challenge his preeminence in central Italy.

Enjoying a front-row seat to this high drama was Machiavelli, who had once again been ordered by the Ten to serve as the Florentine emissary to Valentino's court. He arrived in Imola on the afternoon of October 7, where the Duke had set up headquarters behind the towering battlements of fortress La Rocca. So anxious was he to see the Duke that he presented himself *cavalchereccio,* in the dust-caked clothes he wore on his ride, though, as Valentino quickly determined, he had little to offer but the usual Florentine equivocations.* Machiavelli's mission promised to be particularly unsatisfying since the government's policy was merely to stall for time while it awaited the outcome of the epic struggle just getting underway. Florence's reluctance to commit itself was understandable. Only a few months earlier Machiavelli had been forced to listen while Valentino heaped abuse on the government he served. But the rebels, though now actively courting Florentine aid, were hardly any more attractive as allies. Among their leaders were men like Vitelozzo Vitelli, an avowed enemy of the Florentine state, and Paolo Orsini, kinsman of Piero de' Medici— hardly the kind of neighbors the republic was seeking.†

But if Machiavelli had little of substance to offer the Duke, he was encouraged by Valentino's less belligerent tone. Gone were the tirades he had indulged in during their prior meetings. His Excellency, Machiavelli relayed, "declared that he had always desired the friendship of Your Lordships, and if in this he had failed it was not through his own fault but because of the malice of others." It was a laughable assertion, and Machiavelli knew it. Valentino's sudden amiableness was nothing more than a reflection of his weakened position, but Machiavelli urged his bosses to take advantage of the Duke's vulnerability by striking a deal on favorable terms. He held to this course even after hearing news, coming a week after his

---

* The ostensible reason for Machiavelli's trip was to secure safe passage through Valentino's realm by some Florentine merchants, but it was clear that this minor matter was an excuse to have an emissary in place to keep his eyes and ears on the Duke.

† In his essay "Description of the Method Used by Duke Valentino in Killing Vitellozzo Vitelli, Oliverotto da Fermo, and Others," Machiavelli suggests that Florence was firmly committed to Borgia's side: "But the Florentines, because of their hatred against Vitelli and the Orsini for various reasons, not merely did not join them but sent Niccolò Machiavelli, their secretary, to offer the Duke asylum and aid against these new enemies of his." But the dispatches Machiavelli sent at the time reflect a more equivocal attitude. In his political essays, Machiavelli often distorted the fact to fit his thesis—in this case that Valentino's cunning and ruthlessness, noted by the perceptive Secretary of Florence, would inevitably win the day.

arrival, of the battle of Fossombrone, where Valentino's forces were routed by the rebels. Nothing, it seemed, could shake Machiavelli's confidence in Valentino's star. In his report to the Ten he concluded "his enemies can no longer do much harm to His Lordship." The source of Machiavelli's confidence was largely Valentino himself, whose almost superhuman belief in his own powers rubbed off on the Second Chancellor. Greeting the Florentine emissary with his usual bluster, Valentino laughed off recent reversals, claiming that "with the king of France in Italy and the Pope, our Lord, still living, these two would light such a fire beneath [the rebels] that they would need more water than they possessed to put it out."

The reports Machiavelli sent back to the Ten on an almost daily basis demonstrate his deepening understanding of power politics. Barred from conducting substantive negotiations, he had to content himself with offering his analysis of the increasingly tense situation. His friend Buonaccorsi worried that on occasion his advice was "too forceful," that he should instead stick to a dry narration of the facts, but Machiavelli's bosses found his insights invaluable as they attempted to craft a policy that would provoke neither the dangerous and unpredictable Duke nor his equally formidable rivals.

Steering a middle course between two uncomfortable alternatives remained the government's preferred tack, but the reluctance to follow a bold course was reinforced in this case by the chaos reigning in the halls of the Palazzo della Signoria, great even by the lax standards of the Florentine Republic. Ironically, the current confusion was actually a sign of progress. It resulted from a decision, taken shortly before Machiavelli's departure, to reform a government that all acknowledged was structurally flawed. With the top officials—including the Signoria, the eight priors, and the Gonfaloniere di Giustizia, who made up the chief executive—rotating in and out of office every couple of months, the government consisted of amateurs with little expertise and less courage. Foreign governments complained that decisions arrived at one day were reversed the next, or, more often, were never made at all since the safest course was to avoid taking a difficult stand and to pass the resulting mess along to one's successors. Florentine prestige plummeted as the hapless republic lurched this way and that. Machiavelli later derived a general principle from his unhappy experience in Cesare Borgia's court. "I think taking a stand between two belligerents is nothing short of asking to be hated and despised," he wrote to his friend Francesco Vettori, explaining that both sides would come to regard you as weak and treacherous. It was this policy—or deliberate lack of one—that caused the government of Florence to be looked on, as he so memorably put it, as Sir Nihil.

The only remedy for this fatal lack of direction was to strengthen the chief executive. In September, in a radical departure from past practice, the Great Council voted to make the office of Gonfaloniere di Giustizia a lifetime position. The new Gonfaloniere would be much like the Venetian Doge, an embodiment of the majesty of the state who, through his lifetime tenure and elevation above the daily strife, would provide firm direction to a government deranged by frequent and chaotic elections. After an initial roster of 236 possible candidates was submitted, the people's choice—arrived at on the third ballot—fell to Piero Soderini, brother of the Bishop of Volterra and a man with a long and distinguished career as a diplomat. He owed his election not only to his well-known integrity, but also to the fact that he had spent so much time abroad in service to his country that he had made fewer enemies than most of his peers. In Soderini the Florentine people seemed to have found themselves a wise and scrupulous leader, a man of personal virtue who would put the welfare of the state ahead of family ambition.

Machiavelli welcomed the selection of Soderini. Not only was Machiavelli close to the new Gonfaloniere's brother—the two having served together on the first mission to Valentino—but Piero himself was well acquainted with the Second Chancellor's ability. Agostino Vespucci soon confirmed Soderini's high opinion, passing along the Gonfaloniere's kind words after hearing one of Machiavelli's reports: "The writer who wrote this in his own hand has much talent," Soderini told his colleagues, "is endowed with much judgment, and also no little wisdom." Another friend, Niccolò Valori, was even more emphatic, declaring "I believe he has become your great friend." With such a man in charge, Machiavelli could expect his own career to prosper.

Though Soderini had been elected on September 20, more than two weeks before Machiavelli set out, he did not take office until November 1. In the meantime, little could be accomplished. Machiavelli did his best to deflect Valentino, who was pressing Florence to join him. "Your Lordships write to me about temporizing, not committing you," Machiavelli grumbled, frustrated at being placed in such an awkward position, though he added hopefully that already "the new law [for the Gonfaloniere] has raised the reputation of our city so high that one can scarcely believe it."

Throughout the remainder of October and into November, Valentino and his foes jockeyed for position, while the Second Chancellor tried to evaluate the strengths and weaknesses of the opposing camps. Machiavelli, who used these junkets as an occasion to indulge himself, mixed business with pleasure, wining and dining with the other envoys. It was often hard to distinguish between legitimate government business and partying, and Machiavelli took full advantage of the ambiguity. Between mouthfuls, the ambassadors traded information like merchants at a bazaar, trafficking in gossip and rumor and passing along the more substantial nuggets to their employers back home. "Because courts always include different kinds of busybodies alert to find out what is going on," Machiavelli wrote late in life when he was advising a young man who was about to take up his first ambassadorial posting, "you will profit by making all of them your friends, so that from each one you can learn something. The friendship of such men can be gained by pleasing them with banquets and entertainments; I have seen entertainments given in the houses of very serious men, who thus offer such fellows a reason for visiting them, so that they can talk with them, because what one of them doesn't know another does, and much of the time they all together know everything." Poverty hampered Machiavelli in this regard, but he readily accepted invitations to sup at the well-spread tables of his better funded colleagues.

What he gleaned from these merry gatherings was that Valentino's hand was stronger than it appeared. Though the early victories had gone to the rebels, Machiavelli warned the Ten not to underestimate the resourceful Duke. "[W]hoever examines the quality of one side and the other, knows this Lord to be a man of great vitality, fortunate and full of hope, favored by the Pope and by the King. . . . His adversaries are insecure in their states, and while they were afraid of [Valentino] before they betrayed him, now they are even more so, having injured him thus."

In addition to his audacity and supreme self-confidence, Valentino possessed another quality Machiavelli admired. He was, as he later wrote, "a very skillful dissembler." It was this talent for deception, more than for military strategy, that began to turn the tide in Valentino's favor. Despite his early setbacks he had managed to avoid catastrophe on the field of battle, and with each passing day he gained in stature while in the camp of his adversaries doubt and dissension grew. Particularly unnerving for the rebels was the fact that Valentino continued to enjoy the favor of the French King. He gave tangible evidence of his friendship by placing at Valentino's disposal an additional five hundred lances. With the power of the French crown and the resources of the Vatican behind him, Valentino still had formidable advantages.

Even as he built up his forces, Valentino was pursuing another tack, making conciliatory gestures, floating the idea of an agreement in which he would retain the title of Prince while real power remained in his rivals' hands. "[S]weetly this basilisk whistled," Machiavelli wrote in *The First Decennale,* while the rebels, "these serpents full of poison began to use their claws and with their talons tear one another."

The combination of veiled threats and subtle overtures soon bore fruit. Machiavelli was on hand when a mysterious rider arrived at Valentino's castle in Imola. Though "dressed as a courier," the horseman's disguise was soon penetrated. Word spread through the streets that Paolo Orsini, one of the leaders of the rebellion, had come before the Duke "to excuse and justify what had occurred and to know his Lordship's will and to convey this to the other [rebels]."

To Machiavelli, this was the beginning of the end—a sure sign that Valentino's foes had lost their nerve. The Venetian ambassador in Rome put it even more starkly, concluding "the Orsini might be very sure that they had now cut their own throats." Valentino himself was delighted with the turn of events. He summoned Machiavelli to his room to gloat over his latest coup: "[T]hey write me pleasing letters," the Duke told Machiavelli, "and today Lord Pagolo [Orsini] comes to see me; tomorrow it will be Cardinal [Orsini]. Thus they try to pull the wool over my eyes. I, for my part, will play the game, keep my ears open, and bide my time." On the first of November, after a series of intense negotiations, the two sides signed a truce, agreeing to set aside their differences and resume their interrupted campaign of conquest as if nothing had happened.

What the rebel captains got out of the arrangement, besides "money, robes, and horses," is unclear. Such trinkets were surely a small price for Valentino to pay to bring an end to a potentially fatal revolt; even cheaper were the promises of reconciliation he made, which cost him nothing yet purchased the time he needed to plot his next move. Machiavelli regarded those who fell for such transparent deceits with nothing but scorn: "it is impossible to believe that [Valentino] can forgive the offense, or that they will ever free themselves from fear," he mused. They had violated one of Machiavelli's core principles. "[I]f one must do harm to another," he would elaborate in *The Prince*, drawing a general conclusion from a particular instance, "it must be such that it will not give rise to a vendetta." Not having the benefit of the Second Chancellor's as yet unwritten primer, the rebel captains committed the cardinal error of provoking an angry beast without taking the precaution of first pulling his fangs.

In the meantime, Valentino was more than happy to make use of the military skills of his former opponents, persuading the rehabilitated mercenary generals, now pathetically eager to demonstrate their newfound loyalty, to lead an attack on the city of Sinigaglia, an Adriatic seaport next on Valentino's ever-expanding list of conquests.

While Valentino plotted his revenge, Machiavelli was growing increasingly restless. Fascinated as he was by the political machinations unfolding beneath his eyes, the weeks away from friends and family in Florence were taking a toll. "*Mona* Marietta sent to me via her brother," reported Biagio Buonaccorsi, "to ask when you'll be returning; and she says she doesn't want to write, and makes a thousand complaints, and is upset because you promised her you would stay eight days and no more." With a new baby to care for, feeling lonely and neglected, Marietta had gone to live with her sister and brother-in-law, Piero del Nero—hardly the wedded bliss the young couple might have hoped for.

Adding to these cares were continuing worries over money. Even after Niccolò Valori had secured from Machiavelli's bosses an additional 30 gold ducats he remained short of cash. His junkets always cost him more than he recouped from the parsimonious Signoria; in the vicinity of the court even poor lodgings were exorbitant, as were the robes required to avoid cutting a ridiculous figure. Machiavelli was forced to maintain two separate households on an income barely sufficient to keep one in comfort. As weeks lengthened to months, with no end to the mission in sight, everyone's temper began to fray. Biagio berated Machiavelli for shirking his duties and saddling him with the unpleasant chore of trying to mollify his irate wife. "Stick it up your ass," he began one letter: "Marietta is desperate, and I have spent 44 soldi in silver from your indemnity."

Some of Machiavelli's financial difficulties were his own fault, as Biagio Buonaccorsi suggested. "I wouldn't be at all surprised," he reported, "if your raise is going down the tubes, because here the cry among these chancellors is that you're a cold fish and that you've never shown them any kindness." It is a common refrain throughout Machiavelli's career. With his sharp tongue and prickly personality, he was often his own worst enemy.

He would have soldiered on with more enthusiasm had he been granted any real authority. More than once the Duke called him in only to scold him for his government's fecklessness. Machiavelli returned from these harangues exhausted and discouraged. He begged his employers to replace him with an ambassador granted full power to negotiate a *condotta*. On December 6 he again asked "to relieve the government of this expense, and me of this inconvenience, since for the last twelve days I have been feeling very ill, and if I go on like this, I fear I may have to come back in a basket." Piero Soderini offered his sympathies, but told him he remained indispensable.

To fight off boredom and depression Machiavelli asked Biagio to send him a copy of Plutarch's *Lives,* that ancient compendium of biographies that inspired many a petty tyrant of the Renaissance to imagine himself another Caesar or Alexander. His choice of reading material was likely inspired, at least in part, by his daily sparring matches with the preeminent military figure of the moment, one who might stand comparison with the subjects of Plutarch's biographies. Machiavelli's political philosophy was rooted in comparative biography of the kind at which Plutarch excelled. Rather than treating history as the unfolding of impersonal forces, an approach stressed by political thinkers like Hegel and Marx, Machiavelli grounded his science in the psychology of men, their ambitions, appetites, and animal instincts. His advice to a young diplomat was to focus on the character of the ruler: "I say that you are to observe the nature of the man; whether he is stingy or liberal; whether he loves war or peace; whether fame or any other passion influences him; whether the people love him." Politics as a clash of personalities was an approach that came naturally to someone raised in a city where everyone knew everyone else and where one's political views were shaped by patronage and family rivalries. Summoned almost daily to appear before the charismatic and ruthless Cesare

Borgia, curled up at night with a volume of his beloved Plutarch, history appeared to Machiavelli to be molded by outsized figures who towered like giants above a landscape inhabited by pygmies.

Soon Machiavelli would have fascinating new material to add to the portrait of the tyrant he was already sketching in his mind. In mid-December, Valentino began a tour of his conquered territories. From Imola, the Duke and his army, with the Florentine Second Chancellor in tow, set out for Forli through knee-deep snow, and then south to Cesena. Writing more than a decade later in *The Prince*, Machiavelli recalled his impressions of the states now under the control of the Borgia Duke. He noted that before his conquest the Romagna "was ruled by impotent lords who would sooner exploit their subjects than govern them," and that "seeing that it was necessary to furnish good government to render the province peaceful and obedient to its lord," Valentino appointed a stern and efficient administrator who "brought both unity and order." One of the innovations Machiavelli admired most was Valentino's formation of a citizen militia to serve alongside those grizzled professionals who made up the bulk of his forces. Watching a demonstration by these soldiers, nattily attired in their gold and red uniforms—the Borgia heraldic colors—Machiavelli thought he saw a pale reflection of the armies of the Roman Republic that once had swept across the known world.

The man Valentino had appointed to govern his realm was *Messer* Remirro de Orca, who combined organizational skill with a sadistic streak that left a bloody trail across the Romagna. In praising Remirro (or Ramiro, as he is often called) and the man who employed him, Machiavelli reveals one of the pillars of his political philosophy: a preference for order over anarchy, even when that order was maintained by cruelty. Almost any atrocity could be justified if the end result was an improvement in the lives of the citizens who would be spared the random rapes, murders, and pillage that inevitably followed a breakdown of authority. Observing, as Savonarola had, a world descended into violence and wallowing in corruption, he drew radically different conclusions, based not on some vision of men miraculously transforming themselves into angels but on a hard-headed appraisal of the human animal. Machiavelli recognized, too, that in a dangerous world the greatest disasters were often the result of misplaced kindness. He had already seen how Florentine lenience in dealing with the feuding factions in Pistoia had permitted the bloody strife to continue year after year; if Valentino's methods were more brutal, they were also more effective. "Cesare Borgia was considered cruel," he writes in *The Prince*, "yet his cruelty brought an end to the disorders in the Romagna, uniting it in peace and loyalty. If this is considered good, one must judge him as much kinder than the Florentine people who, in order to escape being called cruel, allowed Pistoia to be destroyed."

Machiavelli was willing to accept an effusion of blood if it resulted in a more orderly state, but he reserved his highest praise for those who achieved security through more subtle means. Thus what happened next greatly increased his admiration for the cunning Duke. Summoning Remirro to join him in Cesena, where he had paused with his army before heading to Sinigaglia, Valentino first set out a banquet for his lieutenant, apparently a reward for a job well done. Drowsy and relaxed, Remirro was completely unprepared when, at a signal from Valentino, armed men rushed into the hall and seized him. Both Machiavelli and the citizens were initially perplexed by this sudden turn of events, as, indeed, was Remirro, who insisted he had done nothing but faithfully serve his lord. But Machiavelli realized that Valentino's apparently arbitrary about-face was actually a brilliant public relations coup: "no doubt [Remirro] will be sacrificed to satisfy the people, whose greatest wish is to see this done," he explained to the Ten.

Machiavelli proved right on the mark. On the 26th he informed his bosses: "*Messer* Remirro this morning has been found cut in two in the piazza, where he remains and where all the people may still see him. The reason for his death is not well known, except that it was pleasing to the Prince, who wishes to show that he can make or unmake men at will, according to their just deserts." In *The Prince*, Machiavelli offers an ever more cold-blooded explanation: "Recognizing that past severities had generated a measure of hatred against him, [Valentino] then determined to free himself of all popular suspicion by demonstrating that if there had been any acts of cruelty they had proceeded not from him but from his minister instead. Having found an occasion to do this, one morning he had Remirro's body, cut in two, placed on view in the public square of Cesena with a wooden block and a blood-stained knife resting beside it. The horror of that spectacle gave the people reason to be both shocked and gratified."

Meanwhile, Paolo Orsini, Vitelozzo Vitelli, and Oliverotto da Fermo anxiously awaited Valentino's arrival in Sinigaglia, twenty miles further along the Adriatic coast. News of Remirro's murder should have warned them against placing their trust in the mercurial Valentino, but if they understood the danger, they still made no attempt to pull their necks from the tightening noose.

Valentino and his army arrived at Sinigaglia on the last day of December. Repeating the pattern that had held since their one decisive victory at Fossombrone, the captains, inexplicably, met strength with weakness. Rather than remaining with their own troops, Orsini and de Fermo apparently decided to demonstrate their good faith by presenting themselves to the Duke accompanied by only a minimal escort. Machiavelli later described the dramatic scene as the former rivals came face to face: "Vitellozzo, Pagolo, and the Duke (Orsini) of Gravina, riding mules, went to meet the Duke, accompanied by a few cavalry. And Vitellozzo, unarmed, in a cloak lined with green, very disconsolate, as though he were aware of his coming death. . . . When these three, then, came into the presence of the Duke and saluted him courteously, he welcomed them with a pleasant face. . . . [Later] having entered Sinigaglia, all of them dismounted at the quarters of the Duke and went with him into a private room, where the Duke made them prisoners." Thus, meekly, did these violent men go to their deaths. Vitellozzo and Oliverotto were strangled in their cells that same night, while Paolo Orsini was spared only long enough to ensure that the Pope's men in Rome first arrested his kinsman, the powerful Cardinal Orsini. The two soon followed Vitelli and da Fermo to the grave, as did many other members of the hated Orsini clan.

One of the first to learn of the executions was the Second Chancellor of Florence, who was summoned to a late-night meeting, where, Machiavelli recorded, the Duke "with the brightest face in the world, expressed his satisfaction at his triumph."

Returning to his modest rooms that night, Machiavelli asked himself: How could such ruthless men allow themselves to be destroyed by Cesare Borgia without offering even token resistance? His conclusion, reached after much thought and spelled out most fully in a notorious chapter of *The Prince*, is that a lie, convincingly told, is among the most powerful weapons in the ruler's arsenal. "Everyone knows how laudable it is," he remarked facetiously, "for a prince to keep his word and live with integrity instead of by trickery. But the experience of our own time shows us that the princes who have accomplished great things are those who cared little for keeping faith with the people, and who used cleverness to befuddle the minds of men. In the end, such princes overcame those who counted on loyalty alone." Though he does not mention him by name, he clearly had Cesare Borgia in mind when he wrote these words. He follows with his famous analogy from the animal kingdom: "Since a prince is required to play the beast, he must learn from both the fox and the lion, because a lion cannot defend himself against snares, nor the fox against wolves."

Over the years Machiavelli's critics have been more outraged by this brazen defense of dishonesty than his advocacy of the judicious use of violence. The caricature of Machiavelli as a sneaky, conniving fellow, cynically using every tool to further his own ends, comes largely from passages extolling the virtue, or at least efficacy, of deception. But, in fact, Machiavelli himself was the least Machiavellian of men. What has tarnished his reputation is not any dishonesty on his part but excessive candor. Everyone knows that politicians often employ deception, that in fact they could hardly function without resorting from time to time to prevarications, half-truths, and outright lies. Few, however, are so open about this peculiar tool of statecraft as the Second Chancellor of Florence, whose reputation as an evil man is due in large part to admitting what everyone knows to be true.

Valentino's great gift was to be able to play the fox as convincingly as the lion. If his foes were equally violent men, they were no match when it came to saying one thing while intending to do the opposite. "Sweetly this basilisk whistled," Machiavelli wrote, as good a description as any for the hypnotic power Valentino held over lesser men.

No one believed that Cesare Borgia was a good man, but success had given him an aura that no amount of pious failure could have conferred. After Sinigaglia, Valentino was hailed as the most accomplished military and political figure in Italy. In the few short years since he had shed his cardinal's scarlet robes, he had compiled a long list of victories on the field of battle, and an equally impressive catalogue of victories won by subterfuge. Now styling himself Cesare Borgia of France, by the grace of God, Duke of Romagna, Valencia, and Urbino, Prince of Andria, Lord of Piombino, Gonfaloniere and Captain-General of the Church, he was approaching the pinnacle of his career.

From Sinigaglia, Borgia turned south again, heading for Rome to rejoin his father. Along the way, almost as an afterthought, he picked off Perugia, home to Gianpaolo Baglioni (who still remained at large), and harassed Siena. Machiavelli, now thoroughly worn out and homesick, was finally relieved of his duties on January 20, 1503, returning to Florence to pick up the pieces of his interrupted life.

In Rome, where Valentino returned toward the end of February, the city's most powerful families were living under a virtual reign of terror as the Pope and his minions tried to squeeze from them every last ducat to fund Cesare's war machine. Most at risk were those with the deepest pockets, in particular the cardinals who had paid handsomely for their offices and now were lucky to escape with their lives. Membership in the Holy College was for sale to the highest bidder, and upon the death of one of these princes of the Church—a misfortune that often seemed closely to follow an invitation to dine at the papal table—the Pope's men would swoop in and confiscate all the deceased's worldly possessions. All but the poorest citizens trembled, "every moment thinking to see the executioner standing behind him."

On the evening of August 5, 1503, Pope Alexander and his son, hoping to escape the heat and dust of the city, made an excursion to the countryside, where they dined at a vineyard belonging to Cardinal Adriano Castellesi. Shortly after returning from the banquet both father and son were stricken with high fevers accompanied by frequent bouts of vomiting. Many jumped to the conclusion that, in an attempt to avoid the fate of so many of his colleagues, Castellesi had slipped poison into his guests' wine. A more likely explanation is that the Borgias had come down with malarial fever, a common peril in the humid Roman summer. While Valentino lay barely conscious in his rooms, the seventy-two-year-old Pope clung to life for almost two weeks, periodically bled and purged by his doctors, before finally succumbing.

Even before his father was laid to rest in his tomb, the apparently solid edifice of Valentino's realm began to crumble. Like all those before him who had tried to convert papal kinship into political power, Cesare Borgia had in fact built on sand. Without the legitimacy conferred by the Holy Father, he had no real claim to the lands seized in his name. Under Alexander's aegis, any brutal act could be forgiven, any conquest justified as a legitimate imposition of papal authority. Without that protective mantle the limitations of such a shortsighted policy were revealed. In his ruthless climb Valentino had made a host of enemies who were only awaiting the first sign of weakness to strike back.

As full of vigor as Alexander had been in life, in death his cadaver decayed with unheard of speed as if all the sins he had committed were eating him from the inside. Nature herself seemed to have turned against the Pope. A stench of corruption rose from his body and wafted through the halls of the Vatican, despite the best efforts of the papal master of ceremonies, Johannes Burchardus, to make him presentable for burial. The Pope's face, he recalled, "had changed to the color of blackest cloth, and [was] covered in blue-black spots; the nose was swollen, the mouth distended, the tongue bent back double . . . the face was more horrifying than anything ever seen."

Though still gravely ill, the resourceful Valentino tried desperately to salvage something from the wreckage. From his sickbed he dispatched his most trusted servant, Miguel de Corella, to the Pope's apartments, where Corella held a knife to Cardinal Casanova's throat until he agreed to hand over the keys to the papal strongboxes. Hauling coin, jewels, and silver worth more than 100,000 ducats, Valentino and a small band of loyalists fled to the security of the Castel Sant' Angelo, and then—as the surviving Orsini descended upon the city to exact their revenge—to his castle of Nepi, in the hills north of Rome. There he hoped to recuperate and ride out what promised to be a tumultuous few months.

Among those bitter enemies who flocked to Rome upon hearing of Alexander's death was the formidable Cardinal Giuliano della Rovere, nephew of Pope Sixtus IV. He had been among those who had challenged Rodrigo Borgia in the conclave of 1492 that elevated the Spanish cardinal to the papal throne, and he had compounded this indiscretion by calling for an investigation into the bribes that had secured the Pope's election.* For the last ten years he had been living in self-imposed exile in France in an effort to escape those unfortunate accidents that claimed so many of his colleagues. With his rival now dead, Giuliano hurried to Rome to seize the prize denied to him once before by the despised Borgia.

---

* In this, Giuliano had apparently forgotten Christ's injunction: "Let he who is without sin cast the first stone." The quantity of bribes distributed on his behalf were almost equally large, if less effective.

The conclave of thirty-eight cardinals that gathered in September proved hopelessly deadlocked, as the traditional rivalry between the Spanish and French factions was exacerbated by events outside the Vatican. The Treaty of Granada that had divided the kingdom of Naples between France and Spain had broken down, and now the two most fearsome armies of Europe were heading toward a climactic struggle that would go a long way toward determining supremacy on the Italian peninsula. What happened in the conclave might well tip the balance to one or the other of the two contending powers. After six days of fruitless argument, made all the more contentious by the sweltering, overcrowded rooms, the cardinals' choice fell to the sixty-four-year-old Cardinal Francesco Todeschini, nephew of the Sienese Pope Pius II. Though widely respected for his piety and patronage of the arts, his virtues counted less than the obvious fact that he was a dying man. This made him particularly acceptable to della Rovere, who, once he determined that the Spanish cabal would block his nomination at any cost, concluded that the aging and ailing Todeschini possessed just the actuarial qualifications he required if he were to consolidate his position. Crowned on October 8 and taking the name Pius III, in honor of his uncle, the gout-ridden Pontiff was too feeble to make the traditional pilgrimage to the Lateran basilica.

In the months following Alexander's death Valentino's empire disintegrated. First the territories adjoining Rome broke free; those in the Romagna, well governed for the most part as Machiavelli noted, remained more steadfast, though it was clear that they, too, would revert to their former allegiances unless Valentino could quickly reassert his dominance. He had ruled by fear and intimidation, but without the resources of the papacy behind him he seemed a far less formidable adversary. Realizing he could accomplish nothing in rustic Nepi, he returned to Rome in October as the first step in rebuilding his fortunes.

But with the Orsini once again in their Roman palaces, Giuliano della Rovere consolidating his support within the College of Cardinals, and the current Pope on his deathbed, friends of Valentino were hard to find. On October 18, less than a month after being elevated to the Throne of Saint Peter, Pope Pius III did what was expected of him and breathed his last. This time Giuliano della Rovere was ready. Though he was already the preferred candidate of the French contingent, he now set about securing the allegiance of the powerful Spanish faction. Showing the remarkable tactical flexibility that would later earn the praise of Machiavelli, he paid a call on Valentino, promising that if he threw the support of the Spanish delegation behind his candidacy, della Rovere would retain the Duke's services as captain-general of the Church. In addition, he would and agree to marry off his nephew, Francesco Maria della Rovere, the current prefect of Rome, to Valentino's daughter. Not surprisingly, given the weakness of his position, Valentino eagerly accepted the terms. It is difficult to see how he could have done otherwise, though Machiavelli believed he had made a fundamental strategic blunder: "[H]e should never have allowed any cardinal he had offended, or who had reason to fear him, to become pope, for men lash out through fear or hatred." On October 31, in a five-hour conclave that must have been close to a record of brevity for meetings usually marked by long-winded speeches and the exchange of cash in the latrines, Giuliano della Rovere was elected Pope, taking the name Julius II.

Machiavelli was again on hand to witness these dramatic events. Upon learning of the old Pope's death, the government had dispatched him to Rome to attend to Florentine interests at this critical juncture. As usual, Machiavelli set out in high spirits. Happy as he had been to return to Florence after months away at Valentino's court, he was just as happy to leave again for a new adventure in the Eternal City. Always restless, he was especially eager to get away because of the petty bickering in the Palazzo della Signoria, which made him despair for his country. The one significant result of his months in Florence was a brief document titled "Some words to be spoken on the matter of raising revenue, after a brief preamble and a few words of excuse." Written in response to the outcry sparked by Piero Soderini's attempts to raise revenues for the republic's armed forces, the speech—probably meant to be delivered by the Gonfaloniere himself in front of the Great Council—captures Machiavelli's passionate patriotism and his disdain for those who would sacrifice their freedom for a few florins. "[A]t present," he said,

> you are incapable of defending your subjects, and you stand between two or three cities, desiring your ruin rather than your

preservation. . . . Remember, at all events, that one cannot always use another's sword, and therefore it were well to keep your own in readiness. . . . For I tell you that fortune will not help those who will not help themselves; nor will heaven itself sustain a thing that is determined to fall. But beholding you free Florentines, with your liberty in your own hands, I will not believe that you desire to fall. For surely I must believe that men born free, and wishing to remain free, will have due respect for liberty!

This harangue, reminiscent of those stirring orations recorded by Livy and Thucydides, shows Machiavelli at his best—a committed republican, blasting his compatriots for their selfishness while their country is starved of the means to defend itself. This episode provides a stark contrast to those infamous passages of *The Prince* where he advocates violence, treachery, and deceit in the name of expedience. But while the tone is different, the motivation is very much the same. Machiavelli's first priority is, as always, the preservation and prosperity of the state; anything that interferes with that—greed and excessive piety alike robbing the nation of much needed vigor—should be resisted by every means possible.

Machiavelli arrived in Rome on October 27, just in time to witness the final machinations leading to the elevation of Giuliano della Rovere to the papal throne. Machiavelli's appointment to this important post—he was addressed in correspondence as "Florentine Secretary and Envoy to the Supreme Pontiff in Rome"—was a testament to Soderini's increasing trust in his friend. The first order of business when he arrived at Julius's Vatican apartments was to alert the new Pontiff to the dangers of Venetian expansion in the north. The Most Serene Republic, Machiavelli explained, was at this very moment taking advantage of the collapse of Valentino's empire to scoop up any state that had been shaken loose, much to the chagrin of the Florentines, who had no wish to see one imperial master replaced by another with even greater resources. Julius was sympathetic, not out of any love for the republic, but because the territories coveted by the Venetians rightfully belonged to the Church.

In Rome, Machiavelli plunged headlong into the kind of balance-of-power politics perfected in Renaissance Italy, where the rise of any one state provoked hasty alliances among all the others to prevent their rival from dominating the peninsula. It was a world of shifting loyalties and sharp betrayals, where today's friend was tomorrow's foe, and where treaties were obsolete before the ink had dried. To that growing class of men who had the difficult job of steering the craft of state through dangerous shoals and unpredictable currents, maneuverability and a sharp-eyed focus on the near at hand succeeded where keeping one's vision fixed on a distant star would lead to disaster. Machiavelli was the first philosopher to speak for these professional diplomats, men without illusions who trafficked in temporary expedients rather than grand abstractions.

In their initial meeting, Machiavelli was subjected to one of those tirades for which the new Pope would soon become famous, though fortunately the target of his wrath was their common enemy, the arrogant Venetians. Having reassured himself as to the direction of Julius's foreign policy Machiavelli paid a call on Valentino. The man he saw in his faded Roman palace was a mere shadow of the triumphant general he had left in Perugia. Ravaged by his illness, he was far less physically imposing, and without the aura that unbridled power conferred, Valentino seemed to shrink to insignificance. Most inexplicable to Machiavelli was the fact that the Duke had fallen into exactly the same trap he had sprung on his enemies only months before, placing his faith in the promises of his adversaries. "[A]lways transported by his daring confidence," Machiavelli wrote to the Ten on November 4, "[Valentino] believes that the words of others are more trustworthy than were his own."

Valentino began by trying to frighten the Florentine envoy with elaborate fantasies of redemption and revenge, but to Machiavelli it was evident he had become dangerously detached from reality. Valentino grew furious when Machiavelli told him that Florence would refuse him safe passage through Tuscany on his planned expedition to recover the territories he had lost in the Romagna. The Florentine Secretary had already sounded out Julius, and knew the Pope had no intention of keeping the promises that had persuaded Valentino to back him in the recent election. "We want the states to return to the Church," Julius explained. "It is our intention to recover them [and although] we made certain promises to the Duke, we intended merely to guarantee his personal safety and his fortune, even though, after all, it was stolen from its rightful owners."

To Machiavelli's ears, Valentino's bluster now sounded like whining. It was a pathetic and disillusioning spectacle. The man Machiavelli had so recently held up as a paragon of the ruthless leader had about him the stench of failure. "I had no lack of things to say in reply, nor would my words have failed me," Machiavelli recalled, "yet I took the course of trying to pacify him, and took leave of him as quickly as possible, for it seemed a thousand years till I could quit his presence." How much had changed since those days in Imola when Machiavelli stood in awe of the great man!

In the end, Valentino's demise was more the stuff of farce than of tragedy. Prevented from leading his army on an overland trek to the Romagna, at the end of November the Duke tried to board a ship at the port of Ostia with the intention of reaching his rebellious empire by sea. This act of disobedience offered Julius just the opportunity he needed to finish off his rival; he ordered that Valentino be arrested and returned to Rome. Machiavelli, for one, was pleased with the news, remarking that "since he is taken, whether he be alive or dead, we need trouble ourselves no more about him. One sees that his sins are gradually bringing him to punishment." Days later, reports arrived that the remainder of Valentino's army was routed by Gianpaolo Baglioni—the one captain who had survived the purge at Sinigaglia—and its commander, Don Michele Corella, sent in chains to Florence. "[T]hus it would seem," wrote Machiavelli to the Ten, "that little by little this Duke is slipping into his grave."

Though Machiavelli's obituary was a bit premature, his assessment was essentially correct. For a time, Valentino pinned his hopes on his fellow Spaniards, who were continuing their victorious campaign against the French, but in the end they, too, had little use for the washed-up son of a dead pope. Deported to Spain, he eventually escaped his imprisonment to serve for a time in the army of his brother-in-law, John of Navarre. He died three years later at the age of thirty-one in an obscure battle in a distant province, largely forgotten by the world that once had trembled at the mere mention of his name.

The catastrophic reversal of fortune for the man who, more than any other, represented for Machiavelli the admirable qualities of leadership—ruthlessness, audacity, cunning, and luck—was unsettling. One can detect in Machiavelli's discomfort the pain that accompanies the shattering of a cherished illusion. Though he had always perceived Valentino's faults, Machiavelli had come to see him as the embodiment of the strength that was so sorely lacking in his own government. If such a man could come to grief, what hope was there for a nation led by timid souls? When he sat down to write *The Prince*, having mulled the matter over for a decade, his final verdict on Valentino is more charitable, though the man's downfall is no less perplexing:

> *Cesare Borgia, called by the masses Duke Valentino, acquired power through his father's fortune and lost it in the same manner. This despite the fact that he employed every art and did all that a prudent and courageous man should do to secure his hold on those territories won by the arms and fortunes of others. . . . [I]f he failed in the end, it was through no fault of his own, since it was born of extraordinary and extreme malice of fortune.*

Extreme malice of fortune! That seems a weak conclusion for someone intent on discovering the laws that govern the rise and fall of men and nations, but Machiavelli was always attuned to the apparent randomness of the universe. In studying the vicissitudes of history, he was often forced to fall back on the image of Dame Fortune, a capricious goddess who bestowed her gifts promiscuously and then plucked them away with equal gusto.

It has often been remarked that the picture of Valentino that Machiavelli paints in *The Prince* is at odds with the fragmentary portrait we can reconstruct from letters and dispatches written at the time. The contrast is particularly striking when we examine the official documents Machiavelli wrote in Rome, where he depicts Cesare Borgia as a broken and pathetic figure. By the time he came to write *The Prince*, Machiavelli had decided to restore much of the luster. Valentino is once again the heroic figure, dominating lesser men through the sheer force of his will; his ad hoc responses to various crises are recast as part of a brilliant plan to confound his enemies and secure his realm. Machiavelli was surely aware that he was straying from the facts in the course of building his larger narrative, but this fiction was conceived in the service of a larger truth. A decade after their last meeting, Valentino had ceased to be the fatally flawed flesh-and-blood creature whose shrunken form and peevish rantings were so distasteful that Machiavelli wanted to flee his presence. He has become "The Prince," prototype of the ruthless tyrant, whose courage and vision will restore Italy to her rightful place among nations.

V I

MEN OF LOW AND POOR STATION

"Nor do I wish it thought a presumption that a man of low and poor
station set out to examine the laws governing the rule of princes."

—MACHIAVELLI, *THE PRINCE*,
DEDICATION TO LORENZO DE' MEDICI

IN THE FALL OF 1502, WHILE HE WAS AWAY AT CESARE
Borgia's court in Imola, Machiavelli met a man, a fellow Tuscan, who was
serving as Valentino's military architect. Machiavelli probably knew him
by reputation, since the fifty-year-old had already achieved some fame
as a painter, first in Florence and later in Milan, where he had served for
many years at the court of Ludovico Sforza. His name was Leonardo and
he was born in Vinci, a village tucked in among the olive groves and vineyards that carpeted the hills west of Florence. When Machiavelli was still
a child, Leonardo had worked as an apprentice in the studio of Andrea
Verrocchio, where he had astonished everyone with his precocious gifts.
The painter and biographer Giorgio Vasari relates the almost certainly
apocryphal story that when the master saw an angel his young assistant
had added to Verrocchio's painting of the baptism of Christ, he set down
his own brushes in despair because he knew he would never be able to
match his pupil.[*]

But if Verrocchio knew talent when he saw it, most Florentines were
less perceptive. Leonardo's years in Florence were unhappy. More estab-

---

[*] The painting, now in the Uffizi Gallery in Florence, clearly reveals the hand of the young Leonardo
in the kneeling angel on the far left. The softness and idealization contrast with the more brittle realism
of Verrocchio's style.

lished artists such as Verrocchio and Botticelli grabbed most of the prestigious commissions, and Leonardo had to settle for the crumbs. In 1476, he was dragged before the magistrates on a charge of sodomy, a traumatic experience that colored his attitude toward the city that gave him his professional start. By 1481, Leonardo had left Florence for Milan, where the polymath, unable to choose among his various interests, promoted himself to Duke Sforza as a musician and military engineer. It was in Milan that Leonardo achieved fame as an artist, producing masterpieces like *The Last Supper*, *The Virgin of the Rocks*, and the massive equestrian statue of the Duke's father, Francesco Sforza.

By the time Machiavelli encountered the middle-aged artist in Imola, however, Leonardo had suffered a string of setbacks and frustrations, punctuated by moments of incandescent triumph. He was, in fact, something of an enigma, a man whose gifts were so enormous that he managed to achieve less than others who deployed with greater efficiency their more modest talents.

Leonardo and the Second Chancellor of Florence were in many ways kindred spirits. Both were ambitious and driven by social and economic insecurity. As the illegitimate son of a prosperous provincial notary, Leonardo never received the education and status that his father's position should have entitled him to. In the introduction to his *Treatise on Painting* he scolds his better educated but less gifted colleagues:

> *I am fully conscious that, not being a literary man, certain presumptuous persons will think that they may reasonably blame me; alleging that I am not a man of letters. Foolish folks! . . . my subjects are to be dealt with by experience rather than by words; and [experience] has been the mistress of those who wrote well. And so, as mistress, I will cite her in all cases.*

Machiavelli, too, was sensitive to the chasm between status and ability. Take, for instance, his dedication to *The Prince*: "Nor do I wish it thought a presumption," he tells Lorenzo de' Medici,

> *that a man of low and poor station set out to examine the laws governing the rule of princes. For just as those who draw landscapes*

place themselves low on the plain to discern the nature of the moun-
tains and high places, and to describe the lowlands they place them-
selves high above, similarly, to know well the nature of the people one
must be a prince and to understand princes one must be of the people.

Both men make a virtue of marginality. Each claims a vantage point that allows him to see what eludes those more comfortably situated; each eschews empty erudition in favor of practical experience. Here is a new kind of man, unburdened by the dead weight of tradition (a university education in one case, wealth in the other) and free to discover new ways of looking at the world. Both Machiavelli and Leonardo spent their lives enduring the snubs of men whose only claim to superiority was an accident of birth. And in both the artist and the bureaucrat there burned a fierce desire to show those upon whom they depended for their livelihoods that they had something unique to offer the world.

Unfortunately, neither man left an account of their initial meeting in Imola, though it is inconceivable that the two compatriots were not at least in casual contact during the months they spent hovering like moths about Valentino's court at the fortress of La Rocca. Thus when, in 1503, the Second Chancellor returned to the thorny problem of reducing the city of Pisa to submission, he recalled Valentino's former engineer and military architect, who had already shown his willingness to find innovative solutions to intractable problems.

The idea of employing artists for military purposes might seem incongruous today, but it was only natural in the Renaissance, when art demanded technical proficiency and practical know-how. Leonardo in particular believed that art and science both dissected nature in order to understand the way the world really worked. In his paintings he put to good use his profound understanding of light, obtained by keen observation and enhanced by experiment, by creating images whose verisimilitude astounded his contemporaries. As a scientist, he was both a visionary and a tinkerer—a spinner of improbable yarns and a builder of ingenious devices. Fascinated by the forces of nature, he sought to harness wind, water, and even sunlight to serve the purposes of mankind.

By the summer of 1503, Leonardo had left the service of Valentino and returned to his native land. He was, as always, seeking new opportunities to test the theories that filled his notebooks and excited his imagination, and attending to the more pressing matter of replenishing his depleted bank account. Approaching members of the government—including, almost certainly, Machiavelli himself, who, as Secretary to the Ten of War was deeply involved in the day-to-day management of military affairs—he presented a plan to defeat Pisa not by use of brute force but by diverting the Arno (the vital artery of both Florence and Pisa), thereby starving the rebellious city of subsistence and commerce.

The notion was not as outlandish as it might seem. In fact the scheme was a culmination of ideas that had long been brewing inside Leonardo's fertile mind. Anyone living near the banks of the capricious Arno, as Leonardo had growing up in the Tuscan foothills, would have witnessed the almost yearly floods that uprooted trees, washed away bridges, and submerged whole neighborhoods. In his series of drawings titled *Deluge*, he envisioned a world engulfed by the watery element, a rain-drenched apocalypse as powerful as anything ever conceived in art. Leonardo dwelled at length on the destructive potential of water, so using a river as an instrument of war must have seemed perfectly natural to him.

To many within the government, less imaginative but more accustomed to managing large-scale public works projects, the scheme seemed far-fetched. The Ten pronounced it "little better than a fantasy." More than half a century earlier, another visionary artist, Filippo Brunelleschi, suggested that the republic might defeat her rival Lucca by diverting the river Serchio so that it flooded the city; the project ended in disaster when Luccan soldiers sabotaged the dam and turned the river back on the Florentines. But Leonardo's plan, presented in a series of detailed maps and drawings, won the support of two critical figures: Machiavelli and, more importantly, Gonfaloniere Piero Soderini.* The fact that he convinced two such practical men to pursue such an unconventional project was a testament not only to Leonardo's powers of persuasion but also to their frustration with conventional approaches that thus far had yielded nothing. After so many disappointments, costly in both blood and treasure, desperation was the mother of invention.

---

* The topographical studies Leonardo made for this project influenced his landscapes, including the bird's-eye view of a river valley that forms the backdrop of the *Mona Lisa*.

Ironically, the Pisans seemed to have more faith in the project than most Florentines. An interrogation of captured residents of the city revealed "that the defenders feared only one thing, that the Florentines would divert the Arno and so dry up its outlet to the sea, depriving Pisa of the help they had been receiving from ships paid for by Lucca, Siena and Genoa." Work on the massive project began late in the summer of 1504. The diversion was to take place at Stagno, a few miles to the south of Pisa, near the port of Livorno, where engineers hoped to create a new mouth for the Arno that would serve the double purpose of starving Pisa and nourishing Florence by opening a navigable passage to the sea that circumvented the old port. The hydraulic engineer Colombino was hired to supervise the two thousand laborers who set to work building weirs and digging ditches.

But as men moved tons of rock and mud, three-dimensional reality began to diverge from the two-dimensional blueprint drawn up by Leonardo. Those on the scene, forced to deal with uncooperative laborers, unenthusiastic supervisors, and constant harassment from Pisan soldiers, cut corners to save money and adapted Leonardo's plans to facts on the ground. Machiavelli was initially reluctant to interfere in technical matters—defending Colombino as "an excellent expert on this hydraulic engineering"—but soon he began to fret about the halfhearted efforts and jerry-built modifications. On September 21 he wrote to the engineers: "Your delay makes us fear that the bed of the ditch is shallower than the bed of the Arno; this would have negative effects and in our opinion it would not direct the project to the end we wish." His concerns proved well founded. At the beginning of October a violent storm damaged the Florentine fleet guarding the mouth of the river and flooded the ditches. A few days later the emboldened Pisans emerged from their defensive works and set about punching holes in the weirs. The labor of months was destroyed in a matter of hours, and the entire project collapsed amidst the usual finger-pointing and recrimination. Francesco Soderini, the Gonfaloniere's brother and newly minted Cardinal, offered his sympathy, begging Machiavelli not to blame himself for the failure: "Notable man and very dear *compare*. It gave us great pain that so great an error should have been made in those waters that it seems impossible to us that it should not have been through the fault of those engineers, who went so far wrong."

Unfortunately, the Cardinal was one of the few willing to go on record to defend the Second Chancellor. No one was more closely associated with Leonardo's discredited project, and he was an easy target for those already unhappy with the regime. Even before the disaster, discontent with Piero Soderini had been growing, particularly within the "aristocratic" faction, led by Alammano Salviati. This was particularly awkward, since Salviati, Piero de' Medici's son-in-law, had been one of Machiavelli's original patrons. Their close ties were evident when, during Machiavelli's embassy to Imola, Salviati had tried unsuccessfully to secure his release from the onerous position. Commiserating with Machiavelli over the disappointing results of his efforts, he signed his letter "your devoted friend." But by 1506, Salviati's feelings had clearly changed, as Biagio Buonaccorsi, always an incorrigible gossip, reported to his friend. "'I have never commissioned anything from that clown [Machiavelli] since I have been one of the Ten,'" a mutual friend overheard Salviati saying, to which Buonaccorsi added conspiratorially: "I could write you many other things, but more when we are together."

The growing friction between Machiavelli and Salviati reflected a widening split within Florence's ruling elite between the aristocratic faction, led by men like Salviati—many of whom were associated with the old Medici regime—and the Gonfaloniere's party, which was increasingly identified with the populists. Salviati had originally supported Soderini, but he had grown disenchanted with the head of state, whose policies—particularly when it came to taxes—he believed favored the *popolani* over magnate families like his. This meant that Machiavelli, who was increasingly seen as the Gonfaloniere's man, was caught uncomfortably between old friends and his current boss. The collapse of the Arno diversion scheme enraged the aristocratic faction further against the head of government, in large part because the money lost on the project had once been in their pockets. Machiavelli, for his part, was fed up with his former patrons. His speech, "Some words to be spoken on the matter of raising revenue, after a brief preamble and a few words of excuse," was directed at men like Salviati, whose patriotism waned as soon as their profits were threatened.

Given the hardening divisions between rival factions within the government, it should be possible to determine where Machiavelli, the most political of men, stood. But in fact it is surprisingly difficult to pin him down. On the question of taxes and the prosecution of the war with Pisa, he certainly stood with the Gonfaloniere, but his dedication in 1504 of the poem *The First Decennale* to Alamanno Salviati reveals that he had not burned his bridges with the *ottimati*. In part this ambivalence can be attributed to his status as a client of powerful men whose favor he had to cultivate. He was the consummate bureaucrat, willing to serve whichever side had the upper hand regardless of ideology. But there was more to this than simple opportunism. He embodied the ethos of the civic functionary, dedicated to the abstract concept of the state whose interests he elevated above loyalty to any individual or party. His ideological slipperiness was a result of his ardent patriotism. As a servant of the republic, he remained as much as possible aloof from political infighting, and while his patrons owed their primary allegiance to powerful clans from which they sprang, Machiavelli favored those he believed put the interests of the nation first. Early on he embraced the *ottimati* when they offered the best chance of restoring the republic after the excesses of Savonarola, but he distanced himself when their selfish opposition to additional taxes threatened the war effort. For all his tactical flexibility, which has enraged generations of critics who see him as a man without principle, he never lost sight of the basic goal—to defend and promote the cause of the Florentine Republic and the Italian people.

The perspective of the government functionary shaped in crucial ways the development of his thought. It allowed Machiavelli to break free from the intellectual framework established by Plato and Aristotle and adapted by philosophers like Thomas Aquinas for the Christian world. For the Greeks and their medieval followers, theories of government were based on the assumption that societies, no matter how corrupt they might be in practice, aspired to some sort of ideal—whether the aristocracy of the mind favored by Plato or the "City of God" imagined in different forms by Augustine and Aquinas. Machiavelli had little patience with such vague abstractions, as he makes clear in *The Prince*. "[I]t seems best to me to go straight to the actual truth of things rather than to dwell in dreams," he declares in a stern rebuke to his predecessors. "Many have imagined republics and principalities that have never been seen nor known to exist. But there is such a chasm between how men actually live and how they ought to live that he who abandons what is for what should be will discover his ruin rather than his salvation."

This simple statement is at the core of Machiavelli's revolutionary approach. It establishes him as the father of modern political science, a field whose proper subject is "the actual truth of things" rather than "dreams." His hardheaded analysis is the source of his originality, as well as all those morally dubious propositions that have troubled later generations. As a bureaucrat who dedicated every waking hour to the state, he took as his starting point the welfare of that impersonal and amoral organism. "For when the safety of one's country wholly depends on the decision to be taken," Machiavelli proclaims, in what amounts to the bureaucrat's Hippocratic Oath, "no attention should be paid either to justice or injustice, to kindness or cruelty, or to its being praiseworthy or ignominious. On the contrary, every other consideration being set aside, that alternative should be wholeheartedly adopted which will save the life and preserve the freedom of one's country." Though Machiavelli did not coin the phrase *raison d'état*, the ideology that animated the careers of statesmen from Richelieu to Kissinger was first articulated by the humble Florentine chancellor.

Machiavelli clearly appreciated Leonardo's engineering skills. What is unclear is whether he appreciated Leonardo's talent in less practical areas. There is little evidence, in fact, that Machiavelli cared deeply about art. Though he was born and raised in a city whose greatest glory was its art and architecture, little in his writing or his life demonstrates a keen interest in either. In his political writings, Machiavelli focuses narrowly on issues of power and governance. Only rarely does his view of society expand to encompass the vast array of activities that people engage in that constitute the core of what makes us human. Perhaps his most glaring oversight is the short shrift he gives to economic factors in determining political structures. One of the few times he looks up to survey the broader terrain comes in a chapter in *The Prince* titled "What a Prince Must Do to Be Esteemed." But even here, cultural endeavors are viewed merely as tools of statecraft: "A prince must show himself a lover of virtue, supporting gifted men and by honoring in the arts. . . . He must, in addition to this, at the appropriate time of year, keep the populace occupied with feasts and spectacles." A similar passage can be found near the end of his *Florentine Histories*, where he summarizes Lorenzo de' Medici's contribution to his native land. "[H]e turned to making his city more beautiful and greater," he notes approvingly. "[H]e kept his fatherland always in festivities: there frequent jousts and representations of old deeds and triumphs were to be seen; and his aim was to keep the city in abundance, the people united, and the nobility honored. He loved marvelously anyone who was excellent in an art; he favored men of letters." In neither passage does Machiavelli show an appreciation of art for art's sake. Instead, art is a tool in the hands of the shrewd leader who employs it to distract the people and retain power.

Reducing art to "bread and circuses" is perhaps a surprising attitude in someone with Machiavelli's creative gifts. He was a more than competent poet and perhaps the greatest prose writer of his day, so one might expect him to possess a greater sensitivity to the arts and artists. But it is clear that the fine arts were, at best, only of secondary importance. He makes his dismissive attitude clear in his preface to Book I of *The Discourses*:

> *When, therefore, I consider in what honor antiquity is held, and how—to cite but one instance—a bit of an old statue has fetched a high price that someone may have it by him to give honor to his house and that it may be possible for it to be copied by those who are keen on this art; and how the latter then work with great industry and take pains to reproduce it in all their works; and when, on the other hand, I notice that what history has to say about the highly virtuous actions performed by ancient kingdoms and republics, by their kings, their generals, their citizens, their legislators, and by others, who have gone to the trouble of serving their country, is rather admired than imitated; nay, is so shunned by everybody in each little thing they do, that of the virtue of bygone days there remains no trace, it cannot but fill me at once with astonishment and grief.*

His most sustained discussion of art, then, is an opportunity to deride those connoisseurs who admire the skill of ancient sculptors who shaped bronze and marble while ignoring those statesmen who were molders of men and morals.

But while Machiavelli exhibited no particular feeling for the visual arts, he could not help but get caught up in a culture where painting, sculpture, and all manner of fine craftsmanship were essential ingredients of everyday life. To the rest of the world Florence was synonymous with high achievement in the arts, and Machiavelli, always attuned to the way his city was perceived abroad, appreciated the favorable impression this artistic achievement made. The fame of artists like Leonardo and Michelangelo, he knew, helped burnish the city's reputation when the conduct of her armies was having the opposite effect. Art in Florence—carried out on an almost industrial scale in large workshops like Verrocchio's or Ghirlandaio's that employed dozens of apprentices churning out altarpieces, portraits, and more ephemeral items for festivals—was a propaganda tool, and this was something Machiavelli understood and cared about deeply.

In the fall of 1503, before his plans to divert the Arno had been finalized, Leonardo was given the commission to fresco the Hall of the Great Council in the Palazzo della Signoria, perhaps the most significant honor the republic could bestow on an artist. The vast room had just been built to house the large assemblies resulting from the Savonarolan reforms of 1494, which had opened up the government to the entire citizen class of Florence. It was thus a potent symbol of the city's republican regime, and it was vital that the art should convey an appropriately patriotic message. That Machiavelli himself was instrumental in securing the commission is suggested by the fact that it was his assistant in the chancery, Agostino Vespucci, who transcribed in Leonardo's own notebook the text on which the painting, *The Battle of Anghiari*, was based. Vespucci's services were probably required since Leonardo's command of Latin was imperfect, but the participation of this civil servant reveals the extent to which the government was intimately involved in every detail of such an important public commission. Whether or not Machiavelli himself conceived the subject for the painting—which commemorated the last major triumph of Florentine arms more than sixty years earlier—its militaristic theme coincided perfectly with the Second Chancellor's own views of a citizen republic sustained by the martial valor of its people.

In fact at the very same moment Leonardo was designing his fresco Machiavelli was drawing up his initial plans for reinstituting a citizen militia, and the martial theme may well reflect an attempt on his part to gin up enthusiasm for this still unpopular undertaking. By recalling past triumphs, Leonardo's painting would restore Florentines' faith in their own valor while reminding them, by way of contrast, how poorly the current crop of mercenary captains stacked up.

Like so many of Leonardo's undertakings, the painting's execution was fraught with difficulty, much of it the artist's own making. Leonardo was easily distracted and easily offended. He dawdled while bureaucrats withheld payment, each side blaming the other for the stalemate. As the process dragged on, Leonardo began to lose interest while the government—now facing the prospect of having invested in another failed venture—grew increasingly impatient with the temperamental genius who never seemed to fulfill his promises. On May 4, 1504, after months of recriminations, a new contract was signed spelling out in greater detail the obligations of each party. The document, which provides a schedule of payments upon the completion of certain benchmarks, ends with the following Latin inscription: "Enacted in the palace of the aforementioned Lords, in the presence of Niccolò son of Bernardo Machiavelli, Chancellor of the aforementioned Lords, and Marco, of ser Giovanni Romenea, citizen of Florence, as witnesses."

Machiavelli's intervention ensured that work would continue, though Leonardo once again failed to live up to expectations. For a time he set to work with renewed vigor, but his penchant for experimentation, and his tendency to lose interest in a project after the initial stages, all but guaranteed failure. Leonardo chafed at the limitations of the fresco technique. This time he mixed oils into the water-based medium, causing the plaster to dry slowly and unevenly. Even before the monumental mural was completed it began sliding from the wall. In a little more than fifty years the painting had deteriorated so badly that it was painted over by that mediocre dauber (and first-rate art historian) Giorgio Vasari.*

Though ultimately a grand failure, *The Battle of Anghiari* offers an instructive illustration of the way the government deployed artists to further

---

* Although *The Battle of Anghiari* must be included among those tragic missteps that marred the artist's career, the lost masterpiece enjoyed a long and productive twilight existence. During the years it remained, damaged but still impressive, on the walls of the Hall of the Great Council, artists studied it attentively and drew inspiration for their own work. Its savage depiction of what Leonardo himself called "the beastly madness" of war, whose violence he captured in a swirling maelstrom of horses and horsemen, changed the course of art history. Among those overwhelmed by Leonardo's conception (in this case the preparatory drawings for the painting, rather than the work itself, which had already disappeared from view) was Peter Paul Rubens, whose brilliant copy of Leonardo's work profoundly influenced the Baroque era.

its political agenda. By depicting a heroic chapter in Florence's history Soderini's regime hoped to wrap itself in past glories, particularly since success on the battlefield had been so conspicuously absent of late.

Indeed, Leonardo was not the only artistic giant whose work on behalf of the Florentine government was less than a success. The Palazzo della Signoria where Machiavelli worked, in particular the Hall of the Great Council, had the distinction of simultaneously playing host to two of the greatest artistic fiascoes of all time, at least if one measures disaster by the distance between promise and achievement. Working alongside Leonardo in 1504 was Michelangelo Buonarotti who had been commissioned to paint *The Battle of Cascina* to complement Leonardo's fresco on the other half of the main wall in front of which the nation's leaders sat in regal splendor. Even more explicitly than the great cavalry clash depicted by Leonardo, Michelangelo's frieze of monumental nudes seems to have been intended to promote Machiavelli's plan for a revived citizen militia. The scene depicts a moment in Florence's last (and more successful) campaign against Pisa in the fourteenth century, when the courage and quick thinking of the Florentine commissioner, Manno Donati, saved the citizen army from a surprise attack after its commander, the mercenary captain Galeotto Malatesta, had taken to his bed. As Donati raises the alarm, the soldiers, according to a contemporary account, "Florentines who had voluntarily joined on horseback in order to do honor to their fatherland," hurriedly pull on their clothes and gird for battle, successfully repelling the enemy attack. Few images could have appealed to Machiavelli as much as this scene of citizens routing a professional army, a vivid illustration of his own political philosophy.

Rarely have two men of such towering genius worked side by side as colleagues and rivals; rarely have two works begun with such great promise ended in such disappointment. Ultimately the two aborted masterpieces complemented each other only in the magnitude of their failure.* While Leonardo's painting began to deteriorate before it was completed, Michelangelo barely got past the initial drawing. Even before he had a chance to transfer the design to the wall he was called away to Rome by

---

* Like Leonardo's *Battle of Anghiari*, Michelangelo's painting had enormous influence through the drawings he made for the project that inspired future generations of artists.

the new Pope, Julius II, who demanded the services of the rising star of Italian art for his own vast projects, a request that Soderini, anxious to maintain cordial relations with his neighbor to the south, could ill afford to ignore.

Fortunately, not everything Michelangelo produced on behalf of his native land was a flop. In fact the commission for the vast fresco was his reward for an earlier spectacular success. Michelangelo had returned to Florence in 1501 after a seven-year absence following the overthrow of the Medici regime.* Six years younger than Machiavelli, Michelangelo had traveled in the same circles before 1494, when Piero de' Medici's expulsion transformed the prospects of the clients of the ruling family. They certainly knew each other and had friends in common, but there is no indication the two men were ever close. In fact if Machiavelli's relationship with Leonardo lacks a certain inspirational quality, the few documented points of contact between Michelangelo and the Second Chancellor are mundane in the extreme, proving that when two great minds meet the results can be trivial. One well-documented encounter came in 1506, when Machiavelli was in Rome on an embassy to Pope Julius. At the time the artist was working for both the Florentine government and the Pope, who had commissioned him to sculpt his tomb. Since Michelangelo was frequently shuttling between Florence and the Eternal City, Biagio Buonaccorsi entrusted him with a menial task: "[T]hus with the sculptor Michelangelo *acting as deputy*," he wrote to Machiavelli, "I have sent you the money for the courier. . . . He told me he would be there next Sunday and would find you, since he also has some of his own business to do." This minor incident says nothing about Machiavelli's appreciation of the artist's talent, but it captures a world in which geniuses were a common enough sight around town that it did not seem strange to employ them as errand boys.

Michelangelo had originally been enticed back to his native city with the promise he would be allowed to work on a legendary block of marble that had lain half ruined in a yard near the Duomo. "This block of marble was nine *braccia*† high," recorded Michelangelo's friend and colleague

---

* Though deeply moved by Savonarola's religious fervor, Michelangelo remained suspect as the protégé of Lorenzo de' Medici. The climate for art had been more favorable in the Rome of Alexander VI than in Florence under the austere rule of the friar.

† A *braccia* (literally "arm") was a Florentine measurement equal to a little under a yard.

Vasari, "and from it, unluckily, one Maestro Simone da Fiesole had begun a giant, and he had managed to work so ill, that he had hacked a hole between the legs, and it was altogether misshapen and reduced to ruin, insomuch that the Wardens of Works of S. Maria del Fiore [in charge of the cathedral], who had the charge of the undertaking, had placed it on one side without troubling to have it finished." Never one to duck a challenge, Michelangelo was also hoping to forestall the commission being offered to Leonardo, the only man he regarded as a worthy rival. After spending time with the magnificent but damaged block, Michelangelo was inspired to carve a figure that would symbolize the republic, an underdog warrior taking on and besting his more powerful adversary. The colossal statue that emerged cut by cut from the marble was the *David*. All Florence followed its progress as diligently as they followed the less happy course of Leonardo's *Battle of Anghiari*. Among those stopping by the stonecutter's yard was the Gonfaloniere himself:

> It happened at this time that Piero Soderini [Vasari wrote], having seen it in place, was well pleased with it, but said to Michelangelo, at a moment when he was retouching it in certain parts, that it seemed to him that the nose of the figure was too thick. . . . [I]n order to satisfy him [Michelangelo] climbed upon the staging, which was against the shoulders, and quickly took up a chisel in his left hand, with a little of the marble-dust that lay upon the planks of the staging, and then, beginning to strike lightly with the chisel, let fall the dust little by little, nor changed the nose a whit from what it was before. Then, looking down at the Gonfaloniere, who stood watching him, he said, "Look at it now." "I like it better," said the Gonfaloniere, "you have given it life." And so Michelangelo came down, laughing to himself at having satisfied that lord, for he had compassion on those who, in order to appear full of knowledge, talk about things of which they know nothing.

Vasari's anecdote recalls Leonardo's dismissal in *The Art of Painting* of "certain presumptuous persons," and Machiavelli's similar claims for the unique perspective of "a man of low and poor station." Soderini comes off as a pompous know-it-all, played for a fool by the humble artist.

These are archetypal stories of the new age in which talented men of the people could dare to match wits against those born into privilege. In the prologue to *La Mandragola*, Machiavelli informs any member of the audience who might wish to disparage his little comedy "that the author, too, knows how to find fault, and that it was his earliest art . . . [nor] does he stand in awe of anybody, even though he plays the servant to such as can wear a better cloak than he can." This is a pugnacious dig at those who think that it is jewels and fine silk rather than quality of mind that defines a person's worth.

Machiavelli, like Leonardo and Michelangelo, belonged to the client class, that vast, restless swarm of the ambitious and the penurious buzzing about their rich and powerful patrons. They are Figaros running rings around the hapless Count. Though none of them consciously strove to shake up the social order, their achievement stands as a reproach to the static hierarchy. Many of the names that have come down through history from this most creative moment are men on the margins of respectability whose ambition was fired by their sense of social insecurity. Michelangelo was descended from the minor but impoverished nobility, the same group from which Machiavelli sprang. (Like Bernardo Machiavelli, Ludovico Buonarotti was both proud and poor, boasting "I never practiced any profession; but I have always up to now lived on my slender income, attending to those few possessions left to me by my forebears.") Michelangelo's disdainful treatment of the Gonfaloniere was the act of a proud man forced to bow to fools who believed that wealth and power entitled them to speak on subjects beyond their competence.

To be fair, those who ruled Florence were keenly aware of the value of men like Leonardo and Michelangelo who could add luster to the state when military and political prestige were sorely lacking. Despite Soderini's quibbles, those in the government and the wider populace immediately recognized the importance of Michelangelo's achievement. The only debate was how best to honor and profit from what everyone recognized was a masterpiece. So vital was the new work to the government's self-esteem that a panel of wise men was convened (including Leonardo, who put aside any feelings of competition with his younger colleague) to determine how best to display the statue. The panel ultimately decided to place the *David* on the platform before the Palazzo della Signoria as the majestic embodiment of the republic. Here, every day on his way to work, Machiavelli passed the sculpture Florentines knew simply as *Il Gigante*, the Giant. It is unlikely the majestic figure inspired in him the requisite feelings of awe and reverence. Well armed with a sense of irony, the Second Chancellor almost certainly regarded with wry amusement the contrast between the heroic ideal displayed outside the door and the petty compromises demanded of those inside.

VII

THE STARS ALIGN

"Each day I discover in you a greater prophet than the Jews or any generation ever possessed."

—FILIPPO CASAVECCHIA TO MACHIAVELLI

ON DECEMBER 28, 1503, ON THE BANKS OF THE GARI-
gliano River some thirty miles north of Naples, the French army in Italy suffered a crushing defeat at the hands of Spanish forces under Gonzalvo de Cordoba. The news, arriving in Florence a few days later, caused near panic in the government palace. The republic's fate had long been linked to the success of the French, and with their ally now retreating before the hostile Spaniards, Florence's future as an independent republic appeared in jeopardy.

The news, however, was not universally bleak. Among the casualties of the battle was Piero de' Medici, who had drowned in the swift-flowing stream while trying to evade capture by the victorious Spanish forces. While Piero's death did not end the threat from the exiled Medici, the new head of the family, his younger brother Cardinal Giovanni de' Medici, was a far more prudent man. Their father was once reported to have remarked: "I have three sons: one is foolish, one is clever, and one is kind." With the foolish son now out of the way, Florentines thought they might have better luck with the clever Giovanni and mild-mannered Giuliano.

For the Second Chancellor and Secretary to the Ten of War, the shift in the balance of power in Italy posed new challenges. With the goal of subjugating Pisa no closer to completion than it had been when Machiavelli first entered office, the beleaguered republic could ill afford to fight on a second front. Should the victorious Spaniards choose to march north, Florence had nothing to block them but a few mercenaries whose performance before the walls of Pisa had given little reason for encouragement. On January 14, 1504, Machiavelli was again dispatched to the court of the French King to "make it clearly understood," according to Niccolò Valori's instructions, "that we are not in a position to gather troops sufficient for our defense, and that accordingly we should be obliged to turn for aid wherever it was to be found." In other words, he was to make it plain to the French that should they be unwilling or unable to help, Florence might be forced to throw herself into the arms of Spain. Fortunately, such a scenario was never put to the test. The Spaniards, it turned out, were stretched too thin both militarily and financially to pursue their advantage. On February 11 the warring nations signed a three-year truce that guaranteed, at least for the time being, the survival of the republic.

But while the immediate threat had dissipated, Florence's position remained precarious. Machiavelli's agitated state of mind at the time is evident in his *First Decennale*, an epic poem on current affairs he completed in November 1504 and dedicated to his early patron, Alamanno Salviati.[*] After chronicling the tumultuous ten years just passed, Machiavelli captures the uncertainty of the times he was living through:

> *[M]y spirit is all aflame; now with hope, now with fear,*
> *it is overwhelmed, so much that it wastes to nothing bit by bit;*
> *because it seeks to know where your ship can sail, weighted with*
> *such heavy weights, or into what harbor, with these winds.*

Likening Florence to a storm-tossed boat unable to steer its own course through turbulent waters, he nonetheless ends on an optimistic note:

> *Yet we trust in the skillful steersman, in the oars, in the sails, in*
> *the cordage; but the voyage would be easy and short if you*
> *would reopen the temple of Mars.*

---

[*] Machiavelli's *First Decennale* was published by his friend Agostino Vespucci at his own expense. Its popularity is suggested by the fact that it was immediately pirated by another printer, much to the chagrin of Vespucci, who stood to lose his investment. The fact that Machiavelli went to the trouble of composing it and having it published reveals that he had not abandoned his earlier literary ambitions.

The "skillful steersman" is Piero Soderini, with whom Machiavelli had struck up a close personal and professional relationship. Most intriguing is the closing line about the "temple of Mars," the first explicit reference to the project that dominated the remainder of his time in office and that would first catapult him to fame as the hero of the reinvigorated Florentine Republic before reducing him to the role of scapegoat, blamed for its sudden collapse.

From the moment he was elected Second Chancellor in the spring of 1498, Machiavelli was consumed by a single idea: How could his beloved republic halt the steady decline of her fortunes? In centuries past she had been the capital of a proud and growing empire; now, with no standing army of her own, she was forced to throw herself into the arms of one protector or another. "[T]he worst thing about weak republics," he wrote in *The Discourses,* "is that they are irresolute, so that all the choices they make, they are forced to make." Instead of being masters of their fate, Florentines had been reduced to pawns in a high-stakes game played by those with little reason to consider their interests. During the reign of Lorenzo de' Medici, adroit diplomacy had masked inherent weakness. The French invasion of 1494 had exposed the impotence of all the states of Italy, but none more starkly than Florence, which for centuries had relied on paid mercenaries to compensate for her own lack of martial vigor. Machiavelli felt the humiliation keenly as he represented the republic in foreign courts, where he was dismissed as a man of no account serving a state that had long ceased to matter on the world stage.

As a careful student of ancient history, Machiavelli knew there was another way. Like many Florentines, he was a great admirer of the Roman Republic, whose citizen soldiers had set out from their farms and shops to conquer the known world. What, Machiavelli asked himself, allowed these simple folk to face down the armies of Sparta and Persia, while his compatriots hardly ever picked up a sword unless it was to avenge a petty insult from a rival family? Florentines had forgotten the ways of war. They had, in his memorable phrase, closed the temple of Mars.

Machiavelli's first mission as Secretary to the Ten of War, in March 1499, had been to the camp of Jacopo of Piombino, where he tried to coax the disgruntled and underpaid *condottiere* from his tent. In the years since, hardly a month passed without a similar incident involving one of

the many mercenary generals in Florentine employ, in which accusations
of treachery on one side were met by countercharges of bad faith on the
other. The most serious ended with the beheading of Paolo Vitelli, though
there must have been many times before and since where Machiavelli felt
that the ax man's services were called for.

Instructed by the Ten to offer Gianpaolo Baglioni a contract, Machiavelli unleashed a diatribe against the man in particular and the breed in
general: "[H]e was like the other pillagers of Rome, who are thieves rather
than soldiers, and whose services are sought for the sake of their names
and influence, rather than for their valor, or the number of men at their
command. Moved as they are by personal interests, the alliances they
make last till it suits their purpose to break them."

By contrast, he observed, armies made up of citizen conscripts fighting
for hearth and home were far more effective. The massive French army
combined a hardened professional force of Swiss pike men with peasants
and laborers levied from the local populace, while the militias instituted
by Cesare Borgia and Remirro that Machiavelli had reviewed during his
tour of the Romagna were an essential ingredient in Valentino's early
success. But Machiavelli's faith in a citizen army went beyond empirical
observation; he had an almost mystical belief in the virtue of the citizen
soldier and a visceral hatred for the hired gun—a conviction that a man
who refused to fight on behalf of his own country was no man at all, and
that a nation that relied on its purse rather than its people would soon be
reduced to slavery. In the final chapter of *The Prince*, Machiavelli urges Lorenzo de' Medici to free Italy from foreign domination, telling him "above
all other things, it is necessary . . . to provide yourself with your own army;
for there cannot be more faithful, truer, or better soldiers than these."
These loyal soldiers stand in stark contrast to those who sell their services
to the highest bidder:

> *Mercenaries and auxiliaries are useless and dangerous, and anyone
> who founds his state on such men will never know stability or secu-
> rity, because they are disorganized, ambitious, without discipline or
> faith. Brave among friends, they are cowards before their enemies.
> They have no fear of God nor loyalty to men. Ruin can be avoided
> only by avoiding action. In peace the prince will be despoiled by his*

own men, in war he will be despoiled by his enemies. The reason for this is that they have no loyalty, nothing that keeps them in the field, but a little bit of money insufficient to make them willing to die for you. They are happy to be your soldiers as long as you avoid war, but when war comes they will desert or flee.

I hardly need to trouble myself persuading anyone of the truth of what I say since Italy's ruin can be traced to no other cause than her reliance, for so many years, on mercenary armies.

For Machiavelli, the use of mercenary armies was not only impractical—it represented an acute moral failing. Free men did not pay others to fight for them but defended their liberty with their blood. "[W]here military organization is good," he wrote in *The Discourses*, "there must needs be good order." Only a corrupt and sybaritic people would stoop to hiring professional soldiers, who inevitably gained a stranglehold over those who employed them. Passionately patriotic and proud of the city's history of independence, Machiavelli concluded that Florence would never equal past glories unless she revived the ancient tradition of the citizen army.

This would require a reversal of almost two centuries of military policy. More importantly, it would involve a radical shift in the way the citizens viewed their obligations to the state. Florentines, as Machiavelli recognized, had long since forgotten the discipline of war; they had grown prosperous and complacent. They paid taxes reluctantly, using all manner of trickery to hide their assets, and then grumbled when the armies they hired on the cheap failed to meet their objectives. Given the generally low sense of civic duty, it was certain they would howl at any attempt to drag them from their comfortable homes to drill on the parade ground and resist any policy that might endanger life and limb on the field of battle.

Perhaps even more difficult to overcome was the near paranoia regarding any policy that led to the arming of the common people. While the prosperous middle class had no desire to take up arms, it was equally averse to placing weapons in the hands of employees who might be tempted to turn on their masters. The uprising by impoverished workers in 1378 known as the Revolt of the Ciompi had instilled in the ruling elite an almost hysterical fear of class warfare. In 1466 a coup against the Medici failed in large part because, according to one eyewitness, they feared "that the little people, all in arms . . . would be so aroused that, having tasted the sweetness of such destruction, would turn against other magnates, thinking in this way to relieve their poverty." If these poor, hungry laborers were conscripted, how long would it be before they asserted their political and economic rights?

Machiavelli understood the difficulties involved, but frustration with the army's recent shameful performance had grown so great that most now admitted there was a problem, even if they still disagreed on a solution. The key figure in all this was the Gonfaloniere. Fortunately, Soderini had come to rely on the Second Chancellor's sound judgment and to appreciate his tireless dedication. Machiavelli had made a convert of Cardinal Francesco Soderini, whose enthusiasm for the project rubbed off on his brother. "Your letter being longer," the Cardinal wrote to Machiavelli, "gave us all the more pleasure, because we now understand more clearly your new military strategy, which corresponds to our hope for the health and dignity of our country, is progressing. . . . And it must be no small satisfaction that it is from your hands that such an honorable undertaking should have begun. So persevere and bring this affair to the desired end."

Even with the support of the Gonfaloniere and the Cardinal, Machiavelli's efforts to institute a civilian militia met with fierce resistance. The rich merchants who made up the bulk of the Great Council refused to arm the urban workforce they regarded as a potentially violent, revolutionary element. Ultimately, Machiavelli was forced to abandon his broader scheme in favor of a more limited one in which the militia was recruited from peasants in the countryside rather than the Florentine proletariat.

With Piero Soderini's blessing, and a grudging wait-and-see approach adopted by the Signoria, Machiavelli began to recruit his army in the winter of 1505–6. He plunged into the work with typical enthusiasm, riding out into the countryside himself to hire captains and draft infantrymen in the village squares and rustic hamlets. His efforts were so successful that by February he was able to march his first recruits through the Piazza della Signoria. The event was described by the apothecary Luca Landucci, who hurried to the square to catch a glimpse of Florence's latest fighting force:

> *There was a muster in the Piazza of 400 recruits whom the Gonfal-*
> *oniere had assembled, Florentine peasants, and he gave them each a*
> *white waistcoat, a pair of stockings half red and half white, a white*
> *cap, shoes, and an iron breastplate, and lances, and to some of them*
> *muskets. These were called battalions; and they were given a con-*
> *stable who would lead them, and teach them how to use their arms.*
> *They were soldiers, but stopped at their own houses, being obliged to*
> *appear when needed; and it was ordered that many thousand should*
> *be made in this way all through the country, so that we should not*
> *need to have any foreigners. This was thought the finest thing that*
> *had ever been arranged for Florence.*

Landucci's testimony indicates that public opinion was turning in favor of the militia. All Machiavelli had to do now was demonstrate their effectiveness in the field. In August he began to test their mettle in small skirmishes in the countryside near Pisa, where their numbers added weight to the mercenary forces besieging the city. Though the exam was not very rigorous—most of the fighting was still left to the professionals—they acquitted themselves admirably in their limited roles.

Even the skeptics in the Great Council were beginning to come around; the militia was given official sanction on December 6, 1506, when the Great Council, by a vote of 841 in favor to 317 opposed, created a new body, the Nine of the Militia, to organize and oversee the newly created force.* When it came time to appoint a chancellor the choice was obvious. Niccolò Machiavelli now added another title to his bulging portfolio. Upon learning of his assistant's election, Piero Soderini congratulated him, and insisted that God must favor the project since "it daily increases and flourishes, in spite of malignant opposition."

As Soderini's letter suggests—and as the vote on the militia, lopsided as it was, confirms—the government and its policies were not without opponents. Machiavelli had his new militia, but there were many, particularly among the *ottimati*, who feared it would become an instrument of tyranny in the hands of a ruler who was aggregating more power every

---

* It couldn't have hurt that the vote was taken in the very room where Leonardo and Michelangelo had been hard at work depicting scenes of the republic's past military glories.

day. In fact many of the ruling families had never reconciled themselves to Soderini. The idea of a Gonfaloniere-for-life appeared to them not much different from a dictator, and while few questioned Soderini's honesty, it was also noted that he did not stint himself when it came to the trappings of office. At one point a florin was issued with the likeness of the Gonfaloniere, a sign, his critics claimed, that he now saw himself as King. Also smacking of regal pretensions was the behavior of his family. As a lifetime appointee it was only natural that his wife should come to live with him in the Palazzo, but this departure from tradition—exacerbated by *Madonna* Soderini's taste for elegant gowns and dinner parties—offended the more traditional-minded, who thought that no serious business could be transacted in proximity to the fairer sex.

Criticism of Soderini's domestic life was a symptom of a deeper anxiety on the part of the *ottimati*, who saw their own power wane as the Gonfaloniere's increased. There was never any indication that he intended to use the militia to intimidate the domestic opposition, but it is not far-fetched to imagine that in time he might have succumbed to the temptation to use a standing army to whip recalcitrant legislators into line.

Signs of growing friction between the *ottimati* and the Soderini executive were apparent in 1507 when Soderini tried to appoint Machiavelli to head an important embassy to the German Emperor-Elect Maximillian I. After vociferous complaints from leading *ottimati* who were afraid the Second Chancellor was too closely allied with the Gonfaloniere, Machiavelli's name was withdrawn in favor of the more aristocratic, better connected, and more independent Francesco Vettori.

Among the great monarchs of Europe, the Holy Roman Emperor (or Emperor of the Romans as he was usually styled before actually receiving the imperial crown from the hands of the Pope) was at once the most exalted and the least powerful. As the heir to Charlemagne, he was the feudal overlord not only of much of central Europe but of northern Italy as well. Unlike his famous medieval predecessors—most notably Frederick Barbarossa and Frederick II—the Renaissance version of the Emperor claimed an authority that was almost limitless in theory and negligible in practice. Should he ever reassert his feudal rights and back up the claim with armed force, as Maximillian was now proposing to do, he could become once again a serious, and seriously disruptive, factor in Italian geopolitics.

As it turned out, keeping an eye on the restless monarch was apparently too much responsibility for Vettori, who was put on the spot when the Emperor demanded from Florence a tribute of 50,000 ducats to help him defray the expense of maintaining his army in Italy. Vettori's letter prompted the Signoria to convene an emergency committee to craft a response. The prospect of emptying their already depleted coffers to finance an adventure from which the best they could hope was to emerge no worse off than they already were, was unappetizing enough. But bowing to the extortionate demand would also enrage the French, who now faced the prospect of being ground to a powder between German and Spanish millstones. With Vettori clearly not up to the job, the government finally agreed to send Machiavelli to stiffen the ambassador's backbone, though only after much grumbling from those who accused him of being Soderini's "puppet."

The mission to Maximillian promised to be another thankless venture. Machiavelli was authorized to offer the emperor 30,000 ducats, going as high as 50,000 if the Emperor proved a hard bargainer, and then only if it was clear that the promised expedition would get off the ground, a questionable proposition given Maximillian's mercurial temper. As usual, the Florentine government was facing a crisis by delaying any real decision, hoping to placate the Emperor without antagonizing the French (an almost impossible task given their mutually incompatible interests) and relying on the Second Chancellor's skills to keep all these mismatched balls in the air.

In December, Machiavelli packed his bags and set out on his journey along snow-choked mountain passes to the Swiss cantons, where the Emperor was trying to conjure up an army and the funds to pay for it. "[I] promise you," he wrote to the Gonfaloniere upon arriving in Bolzano, "that if ever there were a wretched journey, it was the one that I made." Despite the discomfort of the winter weather and poor accommodations, he carefully observed local customs, hoping to discover those secrets that made the Swiss the most feared warriors of the age. "Between Geneva and Constance I made four halts," he later recorded: "The twelve Cantons each contribute four thousand men for the defense of the country, and from one thousand to one thousand five hundred for foreign service. And this because, in the first case, all are by law compelled to bear arms; in the second, namely, when it is a question of going to fight elsewhere, no one need go, save of his own free will."

Later he gathered his observations in a pamphlet titled *Report on Germany*.* The frugal habits of the Swiss offered the starkest possible reproach to the decadent lives of his compatriots: not only were they a free people, governing themselves in their rural hamlets, but they produced a breed of soldier that more than once in recent years had humbled the professional forces the Italians sent against them. Machiavelli paints a largely idyllic portrait of these northern rustics:

> *There can be no doubt of the power of Germany, with her abundance of men, money, and arms. The Germans spend little on administration, and nothing on soldiers, for they train their own subjects in arms. On festival days, instead of playing games, their youth seek diversion in learning the use of the petronel, the pike, and of other weapons. They are frugal in all things, for they affect no luxury in their buildings or their attire, and have but few chattels in their dwellings. It suffices them to have abundance of bread and meat, and to have stoves to protect them from the cold; and he who owns no other possessions, does without them and desires them not. Therefore their country exists on its own produce, without needing to buy from others; and they sell things fashioned by their hands, which are scattered over nearly the whole of Italy, and their gains are all the greater because earned by labor with very little capital. Thus they enjoy their rough life and liberty, and for this cause will not go to war, excepting for great recompense; nor would even that suffice, but for the decrees of their communities.*

Rough life and liberty—these two qualities were intimately connected in Machiavelli's mind. Like the ancient Spartans or the citizen soldiers of early Rome, the Swiss, while possessing little in the way of material comforts, were happy and free, relying on nothing but their own courage and

---

* Machiavelli lumped all the German-speaking regions of Europe under the heading of Germany. This region of central Europe, spreading from the North Sea to the Alps, consisted of innumerable principalities, duchies, and small kingdoms, some loosely confederated, others, like the Swiss cantons, independent.

strength to defend their liberties. They were self-sufficient and self-reliant, a striking contrast to his fellow countrymen, who purchased their ease at the price of their liberty.

Machiavelli was not wholly uncritical. Though their fighting spirit was admirable, the Germans' inability to work together for a common purpose—a quarrelsomeness that the Italians shared, without possessing compensatory virtues—prevented them from achieving greater things. The Emperor commanded enormous resources on paper but was constantly fighting with his vassals "so that it is easy to comprehend why, notwithstanding the great strength of the country, it is in fact much enfeebled."

In truth, Machiavelli is a less than ideal tour guide since he tends to file down the inconvenient edges of any fact until it fits into his preformed thesis. His report is really an argument in the form of a description. It follows a long tradition, dating back at least to Tacitus—who, almost a millennium and a half earlier, drew a similar comparison between the Romans and the rude but virile Germans—in which a traveler from a rich and sophisticated land sings the praises of simple folk he encounters in order to shame his compatriots. For Machiavelli the moral of the story was all too clear. Italians had forgotten the simple virtues of their forebears and unless they mended their ways—in part by relearning the discipline of war as those conscripted into his militias were doing—they were doomed to end their lives as slaves.

Machiavelli's teeth-chattering journey through the mountains would eventually furnish material for the grand theories of power politics he was building in his head. In the meantime, he encountered the usual frustrations that came from serving as the envoy of the Florentine Republic. When he presented himself to the Emperor in Bolzano, Machiavelli's initial offer of 30,000 ducats was met with a curt rebuff. But before he could get down to haggling over sums he needed to divine the Emperor's real intentions. Following the Emperor's court from Bolzano to Trent, Machiavelli struggled to interpret conflicting signals. "It is difficult to forecast events," he wrote to the Ten, explaining the forces pulling in opposite directions that made any prediction perilous: "The Emperor has many worthy soldiers, but he has no money, neither is it apparent from what quarter he will get any, and he is too lavish of that which he has. . . . He is skilled in war, patient of fatigue, but so credulous that many have doubts of the expedition, so that there is matter both for hope and fear. . . . I dwell in uncertainty," he concluded.

The Emperor's indecisiveness was matched only by that of the Florentine government, which was caught somewhere between defiance and abject capitulation. "Your Excellencies have spun so fine a web," Machiavelli complained, "that it is impossible to weave it. . . . You must come to a decision, divine the less dangerous course, and entering upon it, settle your minds in God's name; for by trying to measure great matters like these with compasses, men are led to error."

This was a repetition of Machiavelli's mission to Valentino six years earlier, or, to tell the truth, of almost all the embassies upon which he embarked over the course of his career—an extended variation on themes of evasion and delay. In one particularly candid exchange with his fellow ambassador Luigi Guicciardini, Machiavelli admitted: "It's as if I'm here on a desert island, since I know nothing about anything. Still, to show I'm still alive I invent diligent reports to send to the Ten." Trying to make the best of a bad situation, he wrote to the Gonfaloniere, "I shall do here what little good I can think of, even if my staying here is completely superfluous."

Machiavelli spent more than six months at the court of the German Emperor as, Hamlet-like, the great man attempted to make up his mind. Repeating the frustrations of that earlier mission to the Borgia duke, no matter how often Machiavelli insisted he was accomplishing nothing, his superiors in Florence insisted his presence was essential. At one point suggestions that he be recalled were countered by Vettori, who wrote, "it would be the most inopportune thing in the world to recall Machiavelli . . . it was necessary for him to remain until everything was settled."

On February 4, after receiving word from Pope Julius that he had been granted the title of Emperor, Maximillian entered the cathedral of Trent, accompanied by pompous fanfares and attended by a resplendent guard of honor, and had himself officially invested by the Bishop of Gurk. But, as was often the case with the Emperor, the elaborate ceremony was a substitute for rather than the prelude to decisive action. In the coming weeks troops marched here and there, rumors flew faster than cannonballs, and skirmishing among the forces of Venice, France, and the Emperor did little but inflict misery upon the peasants whose fields were trampled and houses burned. After months filled with sound and fury, word arrived on

June 6 of a grand bargain among the great powers proclaiming a three-year truce. Four days later, Machiavelli headed for home.

Having spent more than half a year at the court of the Emperor pursuing insubstantial rumors, Machiavelli was anxious to return to more manly pursuits. The months spent among the Swiss had only strengthened his conviction that he was on the right track with his citizen army. Now, with the Gonfaloniere's backing, he increased the size and scope of his forces, adding cavalry to the already substantial infantry arm. Machiavelli was so intimately involved with every aspect of the project that those requiring his attention were more likely to find him in camp with the troops than at his desk at the Chancellery.

By the spring of 1509 the war against Pisa, which had dragged on for fifteen grueling years, was finally showing signs of progress. Advances were partly the result of the increased resources brought to bear after the creation of the militia, but also of a change in strategy. After numerous repulses at the walls of Pisa, the commanders reverted to the slow but sure method of starving the city into submission. While Machiavelli's militias stripped the land bare, Genoese corsairs under Florentine command blockaded the sea routes, effectively isolating the beleaguered city. For the better part of the season Machiavelli and his militia were stationed near Lucca, which had earned Florence's wrath by secretly funneling supplies to their Pisan allies. The militia was assigned the task of burning the crops of millet and oats that were finding their way to the hungry residents of the besieged city, and otherwise making life miserable for the civilian population. It was an unpleasant, if not very dangerous, mission that reflected the grim war of attrition now underway. Ever willing to suppress humane considerations when it came to the security of his country, Machiavelli had few qualms about the suffering his troops were inflicting on noncombatants. But he was not alone in harboring bitter resentment toward the enemy. Luca Landucci recounts one story that illustrates the deep-seated hatreds that fueled the war:

> A woman of Pisa came out of the city with her two children and went before the [Florentine] commissary, saying that she was dying of hunger, and had left her mother in Pisa who was almost famished; and the commissary ordered that bread should be given her for herself and her mother and children. Going back into Pisa with the bread,

she told her mother, who was ill from want of food, and on seeing the white bread, the old woman said: What bread is this? And when her daughter told her that she had had it outside, from the Florentines, the old woman cried: Take away the bread of the accursed Florentines; I would rather die!

Though Landucci shows a certain empathy for the plight of Florence's enemies, his compassion extends only so far:

Oh, what grievous sin it is to command that there should be a war! Woe to him who is the cause of it! I pray God to forgive us; although this enterprise of ours is undertaken legitimately: think what is the sin of those who go to war without legitimate cause!

Machiavelli, like Landucci, was convinced that the stubborn Pisans had no one to blame but themselves. Though he admits the hardships of the civilian population of Pisa, he reserves his sympathy for his own troops, who "with great sufferings and much toil, and with much expense . . . starved her." It is difficult today to feel much pity for troops whose job was to starve their Tuscan brothers and sisters, but from Machiavelli's jingoistic perspective Pisa's culpability was so self-evident that it was pointless to waste emotional energy on them. No doubt he would have agreed with General Sherman's observation, made some three and a half centuries later: "War is cruelty, and you cannot refine it." Like Sherman, he believed that what followed from this truism was not that one should attempt to wage war more humanely—the concept of a humane war being a contradiction in terms—but rather that it ought to be prosecuted with sufficient ruthlessness to achieve a swift and decisive victory.

Though Machiavelli had no formal military training (as critics of his *Art of War* will later point out), his zeal for the cause and impatience with what he regarded as halfhearted efforts on the part of his colleagues meant he was ever more deeply engaged in day-to-day military operations. In March of 1509, for instance, he personally supervised the construction of a crossing over the Oseri River, boasting that the job was so well done that "even the horses of Xerxes might ford it." This hands-on approach did not always sit well with those whose job it was to supervise the commanders in the field.

Commissary-General Niccolò Capponi complained to the Ten that Machiavelli frequently overstepped his authority and failed to inform him of his movements. After Capponi lodged an official complaint with the Nine, Biagio Buonaccorsi advised Machiavelli to treat him with more circumspection. "[T]he more powerful must always be right," he explained facetiously, "and it is necessary to treat them with respect. You should be patient and learn how to handle yourself in such circumstances." Patience and tact were two qualities Machiavelli had a hard time summoning when that meant putting up with fools and idlers. But though he continued to step on the sensitive toes of powerful men, he had made himself indispensable to the one person who counted, Piero Soderini, who continued to shield Machiavelli from the barbs of his enemies, even as he reminded him "that the way of this world is to receive great ingratitude for great and good operations." So deep did Machiavelli plunge into the weeds of military tactics that Buonaccorsi began to address him mockingly as "Captain General."

As Pisa slowly crumbled from within, Machiavelli redoubled his efforts, determined not to repeat the mistakes of the past when confident predictions of victory were followed by embarrassing reverses. When the Ten ordered Machiavelli back from the front lines, he pleaded with them to let him stay: "[I]f I wished to avoid fatigue and danger, I should not have left Florence; therefore, I beg your Excellencies to permit me to stay among these camps, and labor with these Commissaries on necessary matters; for here I can be good for something, and there I should be good for nothing, and should die of despair."

The relentless pressure was paying dividends. In March, Machiavelli was ordered to Piombino to meet with a Pisan delegation that had come to explore the possibility of peace. What terms, they asked, were the Florentines willing to offer? "[The Ten]," he told them, "desired obedience, [but] demanded neither their life, their property nor their honor, and would allow them reasonable liberty." Encouraging as these words were, the delegation could not commit to anything. Still, it was becoming increasingly clear that the surrender of Pisa was just a matter of time. With the naval blockade now securely in place and with Machiavelli's militia laying waste to the countryside, Pisa's allies could no longer prolong the contest by resupplying the city. On May 24, Machiavelli and Alamanno Salviati escorted a second delegation of high-ranking Pisans to the Florentine suburb of San Miniato, where they were to meet with government officials to negotiate the terms of surrender. Machiavelli was present on June 1 when the official surrender was signed in the Palazzo della Signoria, affixing his name on the treaty next to that of the First Chancellor, Marcello Adriani. Anxious to be where the action was, Machiavelli hurried back to camp and was among those who watched as hundreds of emaciated citizens broke out of Pisa and entered Florentine lines, where they were fed and clothed.

While Pisan dignitaries finalized terms with their Florentine counterparts, Machiavelli was involved in discussions of his own that would determine exactly how and when the city would be handed over. Perhaps the most important conversation was with a man named Lattanzio Tedaldi, though his expertise was neither political nor military. He was, in fact, an astrologer, and at Machiavelli's request he was charting the planetary orbits to determine the most auspicious moment. On June 5, Machiavelli received his answer. "I would like you," Tedaldi told the Second Chancellor, "to instruct the commissioners that, having decided to take possession of Pisa on Thursday, they should under no circumstances enter before the 12th hour and a half in the morning, but if possible a little after the 13th,* which will be a moment most auspicious for us." Thus, after fifteen long years of blood and toil here on earth, the exact moment of Pisa's fall would be determined by the serene procession of the heavenly bodies.

It might at first seem surprising that a hardheaded realist like Machiavelli should have succumbed to such superstitious nonsense. Though he saw through many of the pieties and prejudices that blinded his contemporaries, he did not free himself entirely from such mumbo jumbo. Astrology was something of an obsession in Renaissance Europe, and while not everyone was convinced—Savonarola condemned it and Pico della Mirandola offered a stinging indictment of the ancient art in his *Disputations Against Astrology*—belief was so widespread that no cornerstone was laid or battle fought without consulting a master of the inscrutable discipline. Even popes were not immune to the superstition, despite condemnation by many Church fathers, who saw astrology as little different from witchcraft. But Machiavelli was no superstitious peasant carrying amulets and chanting spells to ward off evil spirits. He subscribed to the conventional

---

* About 7:30 or 8:00 in the morning, since the hours were counted from the previous sunset.

wisdom of the day that the arc of human life was influenced by cosmic forces, while insisting such forces were not determinative. To believe that our fates are sealed at birth would have made a mockery of his world-view, which was predicated on the notion that individuals could, through strength of will and clarity of mind, forge their own destiny. What point would there be in offering advice to the would-be prince if his fate, and the fate of his subjects, was indelibly written in the stars?

Machiavelli's attitude is suggested by a letter he received from Bartolomeo Vespucci, a famous professor of astrology at the University of Padua, responding to one, now lost, from Machiavelli. "Suffice it that your opinion must be called absolutely correct," Professor Vespucci answered, "since all the ancients proclaimed with one voice that the wise man himself is able to alter the influences of the stars." This, in turn, is a paraphrase of a famous saying of Ptolemy, the ancient astronomer, who declared: "The wise man will control the stars." Charting a middle course between fatalism, on the one hand, and the more acceptably Christian belief in free will was a common intellectual compromise for men of the Renaissance who cherished ancient teachings while still subscribing to the basic tenets of the Church. It was a compromise that appealed to Machiavelli as well since it allowed him to acknowledge the role of what we might call external factors, i.e., those aspects of life over which we have no control, without succumbing to the passivity such beliefs engendered.

In his own writing Machiavelli invokes Fortune, a capricious goddess who stands for the unpredictability of life. When he declares in *The Prince* that "fortune is a woman and in order to be mastered she must be jogged and beaten," he is reiterating, in more colorful language, the point he made to Bartolomeo Vespucci: that powerful men make their own luck.* But they are the exception since "in the world most men let themselves be mastered by fortune." Machiavelli's larger point is that whatever invisible strings tug at us, we ought to live *as if* our fate were in our own hands. This is certainly the way he lived his own life, though when things didn't work out he was apt to take at least a rhetorical swipe at the wicked goddess. On those occasions when things were looking up, however—as they

---

* This same idea is expressed by Cassius in Shakespeare's *Julius Caesar* when he says, "Men at some time are masters of their fates; The fault, dear Brutus, is not in our stars, But in ourselves."

surely were in the summer of 1509—he forgets about *Fortuna* and takes full credit for his success.[*]

Having determined the exact moment with metaphysical precision, Machiavelli saw to the more mundane details that would guide the conquering army as it took possession of the city. Perhaps the most important provision he made was to ensure that the occupying troops were paid in advance so that they would not resort to the looting that victorious armies often regarded as a well-earned bonus after months of hard work.

Florentine forces entered Pisa on the morning of Thursday, June 7, marching in orderly arrays past the gaunt faces of their defeated foes. Riding alongside them was the Second Chancellor, proudly accompanied by members of the militia that owed its existence to his persistence, patriotism, and tireless devotion. It was a moment of triumph for Machiavelli, who had every right to bask in the glow of victory.

Indeed, he had more to be pleased with on that bright June morning than the fact that he had succeeded where others far better versed in the military arts had failed. Having prosecuted the war with utmost vigor, Machiavelli was equally determined to win the peace, and here his careful arrangements paid off as the troops maintained the discipline that would help reconcile the populace to its new situation. Among the Pisans the mood was a mixture of sullenness and relief. If they had been hurt in their pride, at least the immediate future promised to be much more pleasant than the recent past. As Machiavelli made clear to the Pisan delegation in March, Florence was willing to be magnanimous in victory. Property and civil liberties were guaranteed, and while some prominent families chose exile rather than remain in a city now under foreign domination, most adjusted to the new state of affairs.

In contrast to the rather sober mood in Pisa, forty miles to the east in Florence there were scenes of riot occasioned by an excess of high spirits. The arrival of a horseman falsely rumored to be carrying news of the surrender was sufficient to empty the churches as citizens gathered in the squares

---

[*] Machiavelli, with his usual psychological insight, recognizes this as a basic human trait. In "On Fortune" he wrote, "Hence all the evil that comes upon mankind is charged to [Fortune]; but any good that befalls a man he believes he gets through his own worth" (*Chief Works*, II, 746).

to share in the glorious moment, while in the cells of Le Stinche prisoners attacked their guards on the principle that the city's good luck ought to extend
to the least fortunate. In the end, according to one eyewitness, all the prisoners broke free and disappeared into the crowds of revelers.

With the official news, arriving the following day, celebrations were better controlled but equally exuberant. "At about 18 in the afternoon [2 P.M.],"
recorded the apothecary Luca Landucci, "the horseman bearing the olive-
branch arrived with the surrender of Pisa; there was a great *festa*, the shops
being shut, and bonfires made, and illuminations placed on all the towers
and on the *Palagio*."

Landucci makes no mention of Machiavelli's role in bringing about this
joyous day, but his colleagues in the Chancery knew who deserved the victor's laurels. That same day Agostino Vespucci wrote to the Second Chancellor: "If I did not think it would make you too proud, I should dare say
that you with your battalions accomplished so much good work, in such a
way that . . . you restored the affairs of Florence. I do not know what to say.
I swear to God, so great is the exultation we are having that I would write a
Ciceronian oration for you if I had time." Another friend chimed in: "May
a thousand good fortunes result to you from the grand gain of this noble
city, for truly it may be said, that you personally have had a great share in
the matter. . . . Each day I discover in you a greater prophet that the Jews or
any generation ever possessed."

This was heady stuff for Machiavelli, but he understood the character
of his countrymen well enough to know that his current popularity was
likely fleeting. As he often observed, *Fortuna* seemed to enjoy the prospect
of bringing down those she had recently exalted, as if to make the sting of
failure all the more bitter. Indeed this would prove to be the high point of
Machiavelli's career. But his downfall, coming close on the heels of his greatest triumph, was not attributable to some abstract property of the universe,
but rather to a peculiarity of human nature. Years later he would write in
the *Discourses*, "Whoever reads of the doings of republics will find in all
of them some sort of ingratitude in the way in which they deal with their
citizens," something Machiavelli learned from hard experience. He was so
obsessed with the topic that he devoted four chapters to discussing envy in
all its Hydra-like deformity. The problem was particularly acute in Florence,
where military success tended to be regarded with almost pathological sus-

picion—one reason its citizens so rarely achieved it. As Piero Soderini and his faithful assistant rode the crest of popular adulation, those who opposed the regime redoubled their efforts to bring it down.

But it was not only the uncertainty of his own prospects that made this moment less than an unadulterated triumph. As a careful student of history, Machiavelli had reason to believe that Florence would have difficulty holding on to what it had captured. Writing years later in *The Prince*, he offered a pessimistic analysis:

> *He who becomes master of a city accustomed to live in liberty, and who does not destroy it, can expect to be destroyed himself, because the city can always justify rebellion in the name of its ancient liberty and institutions. Neither the span of years nor the benefits received can make the citizens forget. Whatever actions are taken or provisions made, if the inhabitants are neither divided nor dispersed, they will long for what they have lost, and take advantage of every opportunity, as did Pisa after a hundred years of servitude under Florence.*

Machiavelli worried that what he had achieved with Pisa was a classic example of that middle way he so despised. Florence had done more than enough to ensure the undying enmity of a people who had bled and starved in the cause of freedom, without actually depriving them of the means of exacting their revenge. Fifteen years of bitter struggle could not be erased from the minds of a conquered people by handing out a few loaves and allowing them a modicum of self-rule—however necessary these were to the immediate problem of pacification. The thirst for liberty was too strong and the memories of injustice too long, Machiavelli believed, to expect that the events of the summer would form the basis of a lasting peace.

Nor would he salve the conscience of his compatriots by telling them the Pisans were better off under the Florentine yoke. War was cruelty and peace hardly less so as the victors imposed their will upon the defeated. Resentment and fear were the most enduring monuments of such a campaign. Machiavelli offers a bleak epilogue in his *Second Decennale*, highlighting the despair of the loser rather than the triumph of the victor: "And though she was a stubborn enemy, yet, by necessity compelled and conquered, she went back weeping to her ancient chain."

VIII

REVERSAL OF FORTUNE

"[Y]our adversaries are numerous and will stop at nothing."
—BIAGIO BUONACCORSI TO MACHIAVELLI

THE OUTPOURING OF JOY THAT FOLLOWED THE CON-
quest of Pisa was as understandable as it was shortsighted. Florence and
Pisa had been bitter rivals for at least three hundred years, since the up-
start inland power first began to challenge the great seaport as the preeminent city of Tuscany. Florence's original conquest of her ancient foe in
1406 had been the crowning achievement of her centuries-long climb to
imperial status, and Pisa's successful rebellion in 1494 had been a crippling
psychological loss. But what had begun in the Middle Ages as a clash of
titans was now a spat between minnows. Florence was a military nonentity
and Pisa a shadow of her former self. This mutual diminution took place
within the context of a wider demographic and economic shift: Italy was
no longer the vital corridor of commerce from East to West; centers of
banking and trade like Florence and Milan were being marginalized; and
the fleets of Pisa, Genoa, and Venice were overtaken by the Atlantic-based
armadas of Spain and Portugal, and the rising Mediterranean power of the
Ottoman Turks. What Florence had gained from Pisa's recapture was primarily a boost to her self-esteem.

While Florentines dreamed of past glories, France and Spain vied for
supremacy on the peninsula, thrashing about like two great beasts, destroying everything in the vicinity. Cities were ruined almost as an afterthought; governments were overthrown; and along the length and breadth
of Italy, the countryside was despoiled by armies that found it more profit-

able, and a good deal safer, to prey upon the civilian population than to meet their adversaries in battle. Given the potential that Florence herself might well be trampled, her obsession with recapturing her longtime enemy seems myopic.

Spain and France were undeniably the two greatest military powers on the Italian peninsula, but the dominant personality of the moment was Pope Julius II. Born to a poor family in Albiola, a small fishing village near Genoa, he had succeeded his uncle as Cardinal of San Pietro in Vincoli (Saint Peter in Chains) when the latter was elected Pope Sixtus IV(1471–84). Unlike Cesare Borgia, who shed his cardinal's robes before making a career as a soldier, Giuliano della Rovere (as he was called then) strapped his breastplate over his priestly vestments to lead the papal armies against the enemies of the Church. Ascending the throne following a decade-long exile in France during the reign of the Borgia Pope, the sixty-year-old Pontiff demonstrated through his militant defense of papal prerogatives that the passage of years had done nothing to dull his warrior spirit.

In *The Prince*, Machiavelli uses Julius to illustrate a point about the necessity of matching the man to the moment: "Pope Julius II acted impetuously in everything he did. He found the times and the situation conformed so well to this approach that things always ended happily for him." His pugnacious nature, the ferocity that earned him the nickname *Il Papa Terribile* (The Terrifying Pope), may have fit the mood of the times, but his campaign to impose his will on the motley assortment of territories that made up his vast domain seemed likely to unsettle further an already unsettled situation.

Julius was in many ways an admirable figure. He shared with his predecessors—in particular with Sixtus and Alexander—a lust for conquest and an apparent indifference to the spiritual dimensions of his office. But unlike those paragons of the nepotistic impulse, Julius did not look on the Church simply as a vehicle to enrich his own family but as a worthy end in itself. As Machiavelli put it: "Julius not only pursued the same goals [as Alexander] but he added to them. He hoped to win Bologna, defeat the Venetians, and chase the French out of Italy; and in all these endeavors he succeeded—gaining all the more praise since everything he achieved was for the Church, and not for his own private gain." The contrast with Valentino is telling: while the Borgia prince renounced his priestly vows to pursue his own personal aggrandizement, Julius, though equally aggressive, always viewed himself as a soldier toiling on behalf of a revitalized papacy.

In the realm of the arts, where he had the power to command the service of the age's most talented men, he presided over unparalleled creativity, but even here his ambitions were often undermined by a restless spirit that led him to launch grandiose projects only to lose interest to a new enthusiasm. In 1506 he laid the cornerstone for a monumental new edifice to replace the crumbling Basilica of St. Peter (dating from late antiquity), destined to become the largest and most splendid church in Christendom. This was only the first step in a project of urban renewal that was meant to restore Rome to her ancient imperial grandeur. In pursuit of this ambitious goal he summoned Michelangelo from Florence (where he was busy making drawings for *The Battle of Cascina* in the Hall of the Great Council) first to work on his tomb and then to paint the ceiling of the Sistine Chapel.* In art, as in life, Julius was used to getting his way and, surrounded by the greatest geniuses of the age, including the architect Donato Bramante, who created the initial designs for the great basilica, and Raphael, whom he brought to Rome to fresco the chambers and audience rooms of the Vatican, he was largely successful.

In the vastly more complicated realm of Italian politics, where the egos were equally massive but the players more numerous and less tractable, Julius would have a much more difficult time arranging things to his liking. The application of an iron will to issues calling for pliability, nuance, and the capacity to compromise would lead to more tribulation for the already battered nation. But in truth, the problem lay less in the character of the man currently sitting on the papal throne than in the nature of the institution itself. The pope was an anomaly within Italy and unique among the great lords of Europe. He was both the ruler of one of the five major states of the peninsula—jockeying for position with his peers from Milan, Venice, Florence, and Naples—but also the head of Europe's most powerful bureaucracy and spiritual guide for all of Western Christendom.†

---

* The clash of wills and of egos that resulted is memorably evoked in Irving Stone's *The Agony and the Ecstasy.*

† The Pope's title to large swaths of territory in central Italy was based largely on a document known as *The Donation of Constantine.* The document, purportedly dictated by the first Christian emperor of Rome, Constantine I, granted the Pope lordship over large tracts and transformed the Pope into a

Wearing these multiple and mismatched hats, he could not fulfill his role as father to his spiritual flock while protecting his interests as a secular prince; nor could he rule effectively in his own territory when so many of his resources and so much of his attention were directed to far-flung lands. No one saw these contradictions more clearly than Machiavelli, who wrote eloquently about the destructive role of the papacy in Italian history. "It is the Church," he wrote in *The Discourses*,

> *that has kept, and keeps, Italy divided. . . . For, though the Church has its headquarters in Italy and has temporal power, neither its power nor its virtue has been sufficiently great for it to be able to usurp power in Italy and become its leader; nor yet, on the other hand, has it been so weak that it could not, when afraid of losing its dominion over things temporal, call upon one of the powers to defend it against an Italian state that had become too powerful. . . . The Church, then, has neither been able to occupy the whole of Italy, nor has allowed anyone else to occupy it. Consequently, it has been the cause why Italy has never come under one head, but has been under many princes and* signori, *by whom such disunion and such weakness has been brought about, that it has now become prey, not only of barbarian potentates, but of anyone who attack it. For which our Italians have to thank the Church, and nobody else.*

Machiavelli was not alone in his resentment of the Church; in fact his views were fairly typical of Florentines, who too often had suffered at the hands of their erratic neighbor. But he was bolder than most in venting his anger in public, an audacity that won him the eternal hostility of an institution whose many powers included that of branding its critics not as only wrongheaded but positively evil.

Julius's reign added to Machiavelli's argument. The Pope's determination to reinvigorate the Church, though it was a welcome change from the purely selfish policies pursued by Alexander, plunged Italy into new turmoil. The first salvo in his campaign was aimed squarely at Valentino,

---

secular as well as spiritual prince. By Machiavelli's day, many scholars—including most prominently Lorenzo Valla—suspected that the *Donation* was a medieval forgery, but the Pope would not countenance any challenges to its authenticity.

a task in which the Pope's personal inclinations happily aligned with his official duties. With Valentino out of the way, however, others leapt into the vacuum. Quickest to profit from the collapse of Valentino's empire in the Romagna were the Venetians, who swooped in and snapped up the papal dependencies of Faenza and Rimini. This cheeky bit of opportunism inevitably put the Most Serene Republic on a collision course with the new Pope, who had not maneuvered his entire life to obtain the papal tiara only to see his possessions filched by a nation of arrogant merchants.

Florence also had reason to fear the Venetians since a major commercial competitor now stood firmly astride their most important trade routes. One of Machiavelli's tasks during his embassy to Rome in 1503 had been to encourage the new Pope to take a hard line with Venice. In truth, Machiavelli didn't have to work hard to stoke the anger of the Pope, who told him through clenched teeth "that he would in no way tolerate such an injury to the Church." Not content with presenting a dry recitation of his conversation with the Pope, Machiavelli offered the Ten a more expansive vision of what was at stake: "And I make, in short, the following prediction, that what the Venetians have done in seizing Faenza will either open for them a door on to all of Italy, or it will be their ruin."

Perhaps he should have sent this warning instead to Venice, since he seemed to have a better grasp of what they had stirred up than the Venetians did. On December 10, 1508, Julius announced his latest version of a Holy League, this one aimed squarely at the Most Serene Republic of Venice. The new alliance was holy only in the sense that it had been arranged by the Pope; in every other respect it was a cynical arrangement that appealed to the signatories' greed rather than serving any higher purpose. Julius's alliance united long-standing enemies—including the Holy Roman Emperor and the Kings of Spain and France—by promising to each a portion of the rich lands that Venice now held across the length of Italy. To the Pope would go the cities illegally seized in the Romagna; to Emperor Maximillian the mountainous region of the Friuli; Louis coveted the northern cities of Brescia, Bergamo, and Cremona, while Ferdinand of Aragon would acquire the southern Italian ports that Venice had seized as part of her campaign to dominate the Adriatic coastline. The League of Cambrai, as it came to be called, was the most formidable alliance ever forged in Europe, at least on paper, though like any team made up of large egos it suffered from too many would-be leaders and too few willing to be led. Even with this handicap the coalition was strong enough to dominate the forces Venice could bring against them. On May 14, 1509, at Agnadello—near Cremona—league forces under Gian Giacomo Trivulzio routed the Venetians, largely because one Venetian captain, Niccolò Orsini, refused at the critical moment to come to the aid of his colleague Bartolommeo D'Alviano. Though the capital remained safe within its lagoon, "Venice lost in a single day the fruit of eight hundred years of painful toil," as Machiavelli put it in *The Prince*. The Venetian diarist Marino Sanudo recorded the reaction when the news was announced in the Doge's Palace:

> *At twenty-two hours Piero Mazaruol, a secretary, came running in with letters in his hand from the battlefield, with many gallows drawn on them. Thereupon the doge and the savi read the letters and learned that our forces had been routed. And there began a great weeping and lamentation and, to put it better, a sense of panic. Indeed, they were as dead men.*

But while the battle appeared decisive, nothing was ever that simple in the tangled web of Italian politics. In fact the victors were immediately disoriented by their sudden victory, while the magnitude of the disaster steeled the resolve of the defeated. The resilience of the Venetians was demonstrated when, in July, they reconquered Padua. Though Maximillian attempted a quick counterstroke, Machiavelli, remembering his own experience at the imperial court the year before, warned the Florentine ambassadors at the Emperor's court not to make any commitments since Maximillian "very often undid in the evening that which he had done in the morning."

Despite Machiavelli's warnings, the government, deploying its favorite tactic, decided to buy off the Emperor. Adding insult to injury, in November Machiavelli himself was ordered to Verona bearing the second installment of the 40,000 ducats the Florentine ambassadors had promised.

His journey through the territories recently held by the Venetians provided him with one more lesson in the horrors of war. "The invading soldiers have set to robbing and plundering the country," Machiavelli wrote to the Ten, "and I hear and see terrible things such as I have never known of before." He recalled the gruesome scenes he witnessed in his poem "On Ambition":

> *Let him turn his eyes here who wishes to behold the sorrows of*
> *others, and let him consider if ever before now the sun has*
> *looked upon such savagery.*
> *A man is weeping for his father dead and a woman for her*
> *husband; another man, beaten and naked, you see driven in*
> *sadness from his own dwelling.*
> *Oh how many times, when the father has held his son tight in*
> *his arms, a single thrust has pierced the breasts of them both! . . .*
> *Foul with blood are the ditches and streams, full of heads, of*
> *legs, of arms, and other members gashed and severed.*
> *Birds of prey, wild beasts, dogs are now their family tombs—*
> *Oh tombs repulsive, horrible and unnatural!*

As he traveled through the Veneto he observed unrest in both town and country as forces of the Holy League tried to maintain their hold on the territories won from Venice. The resistance of the local population to the foreigners convinced him that his initial assessment had been correct, that the forces of the Emperor and his allies were losing ground and those of Venice were resurgent. Writing to his superiors in the Palazzo della Signoria he offered a cogent analysis of the situation based not on the traditional measures of armies and economic resources, but in terms of a class struggle. Because the Venetians in their empire had protected the *popolo* from exploitation by the local nobility, the peasants and laborers would remain fiercely loyal to their former overlords: "And thus so great a desire of death or vengeance has entered into the souls of these country folk, that they are become more hardened and enraged against the enemies of the Venetians, than were the Jews against the Romans; and it daily happens that some one of them, being taken prisoner, submits to death rather than deny the name of Venice. . . . Therefore, all things considered, it is impossible for those monarchs to hold these lands so long as the peasants have breath."

This conclusion must have surprised his bosses, who, like most well-informed observers, believed that the Battle of Agnadello spelled the end of Venice as a major power. But Machiavelli peered beneath the surface

and discovered deeper currents. In addition to the elements of class warfare that worked against the forces of the league, Venice's resurgence was
abetted by the nature of the coalition arrayed against it, a forced partnership among incompatible partners held together only by a common greed.

Nowhere was this more apparent than in the actions of the Pope himself. Julius had been the driving force behind the coalition, but now that
he had properly chastened the arrogant Venetians he began to regret the
monster he had summoned to do the job. Like Machiavelli, Julius was
an ardent nationalist at heart. His first loyalty was to the church he commanded, but he also cared deeply about the larger Italian nation—an as yet
amorphous concept that was based not so much on political as linguistic
and cultural bonds. No matter how often they were at each other's throats,
Italians remained convinced of their own superiority to those uncultured
louts who despoiled their lands and pillaged their cities. The obvious fact
that they possessed more of the civilized virtues than their tormentors
merely made the humiliation harder to bear. Guicciardini expressed the
common view that, like the ancient Israelites punished by God for their
transgressions, Italians were the authors of their own troubles, for "if these
powers had not been blinded by private greed and had not destroyed the
common weal with shame and harm also to themselves, there is no doubt
that Italy, restored to its pristine glory by their counsels and resources,
would have been safe for many years from the attacks of foreign nations."
Machiavelli shared with his friend and colleague the conviction that Italy's
travails were the outward manifestation of an inner rot, but he also believed in ultimate redemption, a hope to which he gives eloquent voice in
the ringing exhortation that ends *The Prince*:

Against barbarian rage,
Virtue will take the field; then short the fight;
True to their lineage,
Italian hearts will prove their Roman might.

Similar sentiments lodged somewhere in Julius's breast, no matter
how deviously he went about achieving his goal. Having just encouraged foreign powers to help themselves to broad swaths of native soil, he
now made an about-face and launched a campaign in which his former

enemies became his friends, his former allies his sworn enemies. "*Fuori i barbari!*" (Out with the barbarians) was the new rallying cry as he cut a deal with Venice to drive out the Emperor and the French, whom he had previously emboldened.

For Florence the sudden realignment proved particularly uncomfortable. While nominally allied with papal forces, the city had remained on the sidelines during the War of the League of Cambrai—which was just the way the Florentines preferred things. But a war between her traditional ally, France, and her southern neighbor, the Pope, was likely to stretch even Florence's elastic foreign policy to the breaking point.

Trying to ease the strain placed on Florentine diplomacy would occupy Machiavelli for the foreseeable future, but before grappling with these difficult matters he would have to deal with a crisis closer to home. On December 20, 1509, a masked man, accompanied by two witnesses, went to the house of the notary of conservators in Florence to denounce the Second Chancellor and declare that he was, and had always been, ineligible for the office he now held. "[He] contended that having been born of a father, etc.," Buonaccorsi reported to his friend, "you can in no way exercise the office that you hold, etc." Though his friends had rallied around him and, so far, had been able to beat back the challenge, Buonaccorsi urged Machiavelli "not to make a joke of it" since "your adversaries are numerous and will stop at nothing."

The nature of the charge is not spelled out by Buonaccorsi, though apparently the scandal was so well known that it was being talked about "even in the whorehouses." Given the reference to Machiavelli's father, it is likely that his enemies were challenging him on the grounds that Bernardo was *a specchio*, that is prohibited from holding office due to unpaid taxes. Since Niccolò had assumed his father's debts as well as his assets upon Bernardo's death, he, too, his accusers claimed, should be barred from the Palazzo della Signoria.

The timing of the incident is significant. Bernardo Machiavelli's troubles were old news. The fact that they were dredged up at this particular moment suggests a politically motivated attack on the part of the growing, if still largely underground, movement directed at the Gonfaloniere and the man who was now often referred to as Soderini's "hatchet man." The anonymity of the denunciation was disconcerting since Machiavelli had no opportunity to confront his accuser, but it was also reassuring since it implied that the mysterious figure lacked the support to move openly against him. In the end the scandal blew over and Machiavelli remained in his job, but it was an ominous sign.

In June 1510, Piero Soderini sent Machiavelli back to the French court. In the upcoming battle between King Louis and the Pope, Soderini would adopt the usual Florentine policy of delay and distraction, an evasive tactic that, Machiavelli had long ago discovered, always seem to irritate those toward whom it was directed. Though his natural inclination was to back the French, Florence's traditional ally, in his secret instructions Soderini reminded his assistant that "although the Pope as a friend is not worth much, as an enemy he can do much harm." Arriving at Lyons on July 7, Machiavelli dispatched a letter with the usual disclaimer that he expected to achieve nothing "save that of keeping your Excellencies well informed of all that happens from day to day."

Machiavelli's pessimism was well founded. Not surprisingly, Louis had little patience for Florentine equivocations. "[T]here is no way out," Machiavelli informed the Ten after a tense encounter with the king. "[The French] seek to entangle you in this war." On August 9 he wrote again: "Your Excellencies may believe, as they believe the Gospel, that should there be war between the Pope and this sovereign, you will not be able to avoid declaring for one side or the other."

It was not enough, however, to urge his compatriots to take decisive action. An even more critical task was to encourage a little less decisiveness on the part of the French, which he did by reminding the King's advisers how securing an Italian empire always appeared simpler on paper than it proved to be in fact. The problem, as he saw it, was that "if they make war alone, they know what they bring upon themselves; but that if they engage in it with allies, they will have to share Italy with them, and therefore be involved in a greater and more dangerous war among themselves." This is typical of Machiavelli's analysis, which dispenses with all piety and pageantry in favor of a dry account of exactly where each party's interest lay.

It is doubtful whether anyone at the French court appreciated being lectured by this underpaid emissary of a second-rate power, but some at least recognized the wisdom of his words, shifting to a strategy that avoided an all-out military clash. This more cautious approach involved striking the Pope where he appeared strongest—at the aura of sanctity that gave him a standing among the lords of Europe out of all proportion to his tangible assets. Calling for a church council to sit in judgment of the reigning Pontiff, the French intended to raise questions of simony in regard to his election (a charge to which Julius, like all his predecessors, was vulnerable) as well as enumerating other crimes against his holy office. Thus Julius would be forced into a war on two fronts, defending his legitimacy as a spiritual leader while sparring with the French on the field of battle.

Machiavelli returned to Florence in October, much relieved to be done with the onerous and unprofitable mission, though the ill humor of the city was such that he might soon have wished he were back on the road. In the months he had been away discontent with the regime continued to build. The mood had grown so ugly, in fact, that according to one diarist the Eight (in charge of state security) could no longer walk in the streets for fear they would be attacked. The civil discord reflected both a general anxiety about the future and a hardening of differences that had always existed between oligarchic and democratic factions. Soderini was accused of favoring "new men" at the expense of the wealthy clans who traditionally dominated the halls of power, and of being a demagogue who harbored dictatorial ambitions. Nor did the recent success of the Pisan war work entirely to the government's benefit since it increased suspicion that Machiavelli's militia might become an instrument of tyranny.

Opposition to Soderini's regime now began to coalesce around that most magical—and most reviled—name in Florentine history: *Medici*. While there had always been a minority among the elite who favored the return of the city's former ruling family, these men—sometimes referred to as the *bigi*, sometimes as the *palleschi* (named for the red balls, *palle*, that formed the Medici crest)—knew the torment of a love that dared not speak its name. Since the majority still despised the Medici, their secret admirers, though an important constituency within the oligarchic faction, remained little more than a hidden cabal, fearful and conspiratorial. Young pro-Medici hooligans had been among the most militant agitators against Savonarola and his regime, but while they succeeded in destroying the hated preacher, the government that replaced him turned out to be equally hostile to their aims.

In the early days of their campaign the *palleschi* were not helped by the man whose cause they championed. Whenever they seemed to be making progress, Piero de' Medici would engage in some clumsy attempt to overthrow the republican government by force, discrediting his supporters within the city and leading at least a few of them to the gallows. Piero's death was a godsend to Medici sympathizers. Once the family was in the more capable hands of his younger brother, Cardinal Giovanni, the *palleschi* could state their preferences with more candor.

Though the climate now appeared more favorable, the *palleschi* did not entirely abandon their conspiratorial ways. On December 22, 1510, the state police uncovered a plot to assassinate the Gonfaloniere, led by known Medici sympathizer Prinzivalle della Stufa. Though the plot was unraveled before it could get off the ground, it offered further evidence of growing restlessness within the upper reaches of the ruling class.

Machiavelli spent much of the winter of 1511–12 building up the militia, spurred to new exertions by the increasingly dangerous international situation. The war between the Pope and France continued to simmer in the Romagna, next door to Tuscany, with possession of the strategic city of Bologna passing back and forth more than once. In October 1511, Julius declared another Holy League—this time directed at the Most Christian King of France—from the pulpit of the church of Santa Maria del Popolo in Rome, with the ambassadors of Spain and Venice on hand to demonstrate their solidarity.

While Florence hoped to repeat its performance in the League of Cambrai, standing aside to let others do the fighting, France was determined not to let the city off the hook. Louis increased the pressure on the republic by insisting that the church council he was organizing meet in Florentine-controlled Pisa. As far as Florence was concerned the only point to this otherwise futile exercise was to arouse the Pope's fury at Florence for serving as host. Again Machiavelli was dispatched to the court of the French King in an effort to extricate Florence from its predicament. The one heartening sign was that there seemed little stomach among the cardinals for the schismatic council. Most remained either overtly hostile to the project or strangely reluctant to answer their mail. The only ones who showed any enthusiasm were three or four French cardinals, who were regarded as stooges of their King. In his pocket Machiavelli carried a note setting out the difficulties of Florence's situation:

No one shows any wish to attend the Council, and therefore it only serves to irritate the Pope against us; and for this reason we make a request either that it shall not sit at Pisa, or shall at least be suspended for the present. No prelate seems to be coming from Germany; from France very few and very slowly. And it is a matter of universal astonishment to see a Council proclaimed by three Cardinals only, while the few others who were said to adhere to it, dissimulate their opinions and defer their arrival. . . . If, therefore, there should be no hope of agreement between the Pope and the King, and if the latter cannot be persuaded to desist altogether, he should at least be induced to delay for two or three months.

When Machiavelli met with the King in Blois, Louis showed little sympathy for his predicament, demanding that the government of Florence offer safe passage to those few cardinals willing to stick their necks out. Predictably, the Pope retaliated by placing Florence under interdict, a threat that on other occasions had almost brought the republic to its knees. But in the end the council proved to be something of a fiasco and the Pope was soon distracted by more pressing matters: so few cardinals attended that it was more of an embarrassment to the French King than a threat to Julius, who simply ignored the schismatic churchmen.

Frustrated in his attempts to depose the Pope by bureaucratic means, Louis, throwing aside Machiavelli's more cautious counsel, now opted for a frontal assault. In the winter of 1512 a new army of invasion, led by the King's brilliant twenty-three-year-old nephew, Gaston de Foix, marched across the Alps and onto the Lombard plains. Included among the vast host was a token force of three hundred Florentine lances.

On April 12, in fields near the Adriatic port of Ravenna, French forces under Foix met the army of the Holy League led by Ramón de Cardona, Viceroy of Naples. It was the kind of battle Machiavelli approved of—hard-fought and bloody. Of an earlier confrontation he noted with satisfaction that "it was fought with more virtue than any other that had been fought for fifty years in Italy, for in it, between one side and the other, more than a thousand men died." Measured by this dismal standard—between ten and twenty thousand were left dead on the field—the Battle of Ravenna was a notable success. Indeed it bore little resemblance to the typical skirmishes of fifteenth-century warfare, anticipating instead the sanguinary orgies of later centuries.

Throughout the hotly contested battle the small Florentine contingent performed so poorly that the King complained to the ambassador that they failed to pull even their modest weight. His sour mood was provoked, perhaps, by the perplexing and thoroughly discouraging results of the confrontation. Though the French drove the papal army from the field, they lost their young commander, Foix, killed in a skirmish with retreating Spanish infantry. Loss of the dashing general was a blow from which they could not recover, particularly when in the coming months Julius reinforced his army with twenty thousand additional Swiss infantry. Despite their glorious victory, the French were soon, to quote a contemporary witness, "flying like mist before the wind." It was a repetition of 1494, when early French victories were followed by defeat as a combination of local powers, backed by the might of Spain, harried the overextended and overtaxed forces of the King. Parma, Piacenza, and Bologna were lost in quick succession as the French army fled for home. Julius, the "Warrior Pope," had proven himself once again a master tactician. "Out with the barbarians!" was his battle cry, and the sight of the French army turning tail must have filled his heart with joy. But the fact that this victory was accomplished only with the help of many thousands of Swiss and Spanish troops—foreigners who showed no signs of joining their fellow barbarians in departing Italian soil—demonstrates the limitations of the Pope's wider strategic vision, which achieved short-term victories at the risk of long-term goals.

Among the greatest losers to emerge from the French debacle was Florence, whose contingent of three hundred lances had been too meager to please the King but too prominent to avoid becoming a target of papal wrath. News from Mantua, where the members of the league were meeting to divvy up the prizes, turned ominous when Florence's ambassador, Giovan Vittorio Soderini, reported the arrival of Cardinal Giovanni de' Medici and his younger brother, Giuliano. Reciting to all who cared to listen to the long list of missteps and misdeeds by the current government of Florence, the Medici brothers drummed up support for a proposed expedition against their native city. They were joined in this effort by Pope Julius, who publicly called for the resignation of Piero Soderini and his government,

though even with the papal sanction the gathering army seemed less an official campaign than an expedition of freebooters. Offering 10,000 ducats
as a down payment, Cardinal Giovanni finally managed to assemble about
five thousand professional soldiers, hiring the victorious Ramón de Cardona to lead the ragtag band.

This was the direct thrust at Florence that Machiavelli and his colleagues had long feared and had strained every fiber to avoid. But having
backed the wrong horse there was little they could do but gird for battle.
The limitations of diplomacy had been reached, and now they would have
to depend on their own soldiers, who, despite a few notable successes, had
done little to show they could withstand a professional army bent on their
destruction.

To meet the threat, the Eight issued a decree meant to expand the
number of soldiers in the militia and turn them into a fighting force that
could compete on equal terms with the professionals they would soon be
facing: "Seeing the great utility of the Infantry Ordinance [it read], desiring to ensure the safety of the present government and liberty amid the
dangers to which they are now exposed, the Nine are hereby empowered
to enlist under our banners for the entire year 1512, no less than 500 light
horse, armed either with crossbows or matchlocks at the pleasure of the
men; ten percent of the number may be armed with lances." After years of
cautious support, the government was now finally committed to a citizen
militia as the best means of defending their lives and liberty. The task of
preparing their defenses fell once again to Machiavelli, who spent much of
the spring of 1512 in the saddle, traveling about the countryside, recruiting soldiers in Pisa, Arezzo, and Poggio Imperiale, and inspecting the
frontier forts at Valiano and Monte San Savino.

As Spanish forces accompanied by the Medici brothers approached the
borders of Tuscany in August 1512, Florence had reason to hope it might
yet avert disaster. The army led by Viceroy de Cordona was small—num-
bering about five thousand infantry and another two hundred heavily
equipped men-at-arms—far outnumbered by Machiavelli's beefed-up
militia. In addition, the invaders were a motley crew, ill fed and ill supplied. So uncertain was Cordona that victory could be achieved that instead of launching a direct assault on Prato—the city some thirteen miles
north of Florence, where the bulk of the militia was gathered to meet the

invaders—he sent emissaries to the Signoria to see if they might arrive at a negotiated settlement. Their demands, while not unreasonable for an army on the verge of certain victory, seemed harsh when the outcome was uncertain. Cordona insisted not only that the Medici be allowed to return to the city as private citizens, but that Soderini and his pro-French regime be deposed; and, to compensate him for the inconvenience he had already been put through, he demanded a fee of 100,000 ducats—a repetition of the extortion to which Florence was regularly subjected.

Meanwhile, in the increasingly restive capital, Soderini moved against the internal opposition whose disloyalty increased as the distance between the Spanish forces and the city walls shrank. Twenty-five of the most prominent pro-Medici stalwarts, many of whom were in direct contact with the Cardinal and his brother, were rounded up and thrown into prison. Upon learning of the terms demanding his resignation, Soderini called a special session of the Great Council where he offered to sacrifice himself for the sake of peace. "To test the mood of the people," Machiavelli reported in a letter he wrote a month after the events,[*] "[Soderini] assembled the entire council and explained to them what had been proposed, offering to abide by their will. And should they decide that his departure would hasten the restoration of peace, he would return to his home." Soderini almost certainly knew his offer would be rejected. It was one of those grand gestures that politicians often engage in to rally support and garner sympathy, a ploy that apparently proved successful since, as Machiavelli continued, "[e]veryone rejected this and even expressed their willingness to offer up their lives in his defense."

For the moment Florence was buoyed by an uncommon sense of unity and purpose, but beneath the confident surface were gnawing doubts about the city's capacity to withstand the assault. Machiavelli himself admitted: "It was decided initially not to deploy these men in the countryside, because they were not deemed strong enough to resist the enemy." Despite their improved armaments and greater numbers, the militias

---

[*] The letter in which Machiavelli recalls the events leading to the downfall of the Soderini government is addressed simply "To a Noblewoman." Many scholars believe it was written to Isabella d'Este, the brilliant and cultured wife of Francesco Gonzaga, Marquis of Mantua (see Machiavelli et al., *Machiavelli and His Friends*, note 1, p. 495). Others believe it was meant for Alfonsina Orsini, widow of Piero de' Medici.

suffered from a lack of leadership and experience in the heat of battle. Guicciardini, writing with the wisdom of hindsight, was harsher in his judgment, asserting that the forces Florence was relying on for her salvation "were of such a sort, that never in the memory of man had there existed any less worthy of their pay."

With the negotiations at an impasse, Cordona decided to test the mettle of these green troops and assaulted the walls of Prato. But with little in the way of artillery, the attack was repulsed with ease, much to the jubilation of the Florentines. So discouraged was the Viceroy that he almost abandoned the entire campaign. Hoping, however, to salvage one last scrap of honor from what appeared to be a major fiasco, he sent a second delegation to Florence with a proposal to withdraw his forces in exchange for the paltry sum of 3,000 ducats—a far cry from the 100,000 he demanded only a few days earlier—in addition to bread to feed his half-starved troops and a lifting of the banishment of the Medici. Unfortunately, the circumstances that forced Cordona to sweeten the terms made Soderini and his colleagues less inclined to accept them. Years later Machiavelli harshly criticized his old boss's rejection of this proposal, though there is no indication that he spoke up at the time. He discusses Soderini's brave but foolish refusal in *The Discourses* in a chapter titled "Prudent Princes and Republics should be content with Victory, for, when they are not content with it, they usually lose." If what Cordona was offering Soderini was something less than victory, it was, as Machiavelli pointed out, something close to it. Accusing his compatriots of excessive pride, Machiavelli wrote that "[r]ulers of states, when attacked . . . cannot make a greater mistake than to refuse to come to terms when the forces attacking them are a good deal stronger than their own, especially if overtures are made by the enemy."

Of course the problem was that the superiority of the Spanish forces was far from obvious at the time the decision had to be made. Cordona had dropped his most onerous conditions precisely because he himself doubted he could achieve victory. But Machiavelli is correct when he points out that Soderini's rejection was foolhardy. There were in fact plenty of signs that a renewed assault on Prato would yield different results. Florentine stinginess over the years when it came to equipping and training its troops left serious deficiencies in the ranks. The city had agreed to supply squads with matchlocks, for example, but had provided so little ammunition that they were forced to strip lead from the roofs of the houses of Prato to make bullets.

Having received word of the rejection, and with the situation of his army ever more desperate, Cordona decided to make one last attempt on the city. Late in the afternoon of Sunday, August 29, 1512, the Spaniards began bombarding the walls of Prato and managed to create a small gap in the defenses. Where professional troops would have quickly sealed the breach, Machiavelli's green militiamen panicked at the first sight of the Spaniards surging forward, abandoning their posts and leaving the city to the mercy of these half-starved warriors. Like many a besieging army, the victors exacted a fearful revenge on the population whose stubbornness had contributed to their discomfort. Machiavelli recalled the mournful scene: "[A]fter minimal resistance, all fled, and the Spaniards, having occupied the city, then proceeded to sack it and massacre the men, a miserable spectacle of calamity. . . . More than four thousand died; the rest were taken and made, through various means, to pay ransom. Nor did they spare the virgins cloistered in holy sites, which were scenes of rape and pillage."

Catastrophic as this was for the citizens of Prato, it might prove equally calamitous for the Florentines, who were now without means to defend themselves against a foreign army that had just showed its cruelty. Florence might have anticipated some mercy from Cardinal de' Medici, who had no reason to reduce to rubble the city he had spent much of his adult life trying to reclaim, but had the citizens of Florence been able to read a letter he wrote to the Pope a week or so after the sack they would have found little comfort: "The taking of Prato, so speedily and cruelly," he told Julius, "although it has given me pain, will at least have the good effect of serving as an example and a terror to the others."

The "others" were the Florentines, who, much to the Cardinal's satisfaction, seemed to be taking the lesson to heart. "[E]veryone began to fear a sack," Machiavelli recalled, tacitly accepting some responsibility by admitting that the calamity was due largely to "the cowardice of our soldiers." The mood in the city was approaching full-scale panic: respectable women checked themselves into convents; rich merchants fled the city with their valuables; and the guards at the Palazzo della Signoria charged with protecting the government abandoned their posts. Even more encouraging from the Cardinal's point of view were the crowds of *palleschi* who now streamed into the streets and the piazzas proclaiming their devotion to the Medici cause. The old chant *"Palle! Palle!"* rang through the streets and squares of Florence once more. Political fortunes were turned topsy-turvy as Soderini's supporters were shouted down and overwhelmed by the suddenly emboldened adherents of the former ruling family.

Also emboldened was Cordona. When Florentine envoys arrived in Prato, they found that the Viceroy's demands had grown with his victory. Not only did he now insist they pay him 60,000 florins (soon raised to 120,000) for his troubles, but he told them that Soderini must resign and the Medici be immediately reinstated. The proposal was made slightly more palatable by maintaining the fiction that the Medici were to return to the city merely as private citizens, but once inside Florence, surrounded by their jubilant supporters and with Spanish troops within shouting distance outside the walls, no one doubted who the new bosses would be. Though Soderini himself was initially tempted to reject the demand, "relying," as Machiavelli scoffed, "on idle dreams of his own," the ground was swiftly crumbling beneath his feet. Only days earlier Soderini had stood before the Great Council and won overwhelming support for his defiance, but faced with an almost certain repetition of the horrors visited on Prato, public opinion swung decisively against him. A more direct form of pressure was applied when a group of young aristocrats with ties to the Medici broke into the Gonfaloniere's apartments in the palace and threatened to run him through with their swords unless he released their twenty-five imprisoned colleagues. By the morning of Tuesday, August 31, only two days after the fall of Prato, Soderini conceded the game was lost. Rather than engage in what would almost certainly have been a bloody and ultimately unsuccessful resistance, he chose the only sensible course. Summoning Machiavelli, he asked him to approach their mutual friend Francesco Vettori. Though Vettori, who had served with Machiavelli on the mission to the Emperor four years earlier, had ties to the current government, he was also related to the Medici and was known to be sympathetic to their cause. Hurrying to the palace around midday, Vettori met with an evidently shaken Gonfaloniere in his private apartments. Soderini informed him that he had decided to step down but was concerned for his own safety and that of his family. Vettori agreed to allow him the use of his own house during the perilous hours while final arrangements were being made. It was only after the Gonfaloniere had slipped quietly out of the palace that Vettori went before the Signoria and recounted their conversation. At first they refused to depose Soderini, until Vettori explained to them that if he did not resign immediately he would surely be assassinated. No one, in the end, had the stomach for violent confrontation. The *palleschi* were sober in their triumph, supporters of the republican government glum but resigned. A few hours later—accompanied by Vettori and an escort of forty cavalry—Soderini left the city by the Roman Gate and set out on the road that led to Siena and a life of exile.

Machiavelli was not unhappy to see him go. He remained ambivalent about his former boss, believing that he was a genuinely good man but that he lacked the backbone to be a real leader. His most reasoned postmortem on Soderini's career comes in Book III of *The Discourses*: "Piero Soderini . . . conducted all his affairs in a good-natured and patient way. So long as circumstances suited the way in which he carried on, both he and his country prospered. But when afterwards there came a time which required him to drop his patience and his humility, he could not bring himself to do it; so that both he and his country were ruined." He was, in fact, an prime example of a man unable to adapt "in conformity with the times." Machiavelli had little patience for well-meaning incompetents since they often cause more suffering than those who are deliberately cruel. His final verdict was harsh. Upon hearing of Soderini's death in 1522, Machiavelli composed a little verse that suggests a certain contempt for a man whose indecisiveness cost him and his city dearly:

> *The night that Piero Soderini ceased to breathe,*
> *His soul journeyed to the mouth of Hell;*
> *But Pluto cried: "Thou foolish soul,*
> *No Hell for thee! Go seek the Limbo of the babes!*

Though Soderini's regime outlived him by a few days, it was clear to everyone that one era had passed and a new one was beginning. On the first day of September, to the shouts of *"Palle! Palle!"* from the crowds lining the street, Giuliano de' Medici returned to the city of his birth, his beard, which he had recently grown in the Spanish fashion, shaved to demon-

strate his desire to abide by local customs. As he walked the streets of Florence, unaccompanied by those retinues so beloved by powerful men, his
manner was respectful, his dress and comportment modest, winning him
praise among citizens who remembered the high-handed manner of his
brother Piero.

While Giuliano charmed everyone with his affable manner, his supporters, reinvigorated after their years in the shadows, began to flex their
muscle. On the same day that Giuliano returned, and as the new Signoria
prepared to take their seats, Luca Landucci watched as "all the citizens
who considered themselves friends of the Medici, assembled at the door
of the *Palagio* and in the Piazza, all fully armed, and barred every way into
the Piazza." With the *palleschi* mustered menacingly on the doorstep, free
and open debate in the Great Council was impossible.

In fact the government remained rudderless until September 14, when
Cardinal Giovanni de' Medici, accompanied by four hundred lances and
one thousand foot soldiers, made his triumphal entrance to the cheers of
thousands of his supporters. Taking up residence at his boyhood home
on the Via Larga—built by his great-grandfather Cosimo and, until the
plundering that followed the Medici's expulsion, filled to the rafters with
priceless treasures of ancient and modern art—he played the role of the
reluctant suitor dragged back into political life by the tearful supplica-
tions of his fellow countrymen. Two days after his return, the Medici and
their supporters called a *parlamento*, a mass gathering of the citizens in
the Piazza della Signoria where, as if by unanimous acclaim, the people of
Florence called for a committee with special powers to reform the government. This was the oldest trick in the playbook of Florentine politics, one
often exploited by earlier generations of Medici to consolidate their power.
Though ostensibly an exercise in pure democracy, the seething mass, often
surrounded by armed men who made the consequences of dissent immediately apparent, always ratified the wishes of those already in power.
This gathering was no different from its predecessors. With one voice the
citizens of Florence proclaimed their desire for radical reform.

The *Balia*, or special committee, tasked with implementing the reforms
was comprised of forty-five leading citizens (soon expanded to sixty-six),
all of them Medici loyalists. In short order they discarded all the changes
that had occurred since 1494, reinstituting those small councils that had

been the instruments of Medici control and stocking them with their trusted followers. Guicciardini's verdict on the new government is terse. "In this way," he declared in his *History of Italy*, "the liberty of Florence was crushed by force." Even Francesco Vettori, who was sympathetic to the Medici and helped ease them back to power, was critical of the newly constituted government, complaining: "The city was reduced to the point of doing nothing save by the will of Cardinal dei Medici; and this method is the method of perfect tyranny."

As for Machiavelli, the man most closely identified with the exiled Gonfaloniere, his reaction, at least for the moment, was muted. He navigated this latest and most tumultuous storm with the imperturbability with which he had navigated those minor tempests that too often agitated the government for which he worked. Though a political animal through and through, he never regarded himself as a party man. He contemplated the quarrels that consumed his superiors with a disdainful eye, seeing in their petty squabbles the telltale signs of ravenous human ambition, but also determined to rise above them as a devoted servant of the state, whichever party temporarily gained the upper hand. The letter he wrote to an unnamed noblewoman sometime that very month offers the best window into his mood, without the coloring provided by the traumatic events still to come. After describing in rather dry terms the momentous events that had just transpired, the Second Chancellor, apparently still secure in his job, concludes on an optimistic note: "The city remains most peaceful and hopes, with the help of [the Medici], to live no less honorably than in times past, when their father Lorenzo the Magnificent, of most happy memory, governed them."

There may be an element of wishful thinking here. Machiavelli must have suspected that the big brooms currently deployed in the Palazzo might well sweep him out along with much else associated with the former regime. But his hopeful tone reveals something about how Machiavelli saw himself, as the consummate bureaucrat willing and able to serve any government. So great and simple was his patriotism that he could not conceive that anyone would regard him as other than what he was: a devoted servant of the city they all loved. The next few months would disabuse him of his naive assumption and shape his increasingly cynical worldview.

DISMISSED, DEPRIVED, AND TOTALLY REMOVED

*"I should like you to get this pleasure from these troubles of mine, that
I have borne them so straightforwardly that I am proud of myself for
it and consider myself more of a man than I believed I was."*

—MACHIAVELLI TO FRANCESCO VETTORI, MARCH 18, 1513

MACHIAVELLI'S INITIAL OPTIMISM WAS ENCOURAGED
by happy memories of his youthful friendships with members of the
Medici circle, including Giuliano himself, to whom he dedicated one of
his first literary works. Hoping to renew old acquaintances, in the first
days of the new regime Machiavelli wrote at least two letters to Giuliano's
older brother, Cardinal Giovanni de' Medici. Whether this was a sign of
complacency or a desperate attempt to ingratiate himself with those now
in charge, the tone and substance were typical of the man whose profound
psychological insight seemed to desert him when cultivating those who
could help his career. "In the belief that affection may serve as an excuse
for presumption," he began his letter to the head of the Medici family, "I
will venture to offer you this piece of advice." The matter upon which he
offered his unsolicited opinion was a particularly touchy one for the newly
reinstated lords of the city since it had to do with efforts by the family to
take back various properties that had been confiscated following their
exile. While acknowledging the legitimacy of their claims, Machiavelli
explained that "their seizure . . . will generate inextinguishable hatred, for
men feel more grief at the loss of a farm than at the death of a father or
brother, everyone knowing that no change in government can restore a

kinsman to life, but that it may easily cause a restoration of a farm." However sound, this advice was unlikely to be well received by a proud family that had endured more than a decade and a half of exile and felt entitled, at the very least, to reclaim what had been stolen from them.

Given Machiavelli's sensitivity to the myriad ways it was possible to offend and to take offense, it is remarkable how obtuse he was about his own behavior. He always overestimated people's capacity to listen to unpleasant truths, which tended to get him into trouble with his colleagues and contributed to his posthumous reputation as the world's greatest scoundrel. The caricature of Machiavelli as a man without scruple or conscience derives largely from his tendency to speak bluntly those truths that others would acknowledge only in private. Much of what Machiavelli wrote is self-evident—or at least seemed so to him—and it never occurred to him that with the facts clearly on his side he had anything to apologize for. Along with his famous cynicism, Machiavelli possessed a naïveté that assumed any opinion honestly given would be welcomed in the spirit in which it was offered.

The Cardinal was neither the first nor the last man to bristle at Machiavelli's candor, but while disinclined to entertain suggestions from a mid-level civil servant who had until recently been among the most dedicated officials of the government responsible for his exile, Giovanni appeared, at least for the moment, to have judged Machiavelli more a nuisance than a threat.

Not content with offering his opinion on the restitution of lost property, Machiavelli dashed off a second letter in which he offered his insights into the current political situation. Who wouldn't welcome pearls of wisdom, particularly when they came from one as well-placed as Machiavelli to ferret out the hidden motives of his colleagues? The Medici, he concluded, had been away so long that they had forgotten the deviousness of their compatriots, a gap in their knowledge he was only too happy to fill. Warning them to be on guard against those enemies of the former government now posing as Medici loyalists, Machiavelli condemned the *ottimati* as mere flatterers and opportunists "who can come to terms either with this or that government, for the sake of achieving power." Of course Machiavelli could fairly have been accused of the same thing, but his flexibility, as he saw it, was a matter of putting country first, while his rivals valued party over *patria*. They constituted one of those "sects" Machiavelli deplored, the kind of conspiratorial cabal whose quarrelsomeness, he pointed out in his *Florentine Histories*, left "as many dead, as many exiles, and as many families destroyed as ever occurred in any city in memory."

Machiavelli's advice to Cardinal Giovanni is perfectly reasonable and perfectly consistent. While the Medici might benefit in the short run from an alliance with the oligarchs, in the long run they risked not only revolution from below but more insidious threats from among their peers. He expands on this theme in *The Prince*, where the specific dilemma faced by the returning Medici takes the form of a general principle:

> *He who becomes prince through the help of the magnates maintains his position only with more difficulty than the man who becomes prince through the help of the people, because he will find himself surrounded by many who believe themselves his equal. . . . [I]t is not possible to justly satisfy the nobles without injuring others, but it is indeed possible to satisfy the needs of the people, since while the nobles wish to oppress them, they seek only to avoid being oppressed.*

In fact Cardinal Giovanni was well acquainted with the dangers posed by an ambitious nobility, since rebellions against Medici rule had always come from within the ruling elite,* and he might well have given more weight to the argument had it come from another source. As it was, Machiavelli's tactless presumption only added to the voices now clamoring for his dismissal.

On November 7, 1512, two and a half months after Soderini fled the city, Niccolò Machiavelli was thrown out of office. "*Cassaverunt, privaverunt et totaliter amoverunt*" (Dismissed, deprived, and totally removed) read the decree passed unanimously by the Signoria. His friend Biagio Buonaccorsi was fired the same day. Interestingly, their boss, the Chancellor of Florence, Marcello Virgilio Adriani, managed to retain his post, both because he was better connected than Machiavelli and Buonaccorsi but also because his interests were literary rather than political. During

---

* The most serious of these were the revolt of 1466 against Piero and the Pazzi Conspiracy of 1478, both led by disgruntled members of the ruling class.

his tenure in office he had accomplished little and so had stirred up little controversy. It was his underling, the consummate civil servant who had strained every fiber of his being to promote the interests of his country, who got the ax.

More penalties were soon heaped on Machiavelli. The Signoria issued a decree limiting his travel within the territory controlled by Florence and, showing how little they trusted him, demanded that he post a bond of 1,000 lire to guarantee his compliance. Upon further reflection they decided these humiliations were insufficient and banished him from the Palazzo for a year.*

His enemies continued to hound him for another few weeks, before turning their minds to more pressing matters. They had high hopes that an audit of his accounts in office would uncover evidence of corruption, all too common among the underpaid civil servants of the Chancery, but much to their disappointment they came up empty. As he told Francesco Vettori, "my poverty is a testament to my loyalty and honesty."

Angry and dispirited, Machiavelli left Florence for his country house in Sant' Andrea in Percussina, ten miles beyond the southern gates among the rolling hills clad with olive groves and vineyards.† Here, framed by the bare branches of a gray Tuscan winter, he could still see the city to which he had devoted his life and that now seemed content without him. Few visitors stopped by his rustic retreat, and those who did make the journey had little encouraging news to report. The new regime was now in firm control and bent on purging anyone suspected of harboring *popolani* sentiments. Soon, however, the attacks on Machiavelli began to die down. He was no longer a topic of discussion in the halls of the Palazzo but, what was worse, forgotten. The architect of the victory over Pisa, the familiar of popes, kings, and even an emperor, was now a nobody.

But if Machiavelli's name soon dropped from the lips of those who

---

* This final punishment was never enforced since his successors in the Chancery frequently had to suspend the ban in order to consult with him on issues that had been left uncompleted on his desk.

† Machiavelli's house and the village of Sant' Andrea in Percussina still survive much as they were. The house itself, along the road that was once the main thoroughfare through southern Tuscany, leading to the rival city of Siena, is a comfortable but rustic building of stone. It remains as it did in Machiavelli's day surrounded by grapevines and olive trees from which the master of the house made wine, vinegar, and olive oil, both for his own use and to sell in order to supplement his meager income.

wielded power in the state, there were still some who remembered the former Second Chancellor of the Republic of Florence.

Early in February 1513, three months after his dismissal and more than five since the sack of Prato, one Bernardino Coccio, a citizen of Siena, entered the Palazzo della Signoria demanding an immediate audience with the Eight, the committee in charge of state security. Ushered into their presence, he handed them a slip of paper containing the names of twenty citizens of Florence, most of them associated with the former regime. The paper had fallen, *Messer* Coccio told them, from the pocket of a young man named Pietro Paolo Boscoli while the two were guests at the house of the Lenzi family, kinsmen of the Soderini. Since Boscoli had been a vocal opponent of the Medici, the list of names took on sinister contours in the minds of the authorities.

Constables of the Eight quickly arrested Boscoli and his friend Agostino di Luca Capponi. Under torture, they confessed to being involved in a plot to assassinate Giuliano de' Medici and seize the government by force. Giuliano himself never believed the conspiracy amounted to much: "Boscoli and Capponi, young men of good families, but without followers, have been the ringleaders of the conspiracy. They meant to dispossess us; they had fixed the spot, and drawn up a list of persons with whom they thought to find favor." Even though those named were never actively involved in the conspiracy—in fact it was clear the Boscoli and Capponi never even had a chance to contact them—nonetheless they were immediately suspect in the eyes of the still insecure regime.

Seventh on Boscoli's list was Niccolò Machiavelli. The appearance of the former Second Chancellor's name on the slip of paper is hardly surprising since few men were as closely identified with the old regime, but there was never any indication that he had the faintest notion of what was afoot or would have approved had he known. Machiavelli, as we have seen, was hardly a starry-eyed idealist likely to risk his neck in a desperate scheme. Had the conspirators been able to read his mind—or leap a few years into the future when they could have read his words—they would almost certainly have crossed him off the list. Unfortunately, Machiavelli had not yet written the *Discourses*, whose chapter "On Conspiracies" makes clear how little faith he placed in such adventures: "There is . . . no enterprise in which private persons can engage," he writes, "more dangerous or more rash than is this, for it is both difficult and extremely dangerous in all its stages. Whence it comes about that, though many conspiracies have been attempted, very few have attained the desired end." Later in the chapter he makes clear his disdain for such amateurs: "I maintain that one finds in history that all conspiracies have been made by men of standing or else by men in immediate attendance on a prince, for other people, unless they be sheer lunatics, cannot form a conspiracy; since men without power and those who are not in touch with a prince are devoid alike of any opportunity of carrying out a conspiracy successfully." This describes the two unfortunate young men to a tee, and had they approached him with their half-baked plan Machiavelli would surely have dismissed them as the lunatics they were, even had he shared their ideology—a doubtful proposition since his natural inclination was to defer to legitimate authority. Machiavelli, in fact, was the least likely revolutionary, a loyal bureaucrat who preferred to reform the state from within rather than risk the chaos of violent revolution.

None of this could save Machiavelli. Given the uncertainty of the moment, the newly installed government was naturally sensitive to the least hint of sedition. As Machiavelli would shortly observe in *The Prince*: "One must recognize that there is nothing more difficult, nor less likely to succeed, or more perilous to undertake, than to introduce a new system of government, for he who seeks to create a new order makes enemies of all those who profited from the old." As one of those who profited most from the old regime, he was always on the thinnest ice with the new one.

On February 18, armed guards showed up at Machiavelli's door and arrested him. Led to the dismal prison known as Le Stinche, he was thrown into a dark, vermin-infested cell only a few blocks from where he had toiled for so many years on behalf of his beloved republic.

There he languished for twenty-two days in the cold and dark, the lonely hours interrupted only when the cell door clanged open and he was led stumbling into the torturer's chamber. There he was forced to mount a platform, his hands bound tightly behind his back. The rope around his wrists was then knotted to a second cord attached to the wall. When he had been properly trussed, the platform was yanked from under his feet, causing his body to plummet while his arms, still bound behind his back, were wrenched upward, tearing muscle and tendon and dislocating the joint. This favorite Florentine punishment, the strappado, was the same used on many illustrious prisoners before him, from Savonarola, who quickly broke from the excruciating pain, to Paolo Vitelli, who proudly defied his tormentors.

Machiavelli had six appointments with the torturer, "that I bore," he later told Vettori, "with such stoicism, that I am proud and esteem myself more highly than before." Though he confessed nothing—indeed he had nothing to confess—Machiavelli knew that in the current climate mere suspicion of treason was sufficient to justify his execution. Writing to his nephew a few months after his ordeal he acknowledged, "it is something of a miracle that I am alive, because I was deprived of my office and was on the verge of losing my life, which only God and my innocence have saved for me." Despite the constant terror and grim accommodations, he managed to describe the horrific scene in the jaunty little sonnet he composed for Giuliano de' Medici: "One is chained up and another is unironed with a pounding of locks, keys, and bars; another shrieks he is too high above the ground!" Even more irritating than the screams of his fellow inmates, he jokes, is the incessant chanting of paternosters by the pious who stand outside the prison at dawn to give comfort to those about to die.

On the morning of February 23, the pious lifted their voices for Boscoli and Capponi, who were led into the courtyard of the Bargello and beheaded. Still, Machiavelli managed to retain his sense of humor, even if it was of the gallows variety:

> Last night, beseeching the Muses that with
> their sweet cither and sweet songs they would, to console me,
> visit Your Magnificence and make my excuses,
> one appeared who embarrassed me, saying: "Who are you, who
> dare to call me?" I told her my name; and she, to torture me, hit
> me in the face and closed my mouth for me,
> saying: "You are not Niccolò but Dazzo,* since you have your
> legs and your heels bound and you sit here chained like a madman."
> I wished to give her my arguments; she replied to me and said:

---

* Andrea Dazzi, a popular but second-rate literary figure.

"Go like a fool with that comedy of yours in rags."
Give her proofs, Magnifico Giuliano, in the name of High God,
that I am not Dazzo but myself.

The imagery is typical of Machiavelli's sardonic sense of humor. While many poets have called upon the Muses in their moment of need, few have found them to be as belligerent as Machiavelli's sharp-tongued and pugilistic visitor. The Muses, like *Fortuna* herself, are capricious and malicious, not interested in wasting their time on weaklings or fools.

Machiavelli's prison sonnets are not the usual appeals of a condemned man. While they proclaim his innocence, they do so only indirectly, depicting their author as a hapless wretch, a figure of fun rather than pity. Above all, these slight poems provide an emotional release to their author at a particularly painful moment. Machiavelli, as his colleagues at the Chancery attested, was a consummate entertainer, purveyor of off-color stories and satirical portraits. By eliciting laughter, his verses helped relieve his aching heart and, as an added bonus, might even encourage their recipient to conclude that the author was an amusing fellow worth having around.

These prison sonnets also register a profound psychological rupture. Written in the darkest hours of his life, they trace the first tentative steps on a new journey, one that will ultimately bring him far more fame than he could have hoped for had he never suffered misfortune and disgrace. Before the crisis he had made his living and his reputation on the public stage; after, he lived in relative obscurity, forgotten by the state he had served so well and that ultimately scorned him. Before, he had been a man of action; after, a man of words and ideas. It was only following the collapse of his professional career that he transformed himself into a writer and philosopher, discovering hidden talents and blazing trails through uncharted territory. The choice was not his, but he accepted, if only begrudgingly, the hand Fate had dealt him. Even at his lowest point he did not abandon himself to despair. He coped with his sorrows by writing, turning inward and plumbing the depths of his own soul, but also gazing out on the world, casting the same unsparing eye on his fellow man and relishing the human comedy that emerged. If the Muses were an unfriendly lot, Machiavelli never lacked for their company. They were to be his familiar companions for the remainder of his life, inspiring him to climb to creative heights but also cutting him down to size whenever he took himself too seriously.

In the end it was not his poems that won his freedom, nor even the pleading of friends on his behalf. His rescue from the executioner's block came almost as an afterthought, an offhand gesture from that most fickle goddess *Fortuna*, who plucked him from troubled waters and flung him unceremoniously upon the farther shore.

At the very moment Machiavelli was being locked into his cell in Le Stinche, another event occurred in Rome that transformed the political and military map of Europe. Julius, the seventy-year-old "Warrior Pope," was smitten by a sudden attack of malarial fever, dying a few days later, on February 20, 1513. Though all the European powers would have to recalibrate their policies in light of the change in Rome, the impact was likely to be most keenly felt in Florence. Often the fortunes of the republic were determined by the policies and character of the man on the Throne of Saint Peter, and the interregnum between one pope and another was normally a period of great anxiety. This time the mood was subtly different, the usual consternation tempered by the hope that for the first time in history a native son would be elevated. For among the frontrunners for the job was Cardinal Giovanni de' Medici, head of the powerful clan and unofficial boss of the city. No Florentine had ever sat on the papal throne, and to have a native son presiding over the Vatican—particularly one as powerful as Cardinal de' Medici—held out the prospect of a prosperous age where streams of golden ducats would flow through the hands of Tuscan bankers and economic partnership would replace military confrontation.

First, however, Giovanni would have to hurry back to Rome to be included in the conclave. Departing in late February he arrived in time to join his fellow cardinals on March 6. Five days later, after the usual horse-trading and deal-making, the thirty-eight-year-old Giovanni de' Medici was elected, taking the name Leo X. The happy news took only one day to reach Florence, and no sooner was it announced than the city gave itself over to wild celebrations. Shops closed and people poured into the streets; all the church bells of the city were set a-ringing and bonfires kindled in

the squares. In the joy of the moment, feeling invincible and magnanimous, Giuliano de' Medici ordered a mass release of prisoners. Among
them were those survivors implicated in the abortive Boscoli plot, including the former Second Chancellor of Florence.

On March 12, Machiavelli, distressed in body but resilient in spirit,
surrounded by his friends, hobbled from his cell and stood blinking in the
cold light of the Florentine winter. Within a few days he was back on his
farm in Sant' Andrea, enjoying a rare and much needed period of repose
to heal his limbs and adjust to new circumstances.

Machiavelli could be forgiven had he decided to give up politics and
turn his back on the city that had treated him so poorly. Most men would
at least have taken the opportunity to enjoy an extended period of rest. But
Machiavelli was ill-suited to a life of indolence. Boredom and frustration,
as well as more practical concerns, soon roused him from his convales-
cence.

He had, first of all, to take stock of his life and plan for an uncertain
future. The one thing he did not lack for was time to think. Everything
else, however, was in short supply. Even when he was taking home a government salary it had been hard to make ends meet; now he faced a prolonged period of belt-tightening, a particularly grim prospect since, as he
himself admitted, "I am accustomed to spending and cannot do without
spending." The most sensible course would be to make the most of his
meager resources and perhaps invest his profits, but he had no aptitude
for commerce and little interest in the day-to-day management of his
properties. He would much rather speculate about the military strategy of
the Spanish King or the strength of the Swiss mercenaries with his friend
Vettori than drive a hard bargain with a neighbor over the price of timber
or olive oil he was selling from his farm. Shrewd peasants cheated him and
even friends took advantage of his generosity. He was not frugal by nature.
He enjoyed afternoons in the tavern and nights on the town, but now he
would be forced to cut back just when he was most in need of distraction.

Sharing Niccolò's shrinking horizons were the long-suffering Marietta
and their children—eleven-year-old Primavera, ten-year-old Bernardo,
and two younger sons, Ludovico and Guido. They divided their time
between the house in the city and the farm in the countryside, thrown,
for better or worse, in each other's company. If the bustle was a welcome

relief after the solitude of Le Stinche, it was also a reminder of the large and growing household he could now barely feed and clothe. "[F]ortune has left me nothing but family and friends," he wrote to his nephew, "and I make what capital I can from them."

Despite his affection for his wife and children, Machiavelli was hardly the ideal family man. He was too restless and ambitious to find fulfillment in hearth and home and too addicted to illicit pleasures to remain faithful to one woman. Celibacy was never an option for Machiavelli, even for brief periods, and when Marietta wasn't available—and even when she was—he found other means of sexual release. Often this led him into grotesque situations, the salacious details of which he was only too happy to recount to his friends. One particularly unappetizing encounter occurred a few years earlier while he was away in Verona on state business. "[B]linded by matrimonial famine" and "desperately aroused," as he described himself to his correspondent Luigi Guicciardini (brother of the famous historian), he allowed himself to be tempted into a darkened room with the promise of sensual delights. The resulting encounter was something less than advertised: "Having done the deed, and wanting to check out the merchandise, I took a burning ember from the hearth in the room and lit a lamp overhead. The lamp was hardly kindled before it almost fell from my hand. I nearly dropped dead right then and there, the woman was so hideous." The description of the wrinkled, toothless, lice-infested hag that follows is so revolting that one can only hope Machiavelli was exaggerating for comic affect. He concludes his narrative with the equally implausible pledge: "I stake my berth in heaven that as long as I am in Lombardy I'll be damned if I think I shall get horny again."

The letter to Guicciardini captures the earthy side of Machiavelli's humor that he will put to good use in plays like *Clizia* and *La Mandragola*, but it also offers insight into the methods he deployed in his political writings. Whether he was recounting his own sexual misadventures or uncovering the real motives of princes artfully concealed beneath diplomatic doublespeak, Machiavelli demonstrated a willingness to face unflinchingly the seamier side of life. He takes mankind as he finds it, not passing judgment or seeking reformation. (All attempts in this direction were bound to fail, he thought, as amply demonstrated by Savonarola's ill-considered campaigns against vanities and vice.) Depending on one's perspective, his attitude reveals either a generosity of spirit, an empathy with the flawed human animal, or an overeagerness to accommodate our baser instincts. In dealing with personal failings or political machinations, Machiavelli demonstrated a contempt for decorum that has scandalized and intrigued generations of readers.

For Machiavelli, domestic bliss rarely seemed more blissful than when he was many miles away; upon prolonged exposure it inevitably lost its charm. The longer Machiavelli was away, the more he missed his family, often begging his bosses to relieve him so that he might return to them. But when he was home for any length of time, and when there were no great affairs to be dealt with, he grew ill-tempered and longed to be where the action was.

Though there was no longer any important business to keep him in Florence, he often returned to the city house to relieve the tedium of country life. He was not one of those city dwellers who extolled the beauties of the countryside or romanticized the simple folk who tilled the soil. Machiavelli was a cosmopolitan and enjoyed those pleasures, both high and low, the city had to offer. Whenever he was in town he spent much of his time with what he called "*la brigata*," (the gang) a group of old friends who seemed to have as much time on their hands and as little money as he did. Under the circumstances, it is not surprising that they got on each other's nerves. On one occasion Machiavelli was invited to share in a veal roast purchased by Tommaso del Bene. Having rounded up his friends to share a luxurious meal he apparently could not afford, Tommaso then proceeded to charge his fellow diners for the privilege. "We dined," Machiavelli recounted to Vettori, "and when it came time to add up the bill it came to fourteen soldi each. I had only ten on me, so I owed him four. Now every day he pesters me for it. Just yesterday on the Ponte Vecchio he accosted me again."

In addition to chronicling such petty quarrels, Machiavelli regaled his absent friend with amusing tales of their erotic adventures. One companion, whom Machiavelli refers to discreetly only by the nickname "count Orlando," is "obsessed again with a young lad from Ragusa, and has made himself scarce," while another is "slobbering, totally consumed by Gostanza, hanging on her every word—her sighs and her glances, her scents and soft, feminine ways." Machiavelli was too honest to exempt himself from this chronicle of amorous folly. "I have met a creature," he confessed to Vettori, "so kind, so graceful, so noble, both in nature and in bearing, that neither my praise nor my love would be as much as she merits." Though he acknowledged that some might ridicule such a passion in a man approaching fifty (he was actually forty-five at the time), he defended himself on the grounds that, having been disappointed in other walks of life, he was entitled to find consolation in the arms of a woman: "I have found nothing but pain in these other matters, but in love only good and pleasure."

His descriptions of domestic life, by contrast, seem utilitarian, sometimes even grim, as if in the bosom of his family he felt his diminished prospects most keenly. "When dinnertime comes, I sit down with my little troop to eat such food as my poor farm yields. Having eaten, I return to the inn where I usually find the innkeeper, a butcher, a miller, and a couple of kiln workers. With them I waste the rest of the day playing *cricca* and backgammon." When he speaks of his wife and children his tone tends to be unsentimental, as in this brief mention of a family tragedy in a letter to his nephew: "Marietta gave birth to a baby girl, who died after three days. Marietta is well."

This bare-bones account, however, does not furnish an accurate picture of his emotional state. Later in the letter he confesses, "Physically I feel well, but ill in every other respect," an admission all the more poignant for being understated. Much of Machiavelli's gloom—for which he sought distraction in love affairs and seedier encounters—stemmed from feelings of inadequacy occasioned by his unemployment. For a time he could take some satisfaction in having stood up manfully to his ordeal, but soon the vocabulary he uses to describe his situation suggests feelings of decay or emasculation. Imagery of rot, infestation, and impotence crop up with increasing frequency, often in close proximity to references to the family he can barely support. Typical is this passage from a letter to Vettori he wrote in 1514:

Thus I will remain, crawling with lice, unable to find a solitary man who recalls my service or believes I might be good for anything. But it is impossible for me to continue like this, because I am coming apart at the seams and I can see that if God does not show me more favor,

one day I shall be forced to leave my home and find a place as a tutor
or secretary to a governor, if I can find nothing else, or exile myself to
some deserted land to teach reading to children. As if already dead, I
will leave my family behind. They will do much better without me be-
cause I am nothing but an expense. . . . I'm writing to you not because
I want you to worry or trouble yourself for me, but only to unburden
myself, and not to write anymore about these matters since they are
as odious as can be.

These, then, were the pressures—psychological, economic, and professional—bearing down on Machiavelli in the months following his imprisonment. Sick at heart, feeling useless and forgotten, short of money and
with time weighing heavily, he cast about for a project that would remind
those in charge in the Palazzo della Signoria of his singular talents. His
outlook on life was shaped by the gnawing sense of inadequacy that accompanied the loss of his job. "The duty of a father," wrote Leon Battista
Alberti in his *Books on the Family*, "is not only, as they say, to stock the
cupboard and the cradle. He ought, far more, to watch over and guard the
family from all sides." On many of these counts, particularly in regard to
the cupboard, Machiavelli knew he had fallen short of the mark.

For Machiavelli the only way to shore up his dwindling funds and to
restore his self-esteem was to find a way back into government service.
"[S]ince I do not know how to talk about either the silk or the wool trade,
or profits or losses, I have to talk about politics," he explained. The first
step was to mend fences with the Medici family, especially Giuliano, the
effective boss of the city, acting as his brother's agent. Even before his release from prison he had been trying to arouse the sympathy of Giuliano,
hoping to rekindle some spark of affection in his old patron with his witty
poems. A few weeks later he penned a third sonnet for the lord of the city:

I send you, Giuliano, some thrushes, not
because this gift is fine, but that for a bit Your Magnificence
may recollect your poor Machiavelli.
And if you have near you somebody who bites, you can hit him
in the teeth with it, so that, while he eats his bird, to rend others
he may forget.

But you say: "Perhaps they will not have the effect you speak of,
because they are not good and are not fat; backbiters will not eat them."
I will answer such words that I am thin, even I, as my enemies
are aware, and yet they get off me some good mouthfuls.

A few game birds and a bit of doggerel were unlikely to win the favor of Florence's new bosses. Similar presents must have piled up quickly on the threshold of a powerful man's palace, and it is difficult to imagine that Giuliano paid much attention to either the gifts or the giver. To get ahead in Florence usually demanded a greasing of wheels, and Machiavelli was hampered not only by past associations but by his poverty. Still, he tried to make a virtue of necessity, making up in wit what he lacked in other areas. These creatures of skin and bone, like his verses, are a gift of a poor man to a great lord, meager but well meant.

Machiavelli knew that a far more substantial offering would be needed to make an impression on the busy lord of Florence. Even as he was packaging his game birds and little poem to send to the palace on the Via Larga, he was contemplating a far more ambitious undertaking, a little book addressed to Giuliano in which he would distill all he had learned over his years of tireless labor on behalf of the government of Florence. Not surprisingly, given Machiavelli's blunt personality, it would not contain the usual flowery phrases and pious platitudes, but instead insights and difficult truths that others, less honest but more tactful, would neglect to tell him. Machiavelli was a political animal through and through, and in the end had nothing of substance to offer his potential patron other than the fruits of his own peculiar genius.

The work that was beginning to take shape in his mind was *The Prince*, perhaps the most controversial political tract ever written, but for all its notoriety the work had quiet beginnings.* In his own telling, it was both a labor of love but also of consolation:

Come evening, I return to my house and enter my study; on the
threshold I take off my ordinary clothes, covered with mud and dirt,

---

* The letter to Vettori in which he announces "this little study of mine" was written in December 1513, but he indicated it was already nearly complete, which means he must have begun it shortly after his release from prison.

and wrap myself in robes meant for a court or palace. Dressed ap-
propriately, I enter the ancient courts filled with ancient men where,
affectionately received, I nourish myself on that food that alone is
mine and for which I was born; where I am unashamed to converse
and ask them to explain their actions, and where they, kindly, answer
me. And for four hours at a time I feel no boredom, I forget all my
troubles, I have no fear of poverty, or even of death.

Machiavelli went on to explain to his friend, "I am dedicating it to his Magnificence Giuliano," in the hope that "these Medici princes will put me to work." (As it turned out, Giuliano died before Machiavelli completed the work; the final version is dedicated to Giuliano's nephew Lorenzo, son of the late Piero de' Medici.) He had, he thought, much to offer and much to prove: "[T]hrough this work, were it to be read, I hope to demonstrate that during the fifteen years I have been studying the art of the state I have neither slept nor played games. Anyone should be happy to avail himself of one who has profited so much at the expense of others."

The Prince was born in a moment of crisis and out of desperation. As he sat down to write, his career lay in ruins, and the loss of his salary threatened to plunge him into humiliating poverty. If nothing else, alone in his study, surrounded by ghosts of history, the contemplation of eternal truths made him forget his current misery.

X

THE PRINCE

"[S]ince it is my intention to write something useful to those of understanding, it seems best to me to go straight to the actual truth of things rather than to dwell in dreams."

—*THE PRINCE*, XV

MACHIAVELLI INSISTED HE WROTE *THE PRINCE* TO convince the new Medici rulers of Florence to offer him employment, but it is surely one of the most ill-advised job applications of all time. Attempting to ingratiate himself with his would-be bosses by offering to give them a quick tutorial in the secrets of statecraft was presumptuous and unlikely to win over even the most self-effacing lord. "[I]t is customary for those hoping to win the favor of a prince to present him with those things he values most, or that give him most delight," Machiavelli begins, standards by which his own work fell woefully short. Not only is it plain and unadorned, as he himself admits, but it is chock-full of unpleasant truths and blunt assertions that no prince would welcome, no matter how much he might secretly agree with its conclusions. Unlike most of his predecessors, Machiavelli makes little effort to flatter his patron, assuming the brilliance of his insights will be sufficient to recommend his services.

The unsuitability of the manuscript to achieve his stated goals should absolve Machiavelli of the charge that he was a dishonest schemer, cynically manipulating those around him for his own ends. He would not, or could not, alter the substance of his thought even for the sake of salvaging his career. Machiavelli's lack of guile in his own life stands in stark contrast to the course he urges on his patron, which is to practice the art of decep-

tion whenever honesty might prove inconvenient. In fact few works of political philosophy are more sincere than *The Prince*. Whatever one thinks
of the analyses and prescriptions Machiavelli presents, they were not tai-
lored to suit his audience but were instead the result of a compulsion to set
down on paper ideas and attitudes that had long been brewing in his mind
and that, in this moment of personal and professional crisis, he could no
longer suppress.

Despite its tone of scientific objectivity, *The Prince* is a plea for a strong
leader written by a man who was acutely aware of the precarious and humiliating situation he was in.* In a patriarchal society, inability to provide
for one's family was unforgivable, and Machiavelli felt keenly the shame
of his poverty. Disappointed in his hopes, burning with unfulfilled ambition, he wrote a pugnacious work that makes a fetish of strength and oozes
contempt for anything that smacks of weakness or vacillation. "I am wasting away and cannot continue on like this much longer without becoming
contemptible because of my poverty," he tells Vettori, words that show how
much damage his enemies had been able to inflict.

But *The Prince* was not merely a response to personal disappointment.
The humiliation he felt after his disgrace was just a particularly acute
form of a chronic condition. As an impoverished gentleman, Machiavelli
was dependent on the patronage of richer and more powerful men; his
first extant letter was a defense of the "pigmy" Machiavelli against the
"giant" Pazzi, who used their greater wealth and influence to ride roughshod over their neighbors. Throughout his years in the Chancery he was
forced to bow to men who were his social superiors but intellectual inferiors. Feelings of inadequacy, a sense that he was barely hanging on to respectability, characterize Machiavelli from his youth. This insecurity was
only exacerbated by his recent travails. Like most of the creative geniuses
of the age, including Michelangelo and Leonardo, he belonged to the client class, and like them was conscious of his own gifts and chafed at his
dependence on the largesse of his patrons. It is the client's uneasy position

---

* At the same time he was writing *The Prince* Machiavelli was at work on his other great political
tract, *The Discourses on the First Ten Books of Titus Livius*. Some of the harshness, or lack of balance, in
The Prince can be attributed to this division of subject matter between two books, one of which deals
with hereditary, or tyrannical, rule, the other with republics. Machiavelli clearly viewed his two books
in some sense as companion pieces, and, while they are not contradictory, the fact that he wrote two
such contrasting works raises a host of questions that I discuss later.

that is reflected in *The Prince*, its belligerence compensating for feelings of impotence.

Though it would be unfair to dismiss Machiavelli's book as the bitter ranting of a bitter man, it is clear that thwarted ambition gave added urgency to opinions that had long been gestating in his mind. The strength of his convictions came from the intellectual and emotional synergy between his particular circumstances as a marginal figure within the Florentine ruling class and Florence's marginal position in the community of nations. The sting of personal failure combined with the often humiliating conditions he faced in foreign courts—where he was dismissed as an underpaid messenger of a second-rate power, Sir Nihil, as he put it—created in him a contempt for weakness and a worshipful attitude toward those who refused to cower beneath the blows of fortune.

The desire to land a job may have motivated Machiavelli to begin *The Prince*, but once he sat down to write, the form and content were determined by his own obsessions. The ruthless man of action he conjures offers the perfect antidote to his miserable existence. Casting himself in the role of adviser to the prince, he hoped to hitch his failing fortunes to another's rising star.* "Take, then, this little gift, Your Magnificence," Machiavelli urges Lorenzo de' Medici, the ruler of Florence, "in the spirit in which I offer it. Should you read diligently and consider it with care, you will discover therein my deepest desire, which is that You will rise to that greatness which fortune and your own qualities promise. And if Your Magnificence will, from the pinnacle on which you reside, cast from time to time a glance to these lowly places, you will know how unjustly I suffer from a great and continual malice of fortune."

It is not surprising then that the image of the ideal prince he conjures in the pages of this book is characterized by superhuman strength of will, cunning, and ruthlessness—attributes he observed firsthand while serving at the court of Valentino and that stood in stark contrast both to the reality of his own life and of the republic he served for so many years. In *The Prince* Machiavelli seeks redress, or at least finds consolation, for failures both public and private. One might climb further into the thickets of

---

* The dedication to Lorenzo was written after Giuliano's premature death in 1516, but there is no reason to believe Machiavelli's feelings had changed significantly in the interim.

Freudian analysis by claiming that in *The Prince* Machiavelli ritually slays his father, or at least replaces that feckless figure with a man his opposite in every way—strong, where he was weak; ruthless, where he was kind; able to bend the course of history to his will, while Bernardo could barely provide for his own family.

The genius of Machiavelli transformed what could have been a narrowly focused appeal for a political messiah, a strongman to deliver Florence and the rest of Italy from the hands of foreigners, into a universal meditation on the nature of good and evil. Indeed, this slender volume penned by an obscure Florentine civil servant announces the coming of the modern world. Here is a radically new sensibility, one freed from the superstitions and unexamined assumptions that had governed civic life for thousands of years. In *The Prince* Machiavelli sets forth a boldly original conception of history and of human society, with a disdain for conventional morality that scandalized his contemporaries and made his name infamous to future generations. Man, in Machiavelli's formulation, was no longer inscribed within a divinely ordered universe but was, terrifyingly, thrown upon his own resources, forced to grope as best he could through an unforgiving and incomprehensible landscape.

Like all works of revolutionary impact, *The Prince* is a victim of its own success. Many of its most original insights have become commonplace; many of the battles Machiavelli waged against the orthodoxies of his own day seem trivial simply because he routed his enemies so decisively. Like any explorer charting unknown territory, Machiavelli made mistakes, mistakes that were seized upon and corrected by others who followed in his footsteps. But even his harshest critics were guided by the first crude map he had sketched. It is a testament to Machiavelli's gifts as a writer and his penetrating analysis of human motives that a work born from the tangled geopolitics of sixteenth-century Italy can still be read with pleasure and consulted with profit.

The best way to measure the originality of *The Prince* is, paradoxically, to place it once again inside the familiar tradition to which it belonged. Far from being unique, *The Prince* actually adheres to a time-tested form. When Machiavelli sat down to write his book he had a long list of examples to fall back on. He was clearly familiar with his predecessors' work, borrowing from them themes and even chapter headings like "How to Avoid Flatterers" and "Concerning Liberality and Parsimony." Machiavelli's purpose in writing this book was to offer a corrective to those who had come before him, to urge his patron not to be deceived by those philosophers who opined on subjects they knew nothing about and imagined worlds that never were.* Instead, he admonished the young Medici lord, he should heed the advice of a man who had seen politics up close and knew how it really worked: "Since I know that many have already written on these matters, I do not wish to seem presumptuous in writing on them myself, particularly as I intend to depart substantially from what others have said. But since it is my intention to write something useful to those of understanding, it seems best to me to go straight to the actual truth of things rather than to dwell in dreams." In sticking to "the actual truth of things" rather dwelling "in dreams," Machiavelli shatters cherished beliefs about man's place in the world. He discounts, though he never actually denies, the existence of an immortal soul, focusing instead on flesh-and-blood creatures who lived and breathed, toiled and triumphed, suffered and died. Machiavelli was one of the first philosophers since ancient times to treat people not as children of God but as independent adults, forced to make choices without guidance from an all-seeing Father and to suffer the consequences of their mistakes.†

Books purporting to offer a guide to young princelings on the rudiments of statecraft—a genre known as the *specula principi* (mirror of the prince)—had been a staple in Western literature since at least the time of Xenophon and Plato.‡ They survived the transition from the pagan to the

---

* In his play *La Mandragola*, the cuckolded husband is described as a man "who sits all day in his study, understands just books, and can't manage practical affairs" (III, 2, in *Chief Works*, II, 795). Machiavelli disdained scholars with no real experience of the world.

† Perhaps the greatest contrast is with his older compatriot Dante Alighieri, who in addition to writing the greatest poem of the Middle Ages, *The Divine Comedy*, was an important political theorist. In his *De Monarchia* ("On Monarchy") he calls for the establishment of a universal empire based on divine law. "[T]he human race, by living in the calm and tranquillity of peace, applies itself most freely and easily to its proper work," he declares, a vision completely at odds with Machiavelli's conception of a world of ceaseless struggle for power. (*De Monarchia*, excerpted in *Great Political Thinkers*, 252.)

‡ Strictly speaking, the *specula* emerges in the Middle Ages, but these works were based on models like Xenophon's *Cyropaedia* and Isocrates' *To Nicocles*. The philosophical framework was provided by works like Plato's *Republic* and Aristotle's *Politics*.

Christian era with only a slight change in emphasis, reaching their apogee in the high Middle Ages when writers like Dante and Thomas Aquinas tried to reconcile Platonic and Aristotelian notions of government with a worldview based on the teaching of the Gospels. The tradition remained vital in Machiavelli's own day, with distinguished thinkers like Erasmus and Thomas More offering their own variations on a time-honored theme.[*]

The origins of the form can be traced back to Plato's *Republic*, a work that, like all its successors until Machiavelli's fundamental reworking of the genre, is less concerned with the nuts and bolts of governing than with providing readers a vision of the ideal state.[†] Plato is not unaware of the kinds of arguments Machiavelli will make two thousand years later—he places many of them in the mouth of the pompous Thrasymachus, who declares, "I proclaim justice is nothing else than the interest of the stronger"—but he quickly rejects them in favor of an idealism that bears little relation to the way men live. According to Plato, political science was "the knowledge by which we are to make other men good." Machiavelli rejects this description. He insists the only sensible role for political science (a phrase he never uses), is to deal with men as they actually are.

Superficially at least, Machiavelli would seem to have more in common with Aristotle, Plato's pupil, a far more down-to-earth philosopher who based his theories on the study of real states and constitutions. Aristotle criticized Plato as an impossible idealist, noting, sensibly enough, that "the good lawgiver and the genuine politician will have regard both to the 'absolute best' and to the 'best in the circumstances.'" But despite this pragmatic beginning, neither he nor those who followed in his footsteps believed their job was to provide a how-to manual for the aspiring ruler, a task they would have regarded as either trivial or corrupt. Their treatises remained abstract exercises, meditations on the nature of good government. Even when they were written for a living prince, they contained little he could use in the day-to-day management of his affairs. Justice, not power, was their subject—a pointless exercise according to Machiavelli,

---

[*] More's *Utopia*, a fictitious account of a journey to an ideal state, follows many of the conventions and displays many of the attitudes typical of the form.

[†] Plato did in fact attempt to put his notions of a philosopher king in practice by serving as an adviser to his former pupil Dionysus of Syracuse. Predictably, his attempts to replicate abstract philosophy on a messy real-world situation ended in disaster.

who knew that a prince without power has no ability to dispense justice or anything else to his people.

Aristotle gave the classic formulation of the state "as an association of persons formed with a view to some good purpose." Before Machiavelli, very few philosophers questioned the basic premise that man found his fulfillment in the well-run polity. Philosophers were willing to admit that governments often fell short of the ideal in practice, but they never doubted that the common good was the goal toward which human society was striving, and that it was the philosopher's function to point the prince in the right direction. In their writings they define the nature of Justice, the meaning of the Good, and the blessings of Mercy, but ignore the actual conduct of real men and women. The discussion is removed from reality, the advice heavily moralistic and short on practical solutions. What *should be* receives far more attention than what *is*.

Erasmus's *Institutio principis Christiani* ("Education of a Christian Prince") provides perhaps the most useful comparison with *The Prince*. Not only is it almost exactly contemporaneous—written in 1516, it was dedicated to Charles I of Spain (soon to become the Holy Roman Emperor Charles V)—but as a typical, if atypically elegant, example of the form, it offers the strongest possible contrast to Machiavelli's groundbreaking effort. "Wisdom is not only an extraordinary attribute in itself, Charles, most bountiful of princes," Erasmus begins, "but according to Aristotle no form of wisdom is greater than that which teaches a prince how to rule beneficently." From the first line Erasmus sets a high-minded tone for his book. It will deal with qualities like wisdom, clemency, piety, and so on that define the ideal prince; it will ignore the grubby details of actual governance. Had Charles wished to discover any practical advice on how to keep his throne, he would have leafed through its pages in vain.

Machiavelli's approach couldn't be more different. While he doesn't dispense altogether with empty phrases lauding his master's virtue, he insists his work should be useful to his patron, who, he strongly implies, is going to need all the help he can get. Unlike Charles, whose greatness is assured regardless of whether he studies the text set before him, Lorenzo will achieve his rightful place in history only by paying close attention to Machiavelli's counsel: "Should you read diligently and consider [this book] with care, you will discover therein my deepest desire, which is that You will rise to that greatness which fortune and your own qualities promise." For Machiavelli, the issue of greatness remains in question; it lies in the future. "[A]ll things," he declares, "have conspired to show your greatness," but, he insists, "[t]he rest you must do yourself."

The world as pictured in *The Prince* is far more dynamic and uncertain than the one Erasmus contemplated. When he first told Vettori about his latest project, Machiavelli insisted that "it ought to be welcomed by a prince, and *especially by a new prince*"—that is, one who could not count on traditional allegiances or institutions but had to survive by his own wits, often against fierce resistance. Machiavelli had no interest in metaphysics, what he called "dreams," but instead wished to offer sensible rules of thumb to a young lord who faced a difficult road ahead. As Machiavelli explained to his friend, his book will not only define the nature of princely government but will discuss how principalities "are acquired, how they are retained, and why they are lost"—topics that would not have occurred to those writing on behalf of monarchs securely seated on their thrones. To suggest to Charles, or any other monarch who believed himself appointed by divine right, that his rule was precarious would have smacked of treason. In Renaissance Italy, by contrast, such insecurity was the norm. Each despot lived in perpetual fear of the usurper, exhibiting a well-grounded paranoia that helps explain much of the cruelty of the age. As Pope Pius II observed: "In our change-loving Italy, where nothing stands firm, and where no ancient dynasty exists, a servant can easily become a king"—a state of affairs likely to whet the ambition of an impoverished orphan and cause the prince many a sleepless night. All Machiavelli's experience told him that life was unpredictable, and politics—which is merely life played out on a greater stage and for higher stakes—even more so; that the best laid plans of princes and prelates often lead to disaster; and that well-meaning rulers (like Piero Soderini) might forfeit the confidence of their citizens while ruthless tyrants (like Valentino) could win the loyalty of theirs. Given this reality, what's the point of meditating on situations that never arise and offering models of conduct for people too pure ever to have walked the face of the earth? "Many have imagined republics and principalities that never were," he scoffs, dismissing such exercises as pointless speculation.

Erasmus starts with a basic premise: that the prince aspires to rule his subjects as well as he can, and that his instructor need only hold up a model of perfection for his eager pupil to be drawn to it like a moth to a flame.* "Let the teacher paint a sort of celestial creature," Erasmus urges the hypothetical tutor of a future king, "more like to a divine being than a mortal: yea, sent by the God above to help the affairs of mortals by looking out and caring for everyone and everything; to whom no concern is of longer standing or more dear than the state; who has more than a paternal spirit towards everyone; who holds the life of each individual dearer than his own; who works and strives night and day for just one end—to be the best he can for everyone."

To Machiavelli such a picture is laughable. In the course of his career he met many rulers and none of them resembled the celestial creature Erasmus describes. Of course Erasmus's essay doesn't derive from a study of real-life princes but of revered authors, including Aristotle, who wrote in *The Politics*: "[W]e take it for granted that a good ruler is both good and wise, and wisdom is essential for one engaged in the work of the state." Both the Greek philosopher and his Christian disciple predicate their philosophy on the assumption, so deeply held as to remain largely unexamined, that the universe is essentially rational; that it promotes virtue and punishes wickedness; that society yearns to achieve a more perfect union, no matter how far short it falls in practice.† The prince plays a vital role in this divinely ordered universe as God's representative on earth, a shepherd to his flock, a father to his children. As Aquinas expressed it: "The worthy exercise of the kingly office requires . . . excelling virtue and must be requited by a high degree of blessedness." It is through the good prince that the order inherent in the universe is made manifest and the divine plan brought to fruition.

How different is the world Machiavelli conjures! Instead of a rationally ordered universe unfolding according to divine plan, he presents a world governed by caprice, filled with violence, subject to sudden, inexplicable

---

* Erasmus, following Aristotle, makes a distinction between monarchy, which he regards as the best form of government, and tyranny, which is the worst. The good king or prince rules on behalf of his people, while the tyrant, the king's corrupted twin, rules for his own sake. Machiavelli largely ignores this distinction.

† Aristotle, while not subscribing to the Judeo-Christian conception of an all-powerful and perfect deity, believed that nature was rationally and benevolently ordered.

transformations, plunged into chaos and inhospitable to man and all his works. "[A]ll human affairs are ever in a state of flux," he declares, and a prince must be willing to change his course readily since "the things of this world are so variable."* Having observed at close hand the meteoric careers of men like Savonarola and Valentino—not to mention the twists and turns of his own—Machiavelli was keenly aware that nothing is certain but change itself. It is foolhardy to bask in today's success for it will almost certainly be followed by tomorrow's calamity. Presiding over this anarchic muddle we call the world is the trickster goddess *Fortuna*, who "turns states and king-doms upside down as she pleases," and "deprives the just of the good that she freely gives to the unjust." She is an "unstable and fickle deity [who] often sets the undeserving on a throne to which the deserving never attains."†

Faced with such a topsy-turvy world, the very notion of "the good prince" becomes problematic. To Thomas Aquinas, who wrote in his *Commentary on Politics* "No one can be called a good prince unless he is good in the moral virtues and prudent," Machiavelli might well have responded: No one can be a considered a good prince, or any prince at all, who loses his kingdom through a foolish adherence to such platitudes. The very notion of a fixed morality is preposterous in a lawless world. The prince, he insists, "must be prepared to shift according to the winds of fortune and as changing circum-stances dictate. And if possible, as I have already said, he must not depart from the good, but if compelled by necessity he must know the ways of evil."

Necessity, not any abstract notion of the Good, must determine our behavior. The prince must play the hand he is dealt, for he who does not adapt to circumstances is doomed to failure. A prince is successful, Ma-chiavelli says, "when he acts in harmony with the times, and similarly comes to grief when his actions are discordant with them."‡ While most

---

*   Plato, by contrast, believed that change resulted from a profound corruption of the perfect and eternally static universe. "[A]ny change whatever, except from evil, is the most dangerous of all things," he insisted. (*The Laws*, VII, quoted in Wolin, "Plato: Political Philosophy Versus Politics," in *Essays in the History of Political Thought*, 7.)

†   Renaissance philosophers distinguished between Fortune and Providence. Fortune was random, perhaps even malicious, while Providence unfolded according to God's plan. Fortune ruled this world, Providence the next. The difficulty came in explaining the relationship between the two.

‡   Here he paraphrases a letter of September 1506 where he wrote: "The man who matches his way of doing things with the conditions of the times is successful; the man whose actions are at odds with the times and the patterns of events is unsuccessful" (Machiavelli et al., *Machiavelli and His Friends*, 135).

writers asked themselves: What is the best form of government? Machiavelli ponders what he considers to be the only real question: What kind of government, if any, is possible? In a violent and unpredictable world there is no point in dreaming of societies that can never be. Indeed, he spends little time analyzing stable states with established dynasties or ecclesiastical states—which, he remarks with tongue in cheek, "are sustained by superior causes [and so] transcend human understanding"—but instead devotes his efforts to describing the kind of states that were familiar to him, petty principalities insecurely held by upstarts and freebooters. His heroes are those often illegitimate usurpers like Valentino who improvise on the fly and survive on their wits and their courage. They are the men who master capricious fortune. Only by the gravest exertions can we stave off, and then only temporarily, the forces of chaos, Machiavelli insists. Under the circumstances we would be far better served if instead of building models of perfection we concentrated our efforts on cobbling together a serviceable government for the moment, recognizing we must adapt our solutions to evolving circumstances.

Machiavelli was a true child of the Renaissance, shaped by both the values and pathologies of a creative and tumultuous age. His apparent indifference to traditional moral strictures was in large part a response to the chaos he saw all around him. In early-sixteenth-century Italy, kings and princes rose and fell with startling rapidity; conquering armies were quickly conquered in their turn and no state was secure from outside forces or from internal dissension. Nowhere were these lessons as stark as in Florence, whose history was a bloody parade of factional strife of political turmoil. The placid contemplation of ideal states seemed a luxury when governments were collapsing about one's ears and marauding armies burned villages, laid waste the land, and raped and killed with impunity.

For Aquinas and Erasmus, accustomed to a more predictable course, what is at stake for the ruler is simply his virtue—whether he will follow the path of righteousness or of the tyrant. For Machiavelli what is at stake is the more fundamental question of whether or not he will hold on to power. The traditional "mirror of princess" assumes the ruler's place in the hierarchy is secure, the only question being whether he discharges his duties with honor. *The Prince* begins with the assumption that his office and even his life are under constant threat, which makes his virtue rather beside the point. Most of the cruelty advocated in *The Prince* is a result of the insecurity of the ruler's position. "Anyone who gains [new territories] and wishes to hold on to them must do two things," Machiavelli enjoins in a typical passage; "the first is to extinguish the ancient lineage of the previous ruler; the other is to alter neither the law nor the taxes."

This and similarly cold-blooded proposals have sent chills down the spines of generations of readers, but Machiavelli, who had seen close-up both the ruthlessness of princes and the far more devastating consequences of anarchy, cared only about results. "Cesare Borgia was considered cruel," he points out, "yet his cruelty brought an end to the disorders in the Romagna, uniting it in peace and loyalty. If this is considered good, one must judge him as much kinder than the Florentine people who, in order to escape being called cruel, allowed Pistoia to be destroyed." A ruler's first responsibility is to rule, and whatever secures that end can be regarded as just, even if this demands the violation of ethical norms.

Indeed Machiavelli strongly implies that those concerned for their immortal souls might want to find a different line of work. After praising Philip of Macedon as the model of an effective ruler, Machiavelli admits that his policies of ethnic-cleansing were "infinitely cruel, and inimical to society . . . and every man should flee them, preferring to live as a private citizen than to live as a king with such ruin on his account." One can either be a saint or a king, he implies, but not both. He follows with a characteristic warning against the dangers of splitting the difference, a spineless tactic so often pursued by his own government: "Nonetheless, for he who would not wish to follow that first path of goodness, desiring to hold on to what he has, it behooves him to follow the path of evil. But most men prefer to take the middle road, which is most harmful, since they know not how to be completely good nor completely bad."*

---

* Here Machiavelli shows himself to be the temperamental opposite of Aristotle, whose philosophy was based on "the golden mean." "If we were right when in our *Ethics* we stated that Virtue is a Mean," he wrote in *The Politics* (II, 10), "and that the happy life is life free and unhindered and according to virtue, then the best life must be the middle way, consisting in a mean between two extremes." As an example of one such mean, Aristotle calls courage the mean between cowardice and rashness. A preference for moderation was antithetical to Machiavelli's thought.

In the beginning of his *Ethics*, Aristotle declares "that 'the good' is 'that at which all things aim.'" Machiavelli's universe bears little resemblance to the orderly mechanism proposed by Aristotle or the divinely inspired cosmos envisioned by Aquinas or Erasmus.* Fortune is so perverse that even Machiavelli, the most clear-sighted of guides, must on occasion throw up his hands in despair. After analyzing the career of his hero Valentino, Machiavelli admits the limitations of his prescriptions: "Having reviewed all the Duke's actions, then, I would not know how to fault him. Indeed, it seems to me that . . . he should be held up as an example to all those who through fortune or the arms of others have seized the throne. He, possessing greatness of spirit and high ambition, could not have acted otherwise, and it was only the swiftness of Alexander's death, coupled with his own illness, that foiled his designs." If even such a giant as Valentino can come to grief, what hope is there for lesser men?

Such a worldview taken to an extreme would argue for fatalism; passivity is the only rational response to a universe in which the consequences of one's actions are completely unpredictable.† But Machiavelli rejects that conclusion. He had nothing but contempt for pious monks who retired from the world in order to prepare for the next, and little more respect for hedonists who responded to life's travails by losing themselves in meaningless pleasures. He dismissed those who believed "that the prudence of men cannot manage [the affairs of the world], and indeed cannot improve them" and who thought "that there is no point in sweating much over these matters and that they should submit to chance instead." Though the world is ruled by a fickle goddess, it remains in our power to improve the odds:

I believe that even if it is true that fortune governs half our lives, she still allows us to take control of the other half. . . . I compare fortune

---

* In other works, like his famous *In Praise of Folly*, Erasmus seems to come much closer to Machiavelli's conception of a world steeped in vice and wallowing in corruption, but the Dutch humanist always seems to have more faith in the possibility of ultimate redemption.

† One of Machiavelli's contemporaries, the mathematician Gerolamo Cardano, was also grappling with the unnerving fact that the future seemed unpredictable. A compulsive gambler, Cardano was the first man to systematically investigate the laws of probability. His *Book on Games of Chance*, like *The Prince*, seeks to discover a deeper order within apparent chaos. Cardano and Machiavelli found different ways to make sense of a world stripped of the comforting illusion of divine providence.

*to one of those untamed rivers which, when enraged, floods the
plains, uproots trees and topples buildings, and washes the soil from
one place to another.* . . . *[I]n spite of everything, men can still prepare
themselves in times of quiet, erecting dams and levees to channel the
rising waters, so that when the torrent comes it will not prove as destructive.*

Will and chance are in almost perfect balance. Or, to put it more accurately, the two are in constant and dynamic tension since, while equally
matched, each force vies to expand its claim on the world. The great rulers—Moses, Alexander, Romulus, Lycurgus—increase their odds of success through boldness, but also through prudence; they are not afraid to
take risks, but they leave as little to chance as possible. The wise prince
"proves adaptable when unforeseen events occur," a state of affairs, Machiavelli observed, so common as to be the norm.

For all its pessimism Machiavelli's philosophy is ultimately empower-
ing. He insists that man has the capacity, indeed the duty, to shape the
course of his destiny. Though his options are limited by "Fortune in her
furious onrush" who "shifts and reshifts the world's affairs," it is through
the heroic struggle to give form to what is formless that immortality is
achieved. Here the Renaissance belief in the worth of the individual is
applied to real-world situations. "O great and wonderful happiness of
man!" wrote Lorenzo the Magnificent's friend Pico della Mirandola. "It is
given to him to have that which he chooses and to be that which he wills."*
Machiavelli, who lived through more troubled times than Pico, watching
as his people were humiliated and the states of Italy crushed beneath the
boots of foreigners, struck a less hopeful tone, but he continues to urge
ceaseless struggle with fate, even against long odds.

 The force of character that allows a man to resist *Fortuna* Machiavelli
refers to as *virtù*. The term is not to be confused with its English cognate
"virtue," since it does not imply goodness as it is usually understood.
Rather, it is closer to "prowess," the courage and the skill to impose one's

---

* The same idea is expressed in Shakespeare's famous lines: "What a piece of work is a man! How
noble in reason! How infinite in faculty! in form, in moving, how express and admirable! in action how
like an angel! in apprehension how like a god" (*Hamlet*, II, ii).

will on the world.* It was a quality that Valentino, with his "great spirit" and "lofty ambition," possessed in full, though it was not sufficient to save him when abandoned by Fortune. In fact virtue and *virtù* are often incompatible since it is impossible to be an effective leader if one is too squeamish to do the dirty work necessary for achieving and maintaining power. Machiavelli's ideal prince might well have echoed Hamlet in saying, "I must be cruel to be kind," keeping in mind that there is no other judge of *virtù* but success.

"For where men have but little virtue, fortune makes great show of her power," Machiavelli observes in *The Discourses*. *Virtù* is the masculine principle engaged in a perpetual struggle for supremacy with the feminine *Fortuna*. He makes an invidious comparison between the *virtù* of the ancient Romans, who mastered the known world, and the "effeminate" Italians of his own day, who, reared in the gentler ethos of the Gospels, allowed themselves to be mastered by others. The word derives from the Latin *vir*, man, and carries with it the associated ideas of strength and courage. For Machiavelli *virtù* stands for order against the forces of chaos; it is that which holds society together while fickle *Fortuna* seeks to tear it down. His conception does not resemble the static cosmologies typical of the Middle Ages, but embraces the notion of creative destruction as each principle gains a temporary advantage, only to be overcome by its opposite—a model of the world that reflects the dynamism and anxieties of the new age.

---

* The precise meaning of the word *virtù* in Machiavelli's writing is one of the most difficult and controversial issues for both translators and scholars. At times he appears to use it inconsistently—as with the case of the tyrant Agathocles whom he seems to describe, in alternate paragraphs (see *Il Principe*, VIII), as both devoid of *virtù* and an exemplar of the same—and at others merely in his own idiosyncratic way, deliberately contrasting it with the traditional Christian notion of virtue. My own sense of Machiavelli's meaning is that he uses the term in a way that transforms it from a passive quality, a feature of one's character, to an active quality, one that is manifest in action. "Prowess," the ability to impose one's will on the world, often comes closest to the mark, though "boldness" or "virility," a word that shares the same root connoting manliness, are also reasonable variations. As always, Machiavelli is concerned with the result of an idea, not its abstract nature. Virtuous behavior that leads to bad outcomes cannot be condoned, nor should deeds normally described as evil be condemned when they promote the general welfare. Part of the difficulty comes from the fact that while Machiavelli seemed to be clear himself on what he meant, he often employed the term in the usual sense so that he could make a sharper contrast with his own views.

For an interesting discussion of these vexed issues, see Harvey C. Mansfield's *Machiavelli's Virtue*, particularly Chapter 1. The topic has also been adressed by J. H. Whitfield in *Machiavelli*, especially Chapter 6, "The Anatomy of Virtue," by Leo Strauss in his influential *Thoughts on Machiavelli*, and by Friedrich Meinecke in his *Machiavellism: The Doctrine of Raison d'Etat and Its Place in Modern History*.

Though Machiavelli claimed to know nothing about making money, a trait that set him apart from his compatriots, his was a philosophy that came naturally to someone who grew up in a merchant culture driven by entrepreneurs and capitalist gamblers intimately acquainted with cycles of boom and bust. "Everywhere Ambition and Avarice penetrate," he asserts, qualities he observed every day in the bustling markets of Florence. He accepts man for what he is, not condemning the natural drives that medieval philosophers tended to brand as sins. "It is only natural to desire gain," Machiavelli observes, "and when capable men attempt great feats, they will be praised, or at least not blamed." Instead of measuring human behavior in terms of sin and virtue, Machiavelli proposes a different yardstick. "But if they cannot succeed and still persist, here they are in error and deserve to be censured."

Success and failure, then, are the ultimate arbiters of good and evil in Machiavelli's universe. "In all men's acts, and in those of princes most especially," he insists, "it is the result that renders the verdict when there is no court of appeal." One can never judge an act in the abstract but only by observing its consequences in the real world. "[I]t's the part of a prudent man to take the best among bad choices," he said in another context. *The Prince*, filled with tentative solutions to particular problems, offers some guidance for the sensible monarch, while admitting that one can never plan for every contingency. It is predicated on a dynamic conception of society typical of the rags-to-riches-and-back-again economy of capitalism.[†]

Machiavelli's worldview—cynical, secular, and anticlerical—was widely shared among Renaissance Florentines, at least in intellectual circles where classical authors took up more space on a scholar's bookshelves than the writings of the Church Fathers. A similar disdain for conventional attitudes appears in the writings of Machiavelli's friend, the diplomat and

---

[*]   Thomas Hobbes echoes this notion: "The desires and other passions of men, are in themselves no sin. No more are the actions that proceed from those passions, till they know a law that forbids them: which, till laws be made they cannot know; nor can any law be made, till they have agreed upon the person that shall make it" (*Leviathan*, XIII, 83, quoted in Rauch, *The Political Animal*, p. 46).

[†]   In an era before social safety nets and sophisticated economic theory, the cycle of boom and bust was far more painful than it is now. Florentines still recalled with horror the collapse of the great banking firms of the Bardi and Peruzzi in the mid-fourteenth century, a calamity almost as great as the Black Death that followed.

historian Francesco Guicciardini. But while the younger man shared Machiavelli's jaundiced view of the human animal (in fact he often chided Machiavelli for placing too much faith in the wisdom of the people), Guicciardini criticized his friend for going too far. In offering the earliest known critique of *The Prince* he demonstrates his more cautious, more conventional, cast of mind. "It is . . . necessary that the prince should have the courage to resort to extraordinary measures whenever they may be required," Guicciardini acknowledges, "but he should also have the wisdom to neglect no opportunity of establishing affairs with humanity and benevolence, never accepting as an absolute rule the method prescribed by [Machiavelli] who always finds great delight in extraordinary and violent remedies."

In pointing out Machiavelli's love of "extraordinary and violent remedies," Guicciardini captures something of his friend's personality. In private Guicciardini was as irreverent as Machiavelli, but in his public writing he strikes a more diplomatic tone. Machiavelli was less discreet. He clearly meant what he said, but he never used moderate language when vivid phrases would better make his point. "[O]ne should note," Machiavelli declares in a classic formulation, "that hatred may be acquired through good deeds as well as through bad. And so, as I said before, a prince wishing to hold on to his state is often forced to be other than good." The shock provoked by passages like this owes as much to tone as to substance. Machiavelli was one of those tactless people who feel compelled to point out those truths that most are too polite to mention in public.

Of course what Guicciardini, like later critics, found unpalatable was not merely the tone but the substance of Machiavelli's writing. He is particularly uncomfortable with Machiavelli's embrace of the liar's art. "It may also be disputed whether fraud is always a sure means of attaining greatness," says Guicciardini, responding to one of Machiavelli's central points, "because, although grand blows may be struck by deceit, yet the reputation of being a deceiver will afterwards prevent you from accomplishing your purpose"—to which Machiavelli himself would have replied that the best of all possible worlds would be to *appear* honest while yet harvesting the fruits of deception.

•   •   •

Despite the fact that *The Prince* is usually regarded as the despot's hand-book, one early critic dubbing it the guide to "Tyrannical science," Machiavelli's views are far less congenial to despotic rule than those of his more conventional predecessors. Indeed there is an inherent tension in *The Prince* between its stated purpose—which is to aid Lorenzo de' Medici in fulfilling his glorious destiny—and the picture Machiavelli paints of a world teetering on the brink of anarchy. Had he been honest with his patron he would have admitted that the journey he was proposing was hazardous and the destination far from assured. "The universe is so constituted that we never flee one peril without finding ourselves in another," he observes. "But prudence lies in understanding the nature of that peril, and in adopting the least bad as the good." Such a world is inhospitable to absolutist rule predicated on divine right. How can God sanction the rule of one particular man or dynasty when "[n]ot a thing in the world is eternal" and a man "should every hour adjust himself to [Fortune's] variation"? Divine right assumes an orderly hierarchy totally absent from Machiavelli's conception. If God has a plan for this world, Machiavelli has a hard time discerning it.

Even in *The Prince* Machiavelli is not an apologist for despotism. When he calls on Lorenzo to "redeem [Italy] from barbarian insolence and cruelty," he regards this as a short-term solution to a particular crisis. His prince will emerge, if at all, only through guile and struggle. Should he succeed he will need to protect his dominion by exercising constant vigilance and his triumph will only be temporary. Fortune's wheel raises men up, only to plunge them back into the depths. No self-respecting prince would submit himself to such a dreary routine.

Thus despite appearances, and despite the fact that *The Prince* has been embraced by despots from Philip of Spain to Stalin and Hitler, the book offers only the most limited and contingent endorsement of dictatorship. In fact it was his predecessors, those "virtuous" men who have come down through history as saints and sages, who gave aid and comfort to tyrants. Following Aristotle, the tradition of the *specula* assumed that one-man rule was superior. "[G]overnment by one person, being the best, is to be preferred," wrote Aquinas, a logical assumption since he believed earthly government should reflect the Kingdom of Heaven. Machiavelli, by contrast, notes that governments fall into two categories. "All states—all those dominions that once ruled or now rule over men—once were or are now either republics or principalities," he asserts, remaining silent about his preference, clearly spelled out in *The Discourses*, for the former.* Even in *The Prince* he provides only a limited endorsement of despotic rule, telling Lorenzo, "it seems to me that now so many factors point in favor of a new prince"—a statement that carries with it the not so subtle implication that in other times and in other circumstances a more representative form of government is called for. Machiavelli was a realist, willing to tailor his policies and prescriptions to a given situation. Self-government by a broad segment of the citizenry is preferable, he says, but given Italy's debased condition only a strong leader can cure what ails her.

Machiavelli would not have become infamous had he merely been a reluctant pragmatist, advocating the path of virtue as long as he could while admitting that on occasion virtue must be put aside to avert a crisis. But Machiavelli went out of his way to challenge the prevailing wisdom. He took pleasure in scandalizing his readers, standing traditional nostrums on their head and demonstrating how following the recommendations of conventional moralists could lead to disaster. "Everyone knows how laudable it is," he proclaimed with ill-concealed irony, "for a prince to keep his word and live with integrity instead of by trickery. But the experience of our own time shows us that the princes who have accomplished great things are those who cared little for keeping faith with the people, and who used cleverness to befuddle the minds of men. In the end, such princes overcame those who counted on loyalty alone." Despite what "everyone knows," that virtue will triumph and good men will always prosper, Machiavelli demonstrates that the reverse is true. Contemplating the success of Pope Alexander VI, he wrote "a deceiver will never lack victims for his deceptions." In the real world, honesty is praised but deception is rewarded; a place in heaven is reserved for the merciful prince, but only to compensate him for the worldly kingdom he will surely squander.

Not only, Machiavelli insists, does the universe punish the naively virtuous, but we ourselves extol conventional virtues even as we trample

---

* See *Discourses*, III, 9. Even Machiavelli's preference for democracy is practical rather than idealistic, since republics, being more broadly based, can more easily withstand the vicissitudes of Fortune.

underfoot those who practice them. "[T]here is such a chasm between the way men live and the way they ought to live that he who abandons what is for what should be will soon ruin himself rather than secure his preservation. For a man who wishes to always do good will surely be ruined among so many who are not good. Thus it is necessary for a prince wishing to retain power to learn how not to be good, employing this art or not according to need."

In condemning man as essentially wicked, Machiavelli echoes the Christian worldview he otherwise scorned. His harsh view of human nature and belief that only the coercive power of the state could repress humanity's worst instincts mirror the grim assessment of many of the Church Fathers. "Surely, it is not without purpose that we have the institution of the power of kings," Saint Augustine wrote, "the death penalty of the judge, the barbed hooks of the executioner, the weapons of the soldier, the right of punishment of the overlord, even the severity of the good father. All those things have their methods, their causes, their reasons, their practical benefits. While these are feared, the wicked are kept in bounds and the good live more peacefully among the wicked." Machiavelli could not have stated the case for strong government any more boldly, but unlike Augustine and other Church Fathers—or prophetic figures like Savonarola—he did not incorporate humankind's fallen nature into any larger redemptive scheme in which sin was merely the prelude to ultimate salvation.*

Though Machiavelli often uses terms like "evil" to describe people's behavior, this seems more a matter of habit than conviction. Evil or wickedness implies a willful disregard of some higher law, but since Machiavelli is skeptical that such a universal standard exists against which we can measure how far short we have fallen, the term lacks the element of moral censure. In *The Prince* he often struggles to reconcile his natural revulsion against violence with his experience that the most effective leaders are often those who are

---

* The Christian notion of man's wickedness, derived from original sin, was a departure from the mainstream of Greek thought, particularly as expressed in the philosophy of Aristotle, whose views were essentially optimistic. "The function of man is an activity of soul which follows or implies a rational principle" (Aristotle, *Nichomachean Ethics*, 10998a, quoted in Bluhm, "Immanent Good: Aristotle's Quest for the Best Regime," in *Essays in the History of Political Thought*, p. 63). Aquinas revived Aristotle's rationalistic philosophy in a Christian context. "Now the divine law," he wrote, "which is founded on grace, does not abolish human law, which derives from natural reason" (quoted in A. P. D'Entrèves, "Thomas Aquinas," in *Essays in the History of Political Thought*, 100).

least squeamish about employing it. One can sense his ambivalence as he recounts the life of Agathocles, a king of ancient Syracuse: "One cannot call it virtue [*virtù*] to murder one's fellow citizens, to betray one's friends, to live without faith, without piety, without religion," he admits.

> *By such means one may win dominion but not glory. But if one considers Agathocles' prowess [virtù] in first placing himself in peril and then escaping it, and his greatness of spirit in enduring and overcoming adversity, I cannot see why he should be judged inferior to any talented general. Nonetheless, his savage cruelty, inhumanity, and his infinite wickedness will not allow him to be included among those celebrated for their excellence. One should not, then, attribute to fortune or to virtue that which he accomplished without either.*

While making an inventory of the tyrant's many crimes, Machiavelli, in effect, praises Agathocles by damning him only faintly.

Machiavelli is most closely identified with the principle "the ends justify the means," though the exact phrase never appears in his writing. The closest he comes is in a passage in *The Discourses* where he declares: "It is a sound maxim that reprehensible actions may be justified by their effects, and that when the effect is good . . . it always justifies the action." One can argue that this formula is wrongheaded—it may never be possible to get good results from bad actions, since evil will only be met with evil—but not that it is amoral. The worst that one can say is that his morality is utilitarian, geared toward practical results in the here and now rather than obtaining the Kingdom of Heaven.

And what exactly are those ends toward which Machiavelli's famously unpleasant means are pointing us? Over the centuries many have insisted that it is simply power: how to acquire it and how to secure it once acquired. But it is clear that power is not the "good" result for the sake of which Machiavelli is willing to condone "reprehensible actions." This misunderstanding can be attributed to the fact that *The Prince*, his most famous book, focuses almost exclusively on means. It is intended to be a handbook for a practicing politician, and like all how-to manuals it assumes the ends are self-evident and sets them aside in order to concentrate on demonstrating the best way of achieving them.

When Machiavelli does turn to ends rather than means, it is usually to drive home the point that virtuous behavior often leads to bad outcomes, while brutality can sometimes contribute to human welfare. This is not a point of view favored by people of faith because they believe God's plan must be universally good. Machiavelli's philosophy, by contrast, embraces ambiguity and contradiction; it is empirical rather than faith-based, willing to accept the truth that good might come from bad.

The thrust of Machiavelli's ethics is to rescue morality from the theologians. Having witnessed the suffering caused by weakness, corruption, and vacillation, he has nothing but contempt for those holy men who turn their backs on the world to contemplate the purity of their own souls. Though he praises men like Valentino who pursue their ambition openly, he abhors *unnecessary* cruelty. As always, Machiavelli applies a merchant's calculus to morality, toting up the consequences of each action in neat columns of profit and loss: "[A] prince must not care whether he is considered cruel when attempting to keep his subjects loyal and united, because with a few examples he will have shown more mercy than those who, from excessive kindheartedness, allow disorders to continue from which arise murder and rapine. These cause universal suffering, while an execution ordered by the prince harms only one man."

Right and wrong, then, are determined not in the individual conscience but in society, whose ultimate expression is the state and whose preservation, in peace and security, is necessary to human happiness. "It must be understood," he says, "that a prince, especially a newly crowned prince, cannot observe all those things that give a man a reputation for goodness, it often being necessary, for the preservation of the state, to act against faith, against charity, against humanity, against religion." The relevant question for Machiavelli is not whether one's own soul is pure, but whether the choices one makes contribute in the long run to the collective good. Using this social calculus, Machiavelli discovers that many forms of behavior condemned by traditional moralists actually promote the general welfare. This is particularly true in judging the deeds of those entrusted with the care of the state. Murdering potential rivals may be wrong by traditional measures, but it may well spare the people the horrors of civil war. As Cosimo de' Medici, the former strongman of Florence, once remarked: "states cannot be held with *paternosters*."

Like Hobbes a century and a half later, Machiavelli justified drastic measures in the name of security since the alternative was far worse. A well-ordered polity provides a check on human appetites and ambitions that would otherwise run amok, causing untold misery.* "[W]hen the safety of one's country wholly depends on the decision to be taken, no attention should be paid either to justice or injustice, to kindness or cruelty, or to its being praiseworthy or ignominious. On the contrary, every other consideration being set aside, that alternative should be wholeheartedly adopted which will save the life and preserve the freedom of one's country."

These and other similar pronouncements have earned Machiavelli the reputation as father of the concept *raison d'état* (reason of state). Since this doctrine has been deployed by many a regime to justify the suppression of individual liberties, Machiavelli has been accused of being complicit in tyranny. It is a valid criticism up to a point. Machiavelli considers almost any form of government, no matter how oppressive, as worthy of our sacrifice and entitled to our devotion. But the state is not an end in itself. Rather, the state demands our obedience because it is the vital bulwark against the forces of chaos.† To the totalitarian, citizens exist to serve the state, while for Machiavelli the state exists to serve the citizens. His own experience had shown him that oppressive yet well-ordered governments produced far less suffering than permissive governments where neither person nor property was safe, but he also insists that in the long run the most stable and productive societies are those, like the Roman Republic, that promoted liberty and accepted a degree of civil strife as the price for that freedom.‡

Machiavelli is both cynical about and tolerant of human nature. All

---

*   Even John Locke, a philosopher with a greater faith in man's capacity for reasoned behavior, shared Machiavelli's opinion: "if [human appetites] were left to their full swing, they would carry men to the overturning of all morality. Moral laws are set as a curb and restraint to these exhorbitant desires" (Locke, *Essay Concerning Human Understanding*, I, 3, p. 34).

†   Machiavelli's views were echoed by many of the American Founding Fathers, including Alexander Hamilton and John Jay, the first Chief Justice of the Supreme Court, who wrote: "the mass of men are neither wise nor good, and virtue . . . can only be drawn to a point and executed by . . . a strong government ably administered" (John Jay letter to George Washington, June 27, 1786).

‡   This might seem at first to be a contradiction, but it is in keeping with his belief that life is unpredictable. Political systems must be flexible, able to adapt to changing circumstances. This is the hallmark of mixed societies that have evolved through the creative clash among the classes. This theme is more fully developed in *The Discourses*, especially I, iv.

men may be "wicked," as he asserts, but what he really means is that all men are animals who act according to their bestial natures. Where Aristotle declared that what distinguished man from the rest of creation was the exercise of reason,* Machiavelli stresses our kinship with the animals. All living beings are defined by unreasonable appetite, and humans are no exception. We are selfish and self-serving, cowardly, dishonest, and greedy, but Machiavelli refuses to pass judgment. "[I]t is impossible to go against what nature inclines us to do," he says. He accepts our failings, just as he indulged his own vices, preferring to deploy wry humor rather than harsh censure. One vice he lacked was hypocrisy, the vice that justifies all other vices by refusing to recognize in oneself the sins attributed to others.

In the eyes of future generations Machiavelli's greatest crime, the characteristic that has become most closely identified with the term *Machiavellian*, is his disdain for the cardinal virtue of honesty. Machiavelli himself contributed to this perception, boasting on occasion of his own duplicitous nature. Writing to Guicciardini about an elaborate practical joke the two of them were playing on the simple villagers of Carpi, he proclaims: "As for the lies of these citizens of Carpi, I can beat all of them out, because it has been a while since I have become a doctor of this art . . . so, for some time now I have never said what I believe or believed what I said; and if indeed I do sometimes tell the truth, I hide it behind so many lies that it is hard to find." But this is little more than wishful thinking. Machiavelli may have been an admirer of cleverness in others, but he was in fact something of a naïf, offending those around him by telling them exactly what he thought. In fact Machiavelli was among the most honest—even tactless—of men. It is his brutal frankness, not his prevarications, that caused him so much trouble. What kind of liar would make such a confession or publicly announce his belief that deception is often the most effective strategy? It is the deceiver who conceals his art by playing the part of an honest man.

Even more than his advocacy of judicious cruelty, it is his promotion of judicious deceit that has made Machiavelli's name synonymous with villainy. "[A] wise prince cannot keep his word when the situation alters to his

---

* Belief in man's inherent rationality is the basis for Aristotle's entire ethical and political system. "[A]ll associations aim at some good," he begins his *Politics*, "that one which is supreme and embraces all others will have also as its aim the supreme good. That is the association we call the State, and that type of association we call political" (I, I). It is hard to imagine a less Machiavellian statement than this.

disadvantage and when the basis on which he made the pledge no longer holds," he insists. Anticipating in advance the abuse that will come his way, he returns to that critical distinction between the world as it should be, the "fancies" imagined by philosophers, and the world as it really is: "If all men were good, this precept would not be good, but since they are wicked and would not keep faith with you, you need not keep faith with them."

Equally cynical is his contention that a prince who cannot afford to *be* virtuous must nonetheless *appear* to be so: "I know everyone agrees that it would be laudable for a prince to possess every good quality. But since it is not possible to possess them all, or subscribe to them completely—the human condition being what it is—it is necessary to be sufficiently prudent to avoid gaining a reputation for those vices which would cost him his state. . . . For, everything considered, he will discover things which, though seeming virtuous, will cause his ruin, and others which, though seeming wicked, will make him secure and promote his well-being."*

In noting the strategic uses of cruelty and deceit, Machiavelli dismisses millennia of ethical teaching as irrelevant to the way men and women actually live. The revolution achieved by *The Prince* is to engineer a radical shift in perspective away from the God-centered universe of previous thinkers to one in which the human animal takes his place alongside the other beasts in a perpetual struggle for security and the gratification of appetite. "[S]o great is man's ambition that, in striving to slake his present desire, he gives no thought to the evils that in a short time will follow in its wake," Machiavelli observes in a passage that is echoed a century and a half later in the *Leviathan* of Thomas Hobbes.† In *The Discourses*, he offers a similarly bleak assessment: "[H]uman appetites are insatiable, for by nature we are so constituted that there is nothing we cannot long for, but by fortune we are such that of these things we can attain but few. The result is that the human mind is perpetually discontented, and of its possessions is apt to grow weary." The moral architecture of sin and redemption painstakingly constructed over the centuries by the Church has vanished,

---

* Machiavelli offers a variation on this notion in *La Mandragola*: "[M]any times one comes to harm by being too accommodating and too good, as well as by being too bad" (*La Mandragola*, IV, 6, in *Chief Works*, II, 810).

† "I put for a general inclination of all mankind, a perpetual and restless desire of power after power, that ceaseth only in death" (Hobbes, *Leviathan*, XI, 64).

replaced by the empirical methodology of the laboratory. In this new setting the moralist gives way to the political scientist, whose job is not to
condemn human nature but to describe it in order to minimize its most
pernicious effects. Instead of the morally freighted concept of original sin,
Machiavelli offers up the morally neutral concept of human nature, something that must be managed rather than atoned for.

Machiavelli abandons the pose of clinical detachment he has deployed
throughout *The Prince* in the book's stirring final chapter. In "An Exhortation to Free Italy from the Hands of the Barbarians," all the passion that
has been bubbling just below the surface erupts in a brilliant and stirring
peroration in which he paints an abject picture of contemporary Italy and
calls upon the Medici lord to embrace his destiny as the nation's liberator:

> *Almost bereft of life, Italy waits for someone who can salve her*
> *wounds, put an end to the sacking of Lombardy, to the despoiling*
> *of Naples and Tuscany, and heal those sores that have for too long*
> *festered. See how she prays God to send someone who will rescue her*
> *from the cruel and insolent barbarian. See, too, how eager she is to*
> *rally to any banner, so long as there is someone who will raise it.*

Many have discovered in this final chapter the key to Machiavelli's own
redemption. To those who accuse him of being the despot's best friend, his
defenders respond with this moving exhortation, as if to say that every uncomfortable recommendation that preceded it—every defense of violence,
every attempt to justify deceit—can be forgiven (or at least explained) on
the grounds that desperate times called for desperate measures, that only
a leader as stone-hearted and ruthless as Machiavelli's imaginary prince
could save Italy from ruin.

To the extent that Machiavelli justified dictatorship, it is clear that he
thought of it as a temporary expedient. Looking back on Roman history
in *The Discourses*, he remarks: "I claim that republics which, when in imminent danger, have recourse neither to a dictatorship, nor some form of
authority analogous to it, will always be ruined when grave misfortune
befalls them." Tyranny is not the ideal form of government, but sometimes
there is no alternative. Now, Machiavelli would argue, is one of those mo-

ments when only a firm hand on the tiller can steer the nation to safety. With the states of Italy bowed beneath a foreign yoke, only a strong leader possessed of immense courage and foresight and granted extraordinary powers can set free a suffering people. "And although someone may already have given us a glimmer of hope that he had been ordained by God for our redemption," Machiavelli says in an oblique reference to Valentino, "still we saw how at the critical moment he was abandoned by fortune."

Only the house of Medici, he insists, can raise up the banner so recently laid down by the house of Borgia: "Nor at the moment can one see where one may place hope other than in your illustrious house," he tells Lorenzo, "which, blessed by fortune and virtue, favored by God and by the Church, can place itself at the head of this campaign of redemption." But in order to fulfill its glorious destiny, the ruling family of Florence must learn the lessons of history. Here Machiavelli turns to one of his favorite themes: the need for an army of citizen soldiers who fight not for pay but for love of country: "Should your house wish to emulate those great men who redeemed their countries, it will be necessary, above all other things, to furnish yourself with your own army, the foundation of every undertaking; for you cannot possess more loyal, truer, or better soldiers. . . . [C]ommanded by their own prince," he concludes, "Italian valor will defend us from the foreigners."

If Machiavelli were in need of absolution, this final chapter might provide some measure of grace. He was above all an ardent patriot and had nothing but scorn for those corrupt weaklings who had plunged their nations into the abyss. Though his loyalties are no longer parochially Florentine—encompassing now the broader conception of an as yet unrealized Italian nation—his passion for his country, however defined, provides the guiding principle of all his policies.* Much of the apparent harshness of *The Prince* stems from his realization that only a powerful lord, another Valentino, could rescue a people "more oppressed than the Hebrews, more

---

*   In fact Machiavelli never abandoned his Florentine bias. As the final chapter of *The Prince* amply demonstrates, he envisioned Florence as the capital of a newly unified Italian state. This happy outcome was far easier to envision now that a Florentine sat on the papal throne. After the reunification of Italy in the nineteenth century, Florence did serve briefly as the capital. If Machiavelli's parochial Italian nationalism would not bear fruit for centuries, it was enormously influential in the wider context of sixteenth-century Europe, which saw the consolidation and expansion of the great nation-states of France, Spain, and England. By discarding the universalism of medieval philosophy in favor of a worldview that accepted as natural the violent clash of competing states, Machiavelli developed a working political science suitable for kings and diplomats.

enslaved than the Persians, more scattered than the Athenians, without leaders, without order, beaten, despoiled, whipped, trampled, suffering every kind of ruin."

But though Machiavelli's view of the world was shaped by contemporary events, the principles of conduct he lays out in his book have a more universal application. More important than any particular prescription—since each is only tentative, to be adopted as long as it is effective and discarded as soon as it proves faulty—is his perspective, his willingness to face a world where mankind has been left to its own devices. He provides a new moral architecture to replace the tottering edifice based on Christian virtues that were everywhere espoused and nowhere obeyed. He insists that we deal with the world as it is, rather than the world as we wish it were, separating once and for all the role of the political scientist from the theologian, the sociologist from the metaphysician.*

One feature of the world that his predecessors largely neglected but that to Machiavelli was the very heart of the matter was the violent clash between opposing states. Medieval philosophers like Aquinas and Dante recognized that in the real world a prince might rule over limited territory and might be forced to take up arms against an unscrupulous colleague, but this was merely an unfortunate and temporary deviation from the ideal of a universal government sanctioned by God.† Machiavelli, by contrast, cannot conceive of government absent the state of war, calling it "the only art which is of concern to one who commands." He can't be bothered speculating about universal empires filled with happy subjects flourishing under the paternal care of a wise and serene monarch since it is the fact of man's violent nature that makes government necessary in the first place. His is a Darwinian world where a prince must devour his neighbors before they have a chance to feast on him, where war is the normal condition and only the strong and cunning survive.

If critics have detected in Machiavelli a moral slipperiness—a dis-

---

* It is a startling coincidence that *The Prince* and Thomas More's *Utopia* (1516) were written within a few years of each other. If More's book is the culmination of a long tradition of imagining the ideal state that began with Plato, Machiavelli's announces the birth of modern political science.

† Universal government was a more realistic prospect in the Middle Ages when the Holy Roman Emperor was the most powerful monarch in Europe. Dante's *De Monarchia* is a passionate plea for the restoration of peace under the aegis of the heir of Caesar and Augustus.

creditable tendency to tailor principle to circumstance—this is because what mattered to him was not the individual conscience (or soul, to use the term that had greater currency in his own day) but the result of any course of action.* Sometimes he seems to advocate tyranny as the solution to Italy's problems; at other times, particularly in *The Discourses*, he argues at length for republican rule. These are mere details. Machiavelli's originality lies in the ease with which his philosophy—or, more accurately, his *approach*, since *philosophy* implies a consistency he never aspires to—can accommodate both systems. Experience is his guide and expedience his god. One must stick to the path of the good as long as possible, he agrees, but when pursuit of this chimera leads one into treacherous thickets, the ruler must be prepared to abandon this elusive goal and strike out in a different direction.

Machiavelli's letter to Francesco Vettori dated December 10, 1513, indicates that, a mere ten months after his release from prison, he had almost completed his brief tract. But now that he was nearing the end doubts began to creep in: "I have discussed this little study of mine with Filippo [Casavecchia] and whether or not it would be a good idea to present it [to Giuliano], and if it were a good idea, whether I should take it myself or send it to you. Against presenting it would be my suspicion that he might not even read it and that that person [Piero] Ardinghelli might take credit for this most recent of my endeavors." His fear that Ardinghelli, one of Giuliano de' Medici's private secretaries, would take credit for his work suggests that Machiavelli thought he had achieved something notable. In an age before copyright protection, literary theft was a common occurrence, and Machiavelli had every reason to worry that others might claim his ideas as their own.†

In fact Machiavelli never sent the work to Giuliano, perhaps because Vettori's response was discouraging. "When I have seen it," Vettori told him, "I shall tell you my opinion about presenting it or not to the Mag-

---

* Machiavelli often uses the word *animo*, meaning spirit (as in a spirited horse) but rarely, if ever, *anima*, meaning soul.

† In fact this had happened with his *First Decennale*, which was printed in an unauthorized edition in Pistoia (see letter no. 110 in Machiavelli et al., *Machiavelli and His Friends*, p. 121).

nificent Giuliano, as it may seem to me"—a less than ringing endorsement of the project. It may also have occurred to Machiavelli how unsuitable the text was for its intended recipient. In writing *The Prince*, Machiavelli had let his imagination and his hopes run away with him. Giuliano de' Medici, the youngest son of Lorenzo the Magnificent, turned out to have been a man singularly ill adapted to play the role Machiavelli had assigned to him. He was cultured like his father but had none of the great man's passion for statecraft. As one of the principal characters in Baldassare Castiglione's popular *The Courtier*, a sixteenth-century guide to princely refinement and good breeding, Giuliano appears as an affable and sophisticated gentleman, hardly the ruthless leader Machiavelli was dreaming up in the pages of his book.*

Machiavelli was not the only one frustrated in his attempt to refashion the young Medici lord into a great prince. Pope Leo had similar ambitions for his younger brother, and grew impatient as he, too, saw his efforts fall short. Not long after ascending the papal throne Leo had named Giuliano Gonfaloniere of the Church, a position that Cesare Borgia had held before him; following the pattern set by the della Rovere family, he also made Giuliano a feudal lord by marrying him into the French nobility. Giuliano's marriage to Philiberte of Savoy brought him the high-sounding title Duke of Nemours, but it could not light the fire of ambition in a man who preferred books and art to martial glory.

In the end the fun-loving Giuliano could not live up to his résumé. He never fulfilled his brother's expectations as the man who would extend the Medici dominion over north and central Italy, and was even more disappointing to those like Machiavelli who imagined him as the founder of a unified Italian state with Florence as its capital. In 1516 Giuliano succumbed to syphilis, a disease that had been brought to Italy by the invading French army in 1494. He lives on in history through the work of others rather than for anything he himself achieved.†

---

* Ironically, the conversations that Castiglione invents in his book are set in the palace of the Duke of Urbino, the same palace where Machiavelli first encountered Cesare Borgia and where he developed his lifelong fascination with the ruthless man of destiny.

† Giuliano and his nephew Lorenzo are famous for two things: it was to these two mediocrities that Machiavelli dedicated *The Prince*. They are also the residents of Michelangelo's magnificent Medici Tombs in the New Sacristy of San Lorenzo in Florence.

When Machiavelli finally worked up the courage to send *The Prince*, he dedicated it to Lorenzo de' Medici, the Pope's nephew, who now bore the hopes of the family as well as those of Florentine patriots. But Lorenzo proved no more capable than Giuliano. Leo's attempts to create a strong principality in the heart of Italy ruled by the Medici family and strong enough to deter foreign armies foundered even more quickly than Alexander's abortive efforts on behalf of his son. Machiavelli's dream of a unified Italian state would have to wait more than three centuries until a generation of leaders—led by Garibaldi, Cavour, and Mazzini, with Vittorio Emmanuele taking up the mantle discarded by the Medici princelings—inspired by the ideals of the French Revolution and fired by the patriotic exhortation of the Florentine civil servant, would drive the foreigners from native soil. As those nineteenth-century nationalists fought to liberate their nation from the Austrians, many marched into battle with the final words of *The Prince* ringing in their ears:

Against barbarian rage,
Virtue will take the field; then short the fight;
True to their lineage,
Italian hearts will prove their Roman might.

X I

VITA CONTEMPLATIVA

"[F]or the common benefit of all, I have decided to follow a path that has not yet been explored by anyone."

—MACHIAVELLI, *DISCOURSES*, "PREFACE"

MACHIAVELLI WAS SINGULARLY UNSUITED TO THE life of the country squire. Tending to his modest estate felt like an unpleasant chore and he was bored without the stimulating conversation he was used to. His circumstances, he complained, were "sordid and ignominious," and he railed against the malice of fate that had brought him to such a pass. Writing to Vettori, who was currently enjoying the fleshpots of Rome, he offered an account of a typical day, knowing what a sorry contrast his rustic diversions made by comparison:

> *I have been living in the country, and, following these latest broils, I have not spent a total of twenty days in Florence. Recently I have been catching thrushes with my own hands. I'd get up before dawn, prepare the birdlime, and set out with a bundle of birdcages on my back so that I looked like Geta when he came back from the harbor with Amphitryon's books.* I would catch at least two thrushes, six at most. And so I passed all of September. But even this amusement, strange and lowly as it was, dwindled, much to my regret.*

---

* A reference drawn from novella *Geta e Birria*, based in turn on a comedy by Plautus, involving a servant (Geta) who, while delivering books from his master to his home, interrupts his master's wife in an illicit liaison with Jupiter.

For Machiavelli, the modest stone house at Sant' Andrea in Percussina, just off the road that led from Florence to Siena, was like Elba to Napoleon, a place of exile where he could think of nothing but plotting his return to public life. In between trips to the local tavern where he gambled and quarreled with the locals, he vented his feelings in letters to friends and consoled himself by writing on the only subject that mattered to him.

Machiavelli never intended to become a full-time intellectual. A career as a writer was far inferior to, and much less satisfying than, active participation in civic life. He had always been a voracious reader, not only of history but also of the ancient and modern poets. Now, literature and love were among the few pleasures left to him, as he tells Vettori: "Leaving the woods, I go to a spring, and then to one of the spots where I hang my bird nets. In my arm I carry a book: Dante, Petrarch, or one of those minor poets like Tibullus, Ovid. I read of their amorous passions and their loves and recall my own, and lose myself for a while in these happy thoughts."

The writer's life was not entirely new to Machiavelli. Even before he lost his job he occasionally tried his hand at poetry, though even here it was not so much an escape from politics as an alternate route to understanding the subject that interested him most.* In a period of enforced idleness these pursuits took up more of his time and occupied a greater part of his imaginative life. "[T]o live as a malcontent," he wrote in "On Ingratitude or Envy," "would give me more sorrow and more vexation, if it were not that still the sweet strings of my harp, giving forth soft airs, make the Muses not deaf to my singing."

For Machiavelli the company of the Muses was at best a mixed blessing. Throwing himself into his art may have helped soften the blow of his disgrace, but he never lost his taste for the high-stakes drama of politics. In fact he hoped to use his considerable literary gifts to save himself from the literary life. His very identity hung in the balance, since in republican Florence participation in politics defined one's standing as a citizen. To be, as his father had been, excluded from this world was to be only half a man.

Exchanging the *vita activa* for the *vita contemplativa* involved more

---

* His most sustained literary effort to date, the *First Decennale*, was simply a chronicle of contemporary politics in verse form. After his dismissal he tried to complete a sequel, but he left his *Second Decennale* unfinished because he no longer had access to the government documents that served as source material.

than the replacement of one lifestyle with another: each represented an alternative mode of being for the thoughtful man, and their contrasting merits had formed a staple of philosophical argument since at least the time of ancient Greece. A classic paean to the *vita contemplativa* comes from the Roman poet Horace, who depicts the pleasures of the simple life in "Otium" (Repose):

> *He lives happily on a little, on whose frugal table shines the ancestral salt-dish, and whose soft slumbers are not carried away by fear or sordid greed.*
> *Why do we strive so hard in our brief lives for great possessions? Why do we change our country for climes warmed by a different sun? What exile from his fatherland ever escaped himself as well?*

How different Machiavelli's attitude toward the "frugal table"! How quickly would he abandon his rustic retreat for a chance to match wits once again with courtiers and kings. For Machiavelli there is no question which life is more fulfilling or more fit for an intelligent and capable man. Ironically, he makes his most passionate case for the *vita activa* even as circumstances forced him to adopt a way of life more in keeping with its opposite. As he puttered about his farm in Sant' Andrea, his mind remained fully engaged in the life of the city. He pressed friends for any information they could give him about the goings-on abroad, and followed intently the debates in the Palazzo della Signoria. Whenever he was in the city he eagerly participated in those gatherings on the Ponte Vecchio or Old Market where men congregated to discuss the latest diplomatic imbroglio or rumor of war. In a town filled with amateur politicians, he was known about town as a feisty and opinionated debater who pursued a line of inquiry or teased out a thesis until his listeners were exhausted. One can detect a faint echo of those long-into-the-night arguments in his letters with Francesco Vettori. In these back-and-forth exchanges, which often went on for page after page of densely packed script, the retired civil servant seems to delve more deeply into the intricacies of foreign policy than the diplomat. "According to your letter of the 21st," Machiavelli writes, "you would like to know what I think has prompted Spain to make this truce with France," offering in following paragraphs such a tightly woven analysis of the geopolitical situation that Vettori is forced to admit, "you were right and I was mistaken."

All Machiavelli's important political writings date to the period following his expulsion from office, but though he was banished from the Palazzo della Signoria his perspective remains that of the civil servant. This gives his books a unique flavor among the great works of political philosophy. They are pragmatic, acerbic, filled with penetrating insights into matters both great and small, and always faithful to the principles that guided him as an agent of the Florentine government: to provide the clearest, most useful analysis of any situation, free from cant and stripped of illusion.

Perhaps the best way to frame Machiavelli's revolutionary approach is to compare him to the man whose life in many ways most closely paralleled his own. Marcus Tullius Cicero was a Roman statesman who turned to philosophy after being forced from political office in circumstances not dissimilar to those that ended the career of Florence's Second Chancellor. As a Roman consul who found himself on the wrong side of history when he backed Cassius and Brutus in their war with the heirs of Caesar, Cicero was forced to retire to his country villa.* For thousands of years men looked to Cicero's essays for an eloquent defense of the *vita contemplativa*, his authority enhanced by his impeccable credentials as a practitioner of the *vita activa*. Cicero described his coming of age as a philosopher in *De Officiis*:

> *If things had gone better I should never have been devoting my attention to writing, as I do now. No, I would have been delivering public addresses, as I used to in the days when we still had a government. . . . Every scrap of my energy, attention and care used to go to politics. So when there was no such thing as politics any more, it was inevitable that my voice should be heard in the Forum and Senate no longer. Yet how could I let my mind become completely idle? . . . [T]he terrible calamities that have descended on us nowadays have at least made it possible to extract one advantage from the situation. That is to say,*

---

* Like Machiavelli, Cicero worked for a republican government and got into trouble when it was overthrown by tyrannical forces. He was ultimately assassinated—a parallel that must have struck Machiavelli as too close for comfort.

they have given me the opportunity to prepare written accounts of ex-
tremely worthwhile subjects which our compatriots have never known
enough about before.

For Cicero banishment from public life turns out to be a blessing in disguise, allowing him the serenity to turn his mind to timeless truths. Machiavelli, by contrast, thought the life of the mind poor compensation for
what he had lost. Not only is he incapable of summoning Cicero's serenity,
but the source of his frustration lies in something Cicero would not have
understood or sympathized with. "I believe that if His Holiness would
put me to work," Machiavelli pleads with Vettori, "I would not only help
myself but also bring honor and benefits to all my friends." For Machiavelli
"work" and "benefits"* are intimately bound up with "honor," a modern,
bourgeois notion that ran counter to millennia of teaching in which leisure was deemed essential to the cultivation of the noble spirit.† Cicero
considered public life a burden, shouldered only reluctantly out of a sense
of duty to his country; relieved of that burden he is free to return to the
way of life he found most congenial.‡ Machiavelli, showing himself to be
no gentleman, feels useless without his old job. In the wake of their mis-
fortunes both unemployed politicians turned to writing, but while Cicero
leaves behind his former life with few regrets, Machiavelli acts like a jilted
lover still obsessed with the woman who scorned him.

Machiavelli did not share the aristocrat's contempt for honest labor;
indeed, he could hardly afford to. He belonged to the professional class,
which in Florence included notaries, lawyers, and physicians—educated
men who worked for a living and who stood uneasily between the ruling elite and the mass of illiterate workers and peasants. He was a salary

---

* "Benefits," what Machiavelli calls *utili*, are those tangible profits to be made from service to the state.
The highest offices of the land pay only in terms of *honori*.

† The idea that leisure is essential to civilization was first articulated by the ancient Greeks. Plato and
Aristotle both defended slavery as the means by which gentlemen were provided with the freedom to
philosophize. "Indeed, some things are so divided right from birth, some to rule, some to be ruled"
(Aristotle *The Politics*, I, 5). Machiavelli, however, is suspicious of leisure and of the class of men who
live off the labor of others. See, for instance, his claim that "quiet [gives birth] to leisure, leisure to disorder, disorder to ruin" (*Florentine Histories*, V, 1).

‡ Cicero's disdain for the rough and tumble of politics was more rhetorical than real. He continually
involved himself in politics even as he feigned indifference.

man, a "working stiff" to borrow a modern phrase, and embraced the role of a civil servant that a true gentleman would have found degrading. As befit a true professional, he offered his expertise rather than an abstract philosophy suitable for the academy. "[I]n this work I have expressed all that I know and all that I have learned from a long practice and from continual study of the ways of this world," he wrote in the dedication to *The Discourses*, confirming that his natural habitat is the bustling office, not the ivory tower.

For centuries, proponents of the *vita contemplativa* celebrated the simple joys of country life. Machiavelli's famous letter to Vettori in which he first mentions *The Prince* stands the tradition of the bucolic idyll on its head. His version of country life is not marked, like Cicero's, by philosophical reflection but by "a thousand squabbles and angry words," the vitriol not diminished by the insignificance of the stakes. If his status as a property owner raises him above his fellow villagers, relations are marked by rivalry and competition for resources rather than by reverence and awe. Instead of happy shepherds playing their flutes and dreaming of lovely nymphs—a poetic vision favored by aristocratic Florentines like Lorenzo the Magnificent—Machiavelli gives us toothless peasants who cheat at cards and plot to swindle their neighbors. In life, as in his speculative philosophy, Machiavelli deemed it best to stick to the reality of things.

Machiavelli's realism is both aesthetic and substantive. He turns the same unsparing eye on his country neighbors as he does on the great lords of Europe, accepting human nature as he finds it and offering advice on how to prosper in a world populated by scoundrels. And if his view of human nature is unsentimental, it is also generous, accepting, and open to the comedy inherent in daily existence.

The difference between Machiavelli's attitude and that of Cicero is largely one of social standing. Machiavelli can't afford to romanticize the poor peasants who surround him since he is not far removed from their condition. In fact he is engaged in a daily battle to avoid being pulled down to their level. Honest labor is the antidote to a life of shabby indolence, and, conversely, those who live off the toil of others are a threat to good government. In *The Discourses* Machiavelli derides those gentlemen "who live in idleness on the abundant revenue derived from their estates, without having anything to do either with their cultivation or with other forms of labor essential to life. Such men are a pest in any republic . . . but still more pernicious are those who, in addition to the aforesaid revenues, have castles under their command and subjects who are under their obedience. . . . For men born in such conditions are inimical to any form of civic government."

Here Machiavelli shows himself to be a true child of Florence, product of a merchant culture that valued work and carried in its collective consciousness a memory of the battles required to free itself from the grasp of the feudal aristocracy. In particular, he is a product of the Florentine professional class, that pool of educated men dependent on their wealthier patrons for their livelihood. While it is true that many a Florentine merchant wished nothing more than to accumulate enough wealth to retire to a castle in the countryside where he could ape the manners of an idle lord, Machiavelli was never tempted by a life of pampered indolence. Perhaps if he had been richer the pleasures of idleness might have been more appealing, but given his poverty, inactivity meant disgrace.

Machiavelli, for all his financial insecurity, is not a dependent but rather a client, a subtle but important distinction. Unlike Erasmus, who joined the court of Charles V, Machiavelli hoped to sell his services to his social superiors but was never completely under their thumb. His relations with the great and near great of Florence were mediated by his salary, which put him in a subservient position while still leaving him his own man. His condition prefigures that of countless men and women in the following centuries, that great class of salaried professionals who labor in anonymity but whose income permits a modicum of autonomy and self-respect. His work ethic, unsentimental attitude toward his inferiors, and cynicism toward those above him in the pecking order, foreshadow the world to come. One can sense in Machiavelli the bourgeois's fragile vanity, where servility wars with pride and feelings of shame at his neediness are alleviated by a healthy sense of his own abilities.

Machiavelli's insecure status in society goes a long way toward explaining his novel approach to timeworn themes. Gone are those hazy abstractions favored by earlier philosophers, replaced by a hardheaded assessment built on years of experience. "I have no greater gift to offer you," he tells his patron, "than the ability to comprehend in a very brief time all that I, over many years and through much toil and many dangers, have come to learn and understand." What could be further from the *vita contemplativa* than a life of "labors and danger"? It is the fruits of this workaday life that Machiavelli can offer his patron, bringing a professional's coldly calculating eye to material once thought suitable only to learned scholars who rarely left the sanctuary of their book-lined studies.

The Prince was not the only important work that emerged from this most difficult period in Machiavelli's life. Even as he was writing his most famous tract, he was hard at work on a more substantial manuscript whose theme the Medici lords might have found less appealing.* Machiavelli first gives a hint of a second work early in the pages of *The Prince*. "I shall leave out any discussion of republics," he informs his readers, "since I have discussed them at length elsewhere." This casual remark is crucial not only for determining the chronology of his two most important philosophical books (he apparently worked on both simultaneously in the initial period following his forced retirement) but, more importantly, in resolving the apparently contradictory picture each presents of its author. Those who know Machiavelli only through his most famous book tend to consider him an apologist for tyranny, while to those who have dived into the denser material of *The Discourses* he appears a stalwart defender of republican government. Those conversant with both sometimes dismiss him as an opportunist, willing to sell his intellectual virtue to whoever is paying his wages.

Machiavelli's *Discourses*—or to give its full title, *The Discourses on the First Ten Books of Titus Livius*†—is no minor or secondary work. Not only is it considerably longer than *The Prince*, but in its pages Machiavelli gives the fullest account of his political philosophy. He himself considered it his

---

* Machiavelli began *The Discourses* in 1513, the same year he wrote the bulk of *The Prince*, but it is clear that it took him many years to complete. It is dedicated to two men, Zanobi Buondelmonti and Cosimo Rucellai, with whom he became friendly sometime after 1515, after he became a regular attendee of the get-togethers at the Orti Oricellari. There are also references to events, such as the conquest of Urbino (*Discourses*, II, 10, 301), dating to as late as 1517, indicating that Machiavelli was still refining the text at that time.

† Titus Livius (Livy) was a Roman scholar from the reign of Augustus who wrote a monumental history of Rome from its founding to his own day. Only thirty-five of the original 142 books survive. The first ten books, which provide the starting point for Machiavelli's own meditations on government, take us to the third century B.C., just as Rome was poised to become a world power.

most important contribution to political theory, and would certainly have been amused, if not bewildered, to learn that this substantial and erudite work would ultimately be eclipsed by its slighter companion. While *The Prince* is something of a polemic—a brilliant and passionate argument written in response to a personal and political crisis—*The Discourses* presents a reasoned inquiry, based on historical precedents, into the nature of government and a penetrating analysis of how states are formed, how they can be preserved, and what causes them to fail.

The Discourses is in some respects a typical product of Florentine humanism, the intellectual movement that sought to revive the art, language, and literature of the classical past. Inspired by Petrarch's pioneering scholarship in the mid-fourteenth century and primarily associated with Florence, this cultural and literary revival challenged the established order by placing on an equal footing with the teachings of the Church Fathers a body of work of great ambition and sophistication written by men who knew nothing of the Gospels. Rediscovering the depth and breadth of pagan learning and the glories of Greek and Roman art, both excited and unsettled generations of Florentines as accepted wisdom was reexamined in the light of novel ideas—anxieties exploited by fundamentalists like Savonarola, whose preaching satisfied a longing for certainty.

Machiavelli, though he belonged to a generation that had grown up on the great classical texts, was perhaps the first to face squarely the challenge posed by the revival of ancient learning. Most of his contemporaries were content to spend their leisure hours absorbed in a volume of erotic poetry by Ovid or Caesar's history of the Gallic Wars, and then make their way to church to attend Mass, oblivious to the ethical and intellectual acrobatics required to embrace both worldviews. Machiavelli confronts the essential contradiction: that accepting the teaching of the Gospels and simultaneously taking seriously the lessons taught by the pagan philosophers and historians plunged one into a vertiginous world of paradox and moral ambiguity.

The unsettled and unsettling nature of Machiavelli's writing is a product of this clash of mutually exclusive systems of value, one of which makes a claim on our faith, the other on our reason. It is a clash that can be resolved only through deception, that most Machiavellian of expedients:

A prince, therefore, cannot in fact possess all the virtues previously mentioned, but he would do well to appear to possess them. Indeed, I will go so far as to say that should he have all the virtues and observe them at all times it would be positively harmful, though appearing to be virtuous would prove consistently useful. It would serve him to appear pious, faithful, humane, true, religious, and even to be so, but only if he is willing, should it become necessary, to act in the opposite manner. It must be understood that a prince, especially a newly crowned prince, cannot observe all those things that give a man a reputation for goodness, it often being necessary, for the preservation of the state, to act against faith, against charity, against humanity, against religion.

Machiavelli was not the first to recognize that it was impossible for a politician to live according to the precepts set down by Jesus and his disciples, but he was the first to openly endorse *appearing* to live by one set of standards while secretly adopting another. Without explicitly rejecting the faith into which he had been born, he demonstrates time and again which set of values he esteems more.

Machiavelli builds *The Discourses* around one of the key sources of Roman history, Titus Livius's *History of Rome*. It was a text that had particular significance for him. His father, Bernardo, had spent many years compiling an index for a new, multivolume edition and in return for this scholarly effort had received a set of the books, which otherwise he could not have afforded. It was these precious family heirlooms that Niccolò now consulted as the basis for his own monumental undertaking.

In his fascination with ancient, particularly Roman, history, and in his tendency to view his own times through the lens of the distant past, Machiavelli differed little from other well-educated Florentines. But while he and his peers were steeped in the same cultural brew, Machiavelli transformed the common intellectual material of the day into something new. When he showed the still unfinished work to Jacopo Nardi, his friend marveled that it presented "a new argument, never (that I know) essayed by any other." Machiavelli himself believed that what he was attempting constituted a radical departure from the self-consciously antiquarian tomes of his peers. In the preface to *The Discourses* he writes that "for the common benefit of all, I have decided to follow a path that has not yet been explored by anyone," a claim that echoes one made in *The Prince*, where he says "I intend to depart substantially from what others have said."*

In *The Prince* the claim of originality is followed by one of his more startling prescriptions—that the sensible ruler will always strive to *appear* good, while sticking to the good only as long as it proves useful to him. In *The Discourses* the claim of originality involves what appears at first to be a less radical departure from tradition. Machiavelli insists that, while antique forms are widely admired, the substance of the ancients' achievement is neglected. "[I]n the governing of kingdoms, in forming an army or conducting a war, in adjudicating the disputes of one's subjects, or in adding to empire, one finds neither princes, nor republics, nor captains, nor citizens who turn to the ancients for examples," he grumbles.

This might seem like a minor distinction. After all, most educated Florentines were already obsessed with the culture of ancient Greece and Rome, as familiar with the history of the Peloponnesian War as they were with their own recent struggles with Pisa or Milan. In fact religious zealots like Savonarola accused them of being more pagan than Christian. Machiavelli could not disagree more. Admiration for the ancients is superficial, he insists; his compatriots were dazzled by appearances while they failed to probe essentials. The important question to ask is not what made the proportions of the Pantheon so harmonious, but what allowed Alexander to conquer most of the known world with modest numbers of disciplined troops; not which rhyme scheme Virgil employed in *The Aeneid*, but what caused a small village along the marshy banks of the Tiber to grow and prosper until it ruled an empire that stretched from the Euphrates to the Thames:

---

* Machiavelli's opening salvo was mirrored by Galileo in his seminal *Dialogues Concerning Two New Sciences*, where he begins: "My purpose is to set forth a very new science dealing with a very ancient subject." (Quoted in Cassirer, "The Triumph of Machiavellism and Its Consequences," in *Essays in the History of Political Thought*, p. 127.) Galileo, like Machiavelli, was able to topple millennia-old systems of belief through the power of direct observation.

*When, therefore, I consider in what honor antiquity is held, and
how—to cite but one instance—a bit of an old statue has fetched
a high price that someone may have it by him to give honor to his
house . . . and when, on the other hand, I notice that what history
has to say about the highly virtuous actions performed by ancient
kingdoms and republics, by their kings, their generals, their citizens,
their legislators, and by others who have gone to the trouble of serving
their country, is rather admired than imitated; nay, is so shunned by
everybody in each little thing they do, that the virtue of bygone days
there remains no trace, it cannot but fill me at once with astonishment and grief.*

Machiavelli is urging nothing less than a revolution of values to complete
the revolution of taste that has already occurred. While many admired
the beauty of ancient art and the sophistication of its poetry, Machiavelli
believed that his contemporaries failed to grasp that the genius of the ancients lay in the *virtue* (or *virtù*) of the men who plied the chisel and the
pen, and, more importantly, of those who wrote the laws and fought the
battles.* Unless men embrace those ancient virtues, history will continue
on its downward spiral: "[S]ince fortune is changeable, republics and
states also change frequently. And they will go on changing until someone
comes along who is so enamored of antiquity that he arranges things in
such a manner that fortune does not, with every turn of the sun, show
what she is capable of."

But attributing the achievement of the ancients to their virtue
presents a fundamental problem. Though Machiavelli never explicitly
denies his own faith, he observes that those men who knew nothing of
Christ possessed admirable qualities absent among followers of the One
True Faith. As if this weren't dangerous enough, Machiavelli establishes
a causal link between the rise of Christianity and the decline of civic
virtue:

---

* Machiavelli makes a similar point in *The Art of War* when he criticizes the vogue for gardens laid
out in the classical manner by observing: "How much better, then, would those princes have done . . . if
they had endeavored to imitate the ancients in bearing hardships and inconveniences, instead of giving
themselves up to ease and indolence, in performing such exploits as were done in the sunshine and not
in the shade, in following their example while they continued honest and wholesome, and not when
they became dishonest and corrupt" (*The Art of War*, I, 10).

If one asks oneself how it comes about that peoples of old were more fond of liberty than they are today, I think the answer is that it is due to the same cause that makes men today less bold than they used to be; and this is due, I think, to the difference between our education and that of bygone times, which is based on the difference between our religion and the religion of those days. For our religion, having taught us the truth and the true way of life, leads us to ascribe less esteem to worldly honor. Hence the gentiles, who held it in high esteem and looked upon it as their highest good, displayed in their actions more ferocity than we do. . . . Our religion has glorified the humble and contemplative man, rather than men of action. It has assigned as man's highest good humility, abnegation, and contempt for mundane things, whereas the other identified it with magnanimity, bodily strength, and everything else that conduces to make men bold. And, if our religion demands that in you there be strength, what it asks for is strength to suffer rather than strength to do bold things.

If, as Machiavelli asserts, Christianity has "taught us the truth and the true way of life," why do we have so little to show for it? Far from setting us free, the truth in this case has sapped our strength and degraded our spirit. Here Machiavelli reaffirms the dichotomy, so prominent in *The Prince*, between what is "good" and what is "useful." It goes without saying that what is preached in the Gospels is good and true; it is equally obvious that following the example of Christ makes men weak and incapable of managing their affairs. Without the spur of fame and riches, the best among us retire to pursue the perfection of their own souls while corruption and hypocrisy flourish in the world they leave behind. Before the "truth" leads us to our doom, then, we should turn aside and follow instead the crooked paths of deceit.

Because Machiavelli is unwilling to contradict the fundamental tenets of Christian belief, he presents us with a paradox: that good can lead to evil and that progress can be made only by acting as if what is true is actually false. Much of the tension and many of the apparent contradictions in both *The Discourses* and *The Prince* stem from this clash between the Christian faith in which he was raised and which provided a conventional moral frame that not even he could escape, and the pagan virtues of strength, boldness, and civic-mindedness that he admired. This is what Machiavelli demands we confront in his preface to *The Discourses*: the unresolved, and perhaps unresolvable, dissonance between morality and utility. Were Machiavelli a more systematic thinker, he might well have ended up an avowed atheist, but in fact the former Second Chancellor of Florence seems willing to accept paradox. He was too keenly aware of Fortune's puckish sense of humor, too skeptical that universal solutions could accommodate messy reality, to make categorical statements, and while future generations, reading between the lines, have detected in his writings the suggestion that God is indeed dead, Machiavelli himself never went so far.

Do these logical knots reflect Machiavelli's own tortured conscience, or are the occasional nods he makes in the direction of conventional piety merely a concession to the papal censors? Clearly Machiavelli was not a particularly religious man. In one letter Guicciardini teases his friend that "your honor . . . would be darkened if at your age you started tending to your own soul, since having always lived by another creed it would be attributed to your entering a second childhood rather than to any native goodness." When it came to the outward forms of religion Machiavelli was less than diligent in his observance. "On feast days I hear mass," Vettori wrote to his friend, "and do not do as you do, who sometimes doesn't bother." Machiavelli could have pointed out in response that at least he was free of the sin of hypocrisy, since while both men were in the habit of frequenting prostitutes, *he* did not attempt to conceal his vice beneath a veneer of piety.

But for all his irreverence Machiavelli was probably not an atheist. Like many educated Florentines he derided the primitive superstition of his less enlightened compatriots and had nothing but scorn for the ignorant and vice-ridden clergy, feelings that emerge clearly in the character of *Frate* Timoteo, the money-grubbing monk in his play *La Mandragola*. He was also skeptical about much Christian doctrine. But there is no reason to believe he was tormented by these doubts. Metaphysics simply did not interest him, and he may well have retained some vestige of belief simply because he lacked the passion required to demolish it.

•   •   •

What is significant, however, is his insistence that one could not build a functioning society on Christian values. This does not mean that he had no respect for religious institutions. He often cites their social utility while dismissing their beliefs. "It was religion," he claims, "that facilitated whatever enterprise the senate and the great men of Rome designed to undertake." By contrast, Christianity promoted a "pattern of life" that "appears to have made the world weak, and to have handed it over as a prey to the wicked." And while Machiavelli blames this sorry state of affairs on "the pusillanimity of those who have interpreted our religion in terms of idleness not in terms of *virtù*," it is clear that he believes there is something in the nature of Christianity itself that encourages exploitation by corrupt and unscrupulous men. In fact there seems to be an inverse relationship between what is true and what is useful, since the pagan religions he praises as socially beneficial are exactly those that are, at least as far as Machiavelli was concerned, patently false.*

This alone might have been sufficient to earn Machiavelli the condemnation of the Church, but the outrage he provoked from generations of clerics rests on more specific provocations. When, shortly after Machiavelli's death, a prominent cardinal described him as "the finger of Satan," he spoke as a defender of the Church rather than as a theologian. If Machiavelli's attitude toward the most profound issues raised by religion was one of studied indifference, his attitude toward the Church, neighbor to the Florentine Republic in Italy and its frequent political and military rival, was one of barely contained rage. All the potentates of Italy, Machiavelli claims, contributed to the current sorry condition of the country, but the institution that above all others condemned them to misery and ignominy was the Holy Church:†

> It is the Church [he writes in *The Discourses*] that has kept, and keeps, Italy divided. Now of a truth no country has ever been united

---

* Machiavelli praises, for instance, Numa Pompilius, who pretended to receive his law code directly from a nymph in order to give his legislation supernatural sanction (see *Discourses*, I, 11).

† It is unclear whether Machiavelli saw the irony in dedicating *The Prince* to a member of a family whose current power stemmed from the fact that one of the Medici was now the Pope. Any chance that either Giuliano or Lorenzo de' Medici would rally the disunited forces of Italy depended on the resources and influence of the papacy.

and happy unless the whole of it has been under the jurisdiction of one republic or one prince. . . . And the reason why Italy is not in the same position . . . is entirely due to the Church. For, though the Church has its headquarters in Italy and has temporal power, neither its power nor its virtue has been sufficiently great for it to be able to usurp power in Italy and become its leader; nor yet, on the other hand, has it been so weak that it could not . . . call upon one of the powers to defend it against an Italian state that had become too powerful. . . . The Church, then, has neither been able to occupy the whole of Italy, nor has it allowed anyone else to occupy it. Consequently, it has been the cause why Italy has never come under one head, but has been under many princes and signori, by whom such disunion and such weakness has been brought about, that it has now become the prey, not only of barbarian potentates, but of anyone who attacks it. For which our Italians have to thank the Church, and nobody else.

Many Italians would have agreed with Machiavelli in private, even if most were more circumspect about such direct attacks in public.* But Machiavelli went further, attacking the Church not only for its meddlesome role in the temporal realm but also for corrupting religion itself:

[O]wing to the bad example set by the Court of Rome, Italy has lost all devotion and all religion. Attendant upon this are innumerable inconveniences and innumerable disorders; for as, where there is religion, it may be taken for granted that all is going well, so, where religion is wanting, it may be taken for granted the opposite. The first debt which we, Italians, owe to the Church and to priests, therefore, is that we have become irreligious and perverse.

Given this double-barreled assault on Christianity and the Church, it is not surprising that Machiavelli's works were among the first to find their

---

* On this topic, Machiavelli pulled no punches, even in his *Florentine Histories*, a work commissioned by and dedicated to Pope Clement VII: "So henceforward, all the wars waged by the barbarians in Italy were for the most part caused by the pontiffs, and all the barbarians who invaded it were most often called in by them. This mode of proceeding continues still in our own times; it is this that has kept Italy disunited and infirm" (*Florentine Histories*, I, 9, p. 20).

way onto the Papal Index of Prohibited Books in 1559—a grudging admission of the enduring power of his ideas.*

On the most obvious level the difference between *The Prince* and *The Discourses* lies in their subject matter: one book deals with principalities, the other with republics. "All states and all dominions that rule or have ruled over men were once or are now either republics or principalities," Machiavelli declares in the first chapter of *The Prince*, proposing to treat each separately without offering any judgment as to which is better. In 1517 when, at the behest of Pope Leo, he wrote his "Discourse on Remodeling the Government of Florence," he adopted a similarly evenhanded tone, declaring "that in all cities where the citizens are accustomed to equality, a princedom cannot be set up except with the utmost difficulty, and in those cities where the citizens are accustomed to inequality, a republic cannot be set up except with the utmost difficulty."†

Machiavelli's ethic is that of the craftsman, not the ideologue, the ethic of someone who treats ideas as objects that must function in the world and must be judged by the impact they have on the lives of real men and women. Given the fact that men live under both principalities and republics, the only responsible approach is to ensure that each runs as smoothly as possible. In a break with medieval tradition and anticipating modern attitudes, Machiavelli is concerned with the practical effects of an idea rather than its abstract or metaphysical qualities. While he is willing to sell his services to whoever holds the reins of power, he tailors his philosophy to suit his potential employer only to the extent of providing him with such

---

* Direct attacks on the Church and the Pope were not unusual among intellectuals of the era. Erasmus, a more spiritual man than Machiavelli, was no less harsh in his condemnation of a corrupt institution: "[S]ince the Christian Church was founded in blood, strengthened by blood and increased in blood, they continue to manage its affairs by the sword as if Christ has perished and can no longer protect his own people in his own way" (Erasmus, *Praise of Folly*, 59). It is also at this time (1517) Martin Luther nailed his ninety-five theses to the door of All Saints Church in Wittenburg, ushering in the Protestant Reformation.

† Later in the same essay he makes it clear which form is more suited to his beloved Florence: "[I]n order to have a princedom in Florence, where equality is great, the establishment of inequality would be necessary.... [T]o form a princedom where a republic would go well is a difficult thing and, through being difficult, inhumane and unworthy of whoever hopes to be considered merciful and good" (p. 107). Given the recipient of this essay, the statement must be regarded as courageous, if perhaps a bit foolhardy.

knowledge as might prove useful. He approaches politics as a civil servant, proffering his best advice to those responsible for the welfare of the state in the belief that this is the best way to minimize the risk of anarchy.

If Machiavelli can be said to have a political bias it is for order rather chaos. "[I]t is the man who uses violence to spoil things, not the man who uses violence to mend them, that is blameworthy," he insists. Machiavelli had witnessed firsthand the suffering caused by chaos and so is willing to pay almost any price for stability. "Wherever you turn your eyes, you see the earth wet with tears and blood, and the air full of screams, of sobs, of sighs," he wrote after visiting the war-torn Veneto in 1509. His assumption, not always borne out by subsequent history (witness Nazi Germany and Stalinist Russia), is that strong states are less violent than states of anarchy. Since anarchy, Fortuna's gift, seems to be the natural condition of the world, only great diligence and even ruthlessness—qualities associated with masculine *virtù*—can halt the downward spiral.

Though his defense of violence in the pursuit of order might appear to justify the actions of a despot, the bulk of Machiavelli's thought provides little comfort to the would-be tyrant. Machiavelli prefers stability to chaos, but he knows that this is impossible to achieve without tactical flexibility. In a world governed by chance and populated by selfish and ambitious men, government must be built from multiple moving parts if it is to accommodate competing interests. If at all possible power should be dispersed to prevent one man or faction oppressing his fellow citizens.

Despite his ideological flexibility, Machiavelli clearly states his preference for republican government:

> [A] republic has a greater life and enjoys for a longer time good fortune than a principality since, due to the diversity of its citizenry, it can accommodate itself better to changing circumstances than can a prince. For a man who is accustomed to proceed in a certain way never changes, as we have said, and so when times change and no longer suit his ways, he comes to ruin.

Note that his preference is based not on ideology but on the utilitarian grounds that republics are more stable than principalities. If, as Machiavelli asserts, "government by the populace is better than government by princes," this does not blind him to the fact that even the best system occasionally fails.

When a free society grows irredeemably weak or corrupt, the only recourse is for the people to place themselves under the care of a strong ruler. Machiavelli has as little patience with democratic purists as with defenders of tyranny. Examining the history of the Roman Republic, Machiavelli's ideal, he noted that "dictatorship, so long as it was bestowed in accordance with public institutions, and not assumed by the dictator on his own authority, was always of benefit to the state." The argument he puts forward in *The Prince* in favor of a powerful ruler, then, does not contradict the case he makes for republics in *The Discourses.** Rather, the conditions prevailing in Italy represent one of those special cases when "imminent danger" demands a "dictatorship . . . [or] some form of authority analogous to it."

Some have accused Machiavelli of moral relativism: of advocating one set of principles for a certain situation, and a different set when conditions change—an accusation that he would not so much refute as recharacterize as a sensible adaptation to shifting realities. In an imperfect and chaotic world a one-size-fits-all morality is self-defeating. Rigidity is harmful, flexibility beneficial, and because republics embrace a diversity of opinions and interests they are more likely to withstand unexpected blows of Fortune. Ethics, it turns out, is less a matter of hard and fast rules than of playing the odds, of preparing the ground in advance so that good outcomes are more likely than bad. It is here that republican government excels. Princes, no matter how able, tend to be set in their ways, but in a free society each citizen tugs in a slightly different direction, allowing the whole to navigate more nimbly history's wreckage-strewn landscape.

More is at stake in choosing the proper form of government than mere

---

*   Machiavelli does not make the temporary nature of the dictatorship he was advocating explicit in *The Prince*, but in "A Discourse on Remodeling the Government of Florence" (c. 1520), written at the behest of Pope Leo X, he directly, and perhaps rashly, makes just such an appeal. After admitting that at the moment "Florence cannot continue without a director; and since she has to have one, it is much better that he be of the house the people are accustomed to bow down to" (p. 104), Machiavelli assured the head of the Medici family that "[n]ever will the generality of the Florentine citizens be satisfied if the Hall [of the Great Council] is not reopened" (p. 110–11, in *Chief Works*, 1). In this work Machiavelli advises the Pope to use his great prestige to put the government of Florence on a sound footing and then relinquish power, an act, he says, "the most pleasing to God" (p. 114).

survival. Republics are not only more durable, but offer the best hope of promoting the greatest happiness for the greatest number of citizens:

> [F]or it is not the well-being of individuals that makes cities great, but the well-being of the community; and it is beyond question that it is only in republics that the common good is looked to properly in that all that promotes it is carried out; and, however much this or that private person may be the loser on this account, there are so many who benefit thereby that the common good can be realized in spite of those few who suffer in consequence.

But if rule by the people is preferable in normal times, such an inefficient system is ill adapted to times of crisis. "One should take it as a general rule," he argues, "that rarely, if ever, does it happen that a state, whether it be a republic or a kingdom, is either well-ordered at the outset or radically transformed *vis-à-vis* its old institutions unless this be done by one person." Founding a state requires boldness, courage, even ruthlessness—qualities rarely seen in bourgeois democracies. In writing *The Prince*, Machiavelli was hoping to inspire another Lycurgus who would repair the shattered states of Italy, even out of the unpromising material of the Medici heir.

Like the framers of the American Constitution, Machiavelli had a healthy skepticism of human nature. "[I]t must needs be taken for granted," he declared, "that all men are wicked and that they will always give vent to the malignity that is in their minds when opportunity offers." Given our debased nature, the most sensible form of government is one where power is divided among many hands. Each man will still be inclined to pursue his own selfish ends, but excesses will be curbed by the collective efforts of jealous, fearful neighbors.

In *The Discourses*, Machiavelli's system of checks and balances, to use an anachronistic phrase, is most often described as a dynamic tug-of-war between the haves and have-nots, the aristocracy and the people, each of whom has radically different interests and perspectives. "[I]n every republic," he says, "there are two different dispositions, that of the populace and that of the upper class and . . . all legislation favorable to liberty is brought about by the clash between them." Paradoxically, then, stability can be

achieved only by permitting a degree of internal dissension and chan-
neling those passions to constructive ends. In the case of Rome, "good
laws . . . [came] from those very tumults which many so inconsiderately
condemn." By contrast, Machiavelli's native Florence never succeeded in
transforming mutual antagonisms into productive legislation, succumbing instead to the plague of faction. "The enmities in Florence," he wrote,
"were always accompanied by sects and therefore always harmful; never
did a winning sect remain united except when the hostile sect was active,
but as soon as the one conquered was eliminated, the ruling one, no longer
having fear to restrain it or order within itself to check it, would become
divided again." It is obvious that the creative tumult of the kind that was
so constructive in Rome could easily devolve into the pernicious faction of
the kind that was so destructive in Florence, one explanation for history's
violent and unpredictable course.

Machiavelli's analysis, derived from his close study of Roman history,
constitutes a profound rupture with centuries of political thought. Instead
of assuming that comity is the highest political good, he insists that social
tensions are not only inevitable but can even be beneficial. This concept
flows inexorably from his pessimistic view of human nature. He replaces
the ancient ideal, championed by Plato and Aristotle, of a republic of *virtue* with one based on *interest*. To the Greeks, good government resulted
only when high-minded men came together to pursue the common good.
To Machiavelli, who assumes that all men are scoundrels, it is obvious
that this happy moment will never arrive. Instead, good government must
somehow arise from selfish people pursuing selfish ends. By demonstrating that Rome's success was born of the clash between the aristocracy and
the people, each looking out for its own interests, Machiavelli shows how a
well-ordered society can profit when base human nature is exploited to increase the well-being of all. This insight lies at the heart of modern democracy. In *Federalist* No. 51, Madison offers his own version of Machiavelli's
revolutionary idea: "Ambition must be made to counteract ambition. . . .
This policy of supplying, by opposite and rival interests, the defect of better motives, might be traced through the whole system of human affairs,
private as well as public." Democracies, by bringing together "opposite
and rival interests" through the electoral process, place government on a
firmer footing than societies that depend for their survival on the unreli-

able virtue of their people or even their leaders. We don't require that each citizen enter the voting booth as a disinterested servant of the public good. Instead we assume that if each citizen pursues his own advantage, the aggregate will serve the greater interests of all.

This shift from virtue to interest is also the key to capitalism, where selfishness and greed are regarded as the source of our common prosperity. In David Hume's formulation, since "every man is naturally impelled to extend his acquisitions as much as possible," the role of government is to make sure that it is in the "interest, even of bad men, to act for the public good." Once we have accepted Machiavelli's contention that human beings are motivated by a desire for gain and a lust for power, it is incumbent upon those who make the laws to ensure that those drives are put to use in ways that serve society as a whole.

While admitting that political health derives from a creative tension between the haves and have-nots—what Marx would later call the class struggle—Machiavelli, like the good bourgeois he is, makes his allegiance clear:

> [I]f we ask what it is the nobility are after and what it is the common people are after, it will be seen that in the former there is a great desire to dominate and in the latter merely the desire not to be dominated. Consequently the latter will be more keen on liberty since their hope of usurping dominion over others will be less than in the case of the upper class. So that if the populace be made the guardians of liberty, it is reasonable to suppose that they will take more care of it, and that, since it is impossible for them to usurp power, they will not permit others to do so.

These are ideas that would not have seemed out of place in Philadelphia in 1787. Despite his reputation as an apologist for tyranny, there is more of Madison than Mussolini in Machiavelli.

Machiavelli comes even closer to the great architects of American constitutional government in his "Discourse on the Remodeling of the Florentine Government," written around the year 1520 for Pope Leo X. Here he explicitly sets out a three-part structure that largely resembles our own. "I believe it is necessary, since there are three sorts of men . . . that there be also three ranks in a republic," he asserts. Each of these groups is to elect its own representative body: a Signoria, the chief executive, made up of the city's most distinguished citizens; a Council of Two Hundred, representing the merely wealthy; and a Council of One Thousand, speaking for the people.* John Adams, the founder who studied Machiavelli most closely, argued for a similar structure: "When the three natural orders of society are all represented in the government, and constitutionally placed to watch each other, and restrain each other mutually by the laws, it is then only, that an emulation takes place for the public good, and divisions turned to the advantage of the nation."

The similarities are not merely coincidental but stem from a shared belief that human beings are inherently flawed. Wisdom and justice are not the monopoly of any one man, no matter how well intentioned, but are best achieved in the give-and-take of competing interests and points of view.† This is not an approach that would have occurred to either Aquinas or Erasmus, who saw their mission as constructing ideal states so that man might live according to God's plan. But such thinking came naturally to Machiavelli and to Madison, who believed that the job of government was to allow men to live in society by allowing each of us a constructive outlet for our destructive appetites. By shifting his focus from what ought to be to what is, Machiavelli gave birth to political science and transformed speculative political philosophy into a tool that could aid in the practical task of building a civil government.

Machiavelli's jaundiced view of humanity and his tendency to see the present through the lens of the past gives his writing a pessimistic cast. Machiavelli could have found ample backing for his gloomy perspective in the text that served as the basis for his *Discourses*. Writing in the first century

---

*   While Machiavelli's republic would have fallen well short of the universal franchise we have come to regard as the key to democracy, the same criticism could be leveled at Madison's proposals. Both Machiavelli and the Founding Fathers believed the franchise should extend only to property-owning, tax-paying men.

†   See, for example, Madison's *Federalist* No. 10: "As long as the reason of man continues fallible, and he is at liberty to exercise it, different opinions will be formed." And: "The latent causes of faction are thus sown in the nature of man; and we see them everywhere brought into different degrees of activity, according to the different circumstances of civil society."

before Christ, Livy already thought he detected in history a downward trajectory, "the sinking foundations of morality as the old teaching was allowed to lapse, the rapidly increasing disintegration, then the final collapse of the whole edifice, and the dark dawning of our modern day when we can neither endure the vices nor face the remedies needed to cure them." And, like Machiavelli, Livy believed that only by studying the past could we hope to arrest the steep descent: "The study of history is the best medicine for a sick mind; for in history you have a record of the infinite variety of human experience plainly set out for all to see; and in that record you can find for yourself and your country both examples and warnings; fine things to take as models, base things, rotten through and through, to avoid."

History as "the best medicine for the sick mind" could serve as Machiavelli's own motto. Both the Roman historian and the former Second Chancellor of Florence regarded the study of the past not as an antiquarian pastime but as a moral imperative. History is a kind of secular scripture that offers a guide to right living and cautionary tales pointing out the dire consequences of sin. *The Prince* and *The Discourses* jump back and forth between current and ancient events, seeking the common thread and drawing useful lessons from the comparison. In Machiavelli's writing there is no vision of progress; the best we can achieve—if we actually heed those lessons, something Machiavelli often doubts we are capable of because we "lack a proper appreciation of history"—is to learn from our mistakes.

A proper appreciation of history, particularly the history of ancient Rome—the high point of civilization, according to Machiavelli—provides us with the best opportunity to remedy current ills. He justifies his focus on the past by stressing the constancy of human nature: "If the present be compared with the remote past, it is easily seen that in all cities and in all peoples there are the same desires and the same passions as there always were. So that, if one examines with diligence the past, it is easy to foresee the future of any commonwealth, and to apply those remedies which were used of old."

The tragedy of history, or perhaps the farce, lies in the fact that while man's nature is fixed, the world is always in flux: "There are two reasons why we cannot change our ways. First, it is impossible to go against what nature inclines us to. Secondly, having got on well by adopting a certain line of conduct, it is impossible to persuade men that they can get on well by acting otherwise. It thus comes about that a man's fortune changes, for she changes his circumstances but he does not change his ways." Success leads not to success but to failure, as we cling to attitudes and methods that have outlived their usefulness. Thus are the mighty undone and the meek raised up to take their place, only to be humbled in their turn as Fortune's wheel rotates once again.

Because human beings in every place and every time are essentially the same, it is possible to extrapolate the future from the past.* But even with the gift of prophecy, the prospects for mankind are gloomy. An understanding of history's lessons is helpful but the wisdom conferred by careful study of the past cannot overcome the fundamental conditions created by the struggle between human nature, incapable of reformation, and *Fortuna*, incapable of constancy.

In casting his skeptical eye across the vast panorama of human history Machiavelli believes he detects a cyclical rather than a linear structure. He borrows his basic architecture from the ancient Greek historian Polybius, who wrote: "Such is the recurring cycle of constitutions; such is the system devised by nature, according to which constitutional forms change and are transformed and return again to their original state." Machiavelli combines this cyclical structure with the threefold division articulated by Aristotle (monarchy, aristocracy, democracy, or, in their debased form, tyranny, oligarchy, anarchy). "[I]f anyone sets up one of the three first forms of government," Machiavelli observes, "he sets up what will last but for a while, since there are no means whereby to prevent it passing to its contrary, on account of the likeness which in such a case virtue has to vice. These variations are due to chance." It is a theme he returns to in his *Florentine Histories* when he declares: "Thus [states] are always descending from good to bad and rising from bad to good. For virtue gives birth to quiet, quiet to leisure, leisure to disorder, disorder to ruin; and similarly, from ruin, order is born; from order, virtue; and from virtue, glory and good fortune."

Despite his pessimism, Machiavelli does not succumb to fatalistic apathy. As he does in his famous chapter in *The Prince* where he compares

---

* Machiavelli makes the same point in the Prologue to his play *Clizia*, based on an original by Plautus, where he says: "If into the world the same men should come back, just as the same events come back, never would a hundred years go by in which we should not find here a second time the very same things done as now" (*Clizia*, "Prologue" in *Chief Works*, II, 823).

fortune to a raging river, he proposes in *The Discourses* at least a partial solution to the futile repetitions of history. While it is true that no perfect form of government is possible in a world ruled by fickle Fortune, history teaches us that those societies most able to adapt endure and prosper the longest. By adopting a mixed form of government in which the elements of monarchy, aristocracy, and democracy are combined, mankind can slow the turn of Fortune's wheel, if not stop it entirely. Even the most successful states founded on the finest constitutions—such as republican Rome and Sparta after Lycurgus—eventually come to grief. Machiavelli's analysis might be described as organic: birth is merely the prelude to death; growth is inexorably followed by decay. In time, all societies must follow the same dismal path.

Nothing could be more inimical to the Christian view than this endless parade of folly. Instead of the Christian narrative in which human history, born in original sin, ends in the Final Judgment, Machiavelli's history is a Sisyphean exercise in futility. Temporary improvement is possible, but this leads to a complacency that is the prelude to disaster. Notably absent from his narrative is the world-changing death and resurrection of Christ that was to have placed humankind on an entirely new path.[*]

Machiavelli provides no comforting alternative to this redemptive eschatology. In more recent centuries faith in a narrative of spiritual redemption has been replaced by belief in technological or material progress, but the very structure of *The Discourses*, with its constant looping backward toward a past that in most respects shames the present, undermines any reading of history as moving ever forward and upward. At worst, we will continue to ignore the models provided by the great leaders of the past and stumble along blindly. But even if we take to heart the lessons they teach, we will only buy ourselves a temporary reprieve. In either case, *Fortuna* will win in the end, reducing once thriving metropolises to dust and mingling the bones of kings and paupers in the same indifferent ground.

---

[*] Arguing against the cyclical model of history proposed by some ancient philosophers, Saint Augustine explained, "For once Christ died for our sins; and rising from the dead, He dieth no more" (*The City of God*, XII, 13).

The most famous image of Niccolò Machiavelli, it was painted by Tito Santi after the Florentine Chancellor's death. It shows him at the height of his power, in his elegant robes of office. (Erich Lessing/Art Resource, N.Y.)

The Palazzo della Signoria was the residence of the Florentine executive (the Signoria) and the seat of the government. Machiavelli worked here in the offices of the Second Chancery from 1498 to 1512. Its fortresslike exterior suggests the city's violent history. (Miles Unger)

Today, as in the sixteenth century, the Florentine skyline is dominated by the city's great religious edifice, the Cathedral (on the right), with Brunelleschi's soaring dome, and the Palazzo della Signoria (under scaffolding to the left). (Miles Unger)

View of Machiavelli's property Sant' Andrea in Percussina, revealing a typical Tuscan landscape, with rocky terraces and olive groves. (Miles Unger)

This modest farmhouse served as Machiavelli's country retreat. Here in 1513 he wrote *The Prince*. (Miles Unger)

LEFT: Ludovico Sforza was known as *Il Moro* (the Moor) for his swarthy complexion. The scheming Duke of Milan was blamed for inviting the French invasion of 1494. (Scala/Art Resource, N.Y.)

RIGHT: Charles VIII's invasion of Italy in 1494 ushered in a long period of turmoil and humiliation for the Italian people. In Florence, the arrival of the French King contributed to the expulsion of Piero de' Medici and the rise of Savonarola. His rapid conquest of Naples was followed by a dramatic retreat. (Réunion des Musées Nationaux/Art Resource, N.Y.)

The sensual, worldly Rodrigo Borgia, Pope Alexander VI, was the epitome of a corrupt Renaissance Pope. He openly acknowledged his children, including the violent Cesare and beautiful Lucrezia. His feud with Savonarola ultimately ended in the preacher's execution. (Scala/Art Resource, N.Y.)

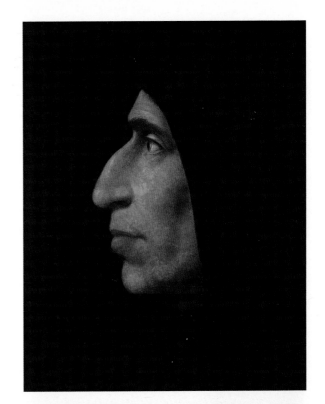

This portrait of Girolamo Savonarola by Fra Bartolomeo captures something of the intensity and asceticism of the Dominican friar who dominated Florentine political, religious, and social life between 1494 and 1498. (Erich Lessing/Art Resource, N.Y.)

The handsome, dashing Cesare Borgia, known as Valentino, was the son of Pope Alexander VI. His boldness, ruthlessness, and early successes were an inspiration for Machiavelli's portrait of an ideal ruler in *The Prince*. (Erich Lessing/Art Resource, N.Y.)

"Il Papa Terribile" (the Terrifying Pope), Julius II—portrayed here by Raphael—spent most of his reign at war, first against the Venetians and later against the French. He was also one of history's great art patrons, commissioning Michelangelo to paint the Sistine ceiling and sculpt his tomb and hiring Donato Bramante to rebuild St. Peter's Basilica. (Scala/Art Resource, N.Y.)

Giovanni de' Medici's election as Pope Leo X on March 11, 1513, led directly to Machiavelli's release from prison. On his accession, he was quoted as saying, "Now that God has given us the papacy, let us enjoy it." In this portrait by Raphael, Leo's cousin Cardinal Giulio de' Medici (later Pope Clement VII) stands on the Pope's right. (Scala/Ministero per i Beni e le Attività culturali/Art Resource, N.Y.)

This engraving of the *Battle of Anghiari* is based on Peter Paul Rubens's copy of Leonardo's lost masterpiece. Even twice removed from the original, this view of the central battle reveals the savagery and energy of Leonardo's original conception. (© The Trustees of the British Museum/Art Resource, N.Y.)

Like Leonardo's battle scene on the adjacent wall of the Hall of the Great Council, Michelangelo's *Battle of Cascina* is known only in copies. Drawings for the fresco became a veritable school for generations of artists. (Foto Marburg/Art Resource, N.Y.)

LEFT: Michelangelo's tomb of Giuliano de' Medici, to whom Machiavelli originally dedicated *The Prince*. (Erich Lessing/Art Resource N.Y.)

RIGHT: Charles V (shown here in painting by Titian) ruled one of history's great empires. He defeated the French king in Italy and, in 1527, sacked Rome. (Erich Lessing/Art Resource N.Y.)

TANTO. NOMINI. NVLLVM. PAR. ELOGIVM
NICOLAVS. MACHIAVELLI
OBIT. AN. A. P. V. CIƆIƆXXVII

Machiavelli's remains were transferred to this impressive monument in Santa Croce from a more modest tomb in the eighteenth century. The Latin inscription reads, "For so great a name, no words will suffice." (Miles Unger)

XII

THE SAGE OF THE GARDEN

*"I believe that the following would be the true way to Paradise—
learn the way to Hell in order to flee from it."*

—MACHIAVELLI TO FRANCESCO GUICCIARDINI

MACHIAVELLI WAS A PESSIMIST BY CONVICTION, BUT his gloomy outlook did little to dampen his zest for life. Indeed, it was his honest appraisal of his own appetites that convinced him that any political theory worthy of the name must account for man's bestial nature. Like many people with a jaundiced view of the world he did not see why this verdict should stop him, or anyone else, from enjoying himself while he could. Even at his lowest moments he never succumbed to despair, and when he was shut out of public life he continued to peer beyond the constricted horizons of his existence. While in the country he collared those who traveled the busy road that passed by his house and pressed them for news of the wider world; in the city he always plunged into the middle of heated discussions over the results of the last election or the latest diplomatic dustup. He was one of those gregarious men who combine a cynical disdain for human nature in the abstract with genuine warmth for people in the flesh. The more Fortune rebuffed him, the more he was inclined to see the comic side of life, discovering in laughter the best antidote to what ailed him. As he wrote to Francesco Vettori, quoting lines of Petrarch:

> So if at times I laugh or sing,
> It is because only thus
> May I give voice to my anguished cries.

It was when his suffering was at its most acute, as in those desperate weeks spent in the dismal Le Stinche prison, that he tended to see the farcical side of life most clearly, consoling himself by composing humorous verses and meditating on the folly of existence. Work gave his life meaning, and he filled the empty hours by picking up his pen and doing battle with the Muses. It is no coincidence that it was in prison that he first referred to himself as a writer, complaining to Giuliano de' Medici, "so the poets are treated!"

Plunging himself into his writing was not the only way he dulled his pain. While he was shackled in his dank cell he longed for the fresh air and simple comforts of Sant' Andrea, but only a few weeks after his release the four walls of his house seemed only a little less confining. He sought distraction in the local tavern, just across the busy road that led to Rome, or, tiring of the boisterous atmosphere, he would tuck a book of poetry under his arm and seek a shady spot to read and spend some time alone with his thoughts. When rustic diversions grew stale he made the ten-mile journey on foot into the city, where he met old friends and caught up on the latest gossip.

Bored and frustrated, Machiavelli found consolation in the arms of women. "[E]very day we go to the house of some girl to restore our vigor," Machiavelli tells Vettori, proof that poverty never pinched so tightly that he could not afford to indulge in those low pleasures to which he had become accustomed.

It is hard not to sympathize with Marietta, forced to stay home with the children during the many nights her husband was in town restoring his vigor in the brothels near the Old Market, while observing that, at least in this regard, Machiavelli was no worse than most of his peers. Florentine wives were expected to patiently tend to hearth and home while their husbands conducted their business and took their pleasures in the wider world. This inequity continued inside the home, where the husband possessed almost unlimited authority over his submissive bride. By the standards of the day, Machiavelli was not an inconsiderate master, his main fault consisting in neglect rather than cruelty. For over twenty-six years of married life, Marietta kept the household running smoothly and saw to the children's basic needs, ensuring that her husband had the leisure and peace of mind to meditate on weightier matters.

Marietta's personality, like that of most of women of the time, remains largely hidden from view. Even with limited information, however, it is clear that Machiavelli's wife was no shrinking violet. She wasn't shy about voicing her displeasure when her husband was away for extended periods, complaining vociferously to the friends he commissioned to drop by and see how she was doing. "Lady Marietta curses God, and says she has thrown away both her body and her goods," wrote Biagio Buonaccorsi during one of Machiavelli's many absences, grumbling that he was forced to bear the brunt of her temper since the real object of her wrath was nowhere to be found.

Machiavelli's fictional portrayals of Florentine wives suggest an unromantic view of the marital state, but his unflattering depictions of the female sex—including his portrayal of *Fortuna* as a cruel and inconstant woman—reflect the ubiquitous misogyny of the age rather than any particular disillusionment with his own marriage. In his novella *The Fable of Belfagor*, Machiavelli's title character is a demon sent by Pluto to investigate whether it is true, as he has heard, that wives are the source of all men's ills. After testing this thesis by marrying a Florentine woman named Onesta, the demon Belfagor quickly returns to the Underworld, claiming he prefers Hell to the torments of the "marriage yoke."

Fortunately, we have more to go on than this bitter assessment. More attractive than the nagging and unreasonable Onesta is Sofronia from his play *Clizia*, a long-suffering woman who is far more sensible and appealing than her lecherous husband, Nicomaco. In fact Machiavelli clearly identifies as much with the wife as with the husband, placing in her mouth cynical views that he might have espoused himself. Told of a monk who had helped a woman conceive, the sharp-tongued Sofronia replies: "A fine miracle, a monk making a woman pregnant! It would be a miracle if a nun should make her pregnant." Even more intriguing in view of Machiavelli's own family life is Sofronia's monologue in which she recalls how Nicomaco's infatuation with a young girl meant that "his affairs are neglected, his farms are going to ruin, his business ventures fail"—a poignant picture of a household turned upside down by a middle-aged man's philandering. The fact that Machiavelli gives the foolish husband a name so similar to his own shows either admirable self-awareness or a deplorable lack of conscience about his own moral lapses.

Marietta's greatest complaint about her husband was that he was so often absent, which suggests she derived a certain amount of pleasure from his company. If Niccolò and Marietta were never soul mates, they remained attentive to each other's needs. Whenever they were apart, each inquired solicitously of the other's health, and just as Marietta made sure to supply her absent husband with everything he needed to make his journeys more comfortable, Niccolò commissioned his friends to look after his family's needs back at home. It is also apparent that despite prolonged absences and frequent infidelities on Niccolò's part, they shared their bed for a considerable time. By 1514 they had six surviving children: four sons (Bernardo, Lodovico, Guido, and Piero), and two daughters (Primavera and Bartolomea).

Machiavelli was an affectionate father, though he was too restless and ambitious to find in family life an adequate substitute for his blighted career. In fact the crowded, laughter-filled house in Sant' Andrea reminded him of responsibilities he could barely meet. One of the most extended glimpses into Machiavelli's intimate feelings comes in a letter he wrote late in life to his son Guido:

> My dearest Guido. I received a letter from you that has given me the greatest pleasure, especially since you write that you have quite recovered; I could not have had better news. If God grant you and me life, I believe that I may make you a man of good standing, if you are willing to do your share. . . . But you must study and, since you no longer have illness as an excuse, take pains to learn letters and music, for you are aware how much distinction is given me for what little ability I possess. Thus, my son, if you want to please me and bring profit and honor to yourself, study, do well, and learn, because everyone will help you if you help yourself.
>
> Since the young mule has gone mad, it must be treated just the reverse of the way crazy people are, for they are tied up, and I want you to let it loose . . . take off its bridle and halter and let it go wherever it likes to regain its own way of life and work off its craziness. The village is big and the beast is small; it can do no one any harm. . . . Greet Madonna Marietta for me and tell her I have been expecting— and still do—to leave [Imola] anyday; I have never longed so much to

return to Florence as I do now, but there is nothing else I can do. Simply tell her that whatever she hears, she should be of good cheer, since I shall be there before any danger comes. Kiss Baccina [Bartolomea], Piero, and Totto [Machiavelli's brother], if he is there. I would dearly appreciate hearing whether his eyes are any better. Live in happiness and spend as little as you can. And remind Bernardo, whom I have written to twice in the last two weeks and received no reply, that he had better behave himself. Christ watch over you all.

The conventional sentiments—fatherly tenderness combined with sensible admonitions to study hard, as well as his surprising empathy for a poor, crazed animal—belie the sinister reputation of the writer of *The Prince.* In fact for all his radical notions, Machiavelli was a rather ordinary man, loving if sometimes selfish, pursuing his own pleasures even as he fretted over his wife's health and his children's prospects.

The other family member who played an important role in Machiavelli's life was his nephew Giovanni Vernacci, son of his sister Primavera. Primavera had died when Giovanni was still a boy, and Machiavelli had taken him in. He looked after Giovanni's interests in Florence while he was away on business, and regarded him as another son. Giovanni, for his part, returned his uncle's affection, addressing him as "Honored and dearest foster father." Machiavelli responded in kind, telling him, "aside from my own children, there is no man I cherish more than you."

But family was never the focus of Niccolò's attention or even the center of his emotional life. One of his favorite haunts was the shop of Donato del Corno, "at the sign of the horn," a place with a reputation as a homosexual hangout. It is unclear whether Machiavelli himself indulged in an occasional illicit tryst with boys (a vice regarded by some as peculiarly Florentine), but he was certainly tolerant of such behavior in his friends.* Machiavelli's easygoing attitude was widely shared by men of his class. More prudish Florentines may have condemned such behavior as unnatu-

---

* He was less tolerant when it came to his own son, Lodovico, who, according to Vettori, "has a boy with him" who "plays with him, sports with him, walks about with him, whispers in his ear; they sleep in the same bed" (April 16, 1523, in Machiavelli, et al., *Machiavelli and His Friends*, no. 281, p. 349). While Vettori was inclined to laugh it off as youthful indiscretion, Machiavelli seems to have been upset by what he believed was taking place.

ral—and on occasion those caught in the act were severely punished—but they did not regard those who engaged in same-sex encounters as men who differed in any fundamental way from their peers. Homosexuality was just another vice, like masturbation or visiting prostitutes, and not a deep-seated expression of one's true nature.

In any case, it is clear that women remained the focus of Machiavelli's sexual attention. He was always an unapologetic sensualist. Hypocrisy was far worse than promiscuity in his view. "It is certainly an amazing thing to contemplate how blind human beings are when it comes to their own sins, and how fiercely they persecute those they don't possess," Machiavelli wrote to Vettori. Commiserating with his friend after a mild scandal erupted over his sexual peccadilloes, Machiavelli continued:

> And to put it more clearly, given your austere disposition, if it had been I—who enjoy as much as any man the caresses of a woman— who had stumbled into the room: as soon as I'd seen what was up, I would have said: "Ambassador, you will make yourself ill; I don't think you're allowing yourself sufficient diversion. Here there are neither boys nor girls. What kind of whorehouse is this anyway?

Professional disappointment drove Machiavelli to seek distractions outside his own home. After 1512, he plunged into a series of torrid love affairs. Some of the objects of his passion were courtesans—like the curly-haired beauty Lucretia, known as *La Riccia*, with whom, an anonymous accuser claimed, he had engaged in "an unnatural sex act," or the singer Barbera Raffacani "who," according to Guicciardini, "like all her kind, seeks to please all and to *seem* rather than to *be*." Others, like the sister of his neighbor Niccolò Tafani, were women of respectable birth.*

Machiavelli found in these women's beds a sexual excitement he no longer found with Marietta, but there was more to these encounters than physical release. Lust sometimes led to love, an emotion that both elated and exhausted him, as he reveals in an unusually lyrical passage from a letter to Vettori:

---

* The identity of his lover at this time can only be guessed, but it seems likely that it was Tafani's sister, since in a letter written a few months after revealing his affair, he urges Vettori to help her arrange a divorce from her husband, who was living with his mistress in Rome. (See letter no. 240 in Machiavelli et al., *Machiavelli and His Friends*, p. 295.)

[W]hile in the country I have met a creature so kind, so graceful, so noble, both in nature and in bearing, that neither my praise nor my love would be as much as she merits. I should tell you, as you told me, how this love began, how Love caught me in his nets, where he spread them, and what they were made of. You will see that they were nets of gold, woven by Venus and hung among the flowers. They were so soft and gentle that even though a hard heart could have severed them, I had no wish to do so. . . . . Suffice it to say that, although I am nearly fifty [he was then only forty-five], I am no longer bothered by the heat of the day, nor am I exhausted by the rough roads or frightened by the dark hours of the night. . . . . I have left behind all my troubles, and nothing in the world would induce me to seek again my freedom. I have banished, then, any thought of matters great and grave, and no longer take delight in reading of the ancients or of more recent doings. All has been transformed into sweet dreams.

It is hard to believe that even a few years earlier Machiavelli would have allowed himself to be so thoroughly unhinged by a woman's charms. Love, in this case, was an obsession that took hold in a man who had little else to occupy his mind and engage his heart.

Vettori, who was used to his friend's many moods, suspected that talk of abandoning his life's work for the "tender thoughts" of love was a sign of despondency, and he tried to lift Machiavelli's flagging spirits by engaging him in "the old game" of geopolitical chess. With the King of France vying with his old enemies the Spaniards for possession of Milan, what policy should the Pope adopt? "With your prudence and intelligence and experience, you will be better able to understand what I have tried to say," the ambassador wrote, playing on his friend's vanity. And Machiavelli, showing that love had not entirely addled him, rose to the bait, delivering in reply a lengthy and carefully reasoned dissertation on the current balance of power.*

---

* Machiavelli ultimately concluded that the Pope should back the French since they would demand less in victory than the Spanish. The worst possible course would be "remaining neutral," which was never "useful to anyone confronted with these conditions" (Machiavelli to Vettori December 10, 1514, no. 241 in Machiavelli et al., *Machiavelli and His Friends*, pp. 295–302). Of course it was exactly this middle way that the Pope preferred.

Machiavelli was amused when he saw how easily Vettori steered him from one obsession to another, but he also thought he detected in his fleeting passions a larger truth about human nature:

> *Anyone who read our letters, my honored friend, and saw their variety, would be greatly astounded, because it would appear at first that we were serious men, deeply engaged in serious matters, and that in our breasts resided nothing that did not bespeak sincerity and grandeur. But then, turning the page, he would discover that these same men are frivolous, inconstant, lascivious, and absorbed in trivial things. And if this manner seems to some undignified, to me it seems laudable: because we are imitating nature, which itself is changeable, and whoever imitates nature cannot be blamed. And though we have grown accustomed to dealing with such varied matters over the course of several letters, this time I wanted to do it in just a single one, as you will see if you read the next page.*

This lighthearted letter reveals the cast of Machiavelli's thought as clearly as any of his more substantial works. "*[W]e are imitating nature, which itself is changeable, and whoever imitates nature cannot be blamed,*" he tells Vettori, as succinct an exposition of his philosophy as one will find in all his writings.

Although Machiavelli enjoyed the pleasures of the flesh, he could never be satisfied without the stimulation of the mind. He called Love "that little thief," and even in the heat of erotic passion he strained against invisible bonds. "I fear for my liberty," he wrote Vettori about his latest lady love, "nor can I conceive of any way to unchain myself." But even as he wrote these words he was seeking a key that would unlock Venus's enervating trap. He craved mental exercise, something apparently more difficult to come by in Florence than carnal knowledge, and he prowled the streets in search of intellectual equals, men with whom he could share the ideas that were churning in his fertile brain.

By the winter of 1515, Machiavelli had reached rock bottom. It was a period when, as he confided to his nephew, "fortune has left me nothing but my family and my friends." A few months earlier he had hoped that, through the strenuous efforts of Francesco Vettori's brother Paolo, he might finally find a position with Giuliano de' Medici. But this wish was shot down by the papal secretary, Piero Ardinghelli, who urged Giuliano to "write to [Paolo] on my behalf that I advise him not to have anything to do with Niccolò."

Machiavelli took this latest setback philosophically, telling himself that since Fortune's wheel never ceased its motion he had only to wait until it turned again. And, in fact, with the coming of spring a few green shoots began to appear in an otherwise bleak landscape. It was during that expectant season that he began attending informal gatherings at the garden belonging to the Rucellai family. Here, some of Florence's most brilliant and learned men came to dine at their host's well-appointed table and discuss erudite matters,* and here among the cypresses and laurel Machiavelli rediscovered the camaraderie he missed from his days in the Chancery.

Machiavelli quickly shook off the cobwebs that clung to him after years of forced retirement and showed he had lost none of his acerbic wit. He was made much of by the mostly younger gentlemen he began to call his "noontime friends" (presumably to distinguish them from the more disreputable companions of the midnight hour), who regarded him as something of a mentor, while he was reinvigorated in their youthful company. With their encouragement he picked up *The Discourses*, begun a couple of years earlier and then set aside, dedicating it to his newfound friends of the garden Cosimo Rucellai and Zanobi Buondelmonti.

In exchanging the low company of Donato del Corno's shop for the more rarefied atmosphere of the Rucellai gardens, Machiavelli was moving up in the world. Not only was he now warmly received by Florence's cultural elite, but he found himself nearer the centers of power than he had been for years. Drawn to this luminous oasis of thought and culture as a moth to a flame, Machiavelli discovered the pleasures and the perils of hovering too close to the light.

The Orti Oricellari, as the Rucellai gardens were called, had for decades

---

* Such gatherings had long been a hallmark of Florentine intellectual life. In the late fourteenth century, leading citizens like Palla Strozzi and Cosimo de' Medici had attended talks at the Camaldolese monastery given by Ambrogio Traversari. The famous "Platonic Academy" sponsored by Lorenzo de' Medici was, similarly, less a formal institution than a gathering of like-minded intellectuals who met to discuss the great philosopher's work at Marsilio Ficino's villa at Careggi. After Lorenzo's death, Bernardo Rucellai played host to the Platonic meetings at his garden.

stood at the heart of the city's intellectual life.* The piece of land, near the Porta al Prato just inside the city's western walls, had originally been purchased by Bernardo Rucellai at the end of the previous century. At the time, the wealthy Bernardo had been among the most influential citizens of Florence, promoted to the highest ranks after marrying Lorenzo the Magnificent's sister, Nanina. But his political fortunes waned with the expulsion of his wife's family and with the rise of the popular government, to which he was vehemently opposed. Disillusioned with politics, Bernardo turned his energies toward less practical pursuits. Behind the high walls of his impeccably landscaped garden he created a green retreat in the bustling urban center, and established an informal academy where the best philosophers and writers could converse while wandering arm in arm among the exotic shrubs and drawing inspiration from the antique statues scattered among the foliage.

But while Bernardo withdrew from active participation in government, he had not entirely abandoned politics. In Florence the line between intellectual theorizing and political action was always porous, and those humanists who congregated in Bernardo's gardens naturally tended to reflect their host's oligarchic prejudices. During the final years of the Soderini government, the Orti Oricellari became a hotbed of pro-Medici agitation. Bernardo and his friends, in fact, were instrumental in facilitating the Medici's return, secretly funneling funds to Giovanni, Giuliano, and their allies.

Given the fact that no one was more closely associated with the departing Gonfaloniere than Niccolò Machiavelli, it is not surprising that for years he was shunned by the luminaries who congregated in the Rucellai gardens. But by 1516 the mood in the city had changed and the nature of the conversations at the Orti changed along with it. Bernardo had died in 1514 and his role as cultural impresario was assumed by his grandson Cosimo, a more amiable and broad-minded man.† As Machiavelli described him, the frail Cosimo appeared to have been a scholarly and courteous host. "I never met anyone," he recalled some years after Cosimo's death, "whose heart was more disposed to great and generous actions."

Perhaps more importantly, the resentments that smoldered in the first days following the overthrow of the Soderini government had cooled with

---

* The gardens took their name from a plant, the *orecella*, that had been imported by the Rucellai family and that was used to make a purple dye important for Florence's thriving cloth industry.

† Some have attributed Cosimo's gentle nature to the fact that he was crippled from an early age. He attended gatherings at his garden by being carried about by servants in a specially made litter.

time. The Medici, with Giovanni now sitting on the papal throne, were so firmly ensconced that the *ottimati*, the Rucellai included, no longer felt threatened by a rising tide of populist feeling. In this more relaxed atmosphere, under the aegis of the urbane Cosimo, thoughts turned from contemporary politics to more arcane matters.

It is unclear exactly how Machiavelli first fell in with his "friends of the cool shade." Many, like Anton-Francesco degli Albizzi and Zanobi Buondelmonti, belonged to the great magnate families of the city, and in their company the middle-aged former Second Chancellor must have cut a somewhat shabby figure. But by now his writings, which had been circulating for years among his friends—particularly the manuscript of the still unpublished *Prince* and perhaps a rough draft of *The Discourses*—were attracting a wider audience and exciting comment among a new generation of intellectuals. While wealth counted for something among the habitués of the Orti, a brilliant mind more than made up for a suspect pedigree. Machiavelli was welcomed into their lunchtime gatherings where, in his threadbare robes, he held forth surrounded by an admiring crowd of fashionable youths—no longer the disgraced civil servant but a modest legend, a brilliant conversationalist, wit, and provocateur.

Machiavelli's attendance at these largely literary gatherings also reflects a subtle change in his own expectations. Though he continued to angle for a government job—and believed his well-connected friends might prove useful in this regard—the fact that he became such a regular at the Rucellai gardens shows he had come to terms with his role as a man of letters. It was as a writer and intellectual, rather than as the former Second Chancellor (a part of his résumé that might have hurt more than it helped), that Machiavelli was included in this sophisticated company.

Machiavelli has left us a description of these gatherings in *The Art of War*, which purports to be an account of a conversation between the commander of the papal army, Fabrizio Colonna, and Cosimo Rucellai that took place in the Orti Oricellari in the summer of 1516[*]:

---

[*] Such philosophical dialogues date back to the time of Plato. The form was revived in the Renaissance, when it was used by writers like Bartolomeo Scala, who turned Niccolò's father into a character in one of his dialogues (see Chapter 2), and Cristoforo Landino, who set his *Disputationes Camaldulenses* in a rustic monastery near Florence.

Fabrizio freely accepted the invitation and came to the gardens at the appointed time, where he was received by Cosimo, and some of his most intimate friends—among whom were Zanobi Buondelmonti, Battista della Palla and Luigi Alamanni. These young men—whose virtues and good qualities are so well known to everybody that it would be altogether unnecessary to say anything here in praise of them—were very dear to Cosimo, were of the same disposition, and were engaged in the same studies.

To be as brief as I can, then, Fabrizio was regaled there with every possible demonstration of honor and respect. But after the end of the entertainment and usual formalities, which generally are few and short among men of sense who are more desirous of gratifying the rational appetite, and since the days were long and the weather intensely hot, Cosimo under a pretext of avoiding the heat, took his guests into the most retired and shady part of the gardens. Then, when they had all sat down—some upon the grass, which is very green and pleasant there, and some upon seats placed under the loftiest trees—Fabrizio said it was a most delightful garden.

While the conversation that follows—in which Machiavelli uses Colonna as the mouthpiece for his own theories of modern warfare—is pure invention, it was based on those afternoons spent in the shade of Cosimo's garden.

As a denizen of the Orti, Machiavelli reinvented himself. He greeted the change in career with a rueful smile and a shrug. The writer's life was not his first choice, but after years of frustration at least it offered him an outlet for his talent and ambition. A most revealing insight into his state of mind comes at the beginning of *The Discourses*, dedicated "not to those who are princes, but [to] those who, on account of their innumerable good qualities, deserve to be; not those who might shower on me rank, honors and riches, but those who, though unable, would like to do so."

How different this is from the dedication to *The Prince*! All hints of servility vanish as Machiavelli addresses his colleagues rather than his master. These were men with whom he had a relationship based on mutual respect rather than on need. In fact, in praising Rucellai and Buondelmonti, Machiavelli takes a swipe at the de facto lord of the city. We are living in a topsy-turvy world, he suggests, in which private citizens are fit to be kings, while those who actually rule deserve to molder in obscurity.

Machiavelli's disillusionment with Lorenzo de' Medici, following a similar disappointment with his cousin Giuliano, was not based merely on personal frustration. True, the arrogant princeling had spurned all his overtures. (There is even a story, probably apocryphal, that when Machiavelli finally worked up the nerve to present *The Prince*, the Medici lord ignored him in favor of a client who had come with a pair of hunting dogs.) More importantly, by 1517 the man whom Machiavelli had imagined as Italy's savior had demonstrated he was as selfish, arrogant, and incompetent as his father, the hapless Piero. In 1514, shortly after completing *The Prince*, Machiavelli wrote that the Medici heir "has filled the entire city with high hopes," but in the space of only a year or two Lorenzo had squandered all that goodwill. While his uncle the Pope urged him to act modestly, he paraded about the city surrounded by a large entourage of equally arrogant young men. He preferred to go hawking rather than attend to state business, and otherwise did his best to make himself obnoxious to his compatriots. Disgusted with the current state of his beloved republic, and disappointed in his own hopes, Machiavelli, like most of the men who enjoyed the hospitality of Cosimo Rucellai, turned inward, meditating on the vast cycles of history while leaving the here and now to take care of itself.

Inspired by the witty conversations of the garden Machiavelli composed a satirical poem (based loosely on a novella by the Roman writer Apuleius) titled *The Ass*, which he read aloud at their meetings as the verses flowed from his pen. Though a decidedly secondary work, *The Ass* captures Machiavelli's mordant wit better than his more learned treatises. Placing himself in the character (and the body) of a beast, the author offers his insights on the human animal. "And our ass," he writes in a barely disguised autobiographical allegory, "who has trodden so many of the stairs of this world to observe the mind of every mortal man . . . heaven itself could not prevent him from braying."

A letter he wrote to one of his new friends, Luigi Alamanni, in December 1517, shows just how much he had begun to relish his new role as a literary wit: "These days I have been reading Ariosto's *Orlando Furioso*. The poem on the whole is fine, with many marvelous passages. If you see him there [in Rome], give him my regards and tell him that my only complaint is that, having mentioned so many poets, he has left me out like a dog, and that he has treated me shabbily in his *Orlando*, something I would never do to him in my *Ass*." Of course Machiavelli's complaint is made in jest, but like his ironic barb in the first of his prison sonnets ("so the poets are treated!") his self-deprecating humor carries a real sting. By now he was well acquainted with disappointment—as he said in his poem, "I do not mind bites or blows as much as I did, having come to resemble the [ass] I sing"—and if Ariosto chose to overlook his contribution to letters, he had come to expect nothing better.

Machiavelli's literary gifts were comic rather than tragic, which might seem odd given his bleak view of the human condition. But comedy is the art of low expectations. While tragedy implies at least the potential for nobility in human nature, comedy traffics in the baser human instincts, territory with which Machiavelli was intimately acquainted. Machiavelli would not have been a comic genius had he thought well of people, but he would also have failed to elicit laughter had he condemned them too harshly. The comedian must be attuned to human frailty, but also possess the gift of empathy. The characters Machiavelli creates in his literary works are all flawed, to say the least. But so is he—and so are we. To say that his conception of the world is comic does nothing to minimize the seriousness of his message. Machiavelli's pessimism is tempered by acceptance, his illumination of the dark corners of the human heart accompanied by an appreciation for the richness and unpredictability of our shared experience. Even his most scholarly essays have a satirical edge, and his most farcical satires a serious point. In all his writing cynicism is married to a generosity of spirit; the foibles of the human animal are exposed, but his response to this parade of deformities is not outrage but rather amused affection.

Machiavelli's skepticism feeds his humanity. Even his harshest prescriptions are of limited scope since he has no faith in utopian schemes. Those who have used Machiavelli's concept *raison d'état* to justify gulags and concentration camps misunderstand the nature of his theories. States, he insists, function best when they allow for dissent and accept the legitimacy of competing interests. In attempting to improve the human condition we can at best effect only marginal and temporary changes. Machiavelli is the natural enemy of anyone who, like Savonarola or Lenin, would seek to perfect the human condition.

Machiavelli's genius shines through in his comedic masterpiece *La Mandragola* ("The Mandrake"), often called the greatest comedy in the Italian language. In this sex farce Machiavelli's sharp wit is on full display, but also his humanity, his ability to probe the depths of the human soul and find both good and bad. We laugh at the ridiculous antics of the characters onstage, and the laughter is more heartfelt because we recognize ourselves and our neighbors in their weakness and self-deception. Better him than us, we think as we watch *Messer* Nicia, the foolish husband of the beautiful Lucretia, unwittingly facilitate his own cuckolding with Callimaco, her handsome young lover. The old man is crass as well as gullible, but his motive—to have his wife bear him a son who will carry on the family name—is one we can all sympathize with. Siro, the clever servant, and *Frate* Timoteo, the corrupt priest, are stock comic types, and the plot, hinging on the supposedly miraculous properties of a potent but deadly fertility potion (concocted from the mandrake root), is formulaic, but Machiavelli weaves the tale so deftly and molds his characters with such skill that the play pulses with life.

La Mandragola is both hugely entertaining and sharply revealing of the man who wrote it. Machiavelli begins by speaking directly to the audience, a strategy that makes the author a character in his own play:

> *The writer is not very famous, yet if you do not laugh, he will be ready to pay for your wine. A doleful lover, a judge by no means shrewd, a friar living wickedly, a parasite the darling of Malice will be sport for you today.*
>
> *And if this material—since really it is slight—does not befit a man who likes to seem wise and dignified, make this excuse for him, that he is striving with these trifling thoughts to make his wretched life more pleasant, for otherwise he doesn't know where to turn his face, since he has been cut off from showing other powers with other deeds, there being no pay for his labors.*

Having exposed himself to the potentially jeering crowd, he then proceeds to caution his listeners that he can give as good as he gets:

*Yet if anyone supposes that by finding fault he can get the author
by the hair and scare him or make him draw back a bit, I give any
such man warning and tell him that the author, too, knows how to
find fault, and that it was his earliest art; and in no part of the world
where* sì *is heard [i.e., where Italian is spoken] does he stand in awe
of anybody, even though he plays the servant to such as can wear a
better cloak than he can.*

Here is Machiavelli as he must have appeared in life, in Donato del
Corno's shop or in the garden of the Rucellai—both pugnacious and self-
deprecating, telling tales at his own expense the better to disarm as he aims
a few well-timed blows in your direction. His life is wretched, he admits,
and his art little better. He has been reduced to hack work, forced to traffic
in low comedy since he has found no market for his pearls of wisdom. But
don't think for a minute that because he's down on his luck he'll stand for
any nonsense. Finding fault was his earliest art and, like writers in every
age, he knows how to wound and even kill with the sharp point of his pen.

Machiavelli's world is chiaroscuro, a shadowy landscape redeemed by
sporadic incandescence. He begins the play with a song that captures his
tragicomic view of life:

*Because life is short
and many are the pains
that every man bears who lives and stints himself,
let us go on spending and wasting the years as we will,
for he who deprives himself of pleasure
only to live with labor and toil
does not understand the world's deceits,
and what ills and what strange events
crush almost all mortals.*[*]

He was no mindless hedonist, but Machiavelli was even more scornful of
those ascetics who thought that the solution to all life's problems was to

---

[*] Of course the sentiments did not originate with Machiavelli. They mirror closely Lorenzo de' Medici's famous carnival song: "How beautiful is youth that quickly flies away. He who would be happy, let
him, for of tomorrow no one can say."

mortify the flesh. Life is hard enough, he insists, without denying yourself the pleasures it offers. When the virtuous Lucretia finally yields to her lover, she offers a telling rationale. "Your cleverness," she explains to Callimaco, "my husband's stupidity, my mother's folly, and my confessor's rascality have brought me to do what I never would have done myself." Like the clever prince, Lucretia applies a flexible morality to a corrupt world. For Lucretia to honor her marriage vows when her husband is both stupid and inconsiderate makes no more sense than a prince keeping his word with enemies who have no intention of keeping theirs.

Among the most memorable characters in the play is the greedy *Frate* Timoteo. Happy as he is to sell his services to the highest bidder, Timoteo is not simply a caricature. In a rare moment of self-awareness he confesses that "[I] put my finger in a sin, then . . . my arm and my whole body." Machiavelli, with his usual psychological penetration, depicts the monk as a man who is aware of his errors but lacks the will to correct them. Wondering aloud how he got himself in this predicament he concludes, in words that echo certain passages in *The Prince*, "many times one comes to harm by being too accommodating and too good, as well as by being bad."*

Despite the vast difference between *The Prince* and *La Mandragola*—not the least of which is the fact that one is meant to instruct, the other to entertain—they reflect the same worldview. In each work deceit triumphs and old-fashioned virtues are portrayed as either naive or destructive. If the prince is justified in using every means, including cruelty and lies, to preserve his state, and the lover is rewarded rather than punished for his duplicitous scheme, this is because the author is concerned with the world as it is rather than as it should be. He is above all a realist, and what he sees when he wipes away the obscuring film of piety is a world in which each seeks his own advantage and uses any means necessary to achieve his ends. Neither work makes any sense unless the human animal is conceived of as self-serving. To put it another way: with subjects who behave like the characters in *La Mandragola*, any prince who is not equally clever will quickly lose control of his kingdom.

---

* See, for example Chapter XV of *The Prince* where he declares "for a man who strives after goodness in all his acts is sure to come to ruin," or Chapter XIX where he says that "hatred may be engendered by good deeds as well as by bad ones."

A few years after writing *La Mandragola*, Machiavelli returned to the stage with another comic offering. Written to please his latest mistress, the singer and actress Barbera Raffacani, *Clizia* is a broad sex farce adapted from a play by Plautus and set in contemporary Florence (rather than ancient Athens). In his prologue Machiavelli justifies the shift of time and locale by returning to a point he made repeatedly in *The Discourses*: "If into the world the same men should come back, just as the same events come back, never would a hundred years go by in which we should not find here a second time the very same things done as now." Futile repetition, a predicament brought about by the inability to learn from our mistakes, is the essence of comedy.* It is also an essential ingredient in Machiavelli's political philosophy. Try as we might, we cannot overcome our nature, and when faced with the same situation, we will fall into the same errors.

The plot of *Clizia* revolves around the rivalry between the elderly Nicomaco and his son Cleander for the love of the beautiful Clizia, Nicomaco's ward. The hilarious picture of a middle-aged husband turning his life upside down as he lusts after a young beauty comes uncomfortably close to Machiavelli's own situation. Like *The Ass* and *La Mandragola*, *Clizia* contains a large element of self-mockery. "It remains for me to tell you," says Machiavelli,

> that the author of this comedy is a man of great refinement, and he would take it badly if you should think, as you see it acted, that there is anything immodest in it. Comedies exist to benefit and to please the audience. It is certainly very helpful for anyone, and especially for young men, to observe an old man's avarice, a lover's madness, a servant's tricks, a parasite's gluttony, a poor man's distress, a rich man's ambition, a harlot's flatteries, all men's unreliability.

Despite the contrast in form and in tone, Machiavelli is revisiting themes set down in grander form in *The Prince*, showing men as they are in order to teach us how to live in the real world. In neither case does the author promise to lead his audience to the Promised Land, but by taking to heart

---

* Karl Marx makes this point when he says: "Hegel remarks somewhere that all great world-historical facts and personages appear, so to speak, twice. He forgot to add: the first time as tragedy, the second time as farce" (from *The Eighteenth Brumaire of Louis Napoleon*).

what he has to say, we can achieve some small measure of control over Fortune's wheel.

In his prologue to *La Mandragola* Machiavelli claims he was forced to turn to farce since he could not make a living by more honorable means, but it seems unlikely that he wrote any of his plays for money. Theater in Italy at this time was rudimentary, confined for the most part to a few aristocratic courts where amateur productions were occasionally staged to entertain the local nobility. The author profited, if at all, by pleasing his patron, who might then find more remunerative work for him to do. Machiavelli wrote *La Mandragola* for the denizens of the Orti Oricellari. The Prologue where he steps onstage to address the audience has the feel of an inside joke meant for friends who knew him well and would appreciate the humor without taking offense at the more pugnacious barbs. The first production was staged for Carnival in 1520 in the Rucellai gardens, with the parts acted out by his "noontime friends" and the scenery painted by Andrea del Sarto and Bastiano (Aristotle) da Sangallo (who had worked with Michelangelo on the Sistine ceiling). Though it was an instant success, it netted him little in the way of material profit. Typical is the response of the artist and art historian Giorgio Vasari, who calls *La Mandragola* "a most amusing comedy" but can't be bothered to provide the name of the man who wrote it.

The first performance of *Clizia* (in 1525) was an equally modest affair, staged in the country villa of Jacopo Falconetti, a wealthy friend of Machiavelli who attracted a diverse crowd to his sumptuous banquets. Known as *Il Fornacciaio* (the baker),* Falconetti was a less sophisticated host than Cosimo Rucellai. Food and wine, both good and plentiful, were the inducements to make the journey to his retreat outside the San Frediano Gate, and Machiavelli, who appreciated both but could not afford to splurge himself, was grateful for his host's generosity. It was here also that he met the voluptuous Barbera Raffacani, a woman whose charm and youth renewed his own animal spirits.

As a patron, Falconetti proved equally generous to his new friend, plowing under part of his garden to build a stage and calling on Bastiano da Sangallo once again to decorate the sets. The play was as great a success with the public as its predecessor, and the citizens of Florence flocked through

---

* He was not a pastry chef, however, but a brickmaker. His country villa housed a large kiln, or "forno."

the Porta San Frediano in large numbers to attend performances. Among those who made the journey to the countryside were the current leading men in the Florentine government, Ippolito and Alessandro de' Medici. According to Vasari, however, it was the painter rather than the playwright who turned the success of the production into florins in his pocket. After painting the scenery for *Clizia*, Vasari recorded, Sangallo "acquired so great a name, that it was ever afterwards his principal profession."

Still, if Machiavelli could not replace his lost civil service salary with income from his plays, other, less tangible benefits accrued. The popular success of *La Mandragola* and *Clizia* confirmed Machiavelli's status as a man of letters. Forgotten was the bureaucrat whose misplaced faith in his citizen army had led to disaster, replaced by the image of the gadfly who held up a funhouse mirror to his fellow citizens, allowing them to laugh at themselves and each other—a cathartic release in which no one, least of all the author himself, was spared.

The fame of Machiavelli's plays, if not the name of their author, quickly spread beyond the walls of Florence. The Venetian Marin Sanudo attended a performance of *La Mandragola* in his native city where "[t]he stage was so full of people that the fifth act was not performed; it was impossible to do so with so many people." Machiavelli accepted his new-won fame with the cautious pleasure of one who has seen too many highs and lows to let the momentary adulation of the crowd go to his head. In any case, he never took his literary endeavors too seriously. When he signed a letter to Francesco Guicciardini with mock pretentiousness "Niccolò Machiavelli, Historian, Comic and Tragic Author," he expected his friend to get the joke.

Ironically, his burgeoning fame as a comic writer opened doors that had long been closed to him. Shortly after *La Mandragola*'s initial run at the Orti Oricellari, Pope Leo heard a firsthand account of the brilliant new comedy, which piqued his interest. It was Machiavelli's friend from the Rucellai gardens, Battista della Palla, who brought the work to Leo's attention. Soon *La Mandragola* was staged for the Pope and his cardinals in the Vatican, a performance that, della Palla told the author, "everyone admires . . . much more than anything else I have brought to Rome with my own hands"—which perhaps says as much about the tastes of the Holy City as the merits of the play.

It is not actually surprising that a racy sex comedy should have won over the Pope when so many of Machiavelli's more serious efforts had failed to make an impression. Leo, like most of his immediate predecessors, was a man of the world who appreciated a fine bottle of *vernaccia* far more than the finer points of theology. When he had first gone to Rome as a thirteen-year-old cardinal, his father had offered him some sensible advice: "Eat plain food and take much exercise, for those who wear your habit, if not careful, easily contract maladies"—advice that the pleasure-loving Giovanni ignored. Raphael's famous portrait reveals a man who did not stint himself; his sharp, shrewd features have been softened by years of indulgent living, the sagging pockets beneath his narrowed eyes hinting at an unhealthy lifestyle. Seated next to his cousin, the brooding Cardinal Giulio, the Pope appears massive yet only half present in the room, his eyes glancing somewhere unseen, his brow furrowed as if he is too preoccupied by pressing matters to remain long. Raphael captures something unsettling about the man, a conspiratorial quality remarked on by his contemporaries who, after a few years of Leo's surreptitious scheming, looked back with nostalgia on the straightforward violence of Julius.

According to popular legend, upon taking his seat upon Saint Peter's Throne Leo remarked to his brother, "Giuliano, now that God has given us the papacy, let us enjoy it." The sybaritic lifestyle of the Pope and his court, and the practice of selling indulgences to help fund it, contributed to the decision by a German Augustinian monk named Martin Luther to nail his Ninety-five Theses to the door of the church in Wittenberg, ushering in the Protestant Reformation. Like Savonarola, Luther was a man who felt an almost physical revulsion at the fallen state of mankind. Machiavelli, no less critical of humanity than the two monks, sought to accommodate man's flaws rather than fight them, to devise practical schemes to deal with impulses that were natural to the human animal.*

With the success of *La Mandragola*, the campaign Machiavelli had begun in prison with the humorous sonnets he composed for Giuliano

---

* In one respect, at least, Luther might be seen to have something in common with Machiavelli. His insistence that clergy should be allowed to marry was an accommodation to human nature that the Italian might well have applauded.

de' Medici finally began to pay dividends. During those agonizing weeks in his dank cell Machiavelli tried to portray himself as a harmless buffoon rather than a mortal threat to the new regime. Now the Pope himself seemed to be coming around. He appreciated clever men as long as they accepted the party line, and Machiavelli was now vouched for by men Leo trusted.

In fact a large part of the credit goes to his friends at the Orti Oricellari, many of whom had close ties to the Medici. Battista della Palla was but one of many distinguished Florentines who took up Machiavelli's cause in Rome, promoting him in ways that Francesco Vettori, for all his affection, never would. Activity on his behalf in Rome was more than matched by efforts in Florence where many of the "friends of the cool shade" were in close contact with the influential Cardinal Giulio de' Medici, the Pope's cousin, who, after the death in May 1520 of Lorenzo de' Medici, was Leo's man in Florence. On March 20, 1520, Lorenzo Strozzi, one of Machiavelli's friends from the Rucellai gardens, brought him to the palace on the Via Larga and introduced him to the Cardinal. After hearing of the meeting, Strozzi's brother Filippo expressed his satisfaction: "I am very glad you took Machiavelli to see the Medici, for if he can get the masters' confidence, he is a man who must rise."

Giulio de' Medici was the illegitimate son of Lorenzo the Magnificent's brother, Giuliano, who had been murdered in the Cathedral during the Pazzi Conspiracy of 1478. Raised in the family palace on the Via Larga after his father's death, the intelligent Giulio had, like his cousin Giovanni, been destined from early in life for holy orders. He had joined his cousins in exile following Piero's expulsion in 1498, serving as Cardinal Giovanni's aide and confidant throughout those difficult years. When Giovanni was elected Pope in 1513, the faithful Giulio reaped his reward, receiving the title Archbishop of Florence and gaining a place in the College of Cardinals. He can be seen in Raphael's portrait standing at the side of the seated Pontiff, his dark, hooded eyes suggesting his introspective and melancholy cast of mind.

With the death of the Pope's nephew Lorenzo in 1520, the capable Giulio was sent back to Florence to run the city on behalf of the Medici family. Unlike the last two candidates for the job, Giulio was a thoughtful and deliberative man, attuned to the sensibilities and prejudices of his people. The feckless Giuliano and the arrogant Lorenzo had soured the populace on Medici rule, and Cardinal Giulio was anxious to restore the family's good name. His uncle, the beloved (at least in retrospect) Lorenzo the Magnificent, had pulled the strings while preserving republican forms, an arrangement that Florentines, attached to their ancient liberties but always fearful of the potential for civic violence, accepted as the price of peace. Lorenzo's son Piero and grandson Lorenzo had failed to grasp this basic element of statecraft, offending their compatriots with their high-handed ways.

Part of Giulio's strategy to improve morale in the city was to solicit proposals for the reformation of the government from the city's leading intellectuals. A cultivated, scholarly man, the Cardinal served as head of the Studio, Florence's university, earning the respect and friendship of many who might otherwise be expected to lead any opposition to Medici rule. Among those he turned to were the habitués of the Orti, Machiavelli included, who, like most of their fellow citizens, had grown disillusioned with a regime marked by extravagance, corruption, and incompetence. "[H]e willingly conversed in his leisure time with men learned in any profession," noted one of Machiavelli's friends approvingly. Whether Giulio's calls for open debate about the republic's future were sincere or part of some subtle scheme to smoke out potential opposition has long been debated. Filippo de Nerli, a frequent guest at the Rucellai gardens, was among the first to ascribe sinister motives to the Cardinal: "Zanobi Buondelmonti and even Niccolò Machiavelli showed their minds very plainly in this way; for I saw their writings, and all went into the hands of the Cardinal, who pretended to value them very highly. . . . He abused the good faith of certain, perhaps over-credulous, citizens, who were all the more easily tricked by seeing that he gave no ear to the complaints and remonstrances of trusty adherents, by who he was warned that he was playing a dangerous game." Despite Nerli's testimony, it is more likely that the Cardinal initially welcomed a free exchange of ideas, and that he reversed course only when he felt his authority was threatened.

Questions about the future of the Florentine government had arisen in part because, with the untimely deaths of Giuliano and Lorenzo, the two most prominent members of the reigning family were men of the cloth,

who technically could not serve as rulers of a secular state.* Before Lorenzo's death, Leo's policy, like that of Pope Alexander before him, had been to
use his office to carve out a powerful principality for his family in central
and northern Italy. "The Pope and his Medici have no other thought than
of increasing the fortunes of their house," wrote the Venetian ambassador
to the Holy See, "and his nephews, unsatisfied with dukedoms, pretend
that one of them ought to be king." Pursuing this nepotistic project, Leo
had brokered his younger brother Giuliano's marriage to a French noblewoman and tried to acquire on his behalf the cities of Modena, Piacenza,
and Reggio. It was this venture that first inspired Machiavelli to conceive
of a revitalized Italian state with Florence as its capital, a dream eloquently
conjured in the last chapter of *The Prince*.† When Giuliano's early death
caused Leo to pin his hopes instead on his nephew Lorenzo, Machiavelli
transferred his loyalty as well, though by now even he must have suspected
it would come to nothing. The project reached a climax when Leo drove
out the ruling Montefeltros of Urbino and brought the strategic duchy
under Medici rule. But Lorenzo proved as flimsy a foundation upon which
to build a dynasty as his uncle, disappointing both the Pope and Florentine
nationalists like Machiavelli who could contemplate a revived Italian nation only as long as their beloved republic stood at its head.

Lorenzo's death not only ended Pope Leo's dreams of a powerful
Medici state at the heart of Italy, but also threatened to undercut the family's authority in its native city. It was in this context that Cardinal Giulio
commissioned Machiavelli's "Treatise on the Reform of the Florentine
Government," written in 1520 and dedicated to Pope Leo. Machiavelli was
elated at finally being able to return to the problems that consumed him,
and he took up the topic with his usual gusto, even if he knew his ideas
were unlikely to be put into practice. Throughout the brief text Machiavelli
walks a diplomatic tightrope, flattering his patrons while trying to nudge
them in the direction of true republican rule. After praising the prudence
of the Pope's ancestors, particularly Cosimo and his grandson Lorenzo
(*Il Magnifico*), Machiavelli gets in a subtle dig at the more recent repre-

---

* There was even some talk of Giulio following the path of Cesare Borgia, forsaking a career in the
Church for that of a secular lord, but Pope Leo rejected the idea.

† Paolo Vettori was chosen to serve as governor on Giuliano's behalf, and it was in this context that
the Vettori brothers sought Machiavelli's counsel.

sentatives: "The Medici who were governing then, since they had been educated and brought up among the citizens, conducted themselves with such friendliness that they gained favor. Now, they have grown so great that, since they have gone beyond all the habits of citizens, there cannot be such intimacy and consequently such favor"—a tactful way of saying that Giuliano and the younger Lorenzo had been insufferable and squandered much of the goodwill their ancestors had built up. Machiavelli's larger point, however, is that given Florentines' love of liberty it would be next to impossible to impose princely rule on them. "[T]o form a princedom where a republic would go well is a difficult thing and, through being difficult, inhumane and unworthy of whoever hopes to be considered merciful and good."

The bulk of the treatise is taken up by Machiavelli's blueprint for a republican government to be established once the Pope and the Cardinal pass from the scene. It follows the familiar three-part structure he normally favored: "there are three sorts of men," he declares, so "there [should] be also three ranks in a republic." Here Machiavelli takes the theories he had developed at greater length in *The Discourses* and applies them to the specific needs of a small republic with a thriving middle class and a history of communal strife. His study of history, both Roman and modern Italian, had convinced him that the most successful governments were those that internalized and accommodated the inevitable clash of competing interests—the kind of controlled chaos that obtains in modern democracies. Again he displays the basic unity of his thought, from comic play to his serious political tract. If comedy is the art of low expectations, democracy is its political counterpart, a system that substitutes an achievable equilibrium for unobtainable perfection.

Nothing came of Machiavelli's proposals or those of his colleagues who had heeded the Cardinal's call to action. In a pattern that would repeat itself throughout the course of Giulio de' Medici's life, boldness was followed by timidity; the promise of a new beginning dissipated in a return to the status quo. It was a pattern that guaranteed disillusionment. Giulio was one of those well-meaning men who know what's right in the abstract but who wilt in the face of harsh reality. When it became clear that he had no intention of restoring the citizens' cherished freedoms, he stoked the very resentment he had hoped to quell.

Though Machiavelli was disappointed by the Cardinal's cowardly retreat, he was not prepared to sever the ties it had taken him so long to establish. The Cardinal continued to hold him in high regard, and even employed him on a couple of minor missions that brought back faint memories of the glory days when Machiavelli had consulted with emperors and kings. In May 1520, he was sent to the ancient Tuscan capital of Lucca on government business. Though the issues at stake were trivial and involved financial matters that were of little interest to him—he was representing a group of rich Florentine creditors in a bankruptcy case—at least he was back in action again. In any case the work does not seem to have been too taxing since he had time in these months away from home to compose a brief "Summary of the affairs of the city of Lucca" and a more substantial *Life of Castruccio Castracani*, the medieval tyrant of that city. Though a minor work, dashed off in the course of a few months and based on secondary material, his friends of the Orti, to whom it was dedicated, "all decided it was a good thing, and well written."

In fact the *Life of Castruccio Castracani* appears merely to have been a trial run for a more ambitious work that was now being promoted by Machiavelli's friends. Looking for a way to help his impecunious friend, Zanobi Buondelmonti had approached the Cardinal with a proposal that he hire the former Second Chancellor to write an official history of Florence, a prestigious commission that would not only place him in the company of such men as former chancellors Leonardo Bruni and Poggio Bracciolini, but also provide him with much needed cash. It seems likely that the project was already under discussion when Machiavelli departed for Lucca and that he submitted the *Life of Castruccio* to the Cardinal as a sample of what he could achieve in the genre.

The work must have pleased the Cardinal because in November he offered Machiavelli the commission. Machiavelli himself wrote up a sample contract: "He is to be hired for ___ years at a salary of ___ per year with the condition that he must be, and is to be, held to write the annals or else the history of the things done by the state and city of Florence, from whatever time may seem to him most appropriate, and in whatever language— either Latin or Tuscan—may seem best to him."

Before sitting down to write in earnest, Machiavelli was employed on another small errand on behalf of the republic. In May 1521 he was chosen to represent the Franciscan Brothers of Florence at the general meeting of the order being held in the provincial town of Carpi in the Romagna. As a diplomatic junket it was hardly more consequential than his mission to Lucca the previous year, but after years in the wilderness even these small signs that he was back in favor were welcome. When he arrived at Carpi, located some seventy-five miles north of Florence on the far side of the Apennines, Machiavelli was instructed to conduct the negotiations on behalf of the Franciscan monasteries of Florence that were seeking independence from the Tuscan chapter.* It was a peculiar mission for a man who had so little religious feeling that many of his friends believed he was a secret atheist. Adding to the irony, he was also tasked by the Wool Guild (which was responsible for overseeing the Cathedral of Florence) with recruiting the popular preacher Fra Rovaio to deliver the Lenten sermons at the Duomo. When Machiavelli explained the nature of his mission, his friend Francesco Guicciardini joked: "It was certainly good judgment on the part of our reverend consuls of the Wool Guild to have entrusted you with the duty of selecting a preacher, not otherwise than if the task had been given to Pachierotto, while he was alive, or to Ser Sano [two well-known pederasts] to find a beautiful and graceful wife for a friend. I believe you will serve them according to the expectations they have of you."

The main interest of this trip to what Machiavelli derisively called "the republic of clogs" (a reference to the Franciscans' humble attire) is the correspondence it generated between the two greatest political thinkers of the age. Guicciardini, fourteen years younger than Machiavelli, was a haughty aristocrat whose disdain for human nature in general was combined with a snobbish contempt for the common people in particular. While both men favored republican government, Guicciardini believed Machiavelli placed far too much faith in the wisdom of the people. "To speak of the people is to speak of madmen, for the people is a monster full of confusion and error," Guicciardini insisted.

---

* When Savonarola managed to wring a similar concession from Pope Alexander on behalf of the Dominicans, the independence he gained was a crucial component of his power.

In his writings Machiavelli combines cynicism with passion; Guicciardini has no better opinion of human nature but his habitual attitude is one of ironic detachment. Guicciardini's cautious approach actually makes him the better historian. His *History of Florence* and *History of Italy* are more accurate than Machiavelli's treatment of the same subjects because he eschews grand pronouncements in favor of a straightforward narration of the facts. While Machiavelli likes to use one small fact as the foundation for vast theoretical structures, Guicciardini doubts that it is possible to draw any firm conclusions from the welter of conflicting data. It is an error, he says, "to wish to speak of the affairs of the world in general terms and according to fixed rules; since nearly all admit of exceptions." After reading what he considered a particularly fanciful passage in *The Discourses*, Guicciardini remarked dryly that many things are "easier to describe in books and in the imagination of mankind, than to carry into practical effect."

The two were drawn together by mutual respect and by their shared patriotism. Each watched with dismay as foreign armies marched across Italy, preparing to hurl themselves at each other in a final desperate bid for supremacy on the peninsula. "The Italians are not strong enough for resistance," Guicciardini despaired, "and capitulation will bring about our enslavement."

On the way to Carpi, Machiavelli stopped in nearby Modena, where his friend had been installed by Pope Leo as governor of Mantua and Reggio, and the two spent many hours discussing the dismal state of Italian affairs and drowning their sorrows in lively conversation lubricated by plenty of fine wine and hearty food. Reluctantly proceeding to the dusty village where the Franciscans had congregated, Machiavelli filled up the dull hours by writing to his recent host, and Guicciardini, his duties as governor apparently not overly taxing, responded in kind.

The exchange of letters from the weeks Machiavelli spent in Carpi have a feeling of whistling past the graveyard as the two men put aside for a moment their dismay at the current political situation to indulge in childish pranks and off-color humor. As Machiavelli admitted to Vettori, he used laughter to hide his tears, and the storm clouds gathering on the horizon gave a slightly frantic quality to their fun. To one of Guicciardini's facetious letters Machiavelli replied:

Magnificent Lord Francesescus Guicciardinis . . . most exalted and most honorable. *I was on the toilet when your messenger arrived, turning over in my mind the absurdities of this world, and trying to figure out just what kind of a preacher I would choose for Florence. He should be one after my own heart, because I am going to be as stubborn about this as I am about my other ideas. And because I have never let my republic down when I could help her out, if not by my actions then with my words, I don't intend to disappoint her now. I know that I am at odds with the opinions of my compatriots, in this as in many other things. They would like a preacher to teach them the way to Paradise, and I'd like to find one who would teach them the way to go to the Devil's lair. . . . [B]ecause I believe that the following would be the true way to Paradise—learn the way to Hell in order to flee from it. Seeing, in any case, how many are taken in by a fraud who hides under the cloak of religion, one can easily imagine how much faith there would be in a good man who walked in truth, and not in lies, treading in the muddy footsteps of Saint Francis.*

Who but Machiavelli could conjure such a scene? Bodily functions and philosophy, heaven and hell, low comedy and high purpose, all are lumped together in a single hilarious image. He is being mischievous certainly, but as always he uses humor to make a serious point. We have no choice, he seems to be saying, but to chart a course through the infernal regions since this is the world we live in. What is *The Prince* if not a practical guide to navigating this blighted landscape? Machiavelli's most helpful roadmap does not actually show us the way to heaven, but merely points out the deepest potholes along the road.

Not the least of the absurdities the two men had to contemplate was Machiavelli's pathetically reduced circumstances, so out of keeping with his abilities and in such stark contrast to his former life. Guicciardini commiserated. "My dearest Machiavelli," he wrote from the comfort of his own official lodgings: "When I read your title as ambassador to the Republic and of friars and recall all those kings, dukes, and princes, with whom you have negotiated in the past, I am reminded of Lysander who, after so many victories and trophies, was given the task of distributing meat to the same soldiers he had once so gloriously commanded."

Most galling to the former Second Chancellor was that the provincial villagers of Carpi had concluded he was a man of no account and were treating him accordingly. Machiavelli was used to being treated as Sir Nihil by kings and emperors, but to be snubbed by men with straw in their hair and manure on their boots was more than he could bear. Writing to Guicciardini he cooked up a ruse to confound the bumpkins who had decided they could save a few ducats by scrimping on his food and lodging. At Machiavelli's prompting Guicciardini sent off a series of important-looking dispatches under official seal, each carried by messenger accompanied by an entourage of armed guards. Machiavelli heightened the effect by hinting that he was at the moment involved in deep negotiations with the Emperor and the King of France. He described to Guicciardini the scene as these simple villagers found themselves caught up in great affairs of state:

> I must tell you that when the crossbowman arrived with your letter and, bowing to the ground, declared that he had been sent expressly to me and in all haste, everyone snapped to attention and created such an uproar that everything was upset, and I was grilled for any news. . . . Soon, they were all standing around with their mouths open and their hats in their hands. I am surrounded as I write, and the more I write the more I am marveled at and seen as one inspired. And I, to make them gape some more, sometimes lift my pen and puff out my cheeks, which just starts them drooling.

Soon Machiavelli was receiving invitations to dine at the homes of the leading citizens, where his hosts would lay for him rustic feast on their finest silver and apologize for the simple fare. He took full advantage of the situation, "gobbl[ing] up," he told Guicciardini, "enough for six dogs and three wolves," and counting up the money he was saving by not having to provide his own meals.

Though the farce enlivened an otherwise thankless mission, Machiavelli was glad to put the walls of Carpi behind him. He was back in Florence by early June. Awaiting him on his arrival were the first proofs of *The Art of War*, just coming off the presses of the printer Filippo di Giunta. This was the one book of Machiavelli's to be published in his lifetime and he was justifiably proud of the accomplishment. Dedicated to Lorenzo

Strozzi, his friend from the Rucellai gardens who had introduced him to Cardinal Giulio, *The Art of War* rehashes many of the themes he had already laid out in *The Prince* and *The Discourses*, proclaiming the superiority of republics to principalities and, as always, the superiority of the citizen militia to mercenary armies. This remains Machiavelli's great obsession: to discourage Italians from employing soldiers-for-hire, rediscover the martial valor of their ancestors, and, with patriotic fire in their eyes, drive the barbarians from their midst.

But for all his passion on the subject, *The Art of War* has held up less well than his other major works. Despite his years organizing and provisioning the citizen militias of Florence, Machiavelli was not a professional military man, and many of his prescriptions are impractical or counterproductive. His disdain for artillery and for military engineering, as well as his preference for infantry over cavalry, derive from his study of Roman history but have little to do with the realities of Renaissance warfare, where cannon and musket were changing the dynamics of battle.

Ultimately, *The Art of War* is significant less for its discussions of tactics or strategy than for Machiavelli's insight that the way a society chooses to wage war profoundly shapes its internal structure. Mercenary armies are the scourge of well-ordered polities because "a good man could not make war his only profession, and . . . no wise prince or governor of a commonwealth would allow any of his citizens to do it." By contrast, armies made up of citizen soldiers, mustered for a brief period at a moment of crisis, are the sinews of a vital organism, fueled by patriotic ardor and unified in a common purpose. When Rome conquered the world she accomplished this with "common soldiers [who] laid down their arms with much more pleasure than they had taken them up," and by "commanders . . . contenting themselves with the honor of a triumph [who] returned with eagerness to their former manner of living."

Machiavelli received from Cardinal Giulio the contract to write a history of his native city in November 1521. He was given a two-year stipend from the University of Florence to complete the work, at the rate of 100 *fiorini di studio,** slightly more than half the salary he earned as the Second

---

* The *fiorino di studio* (florin of the studio) was worth barely half the standard gold florin, a sign that then, as now, academics were expected to spend their prestige when they ran short of hard cash.

Chancellor and Secretary to the Ten. While the money certainly came in handy, just as important for Machiavelli was the opportunity to apply the ideas he had developed in his earlier works to the history of his native land. The commission would prove particularly delicate since his patron's family had played such a crucial and controversial role in the history of the city he was chronicling. His strategy, as he explained to Guicciardini, was to avoid giving offense while still telling the truth as he saw it. It was the same high-wire act he had already practiced in his "Treatise on the Reform of the Government of Florence," and one that, for the most part, he carried out nimbly.

While not a startlingly original work like *The Prince* or *The Discourses*, nor a literary masterpiece like *La Mandragola*, the *Florentine Histories* is solid analytical history, built around the dominant motif of the city's endless factional violence. In *The Discourses* Machiavelli had praised the Romans for their ability to turn civil strife into constructive law, but he viewed the tumultuous history of Florence with a more critical eye. The Roman Republic had used the tension between the classes to forge a new consensus, but the history of Machiavelli's own city was a dismal spectacle of carnage accompanied by no redeeming social evolution. "For the enmities between the people and the nobles at the beginning of Rome that were resolved by disputing were resolved by Florence by fighting," he explains. "Those in Rome ended in law, those in Florence with the exile and death of many citizens; those in Rome always increased military virtue, those in Florence eliminated it altogether."

After laying out this sorry history in gruesome detail, he proceeds to chronicle the rise of the Medici party in the first half of the fifteenth century. Though he admits that the Medici, beginning with Cosimo and continuing with his grandson Lorenzo, systematically dismantled the city's democratic institutions, he portrays this process as a reasonable response to the chaos that preceded it. In effect, the citizens were willing to purchase peace at the price of losing some of their ancient liberties. Machiavelli originally intended to bring his history up to the current moment but he tactfully concluded in 1492 with the death of Lorenzo the Magnificent, happily relieving himself of the difficult task of finding something constructive to say about Giulio's cousin, Piero, and the other younger and less impressive members of the family.

•   •   •

These were relatively happy years for Machiavelli. His sense of isolation lifted with his acceptance into the charmed circle of the Rucellai gardens, bringing him much needed camaraderie and also winning him friends in high places. He was not where he most wanted to be, in the very heart of the action, but at least he was treated with respect, even reverence, by men whose company he enjoyed and who stimulated his ideas. With the success of his comedies he had fame, if not fortune, and a series of passionate love affairs absorbed him when more scholarly pursuits temporarily lost their allure. Even the house at Sant' Andrea seemed less a prison than a refuge where he could work on his history undisturbed but for the pleasant commotion stirred up by young children.

But there were signs the calm would not last. The optimism that had accompanied Giulio de' Medici's arrival in Florence had turned in certain circles into sullen resentment as promised reforms never materialized. Among the most disillusioned were members of the Orti Oricellari, long a bastion of pro-Medici sentiment, and among these the most vehement critics of the regime included Machiavelli's close friends Zanobi Buondelmonti and Luigi Alamanni.

The extent to which Machiavelli himself participated in the whispered conversations is unclear. He was certainly aware that a new dark mood had overtaken the once idyllic—and largely apolitical—gatherings, but he lacked the ideological fire of his younger companions. In any case Machiavelli was never a man of action, particularly when it involved conspiracy against the duly elected authorities. While he certainly shared his friends' aspirations, he remained skeptical of anything that involved potential violence.

Influence, in fact, flowed in the other direction. Buondelmonti, Alamanni, and the other denizens of the Orti had been inspired by the writings of the older man, particularly *The Discourses*, which laid out a convincing case for the superiority of republican government. Once reviled in that aristocratic milieu as the toady of a government with populist leanings, in retrospect the architect of the victory over Pisa seemed an almost heroic figure.

The transformation of the Orti Oricellari from a pro-Medici bastion to a nursery of anti-Medici sedition was typical of the twists and turns of Florentine politics. For the moment there was no danger that inchoate feelings of disenchantment would lead to open resistance. As long as a Medici sat on the papal throne, the alliance between Rome and the *reggimento* in Florence was simply too strong, and the profits accruing to Florentine merchants from increased business too attractive, for the ancient yearning for liberty to congeal into concrete action. All that changed on December 1, 1521, with the unexpected death of Pope Leo following a brief illness. Though only forty-five at the time of his death, the Medici Pope had worn out his welcome and his body through dissipated living. Worse still, he had never met the high expectations that accompanied his election, devoting his energies to aggrandizing his family rather than bolstering the moral reputation of the Church or the prosperity of his native city. Though an intelligent and cultivated man, he was negligent in tending to his spiritual duties and equally negligent when it came to rallying the Italian people to resist the foreign invaders. It was during his reign that Christianity was torn asunder by Luther and his followers—disgusted by the worldly excess they saw in the Vatican—and while the final enslavement of the peninsula did not take place in his lifetime, his corrupt and vacillating policy made such an outcome all but inevitable.

In the ensuing conclave a vigorous battle was waged between supporters of Cardinal de' Medici and Machiavelli's old friend Cardinal Francesco Soderini (brother of the former Gonfaloniere). In the end these two factions fought to a draw, ensuring the election of a colorless Dutchman, Cardinal Adriann Dedel, who ascended the throne on January 9, 1522, with the name Adrian VI.* In Rome the election of this nonentity drew jeers from the crowd outside the Vatican. In Florence the conflict between the two native-born cardinals merely helped widen the fissures that were opening within the ruling elite.

With his position threatened by the death of his cousin, Cardinal Giulio tried to still the voices of discontent by repeating his old trick of inviting proposals for reform. Among those who rose to the bait was Machiavelli (who resubmitted the plan he had drawn up a few years earlier) along with many others who believed the restoration of free institutions

---

* Adrian was also the compromise candidate between supporters of France and of the Emperor, so little known that he offended no one.

and open elections was just around the corner. But as he had three years earlier, Cardinal Giulio backed down at the last minute. Rumors began circulating that instead of restoring their liberties, the Cardinal was preparing to install two Medici bastards—Ippolito, illegitimate son of Giuliano, and Alessandro, love child of Lorenzo—at the head of the government, demonstrating that he viewed Florence as little more than family property.

Early in June 1522 a courier was intercepted by Florentine authorities as he was riding along the road toward Rome. In his saddlebag they found a letter addressed to Battista della Palla (the man who had been instrumental in convincing Pope Leo to stage the first Roman performance of *La Mandragola*) detailing a plot to assassinate Cardinal Giulio and proclaim a restored Florentine Republic. The Roman conspirators included not only della Palla but the two Soderini brothers; the leaders of the conspiracy in Florence were Zanobi Buondelmonti, Luigi Alamanni, and Jacopo da Diaceto, all of them close friends of Machiavelli from the Orti Oricellari. Buondelmonti and Alamanni managed to flee the city ahead of the constables, but other denizens of the Rucellai gardens, including Diaceto and Alamanni's cousin (confusingly also named Luigi) were less fleet of foot. Led in chains to Le Stinche they were subjected to the usual harsh methods employed by the authorities to extract confessions. In an eerie reprise of the failed conspiracy of 1513, Machiavelli's name once again came out during the interrogations. There was even testimony that Buondelmonti had planned to contact him but had been discouraged at the last minute because, as a poor man without connections, Machiavelli was in no position to help.

Cardinal Giulio's retribution was swift, though not, under the circumstances, excessive. Displaying what for him was an unusual decisiveness, he had Diaceto and Luigi Alamanni beheaded in the courtyard of the Bargello, and prevailed upon the Pope to arrest Cardinal Soderini in Rome. (Piero Soderini was spared a similar fate since he died on June 13.) Though Machiavelli himself escaped unscathed, he was understandably distraught at the disaster that had befallen his friends. The "brotherhood of the cool shade" was disbanded once and for all, and with it a happy chapter in his life had closed.

Machiavelli himself never wrote of the disastrous events from the summer of 1522, though one can infer his troubled state of mind from the sparseness of his correspondence during these months. Most suggestive is the brief, bitter epitaph he composed upon learning of Piero Soderini's death:

> *The night that Piero Soderini ceased to breathe*
> *His soul journeyed to the mouth of Hell;*
> *But Pluto cried: "Thou foolish soul*
> *No Hell for thee! Go seek the Limbo of the babes!"*

The sarcastic tone of these lines was almost certainly prompted by Soderini's role in the fiasco. On a personal level Machiavelli had every reason to be loyal to his old boss. In fact Soderini had tried more than once to find employment for his former assistant, offering him a position as secretary to the Republic of Ragusa (modern-day Dubrovnik) and a lucrative sinecure as secretary to the *condottiere* Prospero Colonna. Machiavelli turned down both offers, in part because he was too devoted to his native city to contemplate leaving it for any length of time, and partly because he worried that having dealings with the disgraced Gonfaloniere would cause him trouble with the authorities at home. (At one point he explained to Vettori that he would not visit his old friend for fear that when he returned to the city he would be taken straight to Le Stinche. For all Soderini's kindness to him, and for all the happy memories of their past collaboration, Machiavelli could not forgive this final indiscretion. The disastrous consequences of Soderini's scheming confirmed the verdict pronounced in *The Discourses* that he was a decent man but an ineffectual leader.

Machiavelli's feelings were complicated by the fact that he himself had played a less than heroic role in the tragedy. He had little reason to regret not becoming entangled in his young friends' harebrained schemes; he had always rejected such conspiracies both on practical grounds and on principle. Had Buondelmonti or Alamanni consulted him, he might have referred them to the chapter in *The Discourses* titled "On Conspiracies," where he warns all who would set off down this most dangerous path that "there are very few, if any, who do not themselves get killed in the very act." But he was sympathetic to their cause and it pained him to see them suffer.

In fact he remained on the Medici payroll, retiring to his house in Sant' Andrea to complete work on the *Florentine Histories* commissioned by the very man who had just executed his friends. He felt conflicted, though whether his anger was directed more at the Cardinal or his rash friends is difficult to know. For the most part he seems merely to have escaped into his work and into idle distractions. It was at this time that he began frequenting the villa of Jacopo Falconetti, where he replaced the more cerebral pleasures of the Rucellai gardens with the brickmaker's boisterous bacchanals. It was also at this time that he began his passionate affair with the singer Barbera Raffacani, turning as he often did to the delights of the flesh when the rest of his life seemed to be falling apart. The lighthearted romp *Clizia* was also a product of these listless days. His attitude toward the world and its troubles is summed up in a single line he wrote to his brother-in-law Francesco del Nero. "I'll send your regards to the chickens," he wrote from Sant' Andrea, a wry commentary on his rustic retirement.

NIGHTMARE AND DREAM

"Since [Machiavelli] is unable to remedy the faults of mankind, he will do nothing but laugh at them."

—FRANCESCO GUICCIARDINI TO ROBERTO ACCIAIUOLI

BURYING HIMSELF IN MUSTY ANNALS OF THE PAST, Machiavelli was able to take his mind off the troubles of the present. With ink-stained fingers and stacks of yellowing documents by his side, he delved into the parade of folly that constituted the long and troubled history of his native city. The tramp of armies and roar of cannon were little more than distant rumors, drowned out by the sounds of chickens clucking and scrabbling in the yard below. Now in his mid-fifties, Machiavelli remained physically vigorous (as his gymnastics with the beautiful Barbera suggest) and mentally acute, but he no longer felt the same need to plunge headlong into the maelstrom. Perhaps it was simply that he had learned to live with disappointment. He would accept whatever came his way, willing, as always, to labor on behalf of his native land. But he did not expect to play the same vital role in affairs of state as he had in the reign of Piero Soderini, when the decisions he made could change the course of history.

Machiavelli may have preferred to turn his back on what was happening beyond the fields and orchards of Sant' Andrea, but he could not ignore for long the great events transpiring just beyond the horizon. The tragic farce of the failed plot against Cardinal Giulio had played out against a backdrop of growing menace. In 1516 the kings of Spain and France had signed the Treaty of Noyon, in which the Spaniards recognized the French claim to Milan in return for recognition of their rights in Naples. The treaty brought a rare interlude of calm, but each side was merely biding its time, regrouping and rearming for a more decisive battle.

Now the rivalry threatened to erupt with renewed violence. The two great monarchs of Europe—Francis I, who had succeeded Louis XII in 1515 as King of France, and Charles, who had taken the Spanish throne the following year—had no intention of laying down their weapons until a final decision had been reached. In June 1518 the Flemish-born Charles added to his Spanish throne the title of Holy Roman Emperor. With territories stretching from the North Sea to the Rock of Gibraltar, from the ancient city of Naples to the virgin forests of the New World, Charles V's empire was a vast, unruly patchwork of languages, peoples, and religions.* But despite the difficulties involved in managing such an unwieldy patrimony, Charles had more than enough energy left over to settle old scores with the Most Christian King of France.

One might have hoped, along with Machiavelli, Guicciardini, and countless other Italian patriots, that faced with yet another cataclysmic war on native soil, the states of the peninsula would put aside their own differences long enough to present a unified front against the common enemy. But once again the Italians proved complicit in their own destruction. As they had in 1494, each city-state looked to its own short-term advantage, forging alliances with one or the other of the great powers and switching sides whenever they could cut a better deal.

Machiavelli might well have resigned himself to a placid retirement had Fortuna, a creature of infinite jest, not taken it upon herself to stir the pot once more. In the fall of 1523 history took one of those sudden turns of the kind that made it so difficult to predict the trajectory of a man's life. On September 14, Pope Adrian VI breathed his last, leaving the stage with as little fanfare as he entered it. Like Pius III, who had filled in between the reigns of Alexander VI and Julius II, he had been a stopgap pope, a compromise candidate when the top contenders had battled to a draw. The conclave to which Cardinal Giulio now hurried proved to be one of the most contentious in recent memory. The French King and the Holy

---

* Not least of Charles's headaches were the revolts inspired by Luther and his followers in the northern reaches of his dominions.

Roman Emperor both realized that the new Pope could swing the balance of power in Italy and so they engaged in a bitter proxy war, deploying phalanxes of cardinals inside the Sistine Chapel like well-disciplined soldiers. After more than fifty days, Cardinal Giulio—who had the backing of the Emperor—prevailed over the French cardinals. On November 19, 1523, he was crowned with much pomp in St. Peter's, taking the name Clement VII.

After an interlude of less than two years a Medici was again seated on the papal throne, but there was no reason to suppose that, as far as the people of Florence were concerned, the arrangement—so breathlessly anticipated before the fact—would prove any happier than it had the first time. Having one of their own in the Vatican had merely given the Medici delusions of grandeur; they used their enhanced prestige not to promote the prosperity of their native city but to glorify their own family. Their ambition was embodied in the new tombs Michelangelo was currently working on in the family church of San Lorenzo. Compared to the austere Old Sacristy, which contained the remains of Cosimo and his two sons, the New Sacristy, commissioned by Cardinal Giulio before his departure for Rome, was a grandiose monument to the younger generation of the family. The two tombs of Giuliano and Lorenzo are the work of a genius at the height of his powers, but their marmoreal splendor is out of all proportion to the nonentities who occupy them. The New Sacristy, with its seamless integration of sculpture and architecture, is one of the masterpieces of Renaissance art, but also a testament to the decay of the communal spirit that had animated Florentine life for centuries.

For Machiavelli, Giulio's elevation offered one last chance to make his mark on the public stage. Pope Leo had always regarded the former Second Chancellor with suspicion, but Machiavelli's relations with the new Pontiff were cordial. Over the years he had shown himself a loyal servant, swallowing his pride to take on even the least prestigious assignments, and both his dedication and the quality of his mind continued to impress Clement. Even his association with the conspirators of the Orti proved to be little more than a temporary embarrassment.

With his friend now seated on the papal throne Machiavelli felt reinvigorated. After years spent in dull retirement it was time to dust himself off and see if he might yet make a contribution. By the beginning of 1525 he was close to finishing his *Florentine Histories*. As he had before when he sat with the completed manuscript of *The Prince* on his desk, he asked Vettori whether he should make the trip to Rome and present the work to his patron. "My dear friend," Vettori replied with his usual equivocations:

> *I don't know whether to tell you to come with the book or not, since the times are not conducive to reading and to gift giving. But on the other hand, the night I arrived . . . the pope himself asked after you and whether you had completed the Historia as he anticipated. And when I told him that I had seen part of it and that you had reached the death of Lorenzo, and that it was something that would give satisfaction, and that you wanted to come and bring it to him but, due to the gloomy times, I had dissuaded you, he said to me: "He should have come. I am certain that his books will give much pleasure and be read eagerly." These are the exact words he said to me, but I would not place too much faith in them, since you might come and still find yourself emptyhanded. Given the pope's current state of mind, this could well happen.*

In the case of *The Prince*, Machiavelli had been dissuaded by his friend's less than enthusiastic reception, but this time he ignored Vettori's warning and set out for Rome with the manuscript in his saddlebag. He arrived in the Holy City late in May. Despite Vettori's gloomy prediction, Clement received him warmly and gratefully accepted the work from his hands.*

But, as Vettori correctly noted, the times were not conducive to the leisurely perusal of scholarly tomes. As Machiavelli and the Pope talked in the opulently furnished chambers in the Vatican, the conversation soon turned to the troubles facing the Italian people and the papacy in particular. Though Clement would not admit it, his difficulties were largely due to his own misjudgments. Like his cousin before him, the new Pope proved incapable of sticking to a single farsighted policy, shifting allegiances as easily as other men change their clothes. He had been lifted to the throne on the Emperor's strong arm, but once in power he began to look for ways to wriggle free from Charles's suffocating embrace. Shortly after he took office

---

* The Pope was evidently pleased with what he read since he awarded the author an additional 120 gold ducats.

he secretly allied himself with the French, a policy that looked as if it might pay dividends when in October 1524 Francis arrived in Italy at the head of an apparently invincible army of forty thousand. But, as had happened so often in the past, French dreams were soon dashed on the plains of Lombardy. On February 23, 1525, Francis was routed by imperial forces near the northern Italian city of Pavia, leaving ten thousand of his best soldiers dead and maimed on the field of battle. Worse still for the French cause—and for the Pope who had staked his future on their success—Francis himself was captured and dragged off in chains to a Spanish prison.

With the French army decimated and their King held captive, all Italy lay open to the victorious imperial army. Florence quickly came to terms with the new master of Italy, paying 100,000 ducats for the privilege of not being invaded. But for Pope Clement the consequences were nothing short of calamitous. Even the usually resourceful Guicciardini was at his wits' end: "I well understand that just now every good brain is puzzled," he wrote, "but he who sees that by standing still he will be overwhelmed by destruction, ought to prefer the worst dangers to certain death."

Small wonder, then, that the Pope was preoccupied. But while Clement was despondent, the crisis seemed to have rekindled some of Machiavelli's old fire. Once again he found himself—almost by accident—at the very heart of the action. Believing that Clement's despair provided an opportunity to translate his ideas into concrete action, he filled the Pope's ears with plans, schemes, and theories that he had long ago set down on paper. It was clear, Machiavelli explained, that so long as the Pope had no reliable army of his own he would remain—to borrow a phrase he had used in another context—"an unarmed prophet," a slave to those who could impose their will through powder, shot, and cold steel. The only solution was the creation of a national citizen militia, which to Machiavelli remained the cure for every ill. Humbly reminding the Pope how nobly his small force had acquitted itself before the walls of Pisa (while ignoring their abject failure at Prato), Machiavelli tried to convince Clement that he could mold the villagers and peasants of the Papal States into a fighting force capable of standing up to the Emperor and his Swiss pike men.

As Clement listened he caught some of his guest's enthusiasm. Perhaps it was the delirium of despair, but standing still, as Guicciardini had observed, was not an option. With a sense of renewed purpose the Pope sent

Machiavelli off to the Romagna with instructions to make an inventory of available resources. "[T]he matter is of great importance," read the papal brief Machiavelli carried in his saddlebag, "and on it depends the safety of the Papal States as well as that of the whole of Italy, and practically the whole of Christendom."

Machiavelli set out in high spirits, pleased to be on the road again in the fine summer weather and excited to be taking part in a mission of such vital importance to the future of Italy. He had every reason to be optimistic. Not only did the Pope appear to be fully behind the project, but the recently appointed President of the Romagna, whose cooperation was crucial to the success of the venture, was none other than his old friend Francesco Guicciardini. Unfortunately for Machiavelli, when he arrived in Faenza, capital of the Romagna, he found the phlegmatic Guicciardini less than enthusiastic. In the past Guicciardini had often chided his friend on his too vivid imagination, and this latest proposal struck him as one of those pie-in-the-sky schemes Machiavelli occasionally pursued without regard to practical details. While he did not oppose Machiavelli's goals, he thought current conditions inauspicious for such a bold undertaking. "[I]f it could be brought to the desired fruition," Guicciardini wrote to the papal secretary, "there is no doubt that it would be one of the most useful and praiseworthy things which his Holiness could do." But, he concluded, "if he intends it as a remedy for present dangers, it is a provision which cannot come in time."

In fact Clement had already begun to waver. While Machiavelli enjoyed Guicciardini's hospitality in Faenza, the Pope blew alternately hot and cold. "When I asked him again if His Beatitude had made up his mind," wrote the Pope's adviser, "he replied that he wants to think about it some more."

By the end of the month Machiavelli's initial enthusiasm was gone, undone by the Pope's vacillation. He packed up his bags and headed home for Florence, convinced that the Pope would never make up his mind. It had been a frustrating mission, and Machiavelli returned to his farm disgusted once more with affairs of state that seemed to bring him nothing but aggravation. His brief return to public life merely confirmed his conclusion made years earlier that those who toil on the people's behalf "sow in sand and in water."

The one person Machiavelli apparently did not blame for the failure of his scheme was Guicciardini. His recent sojourn at the presidential palace in Faenza had strengthened a bond that was growing closer with each passing year. It was a relationship built on mutual admiration; however much the two disagreed on specific policies, neither doubted the other's sincerity and genuine passion for the well-being of Italy. It didn't hurt that the wealthy Guicciardini treated his guest royally. Crossing swords with his aristocratic friend was always made more enjoyable by the good food and wine that accompanied their lively debates.

Their friendship was marked by a warmth that went beyond intellectual respect and high-minded ideals. The reserved, aristocratic president of the Romagna and the irrepressible former Second Chancellor, like many who come from varied backgrounds and possessed contrasting temperaments, discovered in their differences a source of both wonder and amusement. When Machiavelli insisted on addressing Guicciardini by his honorific, Guicciardini shot back: "I must warn you that if you address letters to me with 'Illustrious,' I shall address yours 'Magnificent,' and thus, with these reciprocal titles we shall each of us please the other. But soon enough it will turn to mourning when we find ourselves, I say all of us, with our hands full of flies at the end. So decide how much weight you wish to give to titles, measuring mine against those you would delight in having given to you."

Not all their correspondence is marked by similar compliments. In fact they felt sure enough of their mutual affection to goad each other mercilessly. Shortly after Machiavelli returned to Florence, Guicciardini asked his friend to survey a piece of property he had purchased. "[F]or about three miles about, you can see nothing pleasing," Machiavelli began his report. "The house cannot be called bad, but neither would I call it good." It was an assessment made by a poor man who believed that wealth made for careless judgments. But if Guicciardini had no eye for real estate, Machiavelli, according to Guicciardini, had his own blind spot. Pretending to be hurt by his harsh verdict, Guicciardini sent a sharply worded retort. Adopting the persona of the offended estate herself, *Milady Property of Finocchieto*, he wrote:

You are accustomed to your Barbera who, like all of her kind, seeks to please all and to seem rather than to be. However in this case

your eyes, accustomed as they are to meretricious company, are not
satisfied with what is but rather by what seems to be. As long as they
detect some vague hint of beauty, they fail to delve beneath appear-
ances. But you who have read and written so much history and seen
so much of the world should be able to discern that another mode of
adornment, another beauty, a different manner of making oneself up
and of presenting oneself is sought in a woman who lives with every-
one and loves no one.

Bringing up the less than chaste habits of his mistress might seem like hit-
ting below the belt, but if Machiavelli felt the need to leap to the defense
of his lady love that letter has not come down to us. Instead, when he next
writes to Guicciardini it is to offer him a recipe to relieve his constipation,
repaying him for all the delicacies he had consumed at his table with a
concoction of bitter aloe, saffron, and Armenian bole.

Though Machiavelli returned to Florence having achieved little, his
efforts did not go unrecognized. In September 1525 his name was finally
added to the electoral rolls, making him a full-fledged citizen of the republic he had served for so long. Though his friends teased him that the honor
had been won through the charms of his mistress Barbera, it is more likely
that it came at the urging of the Pope, who perhaps felt bad that he had put
Machiavelli through so much trouble for nothing. In any case the honor
was largely empty since real power was jealously held by Cardinal Passerini da Cortona, sent by Clement to supervise the two Medici bastards,
Ippolito and Alessandro, who governed much as their fathers had—with a
combination of arrogance and incompetence that marked all the descendants of *Il Magnifico.*

Machiavelli seemed to regard being *imborsato* (having his name placed
in the electoral bags) as little more than a consolation prize and was determined not to let politics rule his life. In October his oldest son, Bernardo,
came down with "double tertian fever," and as long as he was in danger
Machiavelli could think of nothing else. Once his recovery was assured,
Machiavelli's attention turned to other matters, most notably a production of *La Mandragola* that Guicciardini was organizing in Faenza for the
Carnival season of 1526. With the international situation going from bad
to worse, one might have thought that the two greatest political minds of

the day might have had better things to do than worry about the staging of a frivolous comedy, but as Guicciardini noted it was in times such as these that diversions were most welcome. "Honored Niccolò," he wrote, "I shall begin to answer you with the comedy, because it does not seem among the less important things that we have on our hands, and at least it is something over which we have some control, so that it is not a waste of time to think about it, and now more than ever recreation is needed amidst all this tumult." Machiavelli agreed with his friend about the benefits of distraction, but he also knew that laughter is often the most direct path to deeper truths. Trying to explain a particularly obscure passage in *La Mandragola*, Machiavelli told his friend that he should interpret its meaning as: "time is endlessly repeating but we are always the same"—a notion that also lay at the heart of his political philosophy.

As it turned out the performance in Faenza had to be postponed indefinitely.* Laughter might be an antidote to the poison of political strife, but it could not keep reality at bay. Foreign armies, restless and ill-disciplined, roamed the land, feeding themselves by starving the native population, while powerful men hatched schemes for deploying their lethal power. Friends contemplated mutual betrayal, while sworn enemies slipped discreetly into bed together. Rumor and conjecture filled the information vacuum as civilians tried to make sense of a shifting tapestry that followed no discernible pattern. Before he could put the finishing touches on the performance, Guicciardini was swept up in the maelstrom, summoned to Rome on urgent business with the Pope. Machiavelli did not have much time to grumble about the change in plans; soon he, too, would be plucked out of his present idleness to play his own small part in the unfolding drama.

With Francis's calamitous rout at the Battle of Pavia, Charles had become the master of the Italian peninsula. But in the tangled web of European politics no victory was final and no defeat irretrievable. Success, in fact,

---

* The disappointment was more than made up for by a hugely successful run in Venice, where *La Mandragola* was performed before overflow crowds. In a development that must have pleased Machiavelli no end, his comedy was judged by most to be far superior to Plautus's *Menaechmi*, being performed simultaneously to far smaller audiences.

brought to the victor its own set of problems. The Emperor's triumphant troops were a motley assortment drawn from the four corners of his empire, underpaid and underfed; to maintain them in the field indefinitely and preserve their discipline was almost impossible. And even though Charles ruled more territory than any monarch since the Roman Empire was divided between east and west, along with the immense expanse of his realm came an equally long list of troubles, from the fragile colonies of the New World to the religious quarrels of the Old. Charles, in short, was vastly overextended.

What saved the Emperor, at least for the moment, was the fact that his many foes lacked the will or foresight to take advantage of his weakness. Ever since Ludovico Sforza had played his dangerous game with the French King in 1494, the statesmen of Italy had attempted to secure their realms through subterfuge rather than strength of arms, until all virtue was lost and the country reduced to abject servitude. Elaborate plots replaced sound military strategy, the art of conspiracy substituted for martial valor. Pope Clement was only the most nimble practitioner of this sly art, making solemn commitments one day only to break them the next, infuriating everyone with his pusillanimous and devious conduct.* Machiavelli, for one, was thoroughly fed up, telling Guicciardini, "I have to conclude that this gang here will never ever accomplish anything honorable or heroic to justify either living or dying."

One could argue that this is exactly the world he himself had promoted in *The Prince*: "Since a prince is required to play the beast, he must learn from both the fox and the lion, because a lion cannot defend himself against snares, nor the fox against wolves." But what separated the current Pope from the idealized prince he had conceived was that there was too much of the fox and none of the lion in him. There was nothing Machiavelli despised more than weakness, and all the intricate plots and counterplots spun by the Pope and his allies were little more than the desperate ploys of men lacking courage or conviction. With his eyes set firmly on the ultimate objective—the liberation of Italy from the barbarians—Machiavelli was willing to forgive a great deal if it helped achieve his goal. He was,

---

* After Charles's victory at Pavia, Clement was forced to realign himself with the Emperor. But only a few months later he was discovered plotting with the chief minister of the Duke of Milan to betray the Spaniards. When this scheme unraveled he went crawling back once again into the Spanish fold.

however, unsparing toward those who sacrificed the ultimate objective for short-term advantage or who were simply too inept to get from point A to point B without tumbling into a ditch. Had the Pope's erratic course brought freedom to Italy, Machiavelli, like most of his countrymen, would have ignored his faults. As it was, those faults contributed to the looming disaster.

It was a disaster that both Machiavelli and Guicciardini foretold but could not forestall. "I vent my feelings against these princes, who have done everything possible to bring us to this pass," Machiavelli wrote in despair. Guicciardini was hardly more sanguine. "As to public affairs, I do not know what to say because I have lost my bearings. . . . If I am not deceiving myself, we will all be better acquainted with the evils of peace when the opportunity for making war has passed. One never sees anyone who, when bad times approach, did not seek in some way to try and cover himself, except for us, who want to meet them unprotected in the middle of the road."

During these troubled days the two men remained in constant touch, hoping to discover some way out of the morass. In January 1526, to the surprise of many (including Machiavelli), Charles agreed to release the French King in return for territorial concessions and a formal revocation of any claims he had in Italy. Compliance was to be assured by sending two of the French King's sons to Spain and arranging a marriage between Francis and Charles's sister, Leonora. Machiavelli thought the plan was madness on the Emperor's part. "It would be, as I have said, a foolish move for the emperor to release the king," Machiavelli wrote to Guicciardini, though, he added, "it would be smart for the king to promise anything to obtain his freedom." Machiavelli, who had literally written the book on how to behave in such situations, proved prophetic once again. As soon as he safely crossed the Pyrenees, Francis backed out of the agreement, a breach of promise for which the Pope—no stickler in such matters— quickly absolved him on the grounds that it was made under duress.

"[T]here will be war in Italy, and soon," Machiavelli glumly concluded. Since a victory by Charles would reduce them all to servitude, the only op- tion for Italians was to arm themselves and side with France, a course of action with which Guicciardini heartily agreed. In fact the President of the Romagna was already beginning to put such a plan into motion, urging the Pope to make a stand, like Julius before him, for Italian liberty. "Those dreading war should be shown the perils of peace. Over-prudence is now imprudence, and it is no longer possible to undertake measured enterprises. It is indispensable to resort to arms to avoid a peace that makes us slaves." Prodded by Guicciardini and other Italian patriots, the Pope finally signed an anti-imperial pact. The League of Cognac, as this new alliance was called, included France, Venice, Florence, Milan, and the papacy, a coalition that, at least on paper, should have been more than sufficient to stand up to Charles.*

Having made the decision to confront the Emperor, one of the first orders of business was to shore up the crumbling defenses of the Pope's native Florence, which stood directly in the path of any army descending on Rome. Clement, who had received one of the first copies of Machiavelli's *Art of War*, immediately sent for the former Second Chancellor to discuss the state of the city's fortifications. After making a brief inspection, Machiavelli headed to Rome in late April 1526, where he delivered a report titled "Provision for the creation of the office of the five superintendents for the walls of the city of Florence." He remained in the Holy City only a few days, but when he returned to Florence, he carried with him a document from Clement naming him secretary of the new commission in charge of the reconstruction project. "Machiavelli has left with the orders for the supplies and officers to be carried out," Guicciardini wrote to his brother Luigi in Florence: "people are to start the fortifications in the way that you will learn from him. . . . Machiavelli was the man who fostered this plan, hence please be obliged to treat him well during his stay and in the other matters that may be required because he has earned his share full well."

For the first time since he had been thrown out of office fourteen years earlier, Machiavelli held an official position with the Florentine government. And though his new title, Secretary to the Overseers of the Walls (with son Bernardo appointed his assistant), was a far cry from the distinguished Second Chancellor and Secretary to the Ten, securing the defenses of the city he loved was a task worthy of his efforts. Machiavelli took to the work with his usual zeal, walking the miles of the

---

* Henry VIII of England was to have been included in the new alliance but backed out at the last minute.

city's fortifications, supervising the digging of trenches, and overseeing the repair of crumbling towers. "[M]y head is so full of ramparts that nothing else can enter it," Machiavelli told Guicciardini, overjoyed to find himself useful once more.

In the meantime Guicciardini, now invested with the exalted title of *Luogotenente* (Lieutenant-General) of the papal army, hurried north to take charge of the forces of the league. Finding them in disarray, in early July Guicciardini asked Machiavelli to come join him in Piacenza to help instill some discipline in the ragtag army. Reluctantly, Machiavelli set aside the important work on the city's fortifications and hurried to his friend's side, but even he could make little headway. "He came to reorganize the militia," Guicciardini told Roberto Acciaiuoli, Florentine ambassador to France, "but seeing how rotten it is, he has no hope of having any respect from it. Since he is unable to remedy the faults of mankind, he will do nothing but laugh at them."

Here Guicciardini captures in a few deft strokes a perfect likeness of his friend: a man of contradictions, of light and shadow, laughter and tears, prone to outbursts of enthusiasm that were inevitably followed by bitter disappointment. When duty called he did not excuse himself on the grounds that, at fifty-seven, the rigors of travel or camp life were too onerous, or that in the past his service had been flung back in his face. He remained hopeful that this time would be different, and when he saw his best efforts come to nothing, he turned away with a rueful grin and a derisive shrug as if to say that he expected nothing more. Roberto Acciaiuoli, for his part, appreciated the effort though he despaired of the outcome: "I am glad that Machiavelli gave the orders to discipline the infantry," he replied to Guicciardini. "Would to God he might put into action what he has in mind, but I doubt whether it is like Plato's *Republic*." In other words, Machiavelli was too much the dreamer to stand much chance of success. How ironic that he who famously declared he preferred to "stick to the practical truth of things," should turn out to have been an idealist all along!

But it seemed to be his fate in these dark days to be caricatured as a man of ideas with little sense of the way the world really worked. Even a philosopher with both feet planted firmly on the ground was, after all, still only a philosopher, ill equipped to handle practical chores best left to professionals. While in Piacenza he spent some time in the camp of the famous mercenary Giovanni delle Bande Nere (Giovanni of the Black Bands), whose small army was the one truly capable fighting force in the anti-imperial league. According to the writer Matteo Bandello, who claims to have been there, the battle-tested general thought it might be amusing to teach the author of *The Art of War* a lesson. Opening Machiavelli's book to the chapter on infantry drills, Giovanni asked him to attempt to put into practice what he'd written by marching his three thousand men about the parade ground. Machiavelli gamely took up the challenge but, not surprisingly, proved hopelessly out of his depth. The troops were soon milling about in confusion and could only be disentangled by the prompt intervention of their captain. "How great the difference is," Bandello sneered, "between someone who knows and who has not set in operation what he knows and someone who, as well as knowing, has often rolled up his sleeves and . . . has derived his thoughts and mental view from outward deeds."

Poor Machiavelli! The incident was embarrassing, but the test was hardly fair. More than any writer before him, he brought philosophy down off its pedestal to where it could make a real difference in the lives of real people. If his theories did not always stand up to their initial contact with hard fact, he was enough of an empiricist to revise them in light of new data. And for a man with no formal military training he had done surprisingly well by his country, leading Florence to victory against her ancient rival Pisa and helping in the current crisis to defend her against her enemies.*

For the remainder of 1526 the forces of the League of Cognac sparred with those of the Emperor. The league scored a victory with the capture of Cremona, but this was followed by notable reverses, including a revolt in Rome led by the Colonna family that forced the Pope to flee to the fortress of Castel Sant' Angelo. In the wake of this disaster, Clement was obliged to sign yet another humiliating truce with Charles—one he broke almost immediately by ordering the mercenary captain Paolo Vitelli to launch an attack on Spanish-held Naples.

The league suffered an even more grievous blow late in November

---

* One of the main points of *The Art of War* is that amateur soldiers are preferable to professionals. For instance, "a good man could not make war his only profession" (Book I, p. 17). Giovanni's demonstration may have been intended to show Machiavelli the error of his ways.

when Giovanni delle Bande Nere was killed after being struck in the leg by a cannon ball. He had been Italy's ablest commander, a man who Machiavelli believed was capable of leading the papal armies to victory and fulfilling, at least in part, the dream laid out in the final chapter of *The Prince*. Without their finest general, the cause of the Pope, and of Italy itself, seemed more desperate than ever.

Still the conflict dragged on in fits and starts, a kind of endless Purgatory with ultimate victory and final defeat equally inconceivable. Machiavelli was not spared in all this pointless to-ing and fro-ing, traveling to Milan, Cremona, and then in November to Modena, crossing the Apennine passes on horseback in the sleet and bitter cold. This ceaseless motion was beginning to take its toll. He delayed his departure from Modena for a few days to recuperate from the rigors of the trip; when he finally set out for Florence, he was determined to travel by "daily stages" to spare his aching body.

In fact Machiavelli was more fully engaged in government work than he had been for years, but the rewards were ever more meager in terms of both money and prestige. His duties were all the more onerous since they seemed to so little purpose. Despite Guicciardini's capable management, the forces of the league, under the direct command of the dilatory Duke of Urbino, avoided bold action, principally because the Pope himself could not decide between peace and war. In the end he managed to choose the worst possible course, provoking the Emperor's wrath while doing nothing to protect himself from the consequences. Fortunately, as Machiavelli pointed out, his enemies were hardly any better: "[T]he Spaniards could have beaten us several times, and they have not contrived to do so; we could have been victorious, and we have not known how; the Pope believed in a stroke of the pen more than in a thousand soldiers who could have kept him safe."

The "stroke of the pen" Machiavelli referred to was a truce signed between the Pope and the Emperor, the latest in an apparently endless series of treaties each rendered obsolete before the ink had dried. Given this record, no one, except perhaps the Pope himself, was surprised when the agreement failed to halt the advance of the imperial army. Part of the problem was that Clement had signed the pact with representatives of the distant Emperor, while command on the ground was in the hands of Charles, Duke of Bourbon. Whatever deals his master cut with the slippery Pope, Bourbon was more concerned with placating his twenty thousand ill-disciplined and rebellious troops, who were clamoring for blood and plunder. The treaty, Machiavelli noted, was "made in Rome, but not observed in Lombardy." Worse still, in a desperate attempt to show his good faith, Clement had disbanded the forces needed for the defense of the Holy City, "living in Rome," as Machiavelli scornfully put it, "in such a way as to let himself be captured like a child."

Not surprisingly, the Emperor's halfhearted attempts to rein in his rebellious commander were ignored. As Bourbon's army marched southward, the Pope could not even count on the usual last best defense of the papacy—the conscience of troops who might hesitate before lifting a hand against the Holy Father. Though the Emperor was a devout Catholic, many of those who actually did the fighting were Germans—the famed *Landsknechts* led by Georg von Frundsberg—followers of Luther who regarded the Pontiff as the devil incarnate, and most of the rest simply thugs who would help themselves to the maidens and treasures of Rome as compensation for years of hardship. Even Machiavelli succumbed to despair. "[O]bserving the behavior of France and the Venetians, the poor order of our men, seeing how hopeless it is for the pope to sustain the war against the kingdom [of Naples] and the power and stubbornness of our enemies, we judge the war as good as lost."

As the rogue army snaked south for a final reckoning with Clement, Florentines girded for a possible thrust in their direction. In February, the Eight again dispatched Machiavelli to Guicciardini, who was now in Parma, to urge the *Luogotenente* not to abandon his native city in her hour of need. For a man in his late fifties, the prospect of yet another journey on horseback in the dead of winter was daunting, but Machiavelli accepted the mission without complaint. He remained with the papal army as it moved south, from Bologna—knee deep in snow, as he reported—to Forli. It was a dispiriting march. The forces of the league could only tag along behind the imperial battalions, keeping a wary eye on them but doing nothing to halt their progress. Morale suffered and the troops under Guicciardini's command began to melt away. "We began . . . to divide the army at Parma," Machiavelli wrote to the Eight, "and we have been reducing it bit by bit right up to Forli."

By early April the imperial army was only a few days' march from Florence. The situation was sufficiently ominous that Machiavelli instructed Marietta and the children to leave Sant' Andrea and take refuge inside the city walls. On April 17 Guido wrote to his father: "As for the lansquenets, we don't worry about them any more because you have said you would try to be with us if anything happened. And so *mona* Marietta is no longer fretting. We pray that you write to us if the enemy should think of coming and damaging our property, because we still have many things in the country."

Surveying the situation from Forlì, Machiavelli, Guicciardini, along with what remained of the league's forces, were faced with a painful decision: whether to move south to insert themselves between the imperial army and Rome, or to the west, where they could parry a thrust in the direction of Florence. "I do not believe there were ever more troubling matters than these," Machiavelli wrote to Vettori, "where peace is necessary and war cannot be abandoned; and where we have a prince [Clement] on our hands who decides neither for peace nor for war."

Guicciardini was equally disenchanted with his master. On April 16 he made his decision: "I have taken on my own initiative, as I have no assistance from Rome, to send towards Florence all the forces at my disposal." Machiavelli was relieved. "I love *Messer* Francesco Guicciardini," he gushed that same day, adding, as explanation for this sudden outburst, "I love my city more than my own soul."

Returning to Florence a few days later Machiavelli found the city in an uproar. The Pope's irresolution and the misgovernment of his relatives had turned even former allies against the Medici regime. Even the arrival of Guicciardini's troops outside the walls failed to improve matters. Though they were there to defend the city, they behaved more as occupiers and laid waste to the countryside for miles about. Matters came to a head on Friday, April 26, when mobs of young citizens stormed the Palazzo della Signoria and tried to topple the government. Only the intervention of Guicciardini prevented a violent confrontation as he persuaded the young hotheads to turn in their weapons in exchange for a full pardon.

Fortunately for Florence, the Duke of Bourbon turned away at the last minute, the mere appearance of Guicciardini's small army having been sufficient to discourage an assault. Instead, Bourbon and his men, hungry and ill equipped but spurred on by the promise of plunder, made for the undefended gates of Rome. The Duke of Urbino set out after them, but was, as usual, unwilling to risk open battle. Guicciardini, with Machiavelli riding by his side, followed, on hand to witness, but unable to do anything to avert, the disaster they had been warning of for so long.

The ragged imperial army arrived before the walls of Rome on the evening of May 4, 1527. After months, even years, in the field, the soldiers were cruel, desperate men, coarsened by the horrors of war and seething with resentment against civilians who had spent their days in idle comfort while they were exposed to the dangers of the battlefield and the miseries of camp life. Even those Spanish troops who remained within the Catholic faith now viewed Rome and its masters with contempt.

The mood of the besieging army grew more ominous when on the night of May 5 their leader, the Duke of Bourbon, was killed by a harque-bus discharged from one of the towers. According to Benvenuto Cellini, the great sculptor and goldsmith, it was he who fired the fatal shot, aiming at one "whom I remarked to be higher than the rest." It was an implausible, though not impossible, claim and, in any case, whoever was responsible for the Duke's death hardly did the populace of Rome any favors since without their leader the last restraint was lifted from his troops. On May 6, 1527, German and Spanish soldiers poured through the sparsely manned walls and began their bloody rampage. In three days and nights, Christian soldiers managed to inflict more damage on the holy city than the Visigoths had more than a millennium earlier, burning and pillaging, sparing neither holy place nor holy person, scattering relics and putting to the torch countless shrines, bursting into convents and raping the nuns, murdering defenseless women and children, savaging clerics and civilians alike in an unmatched orgy of destruction.

Machiavelli was with Guicciardini in Orvieto, some fifty miles to the north, when he heard "the dreadful news from Rome." He mourned, like all Italians, the destruction of the great capital, but he was hardly surprised. He had seen the horrors of war close up, and it was largely because of these experiences that he placed such a premium on strong leaders and stable states that protected their people from random violence. "Wherever you turn your eyes," he had written after witnessing another battlefield, "you see the earth wet with tears and blood, and the air full of screams, of sobs, and sighs"—a scene now playing out on an even larger scale in Rome.

News of the horrific sack sent shock waves through the capitals of Europe, but nowhere were the reverberations felt more powerfully than in Florence, where the Pope's humiliation shook the already fragile edifice of Medici power. With Clement now a prisoner of the imperial army, the citizens of Florence no longer saw any reason to defer to his representatives. On May 16 Cardinal Passerini was forced to step down; a few days later, he and the two young Medici heirs, Ippolito and Alessandro, were expelled and a new republic proclaimed, completing a thorough but bloodless change of regime.

Machiavelli was an emissary to an army that was now leaderless from a government that no longer existed. As he packed up his bags and prepared to return to his native city, he was torn by conflicting emotions. He rejoiced that the government would now be restored to its ancient republican form, but he was painfully aware that, once again, he had placed himself on the wrong side of history. For someone as politically astute as Machiavelli, it is remarkable how often he seemed to back the losing side, particularly since he was rarely moved by those ideological passions that are so often the undoing of political men. The explanation for this apparent obtuseness is simple. Machiavelli's misfortune was to be a devoted servant of the state in an age when the state was dysfunctional. The same sense of crisis that motivated his greatest writing undermined his political career. In dedicating himself to the country he loved, he was pledging his loyalty to a faithless mistress, as fickle as *Fortuna*, whose whim ruled the fate of all mortals.

One of his companions on his homeward journey recalled that "he heard him sigh many times when he heard that the city was free. I think he was regretting his conduct, because in fact he greatly loved liberty; but he regretted having involved himself with Pope Clement." Were those feelings of regret made more bitter by a sense of guilt? Five years earlier his friends who were willing to risk all in the cause of liberty had been banished or killed while Machiavelli survived and even prospered. Now the roles were reversed; the idealists had won the day, and those too timid to take a principled stand found themselves scorned by the victors.

Whatever his private regrets, Machiavelli believed he had acted in good faith. His unclouded conscience is suggested by the fact that as soon as he arrived in Florence he began to lobby for his old job back. While some regarded this as unmitigated gall on the part of someone who had only a few days earlier been serving the discredited Medici, he maintained that he had been working not on behalf of the regime but on behalf of all Florentines. The walls he had helped repair, the army he had persuaded to place itself between the city and their enemies, had saved Mediceans and republicans alike, and he saw no reason to apologize.

In fact he had some support among the new leaders of the city. Both Lodovico Alamanni and Zanobi Buondelmonti, who had returned following the expulsion of the Medici, spoke in favor of their old friend. They evidently held no grudges for what had happened five years earlier and tried to get the Signoria to reappoint Machiavelli to the vacant office of Second Chancellor. Unfortunately, Alamanni and Buondelmonti were in a distinct minority. Not only had his recent employment by Pope Clement sullied his reputation in the eyes of most Florentines, but by now his writings, though mostly unpublished and circulating only in manuscript form, had made Machiavelli notorious. One contemporary observed: "[The common people] hated him because of *The Prince*: the rich thought his *Prince* was a document written to teach the duke how to take away all their property, from the poor all their liberty; the *piagnoni* regarded him as a heretic; the good thought him sinful; the wicked thought him more wicked or more capable than themselves—so they all hated him."

This was a prelude of things to come. The man with such a wise and forgiving heart would not be forgiven by those he had mocked with his sharp tongue. He was not an evil man, as many of his contemporaries supposed and as history has assumed, but something worse: he was tactless. Pointing out uncomfortable truths turned out to be an unpardonable crime, while the countless acts of cruelty, treachery, and violence to which he bore painful witness—and that he tried to ameliorate through a philosophy rooted in a realistic assessment of human nature—were passed over with barely a yawn. Even before his death he had become notorious for his irreverence and the pleasure he took in exposing the bankruptcy of shopworn pieties. His compatriots split their sides laughing as his comic inventions *Messer* Nicia and Nicomaco strutted about the stage like pompous fools, but when he sought to fashion a theory of politics that might accommodate such flawed specimens, they balked, unwilling to follow his logic to the end. People could forgive almost anything but the shattering of their illusions. For a man who prided himself on his insights into the human heart, who could subtract the resentment derived from the murder of a relative from the resentment engendered by the loss of an estate and find the precise remainder, he was remarkably careless in assessing the effect his words had on others. Above all he was singularly incapable of playing the devious games he recommended to others as the way to get ahead.

Doctors no longer claim that one can die from a broken heart, but even the most scientific physician would admit that crushing disappointment can take a toll on a body already worn out from years of stress and overwork. On June 10, Machiavelli learned that the job of Second Chancellor went to Francesco Tarugi, an undistinguished functionary who had previously served as Secretary to the Eight. Though Machiavelli's failure to get the appointment could hardly have come as a surprise, it was yet another bitter blow. In 1512 he had met disappointment with reservoirs of inner strength. These reservoirs were long since gone, depleted by age and years of frustration. Only two weeks earlier he had been riding about the countryside on the government's business; less than two weeks later he was laid low with abdominal pain brought on, his son Piero believed, by an overdose of the same homemade remedy he had prescribed for his friend Guicciardini. The crisis was sudden and severe, striking down an elderly but still vigorous man in midstride.*

Machiavelli's death has spawned legends as persistent and contradictory as his life. From Piero we have a spare but almost certainly accurate account: "My very dear Francesco," he wrote to his maternal uncle,

I can only weep in telling you that our father, Niccolò, died on the 22nd of this month, from pains in the stomach caused by a medication he took on the 20th. He confessed his sins to Brother Matteo, who

---

* It is impossible to say with any certainty what killed Machiavelli. Some modern theories include a ruptured appendix or a gastric ulcer. It is also likely that the medicine Machiavelli used to treat his stomach problems accelerated his death.

kept him company until his death. Our father has left us in the deep-
est poverty, as you know.

Such a matter-of-fact account, from such an unimpeachable source, might
seem uncontroversial, but those who revere Machiavelli as the great
prophet of atheism dismiss Piero's account of a priest administering last
rites as a pious fiction intended to hide their hero's true nature. But there is
no reason to believe that Piero invented this deathbed scene. Machiavelli,
as we have seen, was a harsh critic of Christianity, but he reserved most of
his scorn for those corrupt priests who took advantage of the weak and the
gullible. He was certainly never a devoted churchgoer, but he conformed
outwardly to the conventions of the day, entering the sacrament of marriage and baptizing his children. There is no reason to believe that in his
final moments he would have defied those traditions to which he had subscribed, if only casually, throughout his life.

In accepting last rites, Machiavelli may simply have been taking the path
of least resistance, but it also possible that, like many nonbelievers, he had a
change of heart as he felt his end approaching. It is likely that as he was faced
with his own imminent death, he was apprehensive and unsure. He could
not fall back on the comfort of simple faith, but neither was he certain that
the soul was merely an illusion conjured by the material body. He was never
doctrinaire, particularly when it came to such vast, inscrutable matters as
life and death, and would not have presumed to know what awaited him in
the world to come.

Easier to discern than the dying man's innermost thoughts is the impact his passing had on those around him. This is most clearly revealed
in a legend that quickly sprang up around his final vigil. The so-called
"Dream of Machiavelli" is almost as old as Piero's letter, but despite the
ancient pedigree it seems too perfectly crafted to be anything but apocryphal. Lying close to death, the story goes, Machiavelli told his friends
who had gathered at his bedside of a dream he had. In his vision he saw
two columns of men. One consisted of miserable wretches dressed in rags.
When he asked who they were, they replied: "We are the saintly and the
blessed; we are on our way to heaven." Then he spied another column,
this one filled with men dressed in fine robes, deep in conversation. As he
approached he recognized many of them: Plato, Plutarch, and Tacitus, all

discussing grave matters of state. When asked what brought them here, they replied: "We are the damned of Hell." Having told his story, Machiavelli turned to his guests and, smiling, declared that it was among these learned men, rather than pious fools, that he hoped to spend eternity.

It is an appealing story but one that, unfortunately, does not ring true. Certainly, the cynical wit was typical of Machiavelli, who rarely missed a chance for mischief; in fact the legend echoes some of his own words, including those famous lines in his letter to Guicciardini where he explains that the best way to get to heaven is to learn the path to hell.* But Machiavelli was no philosopher-saint like Socrates, a creature of superhuman virtue unaffected by the torments of the flesh. He was the first to admit his own weaknesses, and a lofty indifference to adversity was hardly his style. Out of respect for this most down-to-earth of philosophers, who famously declared that he would rather stick to the truth of things than to fancies, one ought to treat this dream as a charming fiction.

The one form of immortality Machiavelli believed in wholeheartedly was the immortality conferred by a famous name. Perhaps this was the only way to better fickle *Fortuna*, whose writ had little sway beyond the grave. Though he could not be sure that *his* name would endure in the world he was now departing, perhaps he took some comfort in the modest but real successes he had already achieved. The one thing he could not have anticipated as he closed his eyes for the last time, in the house of his ancestors near the Ponte Vecchio in the city he loved best in the world, was that his name would not only endure but that history would proclaim him one of the truly remarkable figures of a remarkable age.

---

* It also recalls some lines in *La Mandragola* where the hero Callimaco says, "Don't you know how little good a man finds in the things he has longed for, compared with what he expected to find? On the other hand, the worst you can get from it is that you'll die and go to Hell. But how many others have died! And in Hell how many worthy men there are!" (*La Mandragola*, IV, i, in *Chief Work*, vol. 2, p. 805.)

XIV

FINGER OF SATAN

"Behold here then the end and scope which I have proposed unto myself, that is, to confute the doctrine of Machiavelli."

—INNOCENT GENTILLET, *CONTRE-MACHIAVEL* (1576)

MACHIAVELLI WAS INTERRED IN THE SMALL FAMILY chapel in the Franciscan basilica of Santa Croce, across the Arno River from his house in the city. The ceremony was private, attended by family and friends. In keeping with the life of a man of few means and modest achievements, the tomb was unassuming. Time, it seemed, would soon swallow up the name of the former Second Chancellor of Florence; at best he would be a footnote in the long and illustrious history of the republic he claimed to love more than his own soul but that had repaid his devotion with ingratitude.

This initial neglect might surprise visitors to Florence today who find themselves in a city that has come to embrace her patriotic son. Streets, hotels, and *trattorie* bear his name, and his sardonic likeness peeks out from many a souvenir shop and postcard stall. The change in attitude is embodied at Santa Croce itself, where Niccolò Machiavelli, comic playwright and midlevel civil servant, now resides in a tomb every bit as grand as those dedicated to such other Florentine greats as Cosimo de' Medici, Dante Alighieri, and Michelangelo Buonarotti.* He was moved

---

* Florence has made a habit of first neglecting her famous sons and later regretting it. Dante was exiled from his native land and died in Ravenna, where he was buried. Despite repeated attempts to recover his remains, Florentines have had to content themselves with a cenotaph, located near Machiavelli's tomb in the nave of Santa Croce.

here from his obscure grave in the eighteenth century when the fame he had achieved in the years since his death made his anonymous burial plot seem an embarrassment. The man once dismissed as a second-rate hack willing to sell his principles to whoever would give him a job was now hailed as the great defender of Florentine liberties and a second Moses pointing his compatriots toward the as yet unborn Italian nation.

Unfortunately, the pompous monument captures nothing of the spirit of the man it commemorates. Atop the marble sarcophagus sits a beautiful woman, embodiment of the fatherland, holding a shield that carries a likeness of the former Second Chancellor; the supporting plinth is inscribed *"Tanto nomini nullum par elogium"* ("For so great a name, no words will suffice"), an ironic epitaph given the silence with which his death was greeted at the time. In fact the whole monument smacks of opportunism. It is a begrudging and belated recognition of the genius who had lived among them but whose achievement they could appreciate only after it was pointed out by others.

Florentines can be forgiven their initial neglect on the grounds that in the summer of 1527 they had more important things on their mind. The cause of Florentine liberty, to which Machiavelli had devoted his life, was in peril, and the particular course he had charted very much in disrepute. He had followed a cautious path when the times demanded a more heroic stance. The events that led to his final disappointment were in fact the opening salvo in the last desperate struggle for Florentine independence, and the atmosphere of existential crisis that gripped the city in those days was hardly conducive to a dispassionate reassessment of his career.

Ironically, the government that replaced the discredited regime of Cardinal Passerini and the Medici bastards largely conformed to the model he set out in one of those writings—his "Treatise on the Reform of the Florentine Government," commissioned by Cardinal Giulio in 1520—but this was not sufficient to rehabilitate a reputation tainted by his years of working with the enemy. The Savonarolan Great Council was restored, as Machiavelli had recommended, and those steering committees through which the Medici subverted the normal functioning of government were largely abolished. Real power was placed once again in the hands of the

Gonfaloniere, while his term in office was limited to a single year to prevent him from assuming dictatorial power.

But the new republic was never given a fair chance. It was born in crisis and throughout its three years of existence never knew a minute of peace. This last great experiment in republican rule was doomed from the outset, as was the cause of Florentine independence. The small city-state that had sprung from the medieval commune was an anachronism in the era of the great nation-states. Florentines had taken advantage of the Pope's defeat and imprisonment to throw off the hated yoke, but they remained babes surrounded by hungry wolves. Florence could maintain her independence only as long as the Emperor and the Pope remained mortal enemies, but that happy state of affairs was unlikely to last since it was in the interests of each to seek a modus vivendi.

In December 1527, Pope Clement was released from captivity. Among the most urgent items on his agenda was recapturing his native city. Rapprochement between the two universal rulers of Christendom was facilitated by another geopolitical crisis, one that had begun in far-off England, where King Henry VIII had fallen in love with the charming Anne Boleyn. To marry Anne, Henry had first to divorce his wife, Catherine of Aragon; the fact that Catherine was Charles V's aunt, and that the power to dissolve the marriage lay in the hands of the Pope, meant that the Emperor had a powerful incentive to mend fences with Clement. In June 1529, Clement and Charles signed the Treaty of Barcelona, in which the Emperor pledged military assistance in restoring the Medici to Florence, with the tacit understanding that the Pope would return the favor by refusing Henry's request for a divorce.* In August, Florentines' already slim hopes suffered another dispiriting blow when they learned that their longtime ally, Francis, had signed the Treaty of Cambrai with Charles, renouncing French claims in Italy.

The tiny republic was now effectively isolated. But despite the enormous odds, Florentines pulled together in one final heroic act of resistance. Like the last stand at the Alamo, the siege of Florence in 1530 is a tale of futile courage, a doomed twilight struggle whose romance belies

---

* Clement's rejection of Henry's petition led, of course, to England's break with Rome, far more consequential for world history than the treaty's impact on the independence of Florence.

the ugly reality of suffering, starvation, and disease. Had Machiavelli lived, he almost certainly would have been among the defenders on the walls, lending his expertise to the engineers who were strengthening the ramparts as the imperial army began to surround the city. Instead, overseeing the city's fortifications was another great Florentine patriot, Michelangelo Buonarotti, whose talents, like those of his rival Leonardo, extended to the arts of war.

Not all Florentine patriots, however, stood with the republic against the papal army. Francesco Guicciardini, after some initial indecision, chose to side with the Medici and their Spanish patrons against his native city. Here one sees the essential difference between the aristocratic Guicciardini and his humble friend. Guicciardini belonged to the *ottimati*, the ruling elite of Florence that often found itself torn between fear of Medici tyranny and an even greater terror of the unruly people, while Machiavelli placed his faith in the collective wisdom of the *popolo*. When the government, under the pressure of war, became increasingly radicalized, threatening to ruin the *ottimati* through heavy taxation and outright confiscation, Guicciardini threw his support behind the besiegers.

By the summer of 1530 the blockade by the vastly superior forces of the Pope had reduced the city to near starvation, a condition to which Florentines might have succumbed sooner had the pressure on the food supply not been relieved by the death of thousands from the plague that was ravaging the poorer neighborhoods. In August the people of Florence reluctantly bowed to the inevitable and surrendered. Guicciardini was among the hard-liners in the new regime. In the bloody purge that followed the change in government he advocated the harshest measures against those now condemned as rebels, declaring "if one wishes to put this state on a proper footing, mild measures are useless."

The restoration of the Medici on the strength of imperial arms effectively put an end to Florence as an independent state. Its subservient status was confirmed in 1532 when Alessandro de' Medici was named Duke of the Florentine Republic, a high-sounding title that made him little more than a feudal vassal of the Holy Roman Emperor. The demise of Florence as a sovereign state closed a chapter in European history and in the history of Western civilization. It was in the small city-states of Italy, and Florence in particular, that the intellectual, scientific, and artistic revolution known as the Renaissance was born and flourished. And it was in the small city-state of Florence that Machiavelli learned the secrets of statecraft. The chaotic and often violent political culture, with its factions and class rivalries, temporary alliances and secret cabals, all struggling for control, convinced him that society conformed to no divine plan but was instead shaped and reshaped by personal ambition. In this bustling mercantile metropolis, humankind was revealed as an intensely political animal, hungry for power and jealous of his neighbors—a creature of infinite appetite and infinite possibility.

The contest over the meaning of Machiavelli's writings began even before his death. Shortly after he wrote *The Prince*, and years before it was actually published, Biagio Buonaccorsi wrote to a mutual friend that they must defend him against those who would try "to bite and tear him." Even people accustomed to the worldly, cynical tone of Florentine political discourse found him abrasive and worried that his words could be put to evil uses. When the first Florentine edition of *The Prince* came out in 1532, his publisher offered the weak defense "that those who teach the use of herbs and medicines also give instruction in poisons so that, recognizing them, we may protect ourselves from them."* The notion that *The Prince* was not a handbook of tyranny but rather an exposé of the very thing it appeared to promote is an old one and reflects the degree of discomfort the book stirred even among Machiavelli's friends.

The truth, of course, is at once more subtle and more straightforward. Machiavelli clearly meant what he said in *The Prince*, but this small book represented only one aspect of a more complex body of thought that included *The Discourses* and other heartfelt defenses of republican government. He was neither an ideological democrat nor an apostle of tyranny, but rather a pragmatist who was willing to pursue whatever path seemed to offer the best chance of success at a given moment. He resembled one of those Renaissance mapmakers who, during the century or two before he wrote his seminal works, transformed cartography from a branch of theology—where the earth displayed the Garden of Eden and Jerusalem

---

* *The Discourses* was first published in 1531.

at its center—to a science based on observation and subject to empirical tests. Machiavelli himself pushes the metaphor in his dedication to *The Discourses*, where he begins: "Although owing to the envy inherent in man's nature, it has always been no less dangerous to discover new ways and methods than to set off in search of new seas and unknown lands . . . I have decided to enter upon a new way, as yet untrodden by anyone else." If his methodology was often flawed and his data inaccurate or incomplete, he shares these shortcomings with all who blaze trails through uncharted territory.

Machiavelli is generally credited with founding the new field of political science, but when he is judged by the standards of the discipline he supposedly invented, he sometimes seems to fall short of the mark. Francis Bacon, father of the modern scientific method, never doubted the crucial importance of the Florentine's insights, declaring "we are much beholden to Machiavel and others, that write what men do, and not what they ought to do." Many others who followed in his footsteps faulted Machiavelli for his lack of consistency, but it is unfair to condemn him for not achieving a scientific rigor to which he never aspired. Although he attempted to place the study of politics on a more rational basis, his approach remains anecdotal rather than programmatic, as if he never really abandoned his role as a diplomat and bureaucrat dispensing practical advice for real-world situations.

Unlike his successors—even those whose theories had a far greater impact on the way politics was actually practiced—Machiavelli looms large in the popular imagination, where his name has become associated not only with a particular approach to politics but with a particular type of personality. To describe someone as a Marxist is to define his political views; to describe someone as Machiavellian is to impugn his character. Machiavelli was certainly not the world's first cynic, but he has been so closely identified with a certain kind of unscrupulousness that any manipulative, self-serving behavior is now described as Machiavellian.

Machiavellianism in the popular imagination is little more than an endorsement of underhanded and immoral behavior. This largely inaccurate, or at least simplistic, interpretation is again a function of his pragmatism, an approach that offends those who insist that morality should be based on something more ethereal. One of Machiavelli's most important contributions was to collapse the distinction between theory and practice, the vital first step in transforming the study of politics into a science. While Plato, Aristotle, and Aquinas had dwelt in realms of abstract theory far removed from the places where men lived, Machiavelli took his role of adviser to a practicing politician seriously. As a writer he never really left behind the habits and attitudes he had developed in the Chancery of Florence, where he confronted on a daily basis crises that demanded a realistic assessment of facts. Assuming the worst of both friends and enemies was always the safest course, and in taking this approach he was rarely disappointed. Results were all that mattered. Instead of asking: What course of action should a prince take in order to be considered good? he asked what to him was the more important question: What course of action should a prince take to remain in power, without which his ability to do good vanishes altogether? "It is a sound maxim that reprehensible actions may be justified by their effects," he writes in *The Discourses*, "and that when the effect is good . . . it always justifies the action." This is not an apology for selfishness, but rather a plea that we judge actions not in the abstract but by their consequences. Having spent many years closely observing the powerful, Machiavelli came to the conclusion that those whose actions conformed to traditional notions of virtue often invited calamity, while those who violated those standards often improved the lives of their citizens. Because he promoted what worked instead of what conformed to conventional notions of right and wrong, he provided ammunition to generations of the righteous who preferred to look down on him from their high horse rather than meeting him on his own ground.

At the time of his death Machiavelli was better known as a satirist than as a political writer, particularly in Venice and Rome, where performances of *La Mandragola* were frequent and well received. This reputation changed in the following decades when all his major political works were published in multiple editions, evidence that they had struck a chord with a wider public. The businessmen who ran the small printing houses of the era soon learned that there was a reliable market for his work, and the more controversy the books generated, the more sales improved. By 1559, the *Art of War* had gone through thirteen editions, *The Discourses* twenty-six, *The Prince* seventeen, and the *Florentine Histories* fifteen, so that within a couple of decades of his death Machiavelli was among the biggest selling authors of the day.

In part one can attribute Machiavelli's posthumous success to an obvious but often overlooked aspect of his work: he is simply a wonderful writer.* His Italian is spare, muscular, without those extraneous flourishes and literary devices beloved by his humanist colleagues. "I have not adorned this work," he says in his dedication to *The Prince*, "with sonorous phrases, with pompous or magnificent words, or with any of those ingratiating or irrelevant ornaments with which many are apt to decorate their writings." Such directness makes him a joy to read, but it also gets him into trouble when he exaggerates for effect. Many of his most shocking pronouncements—such as that it is better to be feared than loved, or that good princes must be good liars—turn out to be more nuanced than they at first appear, but as Guicciardini noted, his friend never sacrificed a memorable phrase for the sake of precision.

Machiavelli's writing and his thought are both marked by clarity and directness; he had a gift for penetration, for going straight to the heart of the matter without being distracted by superficialities. Just as in his prose he eliminates unnecessary ornaments of style, in his philosophy he strips away the phony pieties of religion and convention. His goal is always to discover the universal rules underlying the apparent chaos of the world and the truth hidden beneath the fancies spun by his fellow philosophers.

Though the appeal of Machiavelli's writings is universal, they spoke with particular eloquence to the new age whose painful birth pangs he witnessed in the last years of his life. They were a final creative utterance from the passing age of the small city-state republics, but they appeared to be addressed to the world to come—an age of sprawling nation-states proclaiming the divine right of kings. *The Prince* in particular, with its cunning hero ready to resort to any expedient to increase the reach of his power, seemed prophetic of the new world order where great monarchs bestrode the continent, aided by vast bureaucracies that reached deep into the lives of ordinary people. The Machiavellian concept of *raison*

---

* Friedrich Nietzsche, no mean writer himself, praises Machiavelli for "presenting the most serious matters in a boisterous *allegrissimo*" (*Beyond Good and Evil*, 28).

d'état captured the ethos of these newly consolidated states: vast, impersonal, and ubiquitous. His nationalism, while poignant or even pathetic in the context of his native Italy, encouraged monarchs and civil servants in the rising states of Spain, France, and England who were intent on consolidating power over their own subjects as a prelude to projecting that power abroad. Not everyone agreed these innovations were beneficial, but few denied the relevance of the man who seemed able to peer into the future.

Initially it was the Roman Church that led the charge against Machiavelli, its moral authority contributing to the popular image of him as a man in league with the Devil. In 1559 he was among the first writers placed on the first Papal Index of Prohibited Books, a perverse testament to his popularity since the Pope would not have singled him out if no one read him.* It is not surprising that the Pope came down hard on Machiavelli. His anticlericism, a common attitude in Renaissance Florence, was less acceptable in the era of the Council of Trent (1545–63) when the Church responded to the challenge of Protestantism by reforming and clarifying its doctrines and practices. Ambrogio Catharino, who was active at the council that launched the Counterreformation and influenced the decision to ban Machiavelli's works, called him "wholly destitute of religion and a contemner thereof," a common critique among churchmen, who felt themselves already under siege from heretics and had no tolerance for dissent from within the fold.

Machiavelli's inclusion on the Index reflected a growing consensus that he was a wicked man advocating wicked behavior. The first extended anti-Machiavellian diatribe came barely a decade after his death. It was written, perhaps surprisingly, by an Englishman, Cardinal Reginald Pole, whose 1539 *Apologia Reginaldi Poli ad Carolum V* ("Apology of Reginald Pole to Charles V") credits the Florentine's writings with a great and sinister influence. "This poison," he wrote, "is spread through the courts of princes in this man's books which are circulating almost everywhere." The savagery of Pole's attack (he goes on to call Machiavelli an "enemy of the human race" and the "finger of Satan") suggests personal pique as well as

---

*   More than six hundred authors appeared on the papal list. The ban, in any case, was ineffective; more than half the 158 editions of his works in the century after his death were published after 1559.

ideological objections. Pole was convinced that his nemesis at the court of Henry VIII, the king's chief minister, Thomas Cromwell, was a disciple of the devious Florentine, and that it was under his baleful influence the fateful decision to break with Rome was made. Whether Cromwell actually read Machiavelli, Pole's charge is not entirely implausible since two of the pillars of Machiavelli's thought—his anticlericalism and his belief that the state took precedence over the Church—might well have proved useful to Henry in his ongoing struggle with the Pope.

Ironically, the man to whom Cardinal Pole addressed his screed—the Holy Roman Emperor Charles V—was also said to be a disciple of this "son of Satan." According to Francesco Sansovino's 1567 biographical sketch, the Emperor read only three books: Baldassare Castiglione's *The Courtier* and Machiavelli's *Discourses* and *The Prince*. But this peculiar situation, in which Machiavelli was accused of being the evil puppet master controlling both sides in a bitter dispute, was not unusual. Though Pole believed the English Reformation to be the brainchild of the wicked Florentine, it was just as plausible to view the author of *The Prince* as the ally of a Catholic autocrat.

Indeed the fact that Machiavelli was roundly condemned by the princes of the Catholic Church did not prevent him from being savaged by their ideological foes. In the second half of the sixteenth century, as France was plunged into a civil war between Protestants and Catholics, Machiavelli's name was again invoked. The struggle between the Calvinist Huguenots and the Catholics culminated in the Saint Bartholomew's Day Massacre (1572) when mobs, egged on by a royal court that had remained loyal to Rome, assaulted and killed the religious dissenters in their midst. In the ensuing war of words, the prominent Huguenot pamphleteer Innocent Gentillet laid the blame squarely at Machiavelli's door. In his 1589 essay *Contre-Machiavel* ("Against Machiavelli"), Gentillet insisted that the massacre was part of a diabolical plot on the part of the Queen Mother, Catherine de' Medici, and her Italian courtiers, inspired by the writings of Machiavelli. Here the link was ethnic rather than ideological since Catherine was a Florentine, daughter of that same Lorenzo to whom Machiavelli dedicated *The Prince*. "[M]y intent and purpose," Gentillet wrote, "is onely to shew, that Nicholas Machiavell, not long agoe Secretarie of the Florentine commonweale . . . understood nothing or little in this Politicke science whereof we speake: and that he hath taken Maximes and rules altogether wicked, and hath builded upon them, not a Politicke, but a Tyrannical science. Behold here then the end and scope which I have proposed unto myself, that is, to confute the doctrine of Machiavell." Gentillet assumed that because Machiavelli's rules were "altogether wicked" they were necessarily false, an assumption Machiavelli himself would have regarded as quaint. Machiavelli was perhaps the first to confront us with the terrifying thought that something could be both wicked *and* manifestly true.

Because Machiavelli did not promote any particular ideology, both sides in any contest found it easy to smear his reputation. In the next century Edmund Burke could blame "the odious maxims of a Machiavellian policy" for the "democratic tyranny" of the French Revolution, while a hundred years after that, Marx and Engels contended that a "Machiavellian policy" was the hallmark of anti-revolutionary reaction.

More sympathetic were the so-called Commonwealth men, followers of John Locke, who discovered in the Florentine's philosophy a basis for a liberal society: "All these discoveries and complaints of the crookedness and corruption of human nature," wrote John Trenchard and Thomas Gordon in their influential collection of essays, *Cato's Letters*, "are made with no malignant intent to break the bonds of society; but they are made to shew, that as selfishness is the strongest bias of men, every man ought to be upon his guard against another, that he become not the prey of another." These essays, which in turn influenced our own Founding Fathers, rehabilitated Machiavelli as a humane philosopher who laid the foundations of the modern state by recognizing that political institutions could be built only on interest rather than virtue. When Madison insists that "[a]mbition must be made to counteract ambition," he is paraphrasing Machiavelli and, whether he is willing to acknowledge it or not, his contention that democracy forms the only sound basis for good government, "supplying, by opposite and rival interests, the defect of better motives," he marks himself as a true disciple of the cynical Florentine.

Still, what casual readers took away from Machiavelli's writings was not specifically political. More memorable was his attack on traditional morality and his substitution of a new kind of ethics based on self-interest for one based on traditional notions of good and evil.* *Machiavellianism* soon broke free of Machiavelli and of the particular political conditions that molded his thought. Coined in the early seventeenth century, the term (*Machiavellisme* in the original French of its inventor) stood for insincerity and deviousness, no matter the context and no matter the ideology promoted. The descriptive noun was defined by its inventor as "subtle policie, cunning roguerie," a meaning that has endured almost unchanged down to the present century. In this broader sense the adjective "Machiavellian" can be applied to all behavior, not merely to unscrupulous political acts. Voltaire, for example, described Machiavelli's essential lesson as "ruin[ing] anyone who might someday ruin you; assassinat[ing] your neighbor who might become strong enough to kill you"—an approach to life as old as humanity itself and one that bears only the most tenuous resemblance to his actual philosophy.

Machiavelli did not invent a particular way of looking at the world, but he expressed that viewpoint in such stark and vivid prose that he quickly came to stand for a universally recognizable type. He is the cynic with the disdainful grin curling on his lips as he contemplates the folly of the human comedy; he is the puncturer of every gaseous piety, the debunker of every comforting illusion. As soon as his books were absorbed into the collective consciousness Machiavelli became a stock character, his malevolent influence lurking behind every evil scheme and diabolical plot. Elizabethan playwrights in particular found him a useful dramatic prop. His reputation for villainy was so widely accepted that one only needed to invoke his name to conjure up all manner of crime. In *The Jew of Malta*, Christopher Marlowe creates a fictional Machiavelli who embodies the monster without conscience, to whom nothing is sacred and nothing prohibited. "I count religion but a childish toy," he scoffs, "and I hold there is no sin but ignorance." Shakespeare also discovered in Machiavelli an ir-

---

* Machiavelli anticipated Thomas Hobbes, who traced the origin of government to the basic human right of self-preservation. Hobbes's philosophy in turn anticipates the modern liberal tradition in which society is founded on rights rather than duties. (See Leo Strauss, "On the Spirit of Hobbes' Political Philosophy," in *Essays in the History of Political Thought.*) Even a political philosopher as far from Machiavelli's worldview as John Stuart Mill inevitably starts from the premise set down by the Florentine, that human society is ruled by violence and coercion. "The object of this essay is to assert one very simple principle . . . that the sole end for which mankind are warranted . . . in interfering with the liberty of action of any of their number is self-protection" (Mill, *On Liberty*, I, 6).

resistible dramatic device. Richard III, the treacherous schemer who murders his way to the throne, is modeled on the Florentine Chancellor. In *Henry VI, Part 3*, Richard, still Duke of Gloucester, lays out the villainous plot that will eventually win him the crown by declaring:

> *I'll slay more gazers than the basilisk,*
> *I'll play the orator as well as Nestor,*
> *Deceive more slily than Ulysses could,*
> *And like a Sinon, take another Troy.*
> *I can add colors to the chameleon,*
> *Change shapes with Proteus for advantages*
> *And set the murtherous Machevil to school.*
> *Can I do this, and cannot get a crown?*
> *Tut, were it farther off, I'll pluck it down.*

Machiavelli came to embody the dark side of the Renaissance belief in man's infinite potential. The universal genius, the Renaissance man—signaled in Pico's lines "O great and wonderful happiness of man! It is given to him to have that which he chooses and to be that which he wills," or Shakespeare's "What a piece of work is a man! How noble in reason! how infinite in faculty!"—has an evil twin in Machiavelli's prince, whose only cause in life is the gratification of his own selfish desires. Playing Mr. Hyde to all those Dr. Jekylls of the age—revered geniuses like Leonardo, Michelangelo, and Galileo—Machiavelli represents all those who, having thrown off the shackles of religious orthodoxy, believe themselves to be gods.

It is difficult to overestimate the influence of Machiavelli on the development of modern political thought, even though few of his successors openly acknowledged the debt. Indeed, to a large extent modern political science can be viewed as a response to Machiavelli, as an attempt to address the problem of human government in a godless world, without resorting, as the Florentine was said to have done, to immorality. Admitting that Machiavelli perceived with unprecedented clarity the nature of the problem, those who followed in his wake found his solutions inadequate or downright troubling. He was too quixotic, too undisciplined, and, frankly, too cheeky, to fit comfortably within the elaborate theoretical structures they liked to build. Political theorists as diverse in temperament and intent as Thomas Hobbes, John Locke, Jean-Jacques Rousseau, James Madison, and Karl Marx set out in directions and for purposes Machiavelli could hardly have imagined, but each began from the premise established by the Florentine bureaucrat: that politics involves the study of human character and follows patterns that can be discerned by the careful student. Freeing the analysis of power from the metaphysical shackles that had constrained such investigations in the past, Machiavelli set Western civilization on a course of bold innovation. Once he established the principle that the way people governed themselves was open to scientific inquiry, all manner of theories and experiments were permitted. Every attempt to remake society on a new basis, from totalitarian dictatorship to free-love commune, starts from the basic premise Machiavelli first articulated.

Beyond this vast but admittedly amorphous intellectual legacy, Machiavelli is father to a specific strand within the history of political discourse. Terms like *Realpolitik* or *raison d'état*, theories that take a dim view of humanity and advocate strong medicine to curb our appetites, can be traced to Machiavelli's writings, particularly to *The Prince*, where he sets out most forthrightly his bleak vision of our animal nature. Thomas Hobbes's contention that "the dispositions of men are naturally such, that except they be restrained through fear of some coercive power, every man will distrust and dread each other" is pure Machiavelli. Even those who hold the opposite view of human nature—philosophers like Jean-Jacques Rousseau, who believed that humans are naturally good and that it is civilization itself that is to blame for their corruption—owe a debt of gratitude to Machiavelli since it was in refuting his pessimistic vision that their own philosophy came into focus.

The intellectual heirs of Machiavelli call themselves realists or pragmatists; they are skeptical of utopian schemes, insisting that since human beings are naturally fallible, the search for social or political perfection is misguided and even dangerous. Empiricists like Francis Bacon found in him a kindred spirit. John Locke and his American disciples, men like James Madison and Alexander Hamilton, shared with Machiavelli a distrust of human nature and sought to temper our worst excesses by dispersing power, thereby protecting individual liberty from collective tyranny.

Of course other interpretations of Machiavelli's work are possible. Tyrants from Charles V to Napoleon, Hitler, Stalin, and Mussolini were all said to be admirers and to have discovered in his writings useful tips on how to gain and to hold power. But only by rejecting the majority of his thought and by focusing on narrow tactical issues can the despot discover much in Machiavelli that is to his taste. Many a dictator would find Machiavelli's tolerance of cruelty and deceit useful cover for his own crimes, but the larger message—which he would have to ignore—was that such tactics must ultimately serve the greater good. Valentino's cruelty is redeemed by the security he brought to the people of the Romagna; absent this public good he would be nothing but a petty despot.

Those who prefer to see Machiavelli as an apologist for tyranny tend to concentrate on *The Prince* while ignoring passages in *The Discourses* where he clearly states that the seizure of dictatorial powers is legitimate only when the normal tools of government have failed to meet a crisis.* Indeed he consistently shows disdain for the simple, one-size-fits-all solutions that are the essence of totalitarianism. Mixed governments are better than monolithic ones because a system in the hands of many fallible human beings pulling in different directions is more adaptable than one controlled by a single master convinced he can do no wrong. Machiavelli's insistence on the role of chance in human history, and his view that political science can only serve the rather limited purpose of providing a temporary bulwark against the vicissitudes of fortune, provides little to justify totalitarian schemes promising utopia. In a world where, as he says, "all human affairs are ever in a state of flux" what room is there for a Thousand Year Reich?

The misuse of Machiavelli derives in part from his approach, which is aphoristic and epigrammatic rather than systematic. His fondness for memorable phrases and lack of an overall program has allowed readers to pick and choose what they wish from his writings without fear of contradiction. Unlike, for instance, Karl Marx, who also had a gift for the memorable phrase, Machiavelli is not identified with a particular political creed. He is neither liberal nor conservative; he associates as easily with those

---

* See in particular *Discourses*, I., 34, where he says: "I claim that republics which, when in iminent danger, have recourse neither to a dictatorship, nor to some form of authority analogous to it, will always be ruined when grave misfortune befalls them" (p. 196).

on the left as on the right, infuriating both sides with his apparent lack of ideological purity.

In the nearly five hundred years since his death, Machiavelli has almost always been cast in the role of the villain. Even men like Metternich and Bismarck, politicians noted for their unsentimental pursuit of any advantage in the service of the state, would not have described themselves as Machiavellian, though there were many others only too happy to apply that label to them. *Realpolitik* might be acceptable in diplomatic circles, but Machiavellianism implies something more underhanded. When in an interview in *The New Republic* a journalist asked Henry Kissinger, then President Nixon's National Security Advisor, whether he was influenced by Machiavelli's writings, Kissinger felt compelled to deny the charge. Kissinger would admit to being a realist, but not a cynic.*

People in public life who must submit to the verdict of the ballot are leery of being associated with the notorious Florentine, but in other contexts Machiavelli has gained a certain cachet. Anyone who wants to project a no-nonsense attitude, an ability to see through the pious drivel that passes for conventional wisdom or to slay a few sacred cows, will find it handy to invoke his name. Books dispensing advice on how to run a successful business or manage personal relationships often claim insights derived from his writings. His supposed ruthlessness is the perfect antidote to that greatest of sins for the worldly-wise—naïveté. In sophisticated circles there are worse things to be accused of than adopting "subtle policie, cunning roguerie." Confessing an admiration for Machiavelli, we demonstrate we're nobody's fool.

What would Machiavelli himself have made of all this? He would almost certainly be surprised, though probably not dismayed. In life he had been worldly and ambitious, eager to leave something behind by which he would be remembered, and in this he succeeded beyond his wildest dreams. His posthumous fame eclipsed anything he could have antici-

---

* A typical example of the way Machiavelli's name is invoked comes in a recent biography of Karl Rove, George Bush's political adviser, titled *Machiavelli's Shadow*. The author does not mean to imply that Rove seriously studied Machiavelli's philosophy, only that his approach to politics was cynical and devious.

pated, and while he might be perplexed at the strange uses to which his words were put, the uncongenial causes they were used to promote, and the strange bedfellows with whom he has been forced to share eternity, he was sufficiently attuned to the unpredictability of the universe to take it all in stride. Even at his lowest ebb he never lost sight of the comic aspect of his existence, knowing that admitting one's own ridiculousness was the best way to forestall ridicule by others. Surely, he would have regarded his immortal reputation with the same ironic smile. In life it had been his misfortune to be misunderstood and underestimated, and the dead, even less than the living, can choose neither their friends nor their enemies.

But Machiavelli was convinced that the dead had much to tell future generations, if only they took the time to listen. When he sat down to write *The Prince* he claimed he was visited by ghosts:

> *Fitted out appropriately, I step inside the venerable courts of the ancients, where, solicitously received by them, I nourish myself on that food that alone is mine and for which I was born; where I am unashamed to converse with them and to question them about the motives for their actions, and they, out of their human kindness, answer me. And for four hours at a time I feel no boredom, I forget all my troubles, I do not dread poverty, and I am not terrified by death. I absorb myself into them completely.*

Now that he has joined that spectral crowd, we should pay him the same courtesy and be as attentive to his whispered wisdom as he was to the words of those who came before him.

NOTES

PROLOGUE: THE MALICE OF FATE

Page

2 *"And as for turning my face toward fortune"*: Machiavelli et al., *Lettere Familiari*, 226–27.

2 *"I have, Giuliano"*: Machiavelli, *Chief Works*, II, 1013.

3 *"What gave me most torment"*: Ibid.

4 *"post res perditas"*: Machiavelli et al., *Machiavelli and His Friends*, 197.

4 *"Hence often you labor in serving"*: Machiavelli, *Chief Works*, II, 744.

5 *"I can tell you nothing else in this letter"*: Machiavelli et al., *Lettere Familiari*, 306.

5 *"I wander over to the road by the inn"*: Ibid., 307–8.

5 *"Having eaten"*: Ibid., 308.

6 *"for fortune is a woman"*: Machiavelli, *The Prince*, 86.

6 *"my loyalty and honesty are proven by my poverty"*: Machiavelli et al., *Lettere Familiari*, 310.

7 *"I love my city more than my own soul"*: Ibid., 525.

8 *"fortune has arranged it"*: Ibid., 229.

8 *"I am wasting away"*: Ibid., 310.

8 *"Come evening, I return to my house"*: Ibid., 308–9.

9 *"an enemy of the human race"*: Anglo, *Machiavelli: The First Century: Studies in Enthusiasm, Hostility, and Irrelevance*, 126.

I. BORN IN POVERTY

Page

13 *"I was born poor"*: Machiavelli et al., *Lettere Familiari*, 227.

13 *loggia known as the* chorte di Machiavelli: Atkinson, *Debts, Dowries, Donkeys*, 56.

14 *Bernardo, in recognition of his role as fatherly protector*: Ibid., 38.

14 *"friend and familiar"*: Ibid., 151.

14 *"Well, let them be"*: Atkinson, "Niccolò Machiavelli: A Portrait," in *The Cambridge Companion to Machiavelli*, 14.

15 *"pygmies . . . attacking giants"*: Machiavelli et al., *Lettere Familiari*, 4.

15 *"And whoever would wish justly to weigh"*: Ibid., 3.

15 *"a man who doesn't have pull with the government"*: Machiavelli, *La Mandragola*, in *Chief Works*, II, 788–89.

17 *"a man of low and poor station"*: Machiavelli, *Il Principe*, 84.

18 *among the prominent Guelphs*: Atkinson, *Debts, Dowries, Donkeys*, 27.

19 *"through Hell [Florence's] name is spread abroad"*: Dante, *Inferno*, XXVI.

19 *"notable" citizen families of the Oltrarno neighborhood*: Atkinson, *Debts, Dowries, Donkeys*, 27.

20 *"if in any other republic there were ever notable divisions"*: Machiavelli, *Florentine Histories*, 6–7.

20 *"in my judgment no other instance appears"*: Ibid., 7.

20 *"[H]aving eliminated their nobility"*: Ibid., I, 50.

21 *Three Majors*: Herlihy, Klapisch-Zuber, and Mohlo, *Online Tratte of Office Holders, 1282–1532.*

21 *purchased by the family from the powerful Pitti clan*: Pitti, *Diario of Buonacorso Pitti*, in *Two Memoirs of Renaissance Florence*, 21.

21 *where Niccolò would retire to write* The Prince: Atkinson, *Debts, Dowries, Donkeys*, 31.

22 *patronage rights over the small chapel of San Gregorio*: Ibid., 35.

22 *payment for a delivery of spring lambs for Easter*: Bernardo Machiavelli, *Libro di Ricordi*, 28–30.

22 *a dealer in secondhand clothes*: Atkinson, *Debts, Dowries, Donkeys*, 63.

22 *"messer Bernardo . . . practices no gainful employment"*: Ibid., 53.

23 *"I have never practiced any profession"*: Condivi, *The Life of Michelangelo*, 13.

24 *"all the cities and mountains and rivers that are mentioned"*: Bernardo Machiavelli, *Libro di Ricordi*, 14.

24 *"He spent his time as a good man should"*: Machiavelli, *Clizia*, in *Chief Works*, II, 835–36.

25 *while she was living under Bernardo's roof*: Bernardo Machiavelli, *Libro di Ricordi*, 15ff.

26 *"For it often happens that men who are just"*: Atkinson, *Debts, Dowries, Donkeys*, 152.

26 *"Above all else stick together with your neighbors and kinsmen"*: Kent, *The Rise of the Medici Faction in Florence, 1426–1434*, 17.

30 *"This is an age of gold"*: Schevill, *History of Florence*, 416.

31 *"The city enjoyed perfect peace"*: Guicciardini, *The History of Florence*, IX.

31 *"Florentines lived in very great prosperity"*: Machiavelli, *Florentine Histories*, VIII, 36.

31 *"discordant Italy opened into herself"*: Machiavelli, *First Decennale*, in *Chief Works*, III, 1445.

32 *"Maestro Matteo, master of grammar"*: Grendler, *Schooling in Renaissance Italy*, 76.

33 *"For when a child of tender years begins to understand"*: Machiavelli, *Discourses*, III, 46.

33 *"We call these studies liberal"*: Vergerio, "The Character and Studies Befitting a Free-Born Youth," in *Humanist Educational Treatises*, 14.

34 *"Leaving the woods, I go to a spring"*: Machiavelli et al, *Lettere Familiari*, 307.

34 *"threaten bar keepers"*: Trexler, *Public Life in Renaissance Florence*, 389.

35 *his eyes sparkled with mirth*: Villari, *The Life and Times of Niccolò Machiavelli*, I, 245.

35 *"For now the baby is well"*: Marietta Corsini in Machiavelli et al., *Lettere Familiari*, 114.

36 *"Write to Niccolò Capponi"*: Biagio Buonaccorsi in Machiavelli et al., *Lettere Familiari*, 178–79.

36 *"partly in studies, partly in amusement"*: Machiavelli, *La Mandragola*, in *Chief Works*, II, 778.

37 *"Because life is short"*: Ibid., 776.

37 *"by eagerness for praise and inflamed by love of glory"*: Vergerio, "The Character and Studies Befitting a Free-Born Youth," in *Humanist Educational Treatises*, 4.

II. A SWORD UNSHEATHED

Page

40 *"countless men who, that they might fall to earth"*: Machiavelli, "On Fortune" in *Chief Works*, II, 749.

41 *"O Italy! O Princes!":* Villari, *The Life and Times of Girolamo Savonarola*, I, 334.

41 *"The people of Florence do not think":* Machiavelli, *The Prince*, XI, 105.

41 *"Here come the boys of the friar!":* Landucci, *Diary*, 121.

42 *"a friar of Saint Francis":* Machiavelli et al., *Lettere Familiari*, 313–14.

42 *"suffer fire and sack":* Ibid., 314.

42 *"I didn't actually hear the preacher":* Ibid., 314–15.

42 *"I believe Christ speaks through my mouth":* Martines, *Fire in the City*, 27.

42 *"to give you, as you wished":* Machiavelli et al., *Lettere Familiari*, 4.

43 *"[H]e began with great terrors:* Ibid., 5.

43 *"he follows the mood of the times":* Ibid., 8.

43 *"[H]ad you heard with what audacity":* Ibid., 5.

43 *"But the more they oppressed them":* Ibid., 5–8.

43 *"[H]e seeks to set all of [the people]":* Ibid.

44 *"So, you are allowing Friar Girolamo to preach again":* Martines, *Fire in the City*, 202.

44 *"filled with blood and dead men":* Machiavelli, *First Decennale*, in *Chief Works*, III, 1445.

44 *"But that which to many was far more distressing":* Ibid., 1448.

45 *"With them a flame and a plague":* Guicciardini, *The History of Florence*, XI, 19–20.

46 *"Our Italian princes":* Villari, *The Life and Times of Niccolò Machiavelli*, II, 339.

47 *"discordant Italy":* Machiavelli, *First Decennale* in *Chief Works*, III, 1445.

47 *"because of his dark complexion":* Guicciardini, *The History of Italy*, III, 304.

48 *"for when Italy was left deprived of his advice":* Machiavelli, *Florentine Histories*, VIII, 363.

48 *"He was a haughty and cruel man":* Guicciardini, *The History of Florence*, XI, 21.

49 *where Charles was encamped with the bulk of his army:* Landucci, *Diary*, 58.

49 *"[H]e threw out* confetti": Ibid., 60.

50 *"We're finished!":* Martines, *Fire in the City*, 38.

50 *"kneeling with joined hands":* Landucci, *Diary*, 62.

50 *to signify his role as a conqueror:* Guicciardini, *The History of Florence*, XII, 30.

50 *"Viva Francia!":* Landucci, *Diary*, 66.

50 *"when he was seen on foot":* Ibid.

50 *"a sight in itself very beautiful":* Guicciardini, *The History of Florence*, XII, 30.

51 *"King Charles of France was allowed to conquer Italy with chalk":* Machiavelli, *Il Principe*, XII, 133.

51 *"[Y]our coming has lightened our hearts":* Martines, *Fire in the City*, 50.

52 *"After 1494 when those who had been princes":* Machiavelli, *Discourses*, I, 227.

52 *"[T]he will of God is that the city of Florence":* Martines, *Fire in the City*, 71.

52 *"Now the Florentine people":* Savonarola, "Treatise on the Constitution and Government of Florence," in *Humanism and Liberty*, 237.

54 *"After [the fall of the Medici], the city decided":* Machiavelli, "A Discourse on the Remodeling of the Government of Florence," in *Chief Works*, I, 103.

54 *"Never will the generality of the Florentine citizens":* Ibid., 110–11.

55 *"the Ten Expenders":* Villari, *The Life and Times of Niccolò Machiavelli*, I, 251.

55 *"So all Tuscany was in confusion":* Machiavelli, *First Decennale* in *Chief Works*, III, 1445.

55 *"So with his conquering army":* Ibid., 1446.

56 *"When the report of victory so great":* Ibid.

57 *"We were then pressed to join the league":* Guicciardini, *The History of Florence*, XIII, 47.

57 *"a great slaughter":* *The History of Italy*, IX, 247.

57 *"[Charles] ignored the treat made with us":* *The History of Florence*, XIII, 46.

58 *"scourgings and terrible tribulations":* Ibid., 47.

58 *"false, proud whore"*: Martines, *Fire in the City*, 12.

58 *"[Alexander] was not disturbed by those things"*: Guicciardini, *The History of Italy*, III, 356.

58 *"It is not my habit to seek human glory"*: Martines, *Fire in the City*, 137.

59 *"Long live Christ and the Virgin"*: Landucci, *Diary*, 100–110.

59 *"extinguished the carnal heat of desire"*: Weinstein, *Savonarola and Florence*, 81.

60 *"Thus a great division and violent hatred"*: Guicciardini, *The History of Florence*, XIII, 50.

60 *"[I]t seemed a mistake to me"*: Landucci, *Diary*, 131.

61 *"This man preaches that the Pope is not the Pope"*: Martines, *Fire in the City*, 214.

61 *Backed by Venetian money and a papal blessing*: Guicciardini, *The History of Florence*, XV.

62 *"I could not refrain from weeping"*: Landucci, *Diary*, 126.

62 *"When [the accused] wished to appeal"*: Machiavelli, *Discourses*, I, 221.

63 *"unarmed prophet"*: Machiavelli, *Il Principe*, VI, 106.

63 *"[T]his excommunication is a diabolical thing"*: Martines, *Fire in the City*, 206.

63 *"[H]e seeks to turn all against the supreme pontiff"*: Machiavelli et al., *Lettere Familiari*, 8.

64 *"diverse figures and monstrous animals"*: Martines, *Fire in the City*, 146.

66 *"[W]hen the dispute ended in the Franciscans leaving"*: Landucci, *Diary*, 136.

66 *"To San Marco!"*: Martines, *Fire in the City*, 232.

67 *"Kill the traitor!"*: Ibid., 233.

67 *a man who struck him from behind*: Landucci, *Diary*, 137.

67 *was led from San Marco in irons*: Ibid., 138.

68 *"Regarding my own aim or ultimate purpose"*: Martines, *Fire in the City*, 250.

68 *"[H]e whom we had held to be a prophet"*: Landucci, *Diary*, 139.

69 *"Now listen to me"*: Martines, *Fire in the City*, 259.

69 *the dying men were blessed martyrs*: Landucci, *Diary*, 143.

70 *now seeking to regain its balance after the recent convulsions*: See Rubinstein, "The Beginnings of Niccolò Machiavelli's Career in the Florentine Chancery," 72, for a full discussion of the date of Machiavelli's election.

III. THE CIVIL SERVANT

Page

71 *June 15, 1498, marks a turning point*: Meinecke, *Machiavelli*, 39.

71 *I have set down all that I know*: Machiavelli, *Discourses*, Dedication, 93.

71 *"my knowledge of the actions of great men"*: Machiavelli, *Il Principe*, Dedication, 83.

71 *"it seems best to me to go straight to the actual truth of things"*: Machiavelli, *Il Principe*, XV, 147.

72 *which started at 192 florins a year*: Villari, *The Life and Times of Niccolò Machiavelli*, I, 243–44.

73 *"it is ill living in Florence"*: Ross, *Lives of the Early Medici*, 150–56.

75 *snide comments about their colleagues*: Machiavelli et al., *Machiavelli and His Friends*, 26.

76 *"If I have not written as often as I would have liked"*: Machiavelli et al., *Lettere Familiari*, 13.

76 *"[M]any believed that by overthrowing the friar"*: Guicciardini, *The History of Florence*, XVI, 79.

77 *"[I]f [the* ottimati] *complain that this tax will impoverish them"*: Najemy, *A History of Florence*, 402.

77 *"What a disgusting thing it is"*: Ibid., 406.

77 *"[I]n every republic"*: Machiavelli, *Discourses*, I, 113.

77 *"The reason why all these governments"*: Machiavelli, "A Discourse on the Remodeling of the Florentine Government," in *Chief Works*, I, 103.

78 *"[A] prince is successful"*: Machiavelli, *The Prince*, XXV, 85.

79 *"The rule for our Italian soldiers"*: Landucci, *Diary*, 22.

79 *"A prince must have no other objective"*: Machiavelli, *The Prince*, XIV, 53.

80 *Biagio Buonaccorsi requested that his friend*: Machiavelli et al., *Machiavelli and His Friends*, 19.

81 *"crowded with Florentines"*: Villari, *The Life and Times of Niccolò Machiavelli*, I, 255.

81 *"having thought the matter over in the night"*: Ibid., 255–56.

81 *"had always satisfied her"*: Ibid., 255.

82 *"that spirit of yours, so eager for riding"*: Machiavelli et al., *Machiavelli and His Friends*, 50.

82 *"most highly praised"*: Machiavelli et al., *Lettere Familiari*, 24.

82 *"If you do as I advise"*: Ibid., 20.

83 *"few little parties at Biagio's house"*: Ibid., 34–35.

84 *They were now inside the walls of the city*: Landucci, *Diary*, 159.

84 *about how to punish the rebellious city*: Ibid.

84 *"We have granted the captain"*: Villari, *The Life and Times of Niccolò Machiavelli*, I, 260.

84 *"[H]aving expended up to this date"*: Ibid.

84 *"We should have preferred defeat to inaction"*: Ibid.

85 *some sort of treasonous arrangement with Piero de' Medici*: Ibid., 262.

85 *risked less and promised greater returns*: Ibid.

85 *"this was the end of Pagolo Vitegli"*: Ibid.

85 *"[H]ad it not been for Vitelli's treachery"*: Machiavelli et al., *Lettere Familiari*, 28.

85 *"And in brotherly love"*: Ibid., 29.

87 *"[J]udging the prudence and intelligence of all the others"*: Guicciardini, *The History of Italy*, III, 304.

88 *promised to supply men and money*: Villari, *The Life and Times of Niccolò Machiavelli*, I, 267.

89 *"who had opened the gates"*: Machiavelli, *Il Principe*, III, 88–89.

89 *"So his shrewdness was mocked"*: Machiavelli, *First Decennale*, in *Chief Works*, III, 1450.

89 *at the exorbitant price of 24,000 ducats a month*: Villari, *The Life and Times of Niccolò Machiavelli*, I, 268.

90 *"He who is afraid"*: Ibid., 270.

90 *"It might . . . be well"*: Ibid., 272.

91 *"But when they confronted the Pisans"*: Machiavelli, *First Decennale*, in *Chief Works*, III, 1,451.

IV. SIR NIHIL

Page

93 *"Benefices are sold here like melons"*: Machiavelli et al., *Lettere Familiari*, 44–45.

93 *"who, of all the pontiffs that have ever been"*: Machiavelli, *Il Principe*, XI, 130–31.

94 *"Alexander VI . . . never thought of anything but deception"*: Ibid., XVIII, 157.

95   *"a very mean young man"*: Hibbert, *The Borgias and Their Enemies*, 96.

95   *"shutting himself away in a room"*: Ibid., 107.

96   *"Life has lost all interest for us"*: Ibid., 108.

96   *"Even more than by anger"*: Ibid., 92.

97   *"[I]t would have been safer for her"*: Machiavelli, *Il Principe*, XX, 175.

97   *"This lord knows very well"*: Machiavelli, "Legation 11.40," in *Chief Works*, I, 130.

99   *"The French are blinded by their own power"*: Villari, *The Life and Times of Niccolò Machiavelli*, I, 277–78.

99   *"I don't want to forget to tell you"*: Machiavelli et al., *Lettere Familiari*, 31–32.

100   *"he threatens to erect Pisa"*: Villari, *The Life and Times of Niccolò Machiavelli*, I, 277–78.

100   *"[W]hen the Cardinal of Rouen told me"*: Machiavelli, *Il Principe*, III, 97.

100   *"if the King had conceded everything"*: Villari, *The Life and Times of Niccolò Machiavelli*, I, 278.

100   *"The Pope tries by all means"*: Ibid., 279.

100   *if only Piero de' Medici were restored*: Ibid.

102   *"There can be no proper relation"*: Machiavelli, *The Prince*, XIV, 54.

103   *"not upon their good faith"*: Villari, *The Life and Times of Niccolò Machiavelli*, I, 279.

103   *"[H]e who causes another to become powerful"*: Machiavelli, *Il Principe*, III, 98.

103   *"Every day Ser Antonio's stomach bothers him"*: Machiavelli et al., *Lettere Familiari*, 34.

104   *"When in jest and to relax our minds"*: Machiavelli et al., *Machiavelli and His Friends*, 32.

106   *"I have heard that history is the teacher"*: Villari, *The Life and Times of Niccolò Machiavelli*, I, 296–97.

106   *"[A]s long as the Roman republic continued incorrupt"*: Machiavelli, *The Art of War*, I, 17–18.

106   *"Mercenary captains are either skilled at arms"*: Machiavelli, *Il Principe*, XII, 134.

107   *"The whole morning we heard nothing"*: Landucci, *Diary*, 181.

107   *Florence was forced to buy him off*: Villari, *The Life and Times of Niccolò Machiavelli*, I, 285.

108   *"They killed without pity"*: Hibbert, *The Borgias and Their Enemies*, 182.

110   *"obedience [to her husband]"*: Barbaro, "On Wifely Duties," in Kohl and Witt, *The Earthly Republic*, 193.

110   *"to wish to appear a woman of honor"*: Alberti, *I Libri della Famiglia*, 97.

110   *"I hope I shall never be a husband"*: Machiavelli, *La Mandragola*, in *Chief Works*, II, 792.

110   *"with gentle words"*: Ibid., 790.

111   *"fortune is a woman"*: Machiavelli, *The Prince*, XXV, 86.

111   *"Lady Marietta curses God"*: Machiavelli et al., *Lettere Familiari*, 99.

112   *"My dearest Niccolò"*: Ibid., 114–15.

113   *"I'll go to your house"*: Ibid., 133.

115   *"This Lord is of such splendid and magnificent bearing"*: Machiavelli, *Legazioni, Commissarie, Scritti di Governo*, II, 125.

116   *"We heard that Valentino had sent to say"*: Landucci, *Diary*, 196.

116   *"Well I know that your city"*: Machiavelli, *Legazioni, Commissarie, Scritti di Governo*, II, 120–21.

117   *looting the very people*: Landucci, *Diary*, 199.

118   *"Lucius Furius Camillus entered the Senate"*: Villari, *The Life and Times of Niccolò Machiavelli*, I, 296.

118   *"One can therefore approve"*: Ibid., 297.

118   *"[M]en must either be coddled or destroyed"*: Machiavelli, *Il Principe*, III, 91.

V. EXIT THE DRAGON

Page

121   *"devoured one by one by the dragon"*: Hibbert, *The Borgias and Their Enemies*, 234.

122   *he presented himself* cavalchereccio: Machiavelli, *Legazioni, Commissarie, Scritti di Governo*, no. 174, 195.

122   *"declared that he had always desired"*: Ibid.

123   *"his enemies can no longer do much harm"*: Machiavelli et al., *Machiavelli and His Friends*, 61.

123   *"with the king of France in Italy"*: Machiavelli, *Legazioni, Commissarie, Scritti di Governo*, no. 174, 197.

123   *"too forceful"*: Machiavelli et al., *Lettere Familiari*, 74.

123   *"I think taking a stand"*: Machiavelli et al., *Machiavelli and His Friends*, 304.

124   *"The writer who wrote this"*: Ibid., 50.

124   *"I believe he has become your great friend"*: Ibid., 59.

124   *"Your Lordships write to me about temporizing"*: Machiavelli, *Legazioni, Commissarie, Scritti di Governo*, no. 182, 218.

125   *"the new law [for the Gonfaloniere]"*: Ibid., no. 179, 212.

125   *"Because courts always include different kinds of busybodies"*: Machiavelli, "Advice to Rafaello Girolami when he went as Ambassador to the Emperor," in *Chief Works*, I, 117.

125   *"[W]hoever examines the quality of one side"*: Machiavelli, *Legazioni, Commissarie, Scritti di Governo*, no. 196, 247.

125   *"a very skillful dissembler"*: Machiavelli, "A Description of the Method Used by Duke Valentino in Killing Vitellozzo Vitelli, Oliverotto da Fermo, and Others," in *Chief Works*, 1, 165.

126   *real power remained in his rivals' hands*: Ibid.

126   *"[S]weetly this basilisk whistled"*: Machiavelli, *First Decennale*, in *Chief Works*, III, 388–94.

126   *"dressed as a courier"*: Machiavelli, *Legazioni, Commissarie, Scritti di Governo*, no. 196, 245.

126   *"to excuse and justify what had occurred"*: Ibid., 246.

126   *"the Orsini might be very sure"*: Villari, *The Life and Times of Niccolò Machiavelli*, I, 327.

126   *"[T]hey write me pleasing letters"*: Machiavelli, *Legazioni, Commissarie, Scritti di Governo*, no. 193, 240.

126   *"money, robes, and horses"*: Machiavelli, *Il Principe*, VII, 112.

127   *"it is impossible to belive"*: Machiavelli, *Legazioni, Commissarie, Scritti di Governo*, no. 196, 247–48.

127   *"[I]f one must do harm to another"*: Machiavelli, *Il Principe*, III, 91.

127   *"Mona Marietta sent to me via her brother"*: Machiavelli et al., *Lettere Familiari*, 60.

127   *he remained short of cash*: Machiavelli et al., *Machiavelli and His Friends*, 63.

128   *"Stick it up your ass"*: Ibid., 79.

128   *"I wouldn't be at all surprised"*: Machiavelli et al., *Lettere Familiari*, 97.

128   *"to relieve the government of this expense"*: Villari, *The Life and Times of Niccolò Machiavelli*, 314–15.

128   *"I say that you are to observe"*: Machiavelli, "Advice to Raffaello Girolami when he went as Ambassador to the Emperor," in *Chief Works*, I, 118–19.

129   *"was ruled by impotent lords"*: Machiavelli, *Il Principe*, VII, 112–13.

130   *"Cesare Borgia was considered cruel"*: Ibid., XVII, 151–52.

130 *"no doubt [Remirro] will be sacrificed"*: Machiavelli, *Legazioni, Commissarie, Scritti di Governo*, no. 255, 363.

130 *"Messer Remirro this morning has been found cut in two"*: Ibid., no. 256, 365.

130 *"Recognizing that past severities"*: Machiavelli, *The Prince*, VII, 31–32.

131 *"Vitellozzo, Pagolo, and the Duke"*: Machiavelli, "A Description of the Method Used by Duke Valentino in Killing Vitellozzo Vitelli, Oliverotto da Fermo, and Others," in *Chief Works*, 1, 168.

131 *"with the brightest face in the world"*: Villari, *The Life and Times of Niccolò Machiavelli*, I, 322.

131 *"Everyone knows how laudable it is"*: Machiavelli, *Il Principe*, XVIII, 155.

132 *"Since a prince is required to play the beast"*: Ibid., 156.

133 *"every moment thinking to see the executioner"*: Villari, *The Life and Times of Niccolò Machiavelli*, I, 346.

134 *"had changed to the color of blackest cloth"*: Hibbert, *The Borgias and Their Enemies*, 251.

134 *held a knife to Cardinal Casanova's throat*: Burchardus, *Pope Alexander and His Court*, 180.

136 *"[H]e should never have allowed any cardinal"*: Machiavelli, *Il Principe*, VII, 116.

136 *"[A]t present, you are incapable"*: Villari, *The Life and Times of Niccolò Machiavelli*, I, 339–40.

138 *"[A]lways transported by his daring confidence"*: Ibid., 360.

138 *"We want the states to return to the Church"*: Hibbert, *The Borgias and Their Enemies*, 267–68.

139 *"I had no lack of things to say in reply"*: Villari, *The Life and Times of Niccolò Machiavelli*, I, 360.

139 *"since he is taken"*: Ibid., 364.

139 *"[T]hus it would seem"*: Ibid., 365.

140 *"Cesare Borgia, called by the masses Duke Valentino"*: Machiavelli, *Il Principe*, VII, 109.

VI. MEN OF LOW AND POOR STATION

Page

142 *"I am fully conscious"*: Masters, *Fortune Is a River*, 25.

142 *"Nor do I wish it thought a presumption"*: Machiavelli, *Il Principe*, "Dedication," 84.

143 *Unfortunately, neither man left an account*: Roger Masters chronicles the collaboration between Leonardo and Machiavelli in his book *Fortune Is a River*. Sometimes he goes beyond the available evidence, but his conclusion that the two must have met on numerous occasions in the fall of 1502 seems indisputable.

144 *"little better than a fanstasy"*: Villari, *The Life and Times of Niccolò Machiavelli*, I, 371.

145 *"that the defenders feared only one thing"*: Masters, *Fortune Is a River*, 117.

145 *"Your delay makes us fear"*: Ibid., 130.

145 *"Notable man and very dear compare"*: Ibid., 135.

146 *"your devoted friend"*: Machiavelli et al., *Machiavelli and His Friends*, 79.

146 *" 'I have never commissioned anything from that clown' "*: Machiavelli et al., *Lettere Familiari*, 154.

147 *"[I]t seems best to me to go straight"*: Machiavelli, *Il Principe*, XV, 147.

148 *"For when the safety of one's country"*: Machiavelli, *Discourses*, III, 515.

148 *first articulated by the humble Florentine chancellor*: For an in-depth investigation of Machiavelli as the father of "reason of state," see Friedrich Meinecke's seminal *Machiavellism: The Doctrine of Raison d'Etat and Its Place in Modern History*.

148 *"A prince must show himself a lover of virtue"*: Machiavelli, *Il Principe*, XXI, 180.

149 *"[H]e turned to making his city more beautiful"*: Machiavelli, *Florentine Histories*, VIII, 361.

149 *"When, therefore, I consider in what honor"*: Machiavelli, *Discourses*, I, 97–98.

150 *That Machiavelli himself was instrumental*: See N. Rubinstein "Machiavelli and the Mural Decoration of the Hall of the Great Council of Florence" (pp. 275–85) for a summary of the evidence regarding Machiavelli's participation in the scheme for decorating the Hall.

151 *"Enacted in the palace of the aformentioned Lords"*: Masters, *Fortune Is a River*, 114–15.

152 *"Florentines who had voluntarily joined on horseback"*: Rubinstein, "Machiavelli and the Mural Decoration of the Hall of the Great Council of Florence," 285.

153 *"[T]hus with the sculptor Michelangelo"*: Machiavelli et al., *Machiavelli and His Friends*, 424.

153 *"This block of marble was nine braccia high"*: Vasari, "Michelangelo Buonarotti," in *Lives of the Artists*, II, 653.

154 *"It happened at this time"*: Ibid., 654–55.

155 *"that the author, too, knows how to find fault"*: Machiavelli, *La Mandragola*, in *Chief Works*, II, 778.

155 *"I never practiced any profession"*: Condivi, *The Life of Michelangelo*, 13.

VII. THE STARS ALIGN

Page

157 *"I have three sons"*: Unger, *Magnifico*, 218.

158 *"make it clearly understood"*: Villari, *The Life and Times of Niccolò Machiavelli*, I, 368.

158 *"[M]y spirit is all aflame"*: Machiavelli, *First Decennale*, in *Chief Works*, III, 1457.

158 *"Yet we trust in the skillful steersman"*: Ibid.

159 *"[T]he worst thing about weak republics"*: Machiavelli, *Discourses*, I, 206.

160 *"[H]e was like the other pillagers of Rome"*: Villari, *The Life and Times of Niccolò Machiavelli*, I, 357.

160 *"above all other things, it is necessary"*: Machiavelli, *Il Principe*, XXVI, 193.

160 *"Mercenaries and auxiliaries are useless"*: Ibid., XII, 133.

161 *"[W]here military organization is good"*: Machiavelli, *Discourses*, I, 113.

162 *"that the little people, all in arms"*: Parenti, *Ricordi Storici*, 126–27.

162 *"Your letter being longer"*: Machiavelli et al., *Lettere Familiari*, 165.

163 *"There was a muster in the Piazza"*: Landucci, *Diary*, 218.

163 *"it daily increases and flourishes"*: Villari, *The Life and Times of Niccolò Machiavelli*, I, 409.

165 *Soderini's "puppet"*: Ibid., 460.

165 *"[I] promise you"*: Machiavelli et al., *Machiavelli and His Friends*, 166.

165 *"Between Geneva and Constance I made four halts"*: Villari, *The Life and Times of Niccolò Machiavelli*, I, 462.

166 *"There can be no doubt of the power of Germany"*: Villari, *The Life and Times of Niccolò Machiavelli*, I, 474.

167 *"so that it is easy to comprehend why"*: Ibid., 475.

167 *"It is difficult to forecast events"*: Ibid., 464–65.

168 *"Your Excellencies have spun so fine a web"*: Ibid., 466.

168 *"It's as if I'm here on a desert island"*: Machiavelli et al., *Lettere Familiari*, 191.

168 *"I shall do here what little good"*: Machiavelli et al., *Machiavelli and His Friends*, 167.

168 *"it would be the most inopportune thing"*: Villari, *The Life and Times of Niccolò Machiavelli*, I, 465.

169 *"A woman of Pisa"*: Landucci, *Diary*, 232–33.

170 *"with great sufferings and much toil"*: Machiavelli, *Second Decennale*, in *Chief Works*, III, 1460.

170 *"even the horses of Xerxes might ford it"*: Villari, *The Life and Times of Niccolò Machiavelli*, I, 485.

171 *"[T]he more powerful must always be right"*: Machiavelli et al., *Lettere Familiari*, 179.

171 *"that the way of this world"*: Machiavelli et al., *Machiavelli and His Friends*, 179.

171 *"Captain General"*: Machiavelli et al., *Lettere Familiari*, 177.

171 *"[I]f I wished to avoid fatigue and danger"*: Villari, *The Life and Times of Niccolò Machiavelli*, I, 489.

171 *"[The Ten] desired obedience"*: Ibid., 488.

172 *"I would like you"*: Machiavelli et al., *Lettere Familiari*, 182.

173 *"Suffice it that your opinion"*: Machiavelli et al., *Machiavelli and His Friends*, 103.

173 *"The wise man will control the stars"*: Ibid., 459.

173 *"in the world most men"*: Machiavelli, "On Ambition," in *Chief Works*, II, 739.

175 *"At about 18 in the afternoon"*: Landucci, *Diary*, 235.

175 *"If I did not think it would make you too proud"*: Machiavelli et al., *Machiavelli and His Friends*, 181.

175 *"May a thousand good fortunes result"*: Villari, *The Life and Times of Niccolò Machiavelli*, I, 493.

175 *"Whoever reads of the doings of republics"*: Machiavelli, *Discourses*, I, 179.

176 *"He who becomes master of a city"*: Machiavelli, *Il Principe*, V, 102–3.

176 *"And though she was a stubborn enemy"*: Machiavelli, *Second Decennale*, in *Chief Works*, III, 1461.

VIII. REVERSAL OF FORTUNE

Page

178 *"Pope Julius II acted impetuously"*: Machiavelli, *Il Principe*, XXV, 189.

178 *"Julius not only pursued the same goals"*: Ibid., XI, 131.

180 *"It is the Church"*: Machiavelli, *Discourses*, I, 145.

181 *"that he would in no way tolerate"*: Machiavelli, *Legazioni, Commissarie, Scritti di Governo*, III, 404.

181 *"And I make, in short"*: Ibid., 403.

182 *"Venice lost in a single day"*: Machiavelli, *Il Principe*, XII, 137.

182 *"At twenty-two hours Piero Mazaruol"*: Sanudo, *Venice: Citta Excellentissima*, 174.

182 *"very often undid in the evening"*: Villari, *The Life and Times of Niccolò Machiavelli*, I, 499.

182 *"The invading soldiers have set to robbing"*: Machiavelli, "Legation," in *Chief Works*, II, 738.

183 *"Let him turn his eyes here"*: Machiavelli, "On Ambition", in *Chief Works*, II, 738.

183 *"And thus so great a desire of death"*: Villari, *The Life and Times of Niccolò Machiavelli*, I, 500.

184 *"if these powers had not been blinded"*: Guicciardini, *The History of Italy*, III, 280.

184 *"Against barbarian rage"*: Machiavelli, *The Prince*, XXI, 90.

185 *"[He] contended that having been born of a father, etc."*: Machiavelli et al., *Lettere Familiari*, 196–97.

186 *"although the Pope as a friend"*: Machiavelli et al., *Machiavelli and His Friends*, 195.
186 *"save that of keeping your Excellencies"*: Villari, *The Life and Times of Niccolò Machiavelli*, I, 509.
186 *"[T]here is no way out"*: Machiavelli et al., *Machiavelli and His Friends*, 195.
186 *"Your Excellencies may believe"*: Villari, *The Life and Times of Niccolò Machiavelli*, I, 510.
186 *"if they make war alone"*: Ibid., 510.
188 *Medici sympathizer Prinzivalle della Stufa*: Landucci, *Diary*, 242.
189 *"No one shows any wish to attend the Council"*: Villari, *The Life and Times of Niccolò Machiavelli*, I, 524–25.
189 *"it was fought with more virtue than any other"*: Machiavelli, *Florentine Histories*, VIII, 346.
190 *"flying like mist before the wind"*: Villari, *The Life and Times of Niccolò Machiavelli*, II, 7.
191 *"Seeing the great utility of the Infantry Ordinance"*: Villari, *The Life and Times of Niccolò Machiavelli*, II, 10.
192 *"To test the mood of the people"*: Machiavelli et al., *Lettere Familiari*, 215–16.
192 *"It was decided initially"*: Ibid., 214.
193 *"were of such a sort"*: Villari, *The Life and Times of Niccolò Machiavelli*, II, 12.
193 *"Prudent Princes and Republics"*: Machiavelli, *Discourses*, II, 365.
194 *"[A]fter minimal resistance"*: Machiavelli et al., *Lettere Familiari*, 216–17.
194 *"The taking of Prato, so speedily"*: Villari, *The Life and Times of Niccolò Machiavelli*, II, 14.
194 *"[E]veryone began to fear a sack"*: Machiavelli et al., *Lettere Familiari*, 217.
195 *"relying on idle dreams of his own"*: Ibid.
196 *"Piero Soderini . . . conducted all his affairs"*: Machiavelli, *Discourses*, III, 431.
196 *"in conformity with the times"*: Ibid., 430.
196 *"The night that Piero Soderini ceased to breathe"*: Villari, *The Life and Times of Niccolò Machiavelli*, II, 37.
197 *"all the citizens who considered themselves friends"*: Landucci, *Diary*, 258.
198 *"In this way the liberty of Florence"*: Villari, *The Life and Times of Niccolò Machiavelli*, II, 22.
198 *"The city was reduced"*: Ibid.
198 *"The city remains most peaceful"*: Machiavelli et al., *Lettere Familiari*, 219.

IX. DISMISSED, DEPRIVED, AND TOTALLY REMOVED

Page

199 *"In the belief that affection may serve"*: Villari, *The Life and Times of Niccolò Machiavelli*, II, 26.
199 *"their seizure . . . will generate inextinguishable hatred"*: Ibid., 27.
200 *"who can come to terms"*: Ibid.
201 *"as many dead, as many exiles"*: Machiavelli, *Florentine Histories*, "Preface," 7.
201 *"He who becomes prince"*: Machiavelli, *Il Principe*, IX, 122–23.
202 *"my poverty is a testament"*: Machiavelli et al., *Lettere Familiari*, 310.
203 *"Boscoli and Capponi, young men of good families"*: Villari, *The Life and Times of Niccolò Machiavelli*, II, 34.
203 *"There is no . . . enterprise in which private persons"*: Machiavelli, *Discourses*, III, 398.
204 *"I maintain that one finds in history"*: Ibid., 402.
204 *"One must recognize that there is nothing more difficult"*: Machiavelli, *Il Principe*, VI, 105.

205 *"that I bore it with such stoicism"*: Machiavelli et al., *Lettere Familiari*, 226–27.

205 *"it is something of a miracle"*: Ibid., 246.

205 *"One is chained up and another is unironed"*: Machiavelli, "Sonnet to Giuliano, Son of Lorenzo de' Medici," in *Chief Works*, II, 1013.

205 *"Last night, beseeching the Muses"*: Ibid., 1014.

208 *"I am accustomed to spending"*: Machiavelli et al., *Lettere Familiari*, 356.

209 *"[F]ortune has left me nothing"*: Ibid., 396.

209 *"[B]linded by matrimonial famine"*: Ibid., 194.

210 "la brigatata": Ibid., 232.

210 *"We dined, and when it came time"*: Ibid., 232–33.

210 *"count Orlando"*: Ibid., 233.

210 *"slobbering, totally consumed by Gostanza"*: Ibid., 329.

211 *"I have met a creature"*: Ibid., 360.

211 *"I have found nothing but pain"*: Ibid., 361.

211 *"When dinnertime comes"*: Ibid., 308.

211 *"Marietta gave birth to a baby girl"*: Machiavelli et al., *Machiavelli and His Friends*, 244.

211 *"Thus I will remain"*: Machiavelli et al., *Lettere Familiari*, 356.

212 *"The duty of a father"*: Alberti, *The Family in Renaissance Florence*, I, 36.

212 *"Since I do not know how to talk"*: Machiavelli et al., *Machiavelli and His Friends*, 225.

212 *"I send you, Giuliano, some thrushes"*: Machiavelli, "Third Sonnet to Giuliano, Son of Lorenzo de' Medici," in *Chief Works*, II, 1015.

213 *"Come evening, I return to my house"*: Machiavelli et al., *Lettere Familiari*, 308–9.

214 *"I am dedicating it to his Magnificence Giuliano"*: Ibid., 310.

214 *"[T]hrough this work, were it to be read"*: Ibid.

X. THE PRINCE

Page

215 *"[I]t is customary for those hoping to win the favor"*: Machiavelli, *Il Principe*, "Dedication to Lorenzo de' Medici," 83.

216 *"I am wasting away"*: Machiavelli et al., *Machiavelli and His Friends*, 265.

217 *"Take, then, this little gift"*: Machiavelli, *Il Principe*, "Dedication to Lorenzo de' Medici," 84.

218 *But even his harshest critics:* Leo Strauss uses the memorable phrase "that greater Columbus" to describe Machiavelli's contribution to political science. (Leo Strauss, "On the Spirit of Hobbes' Political Philosophy," in *Essays in the History of Political Thought*, 168.)

218 *can still be read with pleasure:* Books offering to package Machiavelli's philosophy as a guide to modern living remain popular. A few recent examples include: *The New Prince: Machiavelli Updated for the Twenty-first Century* (Dick Morris); *What Would Machiavelli Do: The Ends Justify the Meanness* (Stanley Bing); *Machiavelli on Modern Leadership: Why Machiavelli's Iron Rules Are as Important Today as Five Centuries Ago* (Michael A. Ledeen).

219 *He was clearly familiar with his predecessors' work:* For anyone interested in the topic, a good place to start is Allan H. Gilbert's *Machiavelli's Prince and Its Forerunners*.

219 *"Since I know that many have already written"*: Machiavelli, *Il Principe*, XV, 146–47.

220 *"I proclaim justice is nothing else"*: Plato, *The Republic*, I, in *The Works of Plato*, 18.

220 *"the knowledge by which we are to make"*: Wolin, "Plato: Political Philosophy Versus Politics," in *Essays in the History of Political Thought*, 4–5.

220   "the good lawgiver and the genuine politician": Aristotle, *The Politics*, IV, 150.

221   "as an association of persons": Aristotle, *The Politics*, I, 25.

221   "Wisdom is not only an extraordinary attribute": Erasmus, *Education of a Christian Prince*, "Dedicatory Epistle," 133.

221   "Should you read diligently and consider": Machiavelli, *The Prince*, XXVI, 88.

222   "it ought to be welcomed by a prince": Machiavelli et al., *Machiavelli and His Friends*, 265.

222   "are acquired, how they are retained": Ibid., 264.

222   "In our change-loving Italy": Burckhardt, *The Civilization of the Renaissance in Italy*, I, 21.

222   "Many have imagined republics and principalities": Machiavelli, *Il Principe*, XV, 147.

223   "Let the teacher paint a sort of celestial creature": Erasmus, *Education of a Christian Prince*, 162.

223   "[W]e take it for granted": Aristotle, *The Politics*, III, 108.

223   "The worthy exercise of the kingly office": Aquinas, "On Princely Government," in *Selected Political Writings*, 49.

224   "[A]ll human affairs are ever in a state of flux": Machiavelli, *Discourses*, I, 123.

224   "the things of this world are so variable": Machiavelli, *Il Principe*, X, 128.

224   "turns states and kingdoms upside down": Machiavelli, "On Fortune," in *Chief Works*, II, 746.

224   "No one can be called a good prince": Gilbert, *Machiavelli's Prince and Its Forerunners*, 83.

224   "must be prepared to shift": Machiavelli, *Il Principe*, XVIII, 157.

224   "when he acts in harmony with the times": Ibid., XXV, 187–88.

225   "are sustained by superior causes": Ibid., XI, 44.

226   "Anyone who gains [new territories]": Ibid., III, 90.

226   "Cesare Borgia was considered cruel": Ibid., XVII, 151–52.

226   "infinitely cruel, and inimical to society": Machiavelli, *Discorsi*, I, 49.

226   "Nonetheless, for he who would not wish to follow": Ibid.

227   "that 'the good' is 'that'": Aristotle, *Ethics*, I, 25.

227   "Having reviewed all the Duke's actions": Machiavelli, *Il Principe*, VII, 115.

227   "that the prudence of men cannot manage": Ibid., XXV, 84.

227   "I believe that even if it is true": Ibid., 186–87.

228   "proves adaptable when unforseen events occur": Ibid., II, 13–14.

228   "Fortune in her furious onrush": Machiavelli, "On Fortune," in *Chief Works*, II, 748.

228   "O great and wonderful happiness of man!": Pico della Mirandola, *On the Dignity of Man*, 5.

229   "I must be cruel to be kind": Shakespeare, *Hamlet*, III, IV.

229   "For where men have but little virtue": Machiavelli, *Discorsi*, II, 159.

229   allowed themselves to be mastered by others: Ibid., 104.

230   "Everywhere Ambition and Avarice penetrate": Machiavelli, "On Ambition," in *Chief Works*, II, 735.

230   "But if they cannot succeed and still persist": Machiavelli, *Il Principe*, III, 96.

230   "In all men's acts": Ibid., XVIII, 64.

230   "[I]t is the part of a prudent man": Machiavelli, *La Mandragola*, in *Chief Works*, II, 793.

231   "It is . . . necessary that the prince": Villari, *The Life and Times of Niccolò Machiavelli*, II, 157.

231   "[O]ne should note": Machiavelli, *Il Principe*, XIX, 164.

231   "It may also be disputed whether fraud": Villari, *The Life and Times of Niccolò Machiavelli*, II, 157.

232 "*Tyrannical science*": Anglo, *Machiavelli: The First Century*, 285.

232 "*The universe is so constituted*": Machiavelli, *Il Principe*, XXI, 179–80.

232 "*[n]ot a thing in the world is eternal*": Machiavelli, "On Fortune," in *Chief Works*, II, 748.

232 "*redeem [Italy] from barbarian insolence*": Machiavelli, *Il Principe*, XXVI, 191.

232 "*[G]overnment by one person, being the best*": Aquinas, "On Princely Government," in *Selected Political Writings*, 29.

232 "*All states—all those dominions*": Machiavelli, *The Prince*, I, 13.

233 "*it seems to me that now so many factors*": Ibid., XXVI, 190.

233 "*Everyone knows how laudable it is*": Ibid., XVIII, 155.

233 "*a deceiver will never lack victims*": Ibid., 63.

234 "*[T]here is such a chasm*": Ibid., XV, 147.

234 "*Surely, it is not without purpose*": Deane, "The Political and Social Ideas of St. Augustine," in *Essays in the History of Political Thought*, 90.

234 "*evil*": Machiavelli, *Il Principe*, XVIII, 156.

235 "*One cannot call it virtue*": Ibid., VIII, 118.

235 "*It is a sound maxim*": Machiavelli, *Discourses*, I, 132.

236 "*[A] prince must not care*": Machiavelli, *Il Principe*, XVII, 152.

236 "*It must be understood*": Ibid., XVIII, 157.

236 "*states cannot be held with* paternosters": Viroli, *Niccolò's Smile*, 13.

237 "*[W]hen the safety of one's country*": Machiavelli, *Discourses*, III, 515.

238 "*wicked*": Machiavelli, *Il Principe*, XVII, 153.

238 "*[I]t is impossible to go against what nature*": Machiavelli, *Discourses*, III, 431.

238 "*As for the lies of these citizens*": Machiavelli et al., *Machiavelli and His Friends*, 337.

238 "*[A] wise prince cannot keep his word*": Machiavelli, *Il Principe*, XVIII, 156.

239 "*If all men were good*": Ibid.

239 "*I know everyone agrees that it would be laudable*": Ibid., XV, 148.

239 "*[S]o great is man's ambition*": Machiavelli, *Discourses*, II, 341.

239 "*[H]uman appetites are insatiable*": Ibid., 268.

240 "*Almost bereft of life*": Machiavelli, *Il Principe*, XXVI, 191.

240 "*I claim that republics*": Machiavelli, *Discourses*, I, 196.

241 "*And although someone may already have given*": Machiavelli, *Il Principe*, XXVI, 191.

241 "*Nor at the moment can one see*": Ibid., 191.

241 "*Should your house wish to emulate*": Ibid., 193.

241 "*more oppressed than the Hebrews*": Ibid., 191.

242 "*the only art which is of concern to one who commands*": Mansfield, *Machiavelli's Virtue*, 45.

243 "*I have discussed this little study of mine*": Machiavelli et al., *Machiavelli and His Friends*, 265.

243 "*When I have seen it*": Ibid., 269.

245 "*Against barbarian rage*": Machiavelli, *The Prince*, "Exhortation to Free Italy from the Hands of the Barbarians," 90. Machiavelli is quoting famous lines from Petrarch's "Italia Mia."

XI. VITA CONTEMPLATIVA

Page

247 "*sordid and ignominious*": Machiavelli et al., *Machiavelli and His Friends*, 295.

247 "*I have been living in the country*": Machiavelli et al., *Lettere Familiari*, 306.

248 "*Leaving the woods*": Ibid., 307.

248 *"[T]o live as a malcontent"*: Machiavelli, "On Ingratitude or Envy," in *Chief Works*, II, 740.

249 *"He lives happily on a little"*: Horace, "Otium," ode II, 16.

249 *"According to your letter of the 21st"*: Machiavelli et al., *Machiavelli and His Friends*, 231.

250 *"you were right and I was mistaken"*: Machiavelli et al., *Lettere Familiari*, 247.

250 *"If things had gone better"*: Cicero, *On the Good Life*, 121.

251 *"I believe that if his Holiness"*: Machiavelli et al., *Lettere Familiari*, 234.

252 *"[I]n this work I have expressed"*: Machiavelli, *Discorsi*, "Dedication to Zanobi Buondelmonit and Cosimo Rucellai," 3.

252 *"a thousand squabbles and angry words"*: Machiavelli et al., *Lettere Familiari*, 308.

252 *"who live in idleness"*: Machiavelli, *Discourses*, I, 245–46.

253 *I have no greater gift to offer you"*: Machiavelli, *Il Principe*, "Dedication," 83–84.

254 *"I shall leave out any discussion of republics"*: Ibid., II, 86.

256 *"A prince, therefore, cannot in fact possess"*: Ibid., XVIII, 157.

256 *"a new argument, never (that I know)"*: Villiari, *The Life and Times of Niccolò Machiavelli*, II, 288.

257 *"for the common benefit of all"*: Machiavelli, *Discorsi*, "Preface," 5.

257 *"I intend to depart substantially"*: Machiavelli, *Il Principe*, XV, 146–47.

257 *"[I]n the governing of kingdoms"*: Machiavelli, *Discourses*, "Preface," 98.

258 *"When, therefore, I consider in what honor"*: Ibid., 97–98.

258 *"[S]ince fortune is changeable"*: Machiavelli, *Discorsi*, II, 159.

259 *"If one asks oneself how it comes about"*: Machiavelli, *Discourses*, II, 277–78.

260 *"your honor . . . would be darkened"*: Machiavelli et al., *Lettere Familiari*, 421.

260 *"On feast days I hear mass"*: Ibid., 303.

261 *"It was religion that facilitated"*: Machiavelli, *Discourses*, I, 139.

261 *"pattern of life"*: Ibid., II, 278.

261 *"the pusillanimity of those who have interpreted"*: Ibid.

261 *"the finger of Satan"*: Anglo, *Machiavelli: The First Century*, 126.

261 *"It is the Church that has kept"*: Machiavelli, *Discourses*, I, 145.

262 *"[O]wing to the bad example"*: Ibid., 144.

263 *"All states and all dominions"*: Machiavelli, *Il Principe*, I, 85.

263 *"that in all cities where the citizens"*: Machiavelli, "Discourse on Remodeling the Government of Florence," in *Chief Works*, I, 106.

264 *"[I]t is the man who uses violence"*: Machiavelli, *Discourses*, I, 132.

264 *"Wherever you turn your eyes"*: Machiavelli, "On Ambition," in *Chief Works*, II, 738.

264 *"[A] republic has a greater life"*: Machiavelli, *Discorsi*, III, 187.

265 *"government by the populace is better"*: Machiavelli, *Discourses*, I, 256.

265 *"dictatorship, so long as it was bestowed"*: Ibid., 194.

265 *"imminent danger"*: Ibid., 196.

266 *"[F]or it is not the well-being of individuals"*: Ibid., II, 275.

266 *"One should take it as a general rule"*: Ibid., I, 132.

266 *"[I]t must needs be taken for granted"*: Ibid., 112.

266 *"[I]n every republic"*: Ibid., 113.

267 *"good laws . . . [came] from those very tumults"*: Ibid., 114.

267 *"The enmities in Florence"*: Machiavelli, *Florentine Histories*, VII, 277.

267 *"Ambition must be made to counteract ambition"*: Madison, *Federalist* no. 51, 323.

268 *"every man is naturally impelled"*: Pangle, *The Spirit of Modern Republicanism*, 71.

268 *"[I]f we ask what it is the nobility"*: Machiavelli, *Discourses*, I, 116.

268 *"I believe it is necessary"*: Machiavelli, "Discourse on the Remodeling of the Florentine Government," in *Chief Works*, I, 109.

269 *"When the three natural orders"*: Thompson, "John Adams' Machiavellian Moment," 412.

270 *"the sinking foundations of morality"*: Livy, *Early History of Rome*, I, 30.

270 *"The study of history is the best medicine"*: Ibid.

270 *"lack a proper appreciation of history"*: Machiavelli, *Discourses*, "Preface to Book I," 98.

270 *"If the present be compared with the remote past"*: Ibid., I, 208.

270 *"There are two reasons why"*: Ibid., III, 431–32.

271 *"Such is the recurring cycle of constitutions"*: Polybius, *The Histories*, VI, 220.

271 *"[I]f anyone sets up one of the three"*: Machiavelli, *Discourses*, I, 106.

271 *"Thus [states] are always descending"*: Machiavelli, *Florentine Histories*, V, 185.

XII. THE SAGE OF THE GARDEN

Page

273 *"So if at times I laugh or sing"*: Machiavelli et al., *Lettere Familiari*, 233.

274 *"so the poets are treated!"*: Machiavelli, "Sonnet to Giuliano, Son of Lorenzo de' Medici," in *Chief Works*, II, 1013.

274 *"[E]very day we go to the house of some girl"*: Machiavelli et al., *Lettere Familiari*, 228.

275 *"Lady Marietta curses God"*: Ibid., 99.

275 *"marriage yoke"*: King, *Machiavelli*, 182.

275 *"A fine miracle, a monk making a woman pregnant!"*: Machiavelli, *Clizia*, in *Chief Works*, II, 835.

275 *"his affairs are neglected"*: Ibid., 836.

276 *"My dearest Guido"*: Machiavelli et al., *Machiavelli and His Friends*, 413–14.

277 *"Honored and dearest foster father"*: Machiavelli et al., *Lettere Familiari*, 399.

277 *"aside from my own children"*: Ibid., 404.

277 *"at the sign of the horn"*: Ibid., 233.

278 *"It is certainly an amazing thing"*: Ibid., 322.

278 *"an unnatural sex act"*: Machiavelli et al., *Machiavelli and His Friends*, 492.

278 *"who like all her kind"*: Machiavelli et al., *Lettere Familiari*, 446.

279 *"[W]hile in the country I have met"*: Ibid., 360–61.

279 *"the old game"*: Machiavelli et al., *Machiavelli and His Friends*, 293.

279 *"With your prudence and intelligence"*: Machiavelli et al., *Lettere Familiari*, 363.

280 *"Anyone who read our letters"*: Ibid., 392–93.

280 *"that little thief"*: Ibid., 391.

280 *"I fear for my liberty"*: Ibid., 392.

280 *"fortune has left me nothing"*: Ibid., 396.

281 *"write to [Paolo] on my behalf"*: Ridolfi, *The Life of Niccolò Machiavelli*, 162.

281 *"noontime friends"*: King, *Machiavelli*, 170.

282 *"I never met anyone"*: Machiavelli, *The Art of War*, I, 7.

283 *"friends of the cool shade"*: Ridolfi, *The Life of Niccolò Machiavelli*, 180.

284 *"Fabrizio freely accepted the invitation"*: Machiavelli, *The Art of War*, I, 9.

284 *"not to those who are princes"*: Machiavelli, *Discourses*, "Dedication," 94.

285 *"has filled the entire city with high hopes"*: Machiavelli et al., *Machiavelli and His Friends*, 283.

285 *"And our ass"*: Ridolfi, *The Life of Niccolò Machiavelli*, 166.

286 *"These days I have been reading"*: Machiavelli et al., *Lettere Familiari*, 402–3.

286 *"I do not mind bites or blows"*: Ridolfi, *The Life of Niccolò Machiavelli*, 166.

287 *"The writer is not very famous"*: Machiavelli, *La Mandragola*, "Prologue," in *Chief Works*, II, 777–78.

288 *"Yet if anyone supposes that by finding fault"*: Ibid., II, 778.

288 *"Because life is short"*: Ibid., 776.

289 *"Your cleverness"*: Ibid., V, 819.

289 *"[I] put my finger in sin"*: Ibid., IV, 810.

289 *"many times one comes to harm"*: Ibid., II, 810.

290 *"If into the same world the same men"*: Machiavelli, *Clizia*, "Prologue," in *Chief Works*, II, 823.

290 *"It remains for me to tell you"*: Ibid., 824.

291 the scenery painted by Andrea del Sarto and Bastiano (Aristotle) da Sangallo: Vasari, *Lives of the Painters, Sculptors, and Architects*, II, 432.

291 *"a most amusing comedy"*: Ibid., 431.

292 *"acquired so great a name"*: Ibid., 432.

292 *"[t]he stage was so full of people"*: Sanudo, *Città Excelentissima*, 492.

292 *"Niccolò Machiavelli, Historian"*: Machiavelli et al., *Lettere Familiari*, 465.

292 *"everyone admires . . . much more than anything else"*: Ibid., 410.

293 *"Eat plain food"*: Ross, *Lives of the Early Medici*, 332–35.

293 *"Giuliano, now that God has given us the papacy"*: Sanudo, *Cita Excellentissima*, 180.

294 *"I am very glad you took Machiavelli"*: Ridolfi, *The Life of Niccolò Machiavelli*, 177.

295 *"[H]e willingly conversed in his leisure time"*: Ibid.

295 *"Zanobi Buondelmonti and even Niccolò Machiavelli"*: Villari, *The Life and Times of Niccolò Machiavelli*, II, 353.

296 *"The Pope and his Medici"*: Ibid., 252–53.

297 *"The Medici who were governing then"*: Machiavelli, "A Discourse on Remodeling the Government of Florence," in *Chief Works*, I, 104–5.

297 *"[T]o form a princedom where a republic"*: Ibid., 107.

297 *"there are three sorts of men"*: Ibid., 109.

298 *"all decided it was a good thing"*: Machiavelli et al., *Lettere Familiari*, 414–15.

298 a sample of what he could achieve in the genre: Ridolfi, *The Life of Niccolò Machiavelli*, 181.

298 *"He is to be hired for"*: Machiavelli et al., *Machiavelli and His Friends*, 329.

299 *"It was certainly good judgment"*: Ibid., 335.

299 *"To speak of the people"*: Villari, *The Life and Times of Niccolò Machiavelli*, II, 90–91.

300 *"to wish to speak of the affairs of the world"*: Ibid., 89.

300 *"easier to describe in books"*: Ibid., 155.

300 *"The Italians are not strong enough for resistance"*: Ibid., 500.

301 "Magnificent Lord Francescus Guicciardinis": Machiavelli et al., *Lettere Familiari*, 422–23.

301 *"My dearest Machiavelli"*: Ibid., 427–28.

302 *"I must tell you that when the crossbowman"*: Ibid., 424.

302 *"gobbl[ing] up"*: Ibid., 430.

303 *"a good man could not make war"*: Machiavelli, *The Art of War*, I, 17.

303 *"common soldiers [who] laid down their arms"*: Ibid., 17–18.

304 *"For the enmities between the people"*: Machiavelli, *Florentine Histories*, III, 105.

308 *"The night that Piero Soderini ceased to breathe"*: Villori, *The Life and Times of Niccolò Machiavelli*, II, 37.

308 *he was a decent man but an ineffectual leader*: See especially Machiavelli, *Discourses*, III, 393–94.

308 *"there are very few, if any"*: Ibid., 402.

309 *"I'll send your regards to the chickens"*: Machiavelli et al., *Lettere Familiari*, 435.

XIII. NIGHTMARE AND DREAM

Page

314 *"My dear friend"*: Machiavelli et al., *Lettere Familiari*, 437–38.

315 *"I well understand that just now"*: Villari, *The Life and Times of Niccolò Machiavelli*, II, 500.

316 *"[T]he matter is of great importance"*: Ridolfi, *The Life of Niccolò Machiavelli*, 213.

316 *"[I]f it could be brought to the desired fruition"*: Ibid.

316 *"When I asked him again"*: Machiavelli et al., *Lettere Familiari*, 438.

316 *"sow in sand and in water"*: Machiavelli, "On Ingratitude or Envy," in *Chief Works*, II, 740.

317 *"I must warn you"*: Machiavelli et al., *Lettere Familiari*, 444–45.

317 *"[F]or three miles about"*: Ibid., 441.

317 *"You are accustomed to your Barbera"*: Ibid., 446.

318 *a concoction of bitter aloe, saffron, and Armenian bole*: Ibid., 454.

318 *making him a full-fledged citizen*: Machiavelli et al., *Machiavelli and His Friends*, 365.

318 *"double tertian fever"*: Machiavelli et al., *Lettere Familiari*, 459.

319 *"Honored Niccolò, I shall begin"*: Ibid., 468.

319 *"time is endlessly repeating"*: Ibid., 460.

320 *"I have to conclude that this gang here"*: Ibid., 468.

320 *"Since a prince is required to play the beast"*: Machiavelli, *Il Principe*, XVIII, 156.

321 *"I vent my feelings against these princes"*: Machiavelli et al., *Lettere Familiari*, 465.

321 *"As to public affairs"*: Ibid., 469.

321 *"It would be, as I have said"*: Ibid., 477.

321 *"[T]here will be war in Italy, and soon"*: Ibid., 479.

322 *"Those dreading war should be shown"*: Villari, *The Life and Times of Niccolò Machiavelli*, II, 500–1.

322 *"Machiavelli has left with the orders"*: Machiavelli et al., *Machiavelli and His Friends*, 553.

323 *"[M]y head is so full of ramparts"*: Machiavelli et al., *Lettere Familiari*, 487–88.

323 *"He came to reorganize the militia"*: Machiavelli et al., *Machiavelli and His Friends*, 376.

324 *"I am glad that Machiavelli gave the orders"*: Ibid.

325 *"How great the difference is"*: Ibid.

325 *"daily stages"*: Ridolfi, *The Life of Niccolò Machiavelli*, 325.

325 *"[T]he Spaniards could have beaten us"*: Ibid., 233.

326 *"made in Rome, but not observed in Lombardy"*: Machiavelli et al., *Lettere Familiari*, 523.

326 *"living in Rome"*: Ridolfi, *The Life of Niccolò Machiavelli*, 233.

326 *"[O]bserving the behavior of France and the Venetians"*: Machiavelli et al., *Lettere Familiari*, 523.

326 *"We began . . . to divide the army at Parma"*: Ridolfi, *The Life of Niccolò Machiavelli*, 240.

327 *"As for the lansquenets"*: Machiavelli et al., *Lettere Familiari*, 526.

327 *"I do not believe there were ever more troubling matters"*: Ibid., 525.

327 *"I have taken on my own initiative"*: Ridolfi, *The Life of Niccolò Machiavelli*, 241.

327 *"I love Messer Francesco Guicciardini"*: Machiavelli et al., *Lettere Familiari*, 525.

328 *"whom I remarked to be higher than the rest"*: Cellini, *Vita*, I, 66.

328 *"the dreadful news from Rome"*: Ridolfi, *The Life of Niccolò Machiavelli*, 247.

328 *"Wherever you turn your eyes"*: Machiavelli, "On Ambition," in *Chief Works*, II, 738.

329 *"he heard him sigh many times"*: Ridolfi, *The Life of Niccolò Machiavelli*, 329.

330 *"[The common people] hated him"*: Viroli, *Niccolò's Smile*, 257.

331 *"My very dear Francesco"*: Machiavelli et al., *Lettere Familiari*, 530.

332 *"We are the saintly and the blessed"*: Viroli, *Niccolò's Smile*, 3.

333 *"We are the damned of Hell"*: Ibid.

XIV. FINGER OF SATAN

Page

338 *"if one wishes to put this state on a proper footing"*: Najemy, *A History of Florence*, 462.

339 *"to bite and tear him"*: Anglo, *Machiavelli: The First Century*, 165.

339 *"that those who teach the use of herbs"*: Ibid., 166.

340 *"Although owing to the envy inherent in man's nature"*: Machiavelli, *Discourses*, I, 97.

340 *"we are much beholden to Machiavel"*: Bacon, *Advancement of Learning*, II, 222.

341 *"It is a sound maxim"*: Machiavelli, *Discourses*, I, 132.

342 *"I have not adorned this work"*: Machiavelli, *Il Principe*, "Dedication," 84.

343 *"wholly destitute of religion and a contemner thereof"*: Anglo, *Machiavelli: The First Century*, 169.

343 *"This poison is spread"*: Ibid., 17.

343 *"enemy of the human race"*: Ibid.

344 *"[M]y intent and purpose"*: Ibid., 285.

345 *"the odious maxims"*: Skinner et al., *Great Political Thinkers*, 9.

345 *"All these discoveries and complaints"*: Pangle, *The Spirit of Modern Republicanism*, 32.

346 *"subtle policie, cunning roguerie"*: Anglo, *Machiavelli: The First Century*, 3.

346 *"ruin[ing] anyone who might someday ruin you"*: Ibid., 165.

346 *"I count religion but a childish toy"*: Marlowe, *The Jew of Malta*, "Prologue."

347 *"I'll slay more gazers than a basilisk"*: Shakespeare, *Henry VI, Part 3*, III, ii.

347 *"O great and wonderful happiness of man!"*: Pico, *On the Dignity of Man*, 5, *Portable Renaissance Reader*, p. 478–79.

347 *"What a piece of work is a man!"*: Shakespeare, *Hamlet*, II, ii.

348 *"the dispositions of men are naturally such"*: Rauch, *The Political Animal*, 28.

349 *"all human affairs are ever in a state of flux"*: Machiavelli, *Discourses*, I, 123.

351 *"Fitted out appropriately"*: Machiavelli et al., *Machiavelli and His Friends*, 264.

BIBLIOGRAPHY

ELECTRONIC DATABASES

Online Catasto of 1427. Version 1.3. Edited by David Herlihy, Christiane Klapisch-Zuber, R. Burr Litchfield, and Anthony Molho. [Machine-readable data file based on David Herlihy and Christiane Klapisch-Zuber, *Census and Property Survey of Florentine Domains in the Province of Tuscany, 1427–1480.*] Florentine Renaissance Resources/STG: Brown University, Providence, Rhode Island, 2002.

Online Tratte of Office Holders, 1282–1532. Edited by David Herlihy, R. Burr Litchfield, Anthony Molho, and Roberto Barducci.

NICCOLÒ MACHIAVELLI

The Art of War, trans. Ellis Farneworth. Cambridge, 1965.

Chief Works and Others, 3 vols., trans. Felix H. Gilbert. Durham, 1965.

Clizia, in *Chief Works*, II.

Discorsi sopra la Prima Deca di Tito Livio, Florence, 1886 and 1900.

Discourse on Remodeling the Government of Florence, in *Chief Works*, I.

The Discourses, trans. Bernard Crick, ed., and Leslie Walker. London, 1970.

First Decennale, in *Chief Works*, III.

Florentine Histories, trans. Laura F. Banfield and Harvey C. Mansfield, Jr. Princeton, 1988.

Il Principe. Milan, 1950.

La Mandragola, in *Chief Works*, II.

Legazioni, Commissarie, Scritti di Governo, 4 vols. Rome, 2006.

—— et al. *Lettere Familiari di Niccolò Machiavelli*, ed., Edoardo Alvise. Florence, 1893.

—— et al. *Machiavelli and His Friends: Their Personal Correspondence*, trans. and ed. James B. Atkinson and David Sices. Northern Illinois University Press, DeKalb, 1996.

Opere Minori. Florence, 1852.

The Prince, trans. Daniel Donno. New York, 1966.

Tercets on Ambition, in *Chief Works*, II.

Tercets on Fortune, in *Chief Works*, II.

Tercets on Ingratitude or Envy, in *Chief Works*, II.

PRIMARY

Alberti, Leon Battista. *The Family in Renaissance Florence*, trans. Renée Neu Watkins. Columbia, 1969.

———. *I Libri della Famiglia*. Florence, 1910.

Alighieri, Dante. *The De Monarchia of Dante Alighieri*, trans. Aurelia Henry. Houghton Mifflin, Boston, 1904.

———. *Inferno*, trans. John D. Sinclair. New York, 1939.

———. *Paradiso*, trans. John D. Sinclair. New York, 1939.

———. *Purgatorio*, trans. John D. Sinclair. New York, 1939.

Aquinas, Thomas. *Selected Political Writings*, trans. J. G. Dawson. Oxford, 1948.

Aristotle. *Ethics*, trans. J. A. K. Thomson. London, 1955.

———. *The Politics*, trans. T. A. Sinclair. London, 1962.

Saint Augustine. *The City of God*, trans. Marcus Dodds. New York, 1950.

———. *Confessions*, trans. J. G. Pilkington. New York, 1943.

Bacon, Francis. *Advancement of Learning and Novum Organum*. New York, 1899.

Boethius. *The Consolation of Philosophy*, trans. P. G. Walsh. New York, 2000.

Bracciolini, Poggio. "On Avarice," trans. Benjamin G. Kohl and Elizabeth B. Welles, in *The Earthly Republic: Italian Humanists on Government and Society*, ed. Benjamin G. Kohl and Ronald G. Witt. Philadelphia, 1978.

———. "On Nobility," in *Humanism and Liberty: Writings on Freedom from Fifteenth-Century Florence*, trans. and ed. Renée Neu Watkins. Columbia, 1978.

———. "The Ruins of Rome," in *The Portable Renaissance Reader*, ed. James Bruce Ross and Mary Martin McLaughlin. Middlesex, 1953.

Bruni, Leonardo. *History of the Florentine People*, trans. James Hankins. Cambridge, 2001.

———. *Panegyric to the City of Florence*, trans. Benjamin G. Kohl, in *The Earthly Republic: Italian Humanists on Government and Society*, ed. Benjamin G. Kohl and Ronald G. Witt. Philadelphia, 1978.

Buchard, Johann. *At the Court of Borgia: Being an Account of the Reign of Pope Alexander VI*, trans. Geoffrey Parker. London, 1963.

———. *Pope Alexander and His Court*. New York, 1921.

Buonaccorsi, Biagio. *Diario 1498 all' anno 1512 e altri scritti*. Rome, 1999.

Cardano, Girolamo. *The Book of My Life*. New York, 2002.

Castiglione, Baldassare. *The Book of the Courtier*, trans. George Bull. London, 1967.

Cavalcanti, Giovanni. *Istorie Fiorentine*, ed. G. Di Pino. Florence, 1838–39.

———. *The "Trattato politico-morale" of Giovanni Cavalcanti (1381–1451)*, ed. Marcella T. Grendler. Geneva, 1973.

Cellini, Benvenuto. *Vita*. Milan, 1997.

Chronicles of the Tumult of the Ciompi, trans. and ed. Rosemary Kantor and Louis Green. Victoria, 1990.

Cicero, Marcus Tullius. *On the Good Life*, trans. Michael Grant. London, 1971.

Commines, Philip de. *The Memoirs of Philip de Commines, Lord of Argenton*, trans. Andrew R. Scoble. London, 1855–56.

Compagni, Dino. *Dino Compagni's Chronicle of Florence*, trans. Daniel E. Bornstein. Philadelphia, 1986.

Condivi, Ascanio. *The Life of Michelangelo*, trans. Alice Sedgwick Wohl, ed. Hellmut Wohl. Baton Rouge, 1976.

Dati, Gregorio, and Buonacorso Pitti. *Two Memoirs of Renaissance Florence; the Diaries of Buonacorso Pitti and Gregorio Dati*, trans. Julia Martines, ed. Gene Brucker. New York, 1967.

Dei, Benedetto. *La cronica dall'anno 1400 all' anno 1500*, ed. Roberto Barducci. Florence, 1985.

Erasmus. "An Age of Gold," in *The Portable Renaissance Reader*, ed. James Bruce Ross and Mary Martin McLaughlin. Middlesex, 1953.

———. *Education of a Christian Prince*. Cambridge, 2006.

———. *Praise of Folly*, trans. Betty Radice. London, 1971.

Ficino, Marsilio. *Commentary on Plato's Symposium on Love*, trans. Sears Jayne. Dallas, 1985.

———. *The Letters of Marsilio Ficino*, trans. Language Department, School of Economic Science. New York, 1985.

———. "The Soul of Man," in *The Portable Renaissance Reader*, ed. James Bruce Ross and Mary Martin McLaughlin. Middlesex, 1953.

Guicciardini, Francesco. *Considerations on the Discourses of Machiavelli*, in *Francesco Guicciardini: Selected Writings*, trans. Cecil Grayson. London, 1965.

———. *Dialogue on the Government of Florence*, trans. Alison Brown. Cambridge, 1994.

———. *The History of Florence*, trans. Mario Domandi. New York, 1970.

———. *The History of Italy*, trans. Sidney Alexander. Princeton, 1984.

Hamilton, Alexander, John Jay, and James Madison. *The Federalist: A Commentary on the Constitution of the United States*. New York, 1888.

Hobbes, Thomas. *Leviathan*. Oxford, 1960.

Horace. *Odes and Epodes*. Boston, 1901.

Landino, Cristoforo. *Disputationes Camaldulenses*, ed. Peter Lohe. Florence, 1980.

Landucci, Luca. *A Florentine Diary from 1450 to 1516 by Luca Landucci, Continued by an Anonymous Writer till 1542 with Notes by Iodoco del Badia*, trans. Alice de Rosen Jervis. London, 1927.

Leonardo da Vinci. *The Art of Painting*, trans. Carlo Pedretti. New York, 1957.

———. *Leonardo da Vinci's Advice to Artists*, ed. Emery Kelen. Philadelphia, 1974.

Livy. *Early History of Rome*, trans. Aubrey de Selincourt. London, 1960.

———. *Rome and Italy*, trans. Betty Radice. Penguin, London, 1982.

———. *The War with Hannibal*, trans. Aubrey de Selincourt. Penguin, London, 1965.

Locke, John. *Essay Concerning Human Understanding*. London, 1879.

———. *Two Treatises on Government*. New York, 1947.

Machiavelli, Bernardo. *Libro di Ricordi*. Florence, 1954.

Mill, John Stuart. *On Liberty*. London, 1921.

Montesquieu, Baron de. *The Spirit of the Laws*, trans. Thomas Nugent. New York, 1949.

More, Thomas. *Utopia*. New York, 1992.

Nietzsche, Friedrich. *Beyond Good and Evil*, trans. Walter Kaufmann. New York, 1966.

Parenti, Marco. *Lettere*, ed. Maria Marrese. Florence, 1996.

———. *Ricordi Storici, 1464–1467*, ed. Manuela Doni Garfagnini. Rome, 2001.

Parenti, Piero di Marco. *Storia Fiorentina*. Florence, 1994.

Platina, Bartolomeo. "The Restoration of Rome," in *The Portable Renaissance Reader*, ed. James Bruce Ross and Mary Martin McLaughlin. Middlesex, 1953.

Plato. *The Laws*, in *The Works of Plato*, trans. Benjamin Jowett. New York, 1936.

———. *The Republic*, in *The Works of Plato*, trans. Benjamin Jowett. New York, 1944.

———. *Works of Plato*, trans. Benjamin Jowett. New York, 1936.

Polybius. *The Histories*, trans. Mortimer Chambers. New York, 1967.

Pico della Mirandola, Giovanni. *On the Dignity of Man*. Indianapolis, 1965.

Rinuccini, Alemanno. "Dialogue on Liberty," in *Humanism and Liberty: Writings on Freedom from Fifteenth-Century Florence*, trans. and ed., Renée Neu Watkins. Columbia, 1978.

———. *Ricordi Storici di Filippo di Cino Rinuccini dal 1282 al 1460 colla Continuazione di Alamanno e Neri, Suoi Figli Fino al 1506*. Florence, 1840.

Sanudo, Marin. *Città Excelentissima: Selections from the Renaissance Diaries of Marin Sanudo*, eds. Patricia H. Labalme and Linda L. Carroll, trans. Linda L. Carroll. Baltimore, 2008.

Savonarola, Girolamo. *Lettere e scritti apolegetici*. Rome, 1984.

———. *Liberty and Tyranny in the Government of Men*, trans. C. M. Flumiani. Albuquerque 1976.

———. "Treatise on the Constitution and the Government of the City of Florence," in *Humanism and Liberty: Writings on Freedom from Fifteenth-Century Florence*, trans. and ed. Renée Neu Watkins. Columbia, 1978.

Vasari, Giorgio. *Lives of the Painters, Sculptors, and Architects*, 2 vols. trans. Gaston du C. de Vere. New York, 1927.

SECONDARY

Anglo, Sydney. *Machiavelli: A Dissection*. New York, 1969.

———. *Machiavelli: The First Century: Studies in Enthusiasm, Hostility, and Irrelevance*. Oxford, 2005.

Ascoli, Albert Russell, and Angela Matilde Capodivacca. "Machiavelli and Poetry," in *The Cambridge Companion to Machiavelli*, ed. John M. Najemy. Cambridge, 2010.

Atkinson, Catherine. *Debts, Dowries, Donkeys: The Diary of Niccolò Machiavelli's Father, Messer Bernardo, in Quattrocento Florence*. Frankfurt am Main, 2002.

Atkinson, James B. "Niccolò Machiavelli: A Portrait," in *The Cambridge Companion to Machiavelli*, ed. John M. Najemy. Cambridge, 2010.

Bailyn, Bernard. *The Ideological Origins of the American Revolution*. Cambridge, 1967.

Baron, Hans. *The Crisis of the Early Italian Renaissance: Civic Humanism and Republican Liberty*. Princeton, 1955.

Barthas, Jérémie. "Machiavelli in Political Thought from the Age of Revolutions to the Present," in *The Cambridge Companion to Machiavelli*, ed. John M. Najemy. Cambridge, 2010.

Bernard, John. *Why Machiavelli Matters: A Guide to Citizenship in a Democracy*. Westport, 2009.

Black, Robert. "Machiavelli in the Chancery," in *The Cambridge Companion to Machiavelli*, ed. John M. Najemy. Cambridge, 2010.

Blitz, Mark. "Virtue, Modern and Ancient," in *Educating the Prince*, eds., Mark Blitz and William Kristol. Lanham, 2000.

Blitz, Mark, and William Kristol, eds. *Educating the Prince: Essays in Honor of Harvey Mansfield*. Lanham, 2000.

Bluhm, William T. "Immanent Good: Aristotle's Quest for the Best Regime," in *Essays in the History of Political Thought*, ed. Isaac Kramnick. Englewood Cliffs, 1969.

Bonadeo, Alfredo. "The Role of the 'Grandi' in the Political World of Machiavelli." *Studies in the Renaissance* 16 (1969): 9–30.

Breisach, Ernst. *Caterina Sforza: A Renaissance Virago*. Chicago, 1967.

Brown, Alison. *Bartolomeo Scala, 1430–1497: Chancellor of Florence: The Humanist as Bureaucrat*. Princeton, 1979.

———. "Lorenzo and Guicciardini," in *Lorenzo the Magnificent: Culture and Politics*, eds. Michael Mallet and Nicholas Mann. London, 1996, 281–96.

———. "Philosophy and Religion in Machiavelli," in *The Cambridge Companion to Machiavelli*, ed. John M. Najemy. Cambridge, 2010.

Brown, David Alan. *Leonardo da Vinci: Origins of a Genius*. New Haven, 1998.

Brucker, Gene. *The Civic World of Renaissance Florence*. Princeton, 1977.

———. *Florence: The Golden Age, 1138–1737*. Berkeley, 1998.

———. *Renaissance Florence*. New York, 1969.

Brucker, Gene, ed. *The Society of Renaissance Florence: A Documentary Study*. New York, 1971.

Bullard, Melissa. "The Language of Diplomacy in the Renaissance," in *Lorenzo de Medici: New Perspectives*, ed. Bernard Toscani. New York, 1992, 263–79.

———. "Lorenzo and Patterns of Diplomatic Discourse in the Late Fifteenth Century," in *Lorenzo the Magnificent: Culture and Politics*, eds. Michael Mallet and Nicholas Mann, London, 1996, 263–74.

Burckhardt, Jacob. *The Civilization of the Renaissance in Italy*, 2 vols., trans. S. G. C. Middlemore. New York, 1958.

Butterfield, Herbert. *The Statecraft of Machiavelli*. New York, 1962.

Butters, Humfrey. "Lorenzo and Machiavelli," in *Lorenzo the Magnificent: Culture and Politics*, eds. Michael Mallet and Nicholas Mann. London, 1996, 275–80.

———. "Machiavelli and the Medici," in *The Cambridge Companion to Machiavelli*, ed. John M. Najemy. Cambridge, 2010.

Cabrini, Anna Maria. "Machiavelli's *Florentine Histories*," in *The Cambridge Companion to Machiavelli*, ed. John M. Najemy. Cambridge, 2010.

Carrese, Paul. "The Machiavellian Spirit of Montesquieu's Liberal Republic," in *Machiavelli's Liberal Republican Legacy*, ed. Paul Rahe. Cambridge, 2006.

Cassirer, Ernst. "The Triumph of Machiavellism and Its Consequences" in *Essays in the History of Political Thought*. ed. Isaac Kramnick. Englewood Cliffs, 1969.

Chabod, Federico. *Machiavelli and the Renaissance*, trans. David Moore. London, 1958.

Chamberlin, E. R. *Everyday Life in Renaissance Times*. London, 1966.

———. *The World of the Italian Renaissance*. London, 1982.

Cheetham, Sir Nicolas. *Keepers of the Keys: A History of Popes from St. Peter to John Paul II*. New York, 1983.

Cherubini, Giovanni, et al. *Vivere nel contado al tempo di Lorenzo*. Florence, 1992.

Clark, Kenneth. "The Young Michelangelo," in J. H. Plumb, *The Penguin Book of the Renaissance*. Middlesex, 1961, 99–118.

Courtney, Louise. *The Trumpet of the Truth: An Analysis of Benedetto Dei's Cronica*. Victoria, 1986.

Cox, Virginia. "Rhetoric and Ethics in Machiavelli," in *The Cambridge Companion to Machiavelli*. ed. John M. Najemy. Cambridge, 2010.

Danford, John W. "Getting Our Bearings: Machiavelli and Hume," in *Machiavelli's Liberal Republican Legacy*, ed. Paul Rahe. Cambridge, 2006.

Deane, Herbert A. "The Political and Social Ideas of St. Augustine," in *Essays in the History of Political Thought*. ed. Isaac Kramnick. Englewood Cliffs, 1969.

Denley, Peter, and Caroline Elam, eds. *Florence and Italy: Renaissance Studies in Honor of Nicolai Rubinstein*. Turnhout, 1996.

D'Entrèves, A. P. "Thomas Aquinas," in *Essays in the History of Political Thought*, ed. Isaac Kramnick. Englewood Cliffs, 1969.

Dunning, William Archibald. *A History of Political Theories from Luther to Montesquieu*. New York, 1953.

Ebenstein, William. *Great Political Thinkers: Plato to the Present*. Fort Worth, 2000.

Epstein, David F. "*The Federalist's* Unmixed Republican Government," in *Educating the Prince*, eds. Mark Blitz and William Kristol. Lanham, 2000.

Everitt, Anthony. *Cicero: The Life and Times of Rome's Greatest Politician*. New York, 2001.

Field, Arthur. *The Origins of the Platonic Academy of Florence*. Princeton, 1988.

Findlen, Paula, ed. *The Italian Renaissance*. Malden, 2002.

Fleisher, Martin, ed. *Machiavelli and the Nature of Political Thought*. New York, 1972.

Forde, Steven. "Benjamin Franklin's 'Machiavellian' Civic Virtue," in *Machiavelli's Liberal Republican Legacy*, ed. Paul Rahe. Cambridge, 2006.

Gage, John. *Life in Italy at the Time of the Medici.* New York, 1970.

Ganz, Margery A. "Donato Acciaiuoli and the Medici: A Strategy for Survival in 1400 Florence," *Rinascimento,* 2nd ser., 22 (1982): 33–73.

Garin, Eugenio. *Italian Humanism: Philosophy and Civic Life in the Renaissance,* trans. Peter Munz. Westport, 1975.

Gentile, Sebastiano. "Ficino e il platonismo di Lorenzo," in *Lorenzo de Medici: New Perspectives,* ed. Bernard Toscani. New York, 1992, 23–49.

Gibbons, John P. "How a Liberal Picks a Fight: Marsilius of Padua and the Singular Cause of Strife," in *Educating the Prince,* eds. Mark Blitz and William Kristol. Lanham, 2000.

Gil, Anton. *Il Gigante: Michelangelo, Florence, and the David.* New York, 2003.

Gilbert, Allan H. *Machiavelli's Prince and Its Forerunners: The Prince as a Typical Book de Regime Principum.* New York, 1968.

Gilbert, Felix. "Bernardo Rucellai and the Orti Oricellari: A Study on the Origin of Modern Political Thought," in Felix Gilbert, *History: Choice and Commitment.* Cambridge, 1977.

——. "The Composition and Structure of Machiavelli's *Discorsi,*" in Felix Gilbert, *History: Choice and Commitment.* Cambridge, 1977.

——. *History: Choice and Commitment.* Cambridge, 1977.

——. "The Humanist Concept of the Prince and *The Prince* of Machiavelli," in Felix Gilbert, *History: Choice and Commitment.* Cambridge, 1977.

——. *Machiavelli and Guicciardini: Politics and History in Sixteenth-Century Florence.* New York, 1984.

——. "Machiavelli's *Istorie Fiorentine*: An Essay in Interpretation," in Felix Gilbert, *History: Choice and Commitment.* Cambridge, 1977.

——. "Machiavellism," in Felix Gilbert, *History: Choice and Commitment.* Cambridge, 1977.

——. *The Pope, His Banker, and Venice.* Cambridge, 1980.

——. "The Venetian Constitution in Florentine Political Thought," in *Florentine Studies: Politics and Society in Renaissance Florence,* ed. Nicolai Rubinstein. London, 1968, 463–500.

Goldthwaite, Richard A. *The Building of Renaissance Florence: An Economic and Social History.* Baltimore, 1980.

——. *Private Wealth in Renaissance Florence: A Study of Four Families.* Princeton, 1968.

——. "Schools and Teachers of Commercial Arithmetic in Renaissance Florence." *Journal of European Economic History* 1 (1972): 418–33.

Gombrich, E. H. "The Renaissance Conception of Artistic Progress," in *Norm and Form: Studies in the Art of the Renaissance,* 1, London and New York, 1966.

Gottlieb, Anthony. *The Dream of Reason: A History of Philosophy from the Greeks to the Renaissance.* New York, 2000.

Grafton, Anthony. *Leon Battista Alberti: Master Builder of the Italian Renaissance.* New York, 2000.

Green, Louis. *Chronicle into History: An Essay on the Interpretation of History in Florentine Fourteenth Century Chronicles.* Cambridge, 1972.

Grendler, Paul F. *Schooling in Renaissance Italy: Literacy and Learning, 1300–1600.* Baltimore, 1989.

Grene, David. "Man in his Pride," in *Essays in the History of Political Thought*, ed. Isaac Kramnick. Englewood Cliffs, 1969.

Hale, John R. *Florence and the Medici: The Pattern of Control.* London, 1977.

———. *Machiavelli and Renaissance Italy.* New York, 1963.

———. "Violence in the Late Middle Ages: A Background," in *Violence and Civil Disorders in Italian Cities, 1200–1500*, ed. Lauro Martines. Los Angeles, 1972.

Hancock, Ralph C. "Necessity, Morality, Christianity," in *Educating the Prince*, eds. Mark Blitz and William Kristol. Lanham, 2000.

Hankins, James. "Lorenzo de' Medici as a Patron of Philosophy." *Rinascimento*, 2nd ser., 34, (1994): 15–53.

———. "The Myth of the Platonic Academy. *Renaissance Quarterly* 44 (Autumn 1991): 429–75.

Hawkins, D. J. B. *A Sketch of Medieval Philosophy.* New York, 1947.

Herlihy, David. "Some Psychological and Social Roots of Violence in the Tuscan Cities," in *Violence and Civil Disorders in Italian Cities, 1200–1500*, ed. Lauro Martines. Los Angeles, 1972.

Hibbert, Christopher. *The Borgias and Their Enemies: 1431–1519.* Orlando, 2008.

———. *Florence: The Biography of a City.* New York, 1993.

———. *The House of the Medici: Its Rise and Fall.* New York, 1975.

———. *The Popes.* Chicago, 1982.

Holmes, George. *Florence, Rome and the Origins of the Renaissance.* Oxford, 1986.

———. *The Florentine Enlightenment, 1400–1450.* London, 1969.

Holmes, George, ed. *Art and Politics in Renaissance Italy.* Oxford, 1993.

Hook, Judith. *Lorenzo de' Medici: An Historical Biography.* London, 1984.

Hörnqvist, Mikael. "Machiavelli's Military Project and the *Art of War*," in *The Cambridge Companion to Machiavelli*, ed. John M. Najemy. Cambridge, 2010.

Ilardi, Vincent. "The Assassination of Galeazzo Maria Sforza and the Reaction of Italian Diplomacy," in *Violence and Civil Disorders in Italian Cities, 1200–1500*, ed. Lauro Martines. Los Angeles, 1972.

Jurdjevig, Mark. "Civic Humanism and the Rise of the Medici." *RQ* 52 (Winter 1999): 494–517.

Kahn, Victoria. "Machiavelli's Afterlife and Reputation to the Eighteenth Century," in *The Cambridge Companion to Machiavelli*, ed. John M. Najemy. Cambridge, 2010.

Kallendorf, Craig, ed. *Humanist Educational Treatises.* Cambridge, 2002.

Kelsen, Hans. "Aristotle's Doctrine of Justice," in *Essays in the History of Political Thought*, ed. Isaac Kramnick. Englewood Cliffs, 1969.

Kendall, Willmoore. "John Locke and the Doctrine of Majority Rule," in *Essays in the History of Political Thought*. ed. Isaac Kramnick. Englewood Cliffs, 1969.

Kent, Dale. *Cosimo de' Medici and the Florentine Renaissance: The Patron's Oeuvre.* New Haven, 2000.

——. "The Florentine *Reggimento* in the Fifteenth Century." *Renaissance Quarterly* 28 (1975): 575–638.

——. *The Rise of the Medici Faction in Florence, 1426–1434.* Oxford, 1978.

Kent, D. V., and F. W. Kent. *Neighbours and Neighbourhood in Renaissance Florence: The District of the Red Lion in the Fifteenth Century.* Locust Valley, 1982.

Kent, F. W. "Gardens, Villas and Social Life in Renaissance Florence," in *Renaissance Gardens—Italy.* Victoria, 2001.

——. *Household and Lineage in Renaissance Florence: The Family Life of the Capponi, Ginori, and Rucellai.* Princeton, 1977.

——. *Lorenzo de' Medici and the Art of Magnificence.* Baltimore, 2004.

——. "Patron-Client Networks in Renaissance Florence and the Emergence of Lorenzo as 'Maestro della Bottega,'" in *Lorenzo de' Medici: New Perspectives,* ed. Bernard Toscani. New York, 1994, 279–314.

Kessler, Charles R. "Responsibility in *The Federalist,*" in *Educating the Prince,* eds. Mark Blitz and William Kristol. Lanham, 2000.

King, Ross. *Brunelleschi's Dome.* New York, 2000.

——. *Machiavelli: Philosopher of Power.* New York, 2007.

——. *Michelangelo and the Pope's Ceiling.* New York, 2003.

Kohl, Benjamin G., and Ronald G. Witt, ed. and trans. *The Earthly Republic: Italian Humanists on Government and Society.* Philadelphia, 1978.

Kramnick, Isaac, ed. *Essays in the History of Political Thought.* Englewood Cliffs, 1969.

Kraye, Jill. "Lorenzo and the Philosophers," in *Lorenzo the Magnificent Culture and Politics,* eds. Michael Mallet and Nicholas Mann. London, 1996, 151–66.

Kristeller, Paul. *Eight Renaissance Philosophers.* Stanford, 1964.

——. *The Philosophy of Marsilio Ficino,* trans. Virginia Conant. New York, 1943.

——. *Renaissance Thought and Its Sources.* New York, 1979.

Lamprecht, Sterling P. "Hobbes and Hobbism," in *Essays in the History of Political Thought,* ed. Isaac Kramnick. Englewood Cliffs, 1969.

Lang, Jack. *Il Magnifico: Vita di Lorenzo de' Medici,* trans. Alessandra Benabbi. Milan, 2002.

Larner, John. "Order and Disorder in Romagna, 1450–1500," in *Violence and Civil Disorders in Italian Cities, 1200–1500,* ed. Lauro Martines. Los Angeles, 1972.

Levey, Michael. *Florence, A Portrait.* Cambridge, 1996.

Lubkin, Gregory. *A Renaissance Court: Milan Under Galeazzo Maria Sforza.* Berkeley, 1994.

Lucas-Dubreton, J. *Daily Life in Florence in the Time of the Medici,* trans. Lytton Sells. New York, 1961.

Lyons, David. *Forms and Limits of Utilitarianism.* Oxford, 1965.

Macpherson, C. B. "The Social Bearing of Locke's Political Theory," in *Essays in the History of Political Thought,* ed. Isaac Kramnick. Englewood Cliffs, 1969.

Major, Rafael. "A New Argument for Morality: Machiavelli and the Ancients." *Political Research Quarterly* 60, no. 2 (June 2007): 171–79.

Mallett, Michael. "Pisa and Florence in the Fifteenth Century: Aspects of the Period of the First Florentine Domination," in *Florentine Studies: Politics and Society in Renaissance Florence*, ed. Nicolai Rubinstein. Evanston, 1968, 403–42.

Mallett, Michael, and Nicholas Mann, eds. *Lorenzo the Magnificent: Culture and Politics.* London, 1996.

Mansfield, Harvey. *Machiavelli's Virtue.* Chicago, 1996.

———. *Taming the Prince: The Ambivalence of Modern Executive Power.* New York, 1989.

Manuel, Frank E., and Fritzie P. Manuel. *Utopian Thought in the Western World.* Cambridge, 1979.

Martelli, Mario. "La cultura letteraria nell'età di Lorenzo," in *Lorenzo the Magnificent: Culture and Politics*, eds. Michael Mallet and Nicholas Mann. London, 1996, 167–76.

Martines, Lauro. *April Blood: Florence and the Plot Against the Medici.* Oxford, 2003.

———. *Fire in the City: Savonarola and the Struggle for the Soul of Renaissance Florence.* Oxford, 2006.

———. *An Italian Renaissance Sextet: Six Tales in Historical Context*, trans. Murtha Baca. Toronto, 2004.

———. *Power and Imagination: City States in Renaissance Italy.* Baltimore, 1988.

———. *The Social World of the Florentine Humanists, 1390–1460.* Princeton, 1963.

———. *Strong Words: Writing and Social Strain in the Italian Renaissance.* Baltimore, 2001.

Martines, Lauro, ed. *Violence and Civil Disorders in Italian Cities, 1200–1500.* Berkeley, 1972.

Martinez, Ronald L. "Comedian, Tragedian: Machiavelli and Traditions of Renaissance Theater," in *The Cambridge Companion to Machiavelli.* ed. John M. Najemy. Cambridge, 2010.

Masters, Roger D. *Fortune Is a River.* New York, 1999.

Mattingly, Garrett. *Renaissance Diplomacy.* New York, 1970.

McKeon, Richard, ed. *Selections from Medieval Philosophers.* New York, 1929.

Meinecke, Friedrich. "Machiavelli," in *Essays in the History of Political Thought*, ed. Isaac Kramnick. Englewood Cliffs, 1969.

———. *Machiavellism: The Doctrine of Raison d'Etat and Its Place in Modern History*, trans. Douglas Scott. New Haven, 1957.

Mohlo, Anthony. *Marriage Alliance in Late Medieval Florence.* Cambridge, 1994.

Muir, Edward. *Civic Ritual in Renaissance Venice.* Princeton, 1981.

Najemy, John. *A History of Florence: 1200–1575.* West Sussex, 2006.

Najemy, John M., ed. *The Cambridge Companion to Machiavelli.* Cambridge, 2010.

———. "Society, Class, and State in Machiavelli's *Discourses on Livy*," in *The Cambridge Companion to Machiavelli*, ed. John M. Najemy. Cambridge, 2010.

Ore, Oystein. *Cardano: The Gambling Scholar.* Princeton, 1953.

Pampaloni, G. "Fermenti di riforme democratiche nella Firenze medicea del Quattrocento." *ASI* 119 (1961): 11ff.

Pangle, Thomas. *The Spirit of Modern Republicanism: The Moral Vision of the American Founders and the Philosophy of John Locke.* Chicago, 1988.

Parel, Anthony J. *The Machiavellian Cosmos.* New Haven, 1992.

Parks, Tim. *Medici Money: Banking, Metaphysics, and Art in Fifteenth-Century Florence.* New York, 2005.

Partner, Peter. "Florence and the Papacy in the Earlier Fifteenth Century," in *Florentine Studies: Politics and Society in Renaissance Florence,* ed. Nicolai Rubinstein. Evanston, 1968, 381–403.

———. *Renaissance Rome: 1500–1559: A Portrait of a Society.* Berkeley, 1976.

Pastor, Ludwig. *The History of the Popes from the Close of the Middle Ages.* St. Louis, 1898.

Pernis, Maria Grazia. "The Young Michelangelo and Lorenzo de' Medici's Circle," in *Lorenzo de Medici: New Perspectives,* ed. Bernard Toscani. New York, 1992, 143–63.

Pesman, Roslyn. "Machiavelli, Piero Soderini, and the Republic of 1494–1512," in *The Cambridge Companion to Machiavelli,* ed. John M. Najemy. Cambridge, 2010.

Phillips, Mark. *The Memoir of Marco Parenti: A Life in Medici Florence.* Princeton, 1987.

Pico della Mirandola, Giovanni. *On the Dignity of Man.* Indianapolis, 1965.

Pirolo, Paola. "Su alcuni aspetti della formazione della legenda Medicea: Da Cosimo a Lorenzo," in *Lorenzo dopo Lorenzo: La Fortuna Storica di Lorenzo il Magnifico,* ed. Paola Pirolo, Florence, 1992.

Pirolo, Paola, ed. *Lorenzo dopo Lorenzo: La Fortuna Storica di Lorenzo il Magnifico,* Florence, 1992.

Plant, Margaret. *Renaissance Gardens—Italy.* Victoria, 2001.

Plebani, Eleonora. *Lorenzo e Giuliano de' Medici: Tra Potere e Legame di Sangue.* Rome, 1993

Plumb, J. H. "Milan: City of Strife," in J. H. Plumb, *The Penguin Book of the Renaissance.* Middlesex, 1961, 155–69.

———. "Rome: Splendour and the Papacy," in J. H. Plumb, *The Penguin Book of the Renaissance.* Middlesex, 1961, 189–208.

———. *The Penguin Book of the Renaissance.* Middlesex, 1961.

Pocock, John G. A. "Machiavelli and Rome: The Republic as Ideal and as History," in *The Cambridge Companion to Machiavelli,* ed. John M. Najemy. Cambridge, 2010.

———. *The Machiavellian Moment: Florentine Political Thought and the Atlantic Republican Tradition.* Princeton, 1975.

Polizzotto, Lorenzo. "Lorenzo il Magnifico, Savonarola and Medicean Dynasticism," in *Lorenzo de Medici: New Perspectives,* ed. Bernard Toscant. New York, 1992, 331–55.

Raab, Felix. *The English Face of Machiavelli: A Changing Interpretation, 1500–1700.* London, 1964.

Rabkin, Jeremy. "Things Which Independent States May of Right Do," in *Educating the Prince,* eds. Mark Blitz and William Kristol. Lanham, 2000.

Rahe, Paul A. "Machiavelli in the English Revolution," in *Machiavelli's Liberal Republican Legacy,* ed. Paul Rahe. Cambridge, 2006.

——. "Thomas Jefferson's Machiavellian Political Science," in *Machiavelli's Liberal Republican Legacy*, ed. Paul Rahe. Cambridge, 2006.

——. *Republics Ancient and Modern: Classical Republicanism and the American Revolution.* Chapel Hill, 1992.

Rahe, Paul A., ed. *Machiavelli's Liberal Republican Legacy.* Cambridge, 2006.

Rauch, Leo. *The Political Animal: Studies in Political Philosophy from Machiavelli to Marx.* Amherst, 1981.

Rebhorn, Wayne A. "Machiavelli's *Prince* in the Epic Tradition," in *The Cambridge Companion to Machiavelli*, ed. John M. Najemy. Cambridge, 2010.

Rendina, Claudio. *The Popes: Histories and Secrets*, trans. Paul d. McCusker. Santa Ana, 2002.

Richardson, Brian. *Printing, Writers and Readers in Renaissance Italy.* Cambridge, 1999.

Ridolfi, Roberto. *The Life of Niccolò Machiavelli*, trans. Cecil Grayson. London, 1963.

Rocke, Michael. *Forbidden Friendships: Homosexuality and Male Culture in Renaissance Florence.* New York, 1996.

Roeder, Ralph, "Lorenzo de' Medici," in J. H. Plumb, *The Penguin Book of the Renaissance.* Middlesex, 1961.

——. *The Man of the Renaissance: Four Lawgivers: Savonarola, Machiavelli, Castiglione, Aretino.* New York, 1933.

Roscoe, William. *The Life and Pontificate of Leo X*, 2 vols. London, 1893.

——. *The Life of Lorenzo de Medici, Called the Magnificent.* London, 1889.

Rosen, Gary. "James Madison's Princes and Peoples," in *Machiavelli's Liberal Republican Legacy*, ed. Paul Rahe. Cambridge, 2006.

Ross, Janet. *Florentine Palaces and Their Stories.* London, 1905.

——. *Lives of the Early Medici.* London, 1910.

Roth, Cecil. *The Last Florentine Republic: 1527–30.* London, 1925.

Rubenstein, Richard E. *Aristotle's Children: How Christians, Muslims, and Jews Rediscovered Ancient Wisdom and Illuminated the Dark Ages.* Orlando, 2003.

Rubinstein, Nicolai. "The Beginnings of Niccolò Machiavelli's Career in the Florentine Chancellery." *Italian Studies* 11 (1956): 72–91.

——. "The Beginnings of Political Thought in Florence, A Study in Medieval Historiography." *Journal of the Warburg and Courtauld Institutes* 5 (1942): 198–227.

——. "Florentine Constitutionalism and Medici Ascendancy in the Fifteenth Century," in *Florentine Studies: Politics and Society in Renaissance Florence*, ed. Nicolai Rubinstein. Evanston, 1968, 442–63.

——. *The Government of Florence Under the Medici.* Oxford, 1977.

——. "Machiavelli and the Decoration of the Hall of the Great Council in the Palazzo Vecchio," in *Musagetes: Festschrift für Wolfram Prinz*, ed. R. G. Kecks. Berlin, 1991.

——. *The Palazzo Vecchio, 1298–1532: Government, Architecture, and Imagery in the Civic Palace of the Florentine Republic.* Oxford, 1995.

Rubinstein, Nicolai, et al. *The Age of the Renaissance.* London, 1967.

Rubinstein, Nicolai, ed. *Florentine Studies: Politics and Society in Renaissance Florence.* London, 1968.

Ruggiers, Paul G. *Florence in the Age of Dante.* Norman, 1964.

Scaife, Walter B. *Florentine Life During the Renaissance.* Baltimore, 1893.

Schevill, Ferdinand. *History of Florence, from the Founding of the City Through the Renaissance.* New York, 1961.

———. *The Medici.* New York, 1949.

Skinner, Quentin. *The Foundations of Modern Political Thought.* Cambridge, 1978.

Skinner, Quentin, et al. *Great Political Thinkers: Machiavelli; Hobbes; Mill; Marx.* Oxford, 1992.

Smith, Margaret Michell Barnes. "The Philosophy of Liberty: Locke's Machiavellian Teaching," in *Machiavelli's Liberal Republican Legacy,* ed. Paul Rahe. Cambridge, 2006.

Spackman, Barbara. "Machiavelli and Gender," in *The Cambridge Companion to Machiavelli,* ed. John M. Najemy. Cambridge, 2010.

Spalding, Matthew. "The American Prince? George Washington's Anti-Machiavellian Moment," in *Machiavelli's Liberal Republican Legacy,* ed. Paul Rahe. Cambridge, 2006.

Stoner, James R., Jr. "The Common Law Spirit of the American Constitution," in *Educating the Prince,* eds. Mark Blitz and William Kristol. Lanham, 2000.

Strauss, Leo. "On the Spirit of Hobbes' Political Philosophy," in *Essays in the History of Political Thought,* ed. Isaac Kramnick. Englewood Cliffs, 1969.

———. *The Political Philosophy of Hobbes: Its Basis and Its Genesis,* trans. Elsa M. Sinclair. 1952.

———. *Thoughts on Machiavelli.* Glencoe, 1959.

Sullivan, Vickie B. "Muted and Manifest English Machiavellism: The Reconciliation of Machiavellian Republicanism with Liberalism in Sidney's *Discourses Concerning Government* and Trenchard's and Gordon's *Cato's Letters,*" in *Machiavelli's Liberal Republican Legacy,* ed. Paul Rahe. Cambridge, 2006.

Tarcov, Nathan. "Machiavelli and the Foundation of Modernity," in *Educating the Prince,* eds. Mark Blitz and William Kristol. Lanham, 2000.

Thompson, C. Bradley. "John Adams' Machiavellian Moment." *The Review of Politics* 57 (Summer 1995): 389–417.

Toscani, Bernard, ed. *Lorenzo de Medici: New Perspectives.* New York, 1992.

Trexler, Richard. "Lorenzo de' Medici and Savonarola: Martyrs for Florence." *Renaissance Quarterly* 31 (1978): 293–308.

———. *Public Life in Renaissance Florence.* Ithaca, 1991.

Ullmann, Walter. *Principles of Government and Politics in the Middle Ages.* New York, 1961.

Unger, Miles. *Magnifico: The Brilliant Life and Violent Times of Lorenzo de' Medici.* New York, 2008.

Villari, Pasquale. *The Life and Times of Girolamo Savonarola,* 2 vols., trans. Linda Villari. London, 1888.

———. *The Life and Times of Niccolò Machiavelli*, 2 vols., trans Linda Villari. London, 1898.

Viroli, Maurizio. *Machiavelli*. Oxford, 1998.

———. *Niccolò's Smile: A Biography of Machiavelli*, trans. Antony Shugaar. New York, 2000.

Waley, Daniel Philip. *The Italian City-Republics*. New York, 1969.

Walling, Karl-Friedrich. "Was Alexander Hamilton a Machiavellian Statesman?" in *Machiavelli's Liberal Republican Legacy*, ed. Paul Rahe. Cambridge, 2006.

Watkins, Renée Neu, ed. and trans. *Humanism and Liberty: Writings on Freedom from Fifteenth-Century Florence*. Columbia, 1978.

Wienberger, Jerry. "Metaphysics and Religion: Francis Bacon's Critique of the Ancients," in *Educating the Prince*, eds. Mark Blitz and William Kristol. Lanham, 2000.

Weinstein, Donald. "The Myth of Florence," in *Florentine Studies: Politics and Society in Renaissance Florence*, ed. Nicolai Rubinstein. Evanston, 1968.

———. *Savonarola and Florence: Prophecy and Patriotism in the Renaissance*. Princeton, 1970.

Witt, Ronald. *Hercules at the Crossroads: The Life, Works, and Thought of Coluccio Salutati*. Durham, 1983.

Wolfgang, Marvin E. "A Florentine Prison: Le Carceri delle Stinche." *Studies in the Renaissance* 7 (1960): 148–66.

Wolin, Sheldon S. "Plato: Political Philosophy Versus Politics" in *Essays in the History of Political Thought*. ed. Isaac Kramnick. Englewood Cliffs, 1969.

Young, G. F. *The Medici*. New York, 1933.

Zorzi, Alvise. *Venezia nel secolo di Tiziano*. Milano, 1990.

INDEX